This is the first comprehensive study of Soviet policies in the Middle East. Concentrating on policy developments, Professor Golan analyzes the major Soviet decisions and objectives since the end of World War II until the Gorbachev era. She pays particular attention to the wars and crises of recent years and the often problematic development of political relationships in the region.

Professor Golan begins by demonstrating how, until the end of the Brezhnev period, Soviet policies towards the Middle East were principally influenced by the demands of superpower competition with the USA. This is followed by a series of broadly chronological case studies of the main Soviet alliances such as Syria and South Yemen; and of Sadat's Egypt and Khomeini's Iran. Other issues given specific attention include Soviet attitudes to the Arab–Israeli conflict, the role of communism, the importance of Islam in Soviet–Middle East relations, and the emergence, particularly in the Brezhnev era, of differing Soviet elite opinions on Soviet objectives and policies in this region. This original and important book culminates in a study of Gorbachev's interests, initiatives and 'new thinking' in relation to over all Soviet foreign policy objectives and the role of the Soviet Union in the region.

Galia Golan is Jay and Leoni Darwin Professor of Soviet and East European Studies and Chairperson of the Department of Political Science at the Hebrew University of Jerusalem. She is one of the world's leading experts on the Soviet Union in the Middle East and has published widely including *The Soviet Union and the Palestine Liberation Movement: An uneasy alliance; Yom Kippur and after The Soviet Union and the Middle East crisis: the Soviet Union and national liberation movements in the Third World* and *Gorbachev's new thinking on terrorism.*

Soviet policies in the Middle East

Cambridge Soviet Union Paperbacks: 2

Cambridge Soviet Paperbacks is a completely new initiative in publishing on the Soviet Union. The series will focus on the economics, international relations, politics, sociology and history of the Soviet and Revolutionary periods.

The idea behind the series is the identification of gaps for upper-level surveys or studies falling between the traditional university press monograph and most student textbooks. The main readership will be students and specialists, but some 'overview' studies in the series will have broader appeal.

Publication will in every case be simultaneously in hardcover and paperback.

Also published in this series

Soviet relations with Latin America 1959–1987
Nicola Miller

The Soviet presence and purposes in Latin America are a matter of great controversy, yet no serious study has hitherto combined a regional perspective (concentrating on the nature and regional impact of Soviet activity on the ground) with diplomatic analysis, examining the strategic and ideological factors that influence Soviet foreign policy. Nicola Miller's lucid and accessible survey of Soviet–Latin American relations over the past quarter-century demonstrates clearly that existing, heavily 'geo-political' accounts distort the real nature of Soviet activity in the area, closely constrained by local political, social and geographical factors.

In a broadly chronological series of case-studies Dr Miller argues that, American counter-influence apart, enormous physical and communicational barriers obstruct Soviet–Latin American relations, and that the lack of economic complementarity imposes a natural obstacle to trading growth: even Cuba, often cited as 'proof' of Soviet designs upon the area, is only an apparent exception.

Gorbachev in power
Stephen White

President Gorbachev has captured the imagination of the world. Yet there has been little sustained examination of either his proposals for reform or the experience of *perestroika*. In this book Stephen White provides for the first time a comprehensive and up-to-date account of the initial five years of Gorbachev's leadership.

In an opening chapter, Dr White outlines the historical and political context to Gorbachev's administration and the significant changes that have occurred over the last five years in party leadership. Subsequent chapters cover Gorbachev's political reforms and the process of democratisation; his commitment to *glasnost'*, embracing all areas of the media and creative arts; and the extent to which Gorbachev's economic reforms have been put into practice. Stephen White also explores how Gorbachev has dealt with nationality questions and ethnic communalism as well as the changing role of the Soviet Union in international affairs. A final chapter places Gorbachev's administration within the wider context of the politics of *perestroika* and assesses the problems facing the President as the Soviet Union enters the 1990s.

Soviet policies in the Middle East from World War Two to Gorbachev

GALIA GOLAN
Jay and Leoni Darwin Professor
of Soviet and East European Studies
Chairperson, Department of Political Science,
Hebrew University of Jerusalem

The right of the
University of Cambridge
to print and sell
all manner of books
was granted by
Henry VIII in 1534.
The University has printed
and published continuously
since 1584.

CAMBRIDGE UNIVERSITY PRESS
Cambridge
New York   Port Chester
Melbourne   Sydney

CAMBRIDGE UNIVERSITY PRESS
Cambridge, New York, Melbourne, Madrid, Cape Town, Singapore,
São Paulo, Delhi, Dubai, Tokyo

Cambridge University Press
The Edinburgh Building, Cambridge CB2 8RU, UK

Published in the United States of America by Cambridge University Press, New York

www.cambridge.org
Information on this title: www.cambridge.org/9780521358590

First published 1990
Reprinted 1991
Re-issued in this digitally printed version 2009

A catalogue record for this publication is available from the British Library

Library of Congress Cataloguing in Publication data
Golan, Galia.
Soviet policies in the Middle East: from World War Two to
Gorbachev/Galia Golan.
   p.   cm – (Cambridge Soviet paperbacks: 2)
ISBN 0–521–35332–7. – ISBN 0–521–35859–0 (paperback)
1. Middle East – Foreign relations – Soviet Union.
2. Soviet Union–Foreign relations – Middle East.
I. Title. II. Series.
DS63.2.S65G48 1990
327.47056′09′04–dc20 89–20986 CIP

ISBN 978-0-521-35332-8 Hardback
ISBN 978-0-521-35859-0 Paperback

Contents

Acknowledgments

I should like to thank my research assistants, Brenda Sheffer and Mark Assaraf, whose dedication and diligence have been invaluable to me. The staff and resources of the Hebrew University's Department of Political Science and Mayrock Centre for Soviet and East European Research of the Hebrew University of Jerusalem, as well as the Rand Corporation where I spent part of the time writing this book, were most helpful. The Van Leer Institute of Jerusalem provided most congenial surroundings for the completion of the book.

I should like to dedicate this book to Yuval Hayo and Sagi Tirosh in deep appreciation.

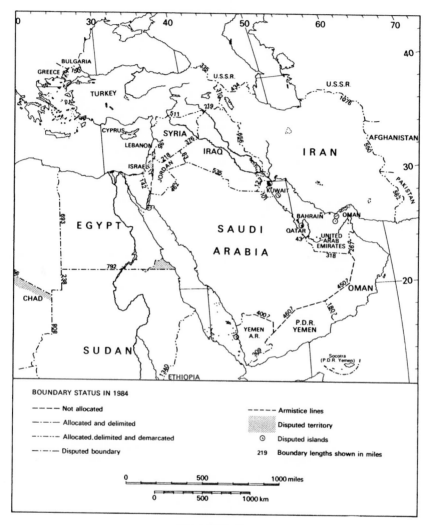

The Middle East

Introduction

The Middle East has never been a region of primary Soviet interest yet it has upon occasion played a role of inordinate significance for Soviet foreign policy-makers. In terms of Soviet foreign-policy priorities, one could posit two constants uppermost in the minds of the Soviet leadership, be it under Stalin, Malenkov, Khrushchev, or Brezhnev. The first would be protection and defence of the Soviet Union; the second would be the East–West (communism versus capitalism) struggle. The interpretation of these two priorities has varied, determining the relative importance as well as the nature of other priorities.

Beginning with a minimalistic, purely defensive approach, the highest priority would go to protecting Soviet borders, or preserving the Soviet homeland from outside attack. That has often been interpreted as the need to maintain a security belt or buffer zone just beyond Soviet borders, that is, the maintenance of friendly regimes and denial of hostile forces in areas just beyond the border. As the traditional invasion route, particularly of major powers, Eastern Europe has taken the highest priority, followed by the borders in the Far East, with China and facing Japan, and then the southern borders in south-west Asia and finally the Middle East, usually in that order. What began as a continental approach, accompanied by a conventional force military doctrine eventually became both a power projection, overseas thrust, accompanied by a doctrine of nuclear deterrence suited to continental as well as global aspirations. Strength in Europe remained the primary concern, as the focal point of both military and industrial power as well as the major theatre of potential conflict, while the United States as the powerful leader of the western alliance became the primary adversary. Asia was second to this, with overseas regions serving only an auxiliary role, although one which nonetheless increased in importance as nuclear warfare reduced the likelihood of war in Europe.

Such military priorities which could very broadly be defined in

1

terms of defence and protection have, of course, been closely connected with if not actually dictated by Soviet competition with other powers, primarily the capitalist West – led by the United States – but in time, also Communist China. Maintenance of the leadership of the world Communist movement in the face of competition from China assumed only slightly lower priority than the ideological struggle with the West. Both competitions entailed the expansion of Soviet influence and, as in the military sphere, this moved from the periphery of Soviet borders outwards and even overseas, for reasons specific to the competition with each opponent. Competition, as well as various interpretations as to just what constitutes strength, had economic as well as military, political, and ideological aspects. While the economic factor itself varied in importance from Soviet leadership to leadership, it did not on the whole alter the overall picture of Soviet priorities. For it too dictated a dominant role for the East–West relationship, be it in a competitive mode through foreign aid to the Third World or détente-related cooperation.

As a Third World region to the south of the Soviet Union, and in part contiguous with it, the Middle East has assumed importance, albeit after that of other border areas, in Soviet defence priorities. It has assumed occasionally more critical importance, however, in the context of Moscow's East–West competition or global role. It is this combination of the competitive and the defence role which has placed the Middle East relatively high within the category of Third World regions. As a region of close proximity to the Soviet Union but of vital interest to the West, it is one in which both super powers have become directly involved, raising the risk-potential of the area itself. This in turn has sporadically catapulted the region to a high-priority position in Soviet foreign policy, in direct connection with the super-power relationship.

This study examines the evolving interests of the Soviet Union in the Middle East and the pursuit of these interests since World War Two. Focusing on Soviet relations with the various actors in the region, up to the rise of Gorbachev in Moscow, particular attention is given to the crises within the Middle East and the often critical decisions connected with them. It is these crises, especially the Arab–Israeli crisis, which provided the Soviet Union with a central vehicle for the pursuit of its interests. But they also highlighted the overriding importance of the Soviet–American rivalry. Local and regional, in addition to the global problems connected with the pursuit of Soviet interests in the area will also be examined, demonstrating the complexity of the issues facing Soviet policy-makers for this region. The area as one of newly independent states, national liberation movements and national minorities; radical and conservative ideologies, Islamic fundamentalism, Arab socialism and communism; pro-western regimes, even one NATO state, and changing internal rivalries and alliances as well as coups, counter-coups, and revolution has posed a continuous challenge for Moscow. The possibility of differing responses and divergent views among Soviet policy-makers themselves is also taken into account in the study of the variegated nature of Soviet policies towards the region.

Gorbachev's approach to these problems and crises marks a change in Soviet Middle East policy, within the overall attempt to transform Soviet foreign policy. This attempt, guided by Gorbachev's 'new thinking' regarding the nature of international relations, the role of the Soviet Union in the world, the Soviet–American relationship, Soviet military doctrine, and the place of the Third World, has clear ramifications for Soviet policies in the Middle East. At the same time, because of its multi-faceted importance, as a region bordering on the Soviet Union, the scene of direct super-power involvement, and as a part of the Third World which holds economic as well as political, ideological and strategic value, the region assumes some importance in Gorbachev's foreign-policy considerations. Thus, the nature of Soviet policy towards the actors and crises within the region may well be an indication, if not a test case, of the depth and significance of the 'new thinking' altogether.

1   Soviet policy-making in the Middle East: from Stalin to Brezhnev

The decision-makers

The Soviet political system was based upon parallel bureaucracies, of the party and the government, with ultimate authority resting within the highest party body. The legitimacy for this authority was found in the Soviet constitution itself, which proclaimed the Communist Party the leading political force in the country. It derived, however, from the Leninist concept of the party and, to some degree, practices introduced by Stalin. Lenin had originally conceived of the idea of a party for the purposes of organizing, educating and leading the proletarian masses who apparently were unaware of their plight and the historic role envisaged for them by Marx and Engels. According to Lenin, imperialism had accorded the capitalist system a respite and enrichment which benefited the workers, albeit temporarily, as well. Class warfare born of the impoverishment of the working class and the decimation of the middle class by cut-throat capitalist competition had given way to class cooperation and the growth of the middle class due to this temporary rise in the standard of living in imperialist capitalist societies. The workers had, in this sense, been lulled to torpor by the satisfaction of their immediate needs (concerning wages, hours, work conditions and the like) achieved through what Lenin derisively termed 'trade unionism'. What was needed was an awakening of the workers to their real needs, which lay with the abolition of private property and the elimination of the capitalist system as such.

The party, that is, a group of professional revolutionaries who understood and could express the real as distinct from transitory interests of the proletariat was the answer to this situation. The party would be built along almost military lines of strict discipline, based on Lenin's concept of democratic centralism. Structured hierarchically as a pyramid, the party would be composed of individual cells at the base, independent of each other as befits the security considerations of an underground organization in the days of the Czar, which would feed information, ideas and proposals upward to the party bodies at the pinnacle. Decisions would then be taken at the top level, where the small leadership was the one body which had a total picture. Once decisions were taken they were disseminated downward and were to be obeyed. Further debate, opposition or appeal was forbidden beyond discussion of implementation only.

' Institutionally the party would be composed of the cells or branches at the bottom, which elected representatives to a party Congress which met periodically (roughly every five years in post-Stalin times). This Congress would in turn elect a Central Committee with a Secretariat to run day-to-day party affairs, and a Politburo (sometimes called a Presidium) to lead the party. Most but not necessarily all members of the Secretariat came to be full or candidate (non-voting) members of the Politburo, which itself was run by the Chairman of the party (at certain times called, rather, Secretary General) who, together with the Politburo was elected by the party Congress.

Once it came to power, the party, as the expression of the real interests of the proletariat, was to assume the commanding positions in the society, in the name of the proletariat. As Stalin later put it, the party, as the organization of those who knew and understood best what was necessary, would function as a general staff, leading society in the interests of the workers. It would do so quite directly, by the placement of party representatives in all institutions and organizations of the society; such representatives would convey the policies decided by the party and ensure their implementation. In this sense, under Stalin's interpretation if not that of Lenin, the various institutions of society, including governmental, scientific, cultural, judicial, legislative and mass organizations or bodies were to become transmission belts for the will of the proletariat, reflecting their interests, as expressed by the party.

This system had further justification in the Marxist explanation of society as divided into production base (means of production and relations to production) and a superstructure consisting of all else (government, science, culture and so forth). In any society, the superstructure was but a reflection or expression of the base, so in a proletarian society it was natural that the superstructure would be of a proletarian nature, just as in bourgeois society, the government, culture and other institutions were bourgeois in nature, serving the ruling bourgeois class and the capitalist form of production.

In this way a parallel party structure grew, at least with regard to the government. For every government ministry or office there came a rough equivalent within the party, in the form of a department or section in the Central Committee. The task of these bodies was to formulate and disseminate party policy, after approval by the superior party organs, namely the Secretariat and, if necessary, the Politburo, to the respective government or other bodies. The latter would also formulate their own proposals as well as provide information, both of which would be disseminated not only vertically within the government bureaucracy but also horizontally to the appropriate party counterpart, be it at the level of ministry department to Central Committee department, for example, or Minister level to party Secretary. The highest governmental level would report to the Politburo, from which it received its guidelines just as the subordinate government bodies received theirs from the subordinate party bodies. Often, though not always, this was achieved through the serving of one and the same person as head of a government bureaucracy such as the Foreign or Defence Ministry or the KGB and as a member of the Politburo, just as sometimes the head of the party and the nominal head of the government were one and the same person.

In the area of foreign affairs, therefore, there was the International Department (ID) of the Central Committee, which, aside from considering and possibly forwarding for approval the policy proposals received from the Foreign Ministry, sent its own recommendations via the responsible party secretary up to the Politburo. The ID had the advantage of receiving information not only from the Foreign Ministry but from its own party representatives and, possibly, other bureaucracies. Certainly the Politburo had the advantage of receiving from and controlling all the bureaucracies, including the army and the security forces, which at lower levels were, like the Foreign Ministry, subordinate to a Central Committee department. Initially the ID was charged with relations with non-ruling Communist parties, parallel to the central committee department dealing with ruling Communist parties. In the 1950s, however, its functions were expanded to include policy regarding all non-Communist states. From this time, until Gorbachev, the ID was headed by candidate Politburo member and party secretary Boris Ponomarev, who was believed to be subordinate to the far more powerful party ideology chief and full Politburo member Mikhail Suslov.

Khrushchev, who expanded the role of the ID, also set up a series of research institutes, some in the party, but most in the Academy of Sciences, which also dealt with international affairs and subjects of foreign policy. The most prestigious and important of these was the Institute for World Economy and International Affairs (IMEMO), but there were also area institutes, such as the Africa Institute, the Oriental Institute, the Far East Institute and, increasingly important, the Institute for the Study of the USA and Canada. The exact role of the research institutes in the making of Soviet foreign policy and their relationship to the ID has been the subject of some question among western observers. The institutes provided research and probably some policy recommendations to the ID, with whom they had a quite close relationship. A number of institute officials and researchers assumed positions in the ID, which itself employed consultants from the institutes as well as, apparently, commissioning research and organizing joint work with them. Some of the heads of the more influential institutes, IMEMO and the USA Institute, achieved party positions as members or candidate members of the Central Committee.

The making of policy with regard to the Middle East was ultimately the task of the party and the final decision-making in the Politburo. It has been far from clear, however, just who in the upper echelons of the party played a particular role with regard to the Middle East. Molotov apparently played a central role regarding policy for the region under Stalin, along with Y. A. Zhdanov in the immediate post-World War Two period. Khrushchev even consulted Molotov at the beginning of the Soviet involvement in Egypt, despite the fact that D. T. Shepilov was then, briefly, Foreign Minister. *Ex officio* the head of the ID, namely Ponomarev, and Gromyko as Foreign Minister even prior to joining the Politburo in 1973, were the most directly involved. Ponomarev and Suslov figured in contacts with Middle Eastern Communists, the former also dealing with national liberation movements. Podgornyi and Kosygin were also directly involved in meetings and contacts as well as decision-making together with Brezhnev. As Defence Minister Grechko was deeply involved, but his successor Ustinov appeared to play a less direct role. Naval commander Gorshkov played a larger role in policy decisions in this region, apparently, than other military figures with the possible exception of air force commander Kutakhov.

Policy proposals conveyed by Ponomarev presumably originated within the Middle Eastern section of the ID, under the supervision of the deputy head in charge of Third World affairs. During much of the Brezhnev period this deputy head was Rostislav Ul'ianovskii, who came from a research institute and dealt with theoretical issues. His

successor, Karen Brutents, had particular responsibility for the Middle
East. The Foreign Ministry appears to have had a great deal of input,
with Middle Eastern section head Poliakov serving as a major negotiator though not a policy-maker. Evgenii Primakov was the senior Soviet
Middle East specialist. First as deputy director of IMEMO and then as
head of the Oriental Institute, Primakov appears to have been a
primary spokesman for the regime's policies on the region in the 1970s
and onward. He may have had some input into decision-making, at
least as an adviser, even in the pre-Gorbachev period.

Soviet Interests in the Middle East

Decision-making as well as the policy proposals or even personal
preferences of those involved were determined by a number of factors.
These included, as was the case with every state, traditional, strategic-
military, economic and political interests. For the Soviet Union,
ideological interests were also relevant if not central, while domestic
public opinion presumably played a smaller role than in western
countries, for example. Differences of opinion, even in the form of
what could be interpreted as bureaucratic politics or pressures may
also have played a role, at least in the Brezhnev era if not earlier. Yet
the relative importance of most of these factors, as we shall see, varied
over the years, from one Soviet leader to the next and within changing
perceptions of East–West relations and the Third World.

The Soviet Union has had a number of traditional interests in the
Middle East, which even predate the Soviet era. The first of these is the
natural interest in a region to the south of its borders, be it on the
borders of the Russian Empire or of the Soviet Union. It has always
been in Russian interests to maintain stable and friendly relations with
the nations on its border. And this, at times, was perceived as
achievable only through the extension of Russian influence, even
control, of the border areas or nations bordering Russia. Minimally,
this was an interest in preventing the domination or presence of
hostile forces on or near the border. A more specific traditional interest
has been the concern for access to and from the Mediterranean Sea via
the Dardanelles and the Bosphorus. These Turkish Straits constitute
the exit route for Russian shipping – commercial or military – from the
Black Sea to the Mediterranean and westward to the Atlantic or
southeasterly through the Suez Canal en route to Asia (including the
Russian Far East). Given Russia's lack of warm water ports, this access
route to the Mediterranean is particularly important. The Turkish

Straits constitute the entry point as well as exit for ships plying the Black Sea. Thus control of this waterway has had great significance for preventing the entry of a foreign, possibly hostile fleet into the Black Sea. These traditional, basically defensive interests in the area were frequently augmented by great power aspirations which sought influence not only for the purpose of preventing a military threat but also to expand power in competition with other countries.

Under Stalin, the pursuit of these interests was determined by the prominence of ideological factors in Soviet foreign policy. In this region as well as other areas adjacent to the Soviet Union, Stalin's post-World War Two policy sought not only to weaken the power of the West, namely Britain, but also to lay the groundwork for what he perceived as the inevitable battle between the Soviet Union and its wartime allies, that is, the ultimate conflict between the Communist world and the capitalist world. His was a bi-polar view of the world, enunciated by Zhdanov at the founding of the Comintern in September 1947 as a two-camp theory. In this view, a country was either socialist or capitalist; the only way to deal with the latter was to work towards its overthrow, that is, preparation for revolution. It was a relatively cautious policy inasmuch as the Soviet Union was economically and militarily inferior to the West. It was also a policy based on a continental military doctrine, disdaining action beyond the Asian and European continents and limiting involvement to the periphery of the Soviet Union. It was, however, mainly the ideological aspect of this policy which led to a period of relative inaction in the Third World, beyond initial efforts in the border states of Turkey and Iran. It barred cooperation with any but socialist regimes and Marxist forces, with only rare, temporary exceptions in the interests of evicting the British (for example, from India or Palestine).

Soviet entry into the Third World began with the death of Stalin in 1953 and the abandonment of the two-camp theory. There have been claims that Stalin himself was contemplating such a change; there was talk at the 1952 CPSU Congress of the need to exploit divisions within the capitalist world – a euphemism from the days of Lenin for cooperating with capitalist states, ostensibly in order to divide them. Whatever Stalin's intentions, the change came only after his death, with the rise to power first of Malenkov and then of Khrushchev. Instead of the two-camp approach, peaceful coexistence was introduced. Without abandoning the competition between capitalism and communism, and the belief in the ultimate victory of socialism, peaceful coexistence shifted this competition to less provocative, less

doctrinaire, and more pragmatic means. Born of the concerns generated by an appreciation of the catastrophic nature of nuclear weapons,
the new foreign policy was to reduce tensions and the possibility of
war, in the belief that wars would inevitably escalate to global nuclear
war.

This had a number of ramifications for the Third World. If direct
East–West confrontation were to be ruled out, the scene of the
competition was to be elsewhere or indirect, that is, a competition for
the Third World. At the same time, because of the dangers inherent in
war, even this competition was to be peaceful, that is, in the form of
economic, political and ideological but not armed competition. Therefore, rather than the both dangerous and often self-defeating demand
for an all or nothing commitment from the new states of the Third
World or the national liberation forces active there, Moscow was
satisfied with the more modest but potentially positive stance of Third
World non-alignment. This was in effect recognition of the possibility
of a third road, by far less demanding and less dangerous.

At the same time, Third World non-alignment or neutrality had
positive aspects for the Soviet Union. Neutrality meant in fact the
refusal to join in alliances with a great power and refusal to grant
military rights and bases. At that point in time, it was the West rather
than the Soviet Union which was seeking overseas bases and the
creation of a network of regional alliances. Moreover, non-alignment
generally implied independence from the former imperialist colonial
rulers, and again it was the West, not the Soviet Union, which was
perceived as imperialist in most of the Third World. Thus, encouragement of non-alignment was virtually encouragement of an anti-
western policy and, therefore, served the Soviet interest of reducing
western power and influence.

Recognition of the value of non-aligned, less than socialist regimes
in the competition with the West carried with it the idea of cooperation
with the new, usually bourgeois nationalist, sometimes even military,
regimes of the Third World. To accommodate this ideologically, there
was a return to the Leninist approach to what in Marxist-Leninist
terms had been called the backward nations. In such countries, where
the proletariat was small or non-existent, forces could be joined with
the nationalists, that is, the national bourgeoisie. As a first step it was
necessary to join in their anti-imperialist, national democratic revolution, and then lead them onward, to the next step, that of proletarian
socialist revolution. This basic idea, or tactic, underwent numerous
interpretations and refinements over the years (discussed below in

chapter 14), but loosely interpreted it provided for cooperation with the new regimes on the basis of a united front, coalition building, evolutionary rather than revolutionary approach.

With these changes in the Soviet attitude and policy towards the Third World, there could be a different approach to the nations and conflicts of the Middle East. States, such as Egypt, which had been rejected because of their bourgeois nationalist regimes could now be considered candidates for Soviet cooperation in Moscow's global competition with the West. Local nationalist struggles could be supported not as an exception but as a rule, with the demand only for an anti-western, not necessarily socialist, orientation. Thus, in the post-Stalin 1950s Soviet traditional interests in the Middle East were joined by the primarily political interest in removing the West from the region even beyond the immediate border by means of active but peaceful competition, in the economic, political and ideological spheres. Encouragement of non-alignment was to be part of this, while revolutionary as well as armed activity was to be limited, in favour of cooperation with the local bourgeois but anti-imperialist governments. While this change in policy was better suited to the realities of the emerging newly independent states, it was the result not so much of these realities as of a new foreign-policy approach altogether in Moscow, born of a different appreciation of the threat of nuclear war and a new appraisal of the place of the Third World in the East–West contest.

In the 1960s Soviet policy in the Middle East appeared to undergo another change as a result of a shift in Soviet interests. Moscow began to seek bases and, by the 1970s, alliances, in apparent contradiction to the encouragement of non-alignment. This was not by any means a return to the Zhdanovist two-camp theory with its ideological counterpart in fomenting Communist revolution. Indeed, ideological interests remained in the secondary position allotted them by Stalin's successors. It might be described as an alteration of the idea of neutrality in order to take advantage of the expulsion of the West from much of the area by securing the Soviets' own, new presence. On the whole, however, the pursuit of bases and alliances was more directly the result of the rise in importance of the Soviets' military-strategic interests in the region in the 1960s.

There had always been an element of military-strategic interest in traditional border security and in the access route through the Turkish Straits to and from the Black Sea. In the 1960s, however, the military interest took unprecedented priority, as a result of changes in the

Soviet military doctrine and posture. A change had been brewing for some time, but a decisive factor may have been the Cuban missile crisis and the shortcomings of Soviet military posture revealed in that crisis. Soviet strategic thinking under Khrushchev had been based upon and focused around nuclear power. While this had been an improvement over Stalin's technological shortsightedness, Khrushchev's strategic approach tended to neglect, to some degree, other considerations such as the conventional forces on the sea and in the air. It also proved to be a serious drain on the Soviet economy.

The placement of medium-range missiles in Cuba was itself an effort to overcome some of these shortcomings, but the Cuban failure glaringly demonstrated the gaps in Khrushchev's nuclear strategy. The crisis revealed Moscow's basic military weakness *vis-à-vis* the United States when it became necessary to find a non-nuclear solution to a nuclear crisis situation some distance away. More generally, it demonstrated Moscow's military weakness at a global level, in contrast to the already apparent American capability to intervene in any number of far-flung theatres of action. While playing a contributory role in Khrushchev's fall from power in 1964, the Cuban failure opened the way for strategic thinking and military development which had in fact already been commenced in a limited fashion. Specifically this was to include the expansion and development of the Soviet fleet, and its forward deployment in the world's seas in an effort to gain Soviet flexibility and increased options.

The intensive expansion of Soviet naval power, which became apparent in the 1960s, was due also to a development which preceded – and probably contributed to – the Cuban missile venture. This was the appearance of the American Polaris nuclear submarine, a seaborne nuclear-weapon (SSBM) launcher to which the Soviets had virtually no answer. It was in part to meet this challenge that the Soviets shifted to forward deployment of their fleet, relying heavily on the development of antisubmarine warfare as well as production of an SSBM capability of their own. Thus, the more general expansion of the Soviet fleet in the pursuit of global flexibility in military-strategic competition with the United States and its allies, combined with the more specific response to the deployment of the Polaris in the Mediterranean Sea, occasioned the opening of the Soviet Mediterranean Naval Squadron in 1964 and, with it, the upgrading of the Middle East in Soviet strategic considerations. The direct connection with the Polaris was evident not only from the timing of the opening of the squadron but also from subsequent developments, for as the Americans placed a modified Polaris and then the Poseidon submarines in the Indian Ocean, thereby targeting Soviet industrial centres from sea-borne launching sites still further away, Soviet ships began to appear on a regular basis in that area as well. And, for all that the Mediterranean Squadron was targeted against the US Sixth Fleet and NATO's south-ern flank, the overall thrust of Soviet military interests in the late 1960s-early 1970s came to be south-south-eastward, in the direction of the Indian Ocean.

The expansion of the Soviet fleet brought with it other Soviet military undertakings, for the Soviets had not developed aircraft carriers. The decision to do so was taken only in the 1960s, with the first two such carriers entering service only in the 1970s. Moscow, therefore, sought not only shore facilities for its fleet but air bases as well for the aircraft necessary to the functioning and protection of the fleet. It was these requirements that transformed the Soviet interest in the Middle Eastern states, specifically Egypt, into a primarily strategic-military one, as Moscow sought multifaceted support facil-ities for its Mediterranean Squadron together with Red Sea–Indian Ocean moorings, for intelligence-gathering as well as other purposes. Egypt was the focal point of this venture, mainly because of the relative stability of its ports and airfields but also because of its geopolitical position in the region and the relative stability of its regime. Thus, prior to the Six-Day War, the Soviets sought port facilities in Egypt and by the late 1960s had undertaken the develop-ment not only of these facilities but of some six air bases as well. With the expulsion of the Soviet military advisers in 1972, and the sub-sequent deterioration of Soviet–Egyptian relations, Moscow sought a strategic alternative in Syria, concentrating on port and air-base access.

The pursuit of Moscow's new strategic-military interest in the Middle East carried with it certain problems which may or may not have been appreciated by the Soviet leadership when undertaken in the early 1960s. For example, the Soviets' appearance in this new role in the region as a super power seeking bases and a military presence threatened to harm Moscow's anti-imperialist image. Aside from the border states Turkey and Iran, the Middle Eastern states had never experienced nor perceived the Russians as imperialist. This relative advantage over the West might now be lost as Moscow pursued its new military objectives with and in these countries. Indeed the Soviet effort might even push these countries back into the hands of the West, or, at least, arouse a greater interest on the part of the western powers in the region and in competing militarily with the Soviets in the region.

At the same time, the pursuit of bases and facilities created a certain vulnerability for the Soviets *vis-à-vis* their Middle Eastern clients. Put in the position of supplicant, the Soviets could become dependent, in a sense, upon the host states and forced to make concessions in order to maintain their presence. This might prove costly to the Soviet Union, in the form of economic and other concessions as well as military aid, particularly should there be an attempt to cancel their assets and presence. It would be difficult both logistically and politically for the Soviets to remain by force in a country beyond the Soviet border area, particularly countries in which the Soviets had no significant political-ideological base of support. Even if logistically possible, it was unlikely that Moscow would want to move troops or combat ships to the region for any lengthy period of time. Nor could it be certain that an attempt to remain by force would not evoke a western military response. Far short of such an eventuality, another military threat existed. If provision of aid and arms to these states were the price Moscow had to pay to enter and remain, there was a great risk that this would in fact encourage and enable these states (particularly the ones locked in ongoing conflict with Israel) to go to war. This in turn ran the risk not only of having Soviet arms systems and possibly personnel harmed, lost or fall into western hands, but also of actually drawing the Soviet Union into an armed conflict and possible confrontation with the United States.

Many of these problems remained even when changes occurred in Soviet strategic-military interests in the region. With the American development of the Poseidon and plans for the even longer-range Trident sea-launched missile, the Indian Ocean, and the states on its periphery, assumed an increasingly important place in Soviet strategic thinking. Moreover, locations further west in the Mediterranean became feasible targets for Soviet military interests once Moscow succeeded in improving its own means of supporting its fleet at sea and larger numbers of long-range aircraft. Thus, by the 1970s, Soviet strategic-military interests, which had dictated the massive move of the Soviet Union into the region in the 1960s, shifted somewhat from the area of the Fertile Crescent (specifically Egypt and Syria) westward and especially southeastward, to the area of the Indian Ocean-Persian Gulf as the latter gradually became the focal point for future superpower confrontation. The advent of the American Rapid Deployment Force in the late 1970s contributed to the increased importance of that area, even as Soviet economic difficulties were dictating something of a cutback in the overseas functions of the Soviet military.

Western naval expert, Michael MccGwire has argued that with the changes in Soviet military doctrine, once again, in the mid-1970s emphasizing theatre (especially European) warfare, Soviet military planning maintained the importance (though possibly reduced) of the Mediterranean down to the Red Sea as part of the southwestern theatre command. This doctrinal shift reduced somewhat the strategic importance of the Indian Ocean–Persian Gulf area, the southern theatre of warfare being of less importance or danger in time of war. Yet ongoing SSBN requirements in the Indian Ocean, the importance of the southern sea route, and the traditional concern for a western (mainly American) move in the Gulf, continued to dictate a primary Soviet interest in the area, perhaps of even higher priority than the eastern Mediterranean. Under Gorbachev, Soviet military doctrine was to change once again, with a significant reduction of the strategic importance of the whole region altogether.

Soviet economic interests in the area have been said to be linked to oil and energy needs, reflecting perhaps the dependence of the western world and Japan upon the energy resources of this region. Much of the Soviet move into the Middle East in the 1960s was explained in the West not by the rise in Moscow's military interest in the area but by what was perceived as a growing Soviet need for Middle Eastern oil. It was argued that the Soviet Union could not keep up with the demand of its own domestic energy needs, which increased at a rate of 8 per cent per year. Nor could it go on providing the vast majority (roughly 80 per cent) of Eastern Europe's needs, (representing 55 per cent of total Soviet oil exports) as it had in the past. At a minimum, Moscow would not be able to maintain its lucrative hard-currency sales of oil and natural gas which represented 40 per cent of Moscow's energy exports and constituted the largest single foreign-currency earner for the country. The main problem could be traced to the lack of a suitable infrastructure and the technological difficulties connected with the extraction and transportation of Soviet oil and gas reserves, located mainly in Siberia. CIA estimates in the 1970s, therefore, predicted that the Soviet Union would become a net importer of oil by the 1980s.

Yet the Soviet Union was the largest producer of oil in the world, producing over 600 million barrels per year. It was the world's second largest exporter of oil, second only to Saudi Arabia, exporting 150 million barrels a year. Some 5 per cent of these exports went to Third

World countries which included even Middle Eastern countries such as Syria, Turkey, Egypt and Yemen. All of the already noted problems with regard to extraction, transportation and rising needs did exist, but certain principles of Soviet foreign policy dictated a search for a solution which would exclude the possibility of dependence upon an outside source for such a vital need.

The solutions were found in a number of measures. As early as the late 1960s Moscow instructed its Eastern European 'clients' to begin purchasing oil elsewhere. This relieved some of the burden of supplying these states, reducing the Soviet share of their oil imports to roughly 65 per cent (although Moscow had to be careful that the economic burden thus created for these weak states did not strain Soviet resources in other ways). Domestically, and perhaps most importantly, the Soviets began a strict energy conservation programme. They thereby succeeded in reducing by half – from 8 per cent to 4 per cent – the yearly rate of increased domestic energy consumption. They also accelerated the development and increased the use of alternative energy sources with some success. They were less successful in seeking outside assistance for the improvement of oil extraction; primarily efforts to conclude agreements with Japan encountered unsurmountable difficulties (mainly political).

Nonetheless, the Soviet Union was not and never became a significant importer of oil. Such imports as there were did not exceed five to six million barrels per year, as distinct from the 150 million exported yearly. There was a brief period in the early 1970s when Moscow did purchase Iraqi and Libyan oil, temporarily, when these states nationalized western companies in their countries and sought new markets until relations with their traditional western partners were once again normalized. Even these Soviet purchases were reduced to a bare minimum when Iraq (in 1973) and Libya (in 1974) began demanding hard-currency payments from the Soviet Union, at the new, higher prices.

There were, however, a number of three-way deals, whereby the Soviet Union exported or imported oil with Middle Eastern states as part of supplies to third parties. For example, the Soviets provided oil and natural gas to Egypt, which in turn exported oil to Japan and India for Moscow; the Soviets exported oil and gas to Europe for the Kuwaitis and the United Arab Emirates, who in turn sent oil to the Far East for the Soviets. Such three-way deals also existed with the Shah's Iran, which supplied southern Russia while the Soviets exported to western Europe. Such arrangements hardly made Moscow dependent upon Middle Eastern imports, any more than they made the Middle Eastern countries dependent upon Soviet imports. Nor were they of a magnitude or nature to account for the increased Soviet presence in the region in the 1960s. Some of these deals fell off with the oil glut of the 1980s; indeed Soviet hard-currency revenues were badly hit by the fall in demand, and prices.

While Soviet economic interests in Middle Eastern oil were of a limited nature, there was a political side to the oil factor, for western Europe and Japan clearly were dependent upon Middle Eastern oil. Presumably, therefore, the Soviets did have an interest in gaining control over this resource, at least to the extent of being able to threaten the regular flow of vital oil supplies to the West and Japan. Disruption of these supplies could produce economic crisis in the western world and aggravate disputes between the western countries. Yet it is not entirely certain that the Soviets were willing to run the risks involved in interfering or even threatening to interfere in the flow of Middle Eastern oil to the West. Disruption of the world oil market might have adverse effects on Soviet involvement in this market as well, just as interference in the transportation routes could have a negative effect on some of Moscow's deals and merchant traffic. More importantly, an attempt at or even a threat of interference would be a high-risk action, bound to arouse a western, specifically American, response even of a military nature.

The Soviet Union did encourage the oil producers to maintain the oil boycott they introduced in 1973, but it clearly did not control or even instigate the move. The states most responsible for and involved in the boycott were not states allied with Moscow; indeed the key countries, Saudi Arabia and the smaller Gulf states, had mostly poor if any relations with Moscow. Libya at the time was still hostile to the Soviet Union and, in any case, did not participate fully in the boycott. Moscow's only real friend among the major oil producers at the time was Iraq, who had nationalized its western companies and was, therefore, temporarily uninvolved in western markets in any case. Moreover, Moscow could not have provided an alternative market for the oil producers, nor suspended its own sales to hard-currency areas. Thus it was hardly a credible champion of the boycott idea. This may have been the reason that although Soviet propaganda applauded the boycott, Moscow made a greater effort to encourage nationalizations. These were a much longer term, politically effective, as well as ideologically sound measure. They did not, however, require the kind of military presence undertaken by the Soviets in the region in the 1960s or after.

There was even a negative side to the Middle Eastern oil issue, from the Soviets' point of view, although it may not have been a determining factor in Soviet considerations at the time. The increased wealth of the oil-producing states led to increased independence and power on their part. This in turn augmented the independence of the less fortunate Arab states, such as Egypt and Syria, whom the oil producers helped; it also enlarged the Arabs' power in the world. Further, the energy crisis of the 1970s drew the United States more deeply into the region, strengthening American willingness to compete with the Soviet Union for influence in the region, out of an interest in protecting the vital needs of America's allies as well as its own interests. Moreover, the boycott of the early 1970s spurred the West to search for alternative sources of energy outside the region, which ultimately succeeded and led to the oil glut of the 1980s, the fall in oil prices, and the blow to Soviet hard-currency revenues.

At its high point, however, the energy crisis did have other, positive, effects on Soviet economic interests in the Middle East. It enhanced the ability of the oil-rich states and their allied beneficiaries to pay for Soviet goods, which in time became increasingly important to the Soviet Union. During the Khrushchev period and even into the Brezhnev–Kosygin period, Soviet economic interests in relations with the Third World had been subordinated to political and strategic interests. Economic competition with the West in the Third World had meant, for the Soviets, competition as to which side could offer Third World states greater economic benefits, easier terms and more impressive projects, rather than concern for profitability, return on investments, favourable trade balances or other strictly economic considerations. By the early 1970s, however, this policy changed. In an effort to improve the Soviet Union's own situation, Moscow began to elevate the economic factor in its foreign-policy considerations, seeking a return on its investments and economic benefits from its involvement.

This was to have two significant results. The first was something of a shift in Soviet trade patterns in the direction of states which could pay. The petro-dollar-rich states of the Gulf fit this description, and increased interest in the Gulf could be discerned with the rise in Soviet emphasis upon economic interests. The second, connected, result was the demand not only for more favourable trade balances, which the Gulf states could provide more readily than the states of the Fertile Crescent (specifically Egypt and Syria), but also a demand for more direct returns. This included a demand for payment for Soviet arms which, previously, had been provided through long-term, low-interest loans (often converted to outright grants or generously extended) or equally generous barter deals. Now, in the early 1970s, came the request for payment, and payment in hard-currency. Indeed arms became a leading Soviet export, bringing in some 20 per cent of Soviet hard-currency earnings (in addition to the 50 per cent brought in by oil exports). In this realm too the oil-rich Gulf states were better able to pay, occasionally providing the wherewithal for the less rich Egyptians and Syrians to meet the Soviets' demands.

These changes in Soviet economic policy, born of the increased attention to economic factors, brought about a gradual shift in Soviet Middle East interest from the area of the Fertile Crescent to that of the Gulf. This coincided roughly with the shift in strategic interests in the same direction. While neither change was total – there continued to be a strategic interest in the Mediterranean area and economic interests were occasionally waived for the sake of important strategic or political gains – they did result in somewhat altered policies towards and diminished emphasis upon the states of the Fertile Crescent, with the exception of Turkey. Moreover, the demand for hard-currency payment for arms greatly limited whatever leverage or influence the Soviets may have hoped to gain from Arab dependence upon Soviet arms in the conflict-ridden Middle East. The riches of the Middle East may have enhanced the Arabs' ability to pay, but it also enhanced their independence, creating the need for greater incentive to make those payments to Moscow rather than western suppliers. Indeed, the pursuit of Moscow's economic interests as defined in the 1970s placed it in direct competition with the West in the one area most difficult for the Soviets, that of commercial ventures. If the lure of easy terms and showpiece projects could no longer be used, Soviet goods and services had to measure up to those of the West. Although, given the needs and structures of the Middle Eastern economies, Soviet failure to compete was not a foregone conclusion. Nonetheless, the new economic objectives did create problems for Soviet policy-makers, in the realm of political as well as economic interests.

Political interests are often closely connected with economic and strategic interests. It is often difficult to determine which precedes which or promotes the other or takes precedence over the other. A military presence, for example, may well be intended to safeguard or promote political or economic objectives, or the reverse may apply. In the mid-1960s and 1970s it would appear that political interests served in effect to promote the Soviets' military-strategic interests in the

Middle East. In the 1950s it had been sufficient to support nonalignment in the interest of removing the West in what was basically a political competition. In the late 1960s and 1970s, however, the Soviet search for a form of alliance, that is, friendship treaties, government-to-government and party-to-party relations, and deeper bonds, may well have been designed to secure the military gains made in the form of bases and naval facilities.

The ideal way to secure these interests, from the Soviet point of view, would be the ascendance of Communist regimes in the countries of the region. Presumably if the Soviet Union could have a Communist regime in one country or another it would welcome it; indeed this was most likely a long-term objective of the Soviet leadership. Post-Stalin Soviet policy, however, indicated that the Soviets realized that such an eventuality was highly unlikely, primarily because of the strength of both nationalism and Islam in the region. They probably also appreciated the risks involved in trying to accomplish such a transformation. The pursuit of such an objective might jeopardize the more immediate military-strategic interests. It might also endanger Soviet interests elsewhere in the Third World, while running the risk of provoking a western response even of a military nature. The Soviet political objective in the Middle East, therefore, was not necessarily Communist regimes but, rather, security for Soviet bases and facilities there and a measure of control sufficient to prevent any danger to the continued enjoyment of these assets.

There were additional, perhaps broader, political interests. Soviet progress in the Middle East, particularly in a politically influential state like Egypt, might facilitate Soviet moves towards other Third World states. Even Soviet interests in obtaining bases elsewhere, for example in the Horn of Africa, might be so served. At the same time, the pro-Soviet camp of those supporting Soviet policies in international bodies and generally in the competition with the West, would be augmented. There was also the added incentive for Moscow of the Sino-Soviet dispute. The Middle East was by no means a significant factor in this dispute; nor was the dispute a central component of Soviet Middle East considerations. Sino-Soviet competition did exist, however, throughout the Third World, including the Middle East, be it at the level of relations with local states, support for radical. and national liberation movements, or influence among local Communists. Therefore, an at least secondary Soviet political interest in the region was a desire to neutralize the Chinese.

Chinese criticism did highlight one serious problem for the Soviets in the political sphere: the issue of détente or, rather, the conflict between détente and the pursuit of Soviet interests in the Middle East. The Chinese accused the Soviet Union of sacrificing the Middle East (and the whole Third World) to its interest in détente, while the United States accused Moscow of ignoring détente in the pursuit of Soviet interests in the Middle East. The actual function of détente in Soviet policy depended to a large degree upon the interpretation of détente. The Soviets had strong economic, military and political interests in East–West détente, but they viewed it as a very broad, highly flexible concept. From their point of view, détente clearly did not come instead of competition with the West and the pursuit of defensive or forward positions *vis-à-vis* the West or strategic interests and bases. Yet it was different from peaceful coexistence in that it called for a degree of cooperation in a number of areas, particularly in the economic sphere. What it sought was to create and maintain an international atmosphere conducive to this cooperation, reducing the risks of confrontation and the costs of the arms race.

Therefore, just as the pursuit of Soviet strategic interests in the region was not to be allowed to lead Moscow into military confrontation with the West, so too the pursuit of Soviet political as well as other interests in the Middle East were not to be permitted to destroy détente. In the case of détente, the parameters, as well as the risks, may not have been as clear, however. It was here that the Soviet interpretation was crucial or, rather, the Soviets' interpretation of Washington's view of détente. Each step taken by the Soviets had to be weighed against the potential conflict with détente, based on an estimate as to how much the United States would tolerate or just how far Moscow might stretch the concept. The situation was complicated by the fact that the United States believed in linkage, defining détente as an all-embracing, binding policy applicable everywhere. The Soviets, however, did not ascribe to linkage. Indeed, under pressure not only from the Chinese, other Communist states such as Cuba and Third World allies, but also from opponents to détente within the Soviet leadership, Moscow devised a formula of the 'divisibility of détente'. This referred to the idea that détente was to be applied at the super-power level while revolutionary activity could continue at other levels. This was meant to answer those, inside and outside the Kremlin, who claimed that the Soviet Union was willing to sacrifice its friends and revolutionary goals for the sake of its relationship with Washington.

There were other problems in the Soviets' pursuit of their political interests. The effort to obtain a degree of control, for example by penetration of the army, the ruling party, the security forces, and the government, tarnished the Soviets' non-imperialist image. The actual presence and behaviour of Soviet personnel contributed to the growing perception of an interfering, imperialist Soviet patron. Moreover, attempts to influence or manipulate internal politics was a risky as well as objectionable aspect of Soviet political involvement. Moscow ran the risk of supporting the wrong elements or moving unwisely. Such moves threatened to jeopardize the future of their broader interests in military or other benefits or, in some cases, their very presence. At the same time, just as the pursuit of strategic interests ran the risk of providing the military wherewithal for a military action detrimental to Soviet regional or global interests, so too the pursuit of political gains could lead to the championing of positions more radical than those of Moscow and counterproductive to broader Soviet interests in the region or globally. There was, of course, the option of employing economic or military measures or sanctions to ensure Soviet interests. Yet there was no guarantee that these would work – indeed they did not – while they also ran the risk of pushing the Soviet client into the waiting arms of the West. Soviet political assistance, like its economic or even military aid, might not be considered as valuable as that of the United States, for example. At the very least, the existence of an alternative to the Soviet Union for the Middle Eastern states, placed the Soviets at a disadvantage *vis-à-vis* their own clients, the latter often raising the ante for a continued Soviet presence or role. This in turn made it increasingly difficult for the Soviets 'to deliver', complicating further their relationship with the states involved, while possibly strengthening the internal divisions in Moscow over central foreign policy issues.

In the late 1970s and early 1980s, with the shift in Soviet military-strategic interests which we have seen, the political interest appeared to take its former position of priority. This was also the result of the increased inroads made by the Americans in the region, at the expense of the Soviet Union, and Soviet concern over the possibility of an American monopoly. The highly competitive approach of Washington in the Middle East, despite détente at the super-power level, prompted a Soviet concentration on blocking American progress. This was sought by means first, of an attempted creation of a bloc of radical nations in the region and, later, beginning in the early 1980s, efforts to broaden support for a Soviet role in Middle East affairs. In both instances, political and economic interests appeared to take priority.

This may also have been due to the change and then possible reduction of the military-strategic interest of the late 1970s-early 1980s as already noted.

Another possible cause for the rise in at least the political factors in Soviet thinking in the late 1970s may have been the return to ideological interests. In addition to the fact that Khrushchev's was simply a more pragmatic approach than that of Stalin, there were quite good reasons for the Soviet Union to avoid an ideological approach to the Middle East. The strength of both nationalism and Islam militated against Communism, and any emphasis upon atheistic Marxism merely highlighted the alien nature of the Soviet Union itself on the Middle Eastern scene. In keeping, therefore, with the Leninist tactics reintroduced by Khrushchev, local Marxists were encouraged to cooperate with the bourgeois nationalist leaders of these states, in effect postponing any revolutionary ideas to some distant future.

In theory, the Communists would be serving this long-term goal inasmuch as they would be helping to create national democracies in which their own activities would become legal and develop, preparing the way for them to take the leadership in transforming their societies to the next stage, that is, socialist development. Their efforts, and image, would be assisted by the benevolent non-imperialist, ostensibly disinterested aid accorded the state by the Soviet Union. In practice, this tactic was by no means to the advantage of the local Communist parties. Some of them were virtually destroyed or dissolved as a result; some were basically neutralized by their limited partnerships with the ruling parties. Many were in fact split, and weakened, by opposition to Moscow's orders.

No essential change in this downgrading of ideological objectives occurred as a result of the difficulties it posed for the local Communist parties. Rather, the change which finally did come, in the 1970s, was the result of the Soviets' own failure to maintain their interests and the loyalty of their clients, specifically the Egyptians. The expulsion of the Soviet military advisers from Egypt in 1972 was perceived as final proof of mistakes which had begun to become apparent with earlier Soviet failures in Ghana and Indonesia. It occasioned a rethinking of Third World policy which tended to the conclusion that a strong organizational framework based on a solid ideological foundation would be a far better way to guarantee a state's loyalty and orientation than reliance upon charismatic leaders and nationalist sentiments. The idea of vanguard revolutionary parties based on Marxism-Leninism was therefore proposed in what could be viewed as a return to the ascendancy of the ideological factor in Soviet Third World policy.

Theoretically this entailed a radicalization of Soviet policies, despite the potential costs in terms of other interests in the Third World or even at the super-power level. To the degree that it was put into practice, or believed by local regimes to have been put into practice, the pursuit of ideologically purer regimes carried with it some risks. While it might produce the desired results, which it did to some degree in Africa, it could alarm local allies as well as other countries, including the West. Such alarm might then upset whatever balance had been achieved between local, even revolutionary, regimes and the Communists, leading to even greater difficulties for local Communists than the previous, more pragmatic but cautious policy had.

There were, therefore, differences of opinion within Soviet foreign-policy circles as to the advisability of this policy, particularly, as they argued, in view of the continued absence of suitably large proletarian bases for such parties in the Third World. Indeed the policy was barely applied, if at all, to the Middle East where other considerations continued to take priority. Yet this issue points to another set of considerations which may have influenced Soviet policies towards and within the Middle East: differences of opinion or policy preferences within the Soviet foreign-policy elite. Such differences were discernible on the broadest issue of foreign policy, that of East–West relations and détente, with many ramifications with regard to Third World policy in general and Middle East policy in particular.

As we have seen, the idea of the 'divisibility of détente' was a Brezhnev response to a number of opponents of détente even within the Soviet Communist Party (CPSU) Politburo. This opposition did not necessarily originate with advocacy of greater involvement in the Third World. It is true that most of the supporters of détente, such as Kosygin and Andropov, also held what could be called a 'Soviet-Union-first' approach. This was a preference for Soviet needs, particularly in the economic sphere, over costly foreign entanglements and risk-taking which might impede the economic aspect of détente relations with the West so crucial to Soviet economic development. There was also the view, often overlapping with this 'Soviet-Union-first' approach, that involvement abroad, particularly in conflict situations, ran the risk not only of damaging détente but of provoking world war. Indeed many who espoused this view, including Andropov as well as many leading party and institute theoreticians and even some military figures, often argued that détente eliminated the need for heavy Soviet (particularly military) involvement abroad, for it restrained the West and thus created the conditions for indigenous, peaceful change in the Third world. The absence of détente, however, need not change the attitude towards Soviet involvement, for an aggressive West, as distinct from a restrained West, rendered involvement too dangerous.

The anti-détentists, particularly in the military, argued that the West was inherently aggressive and, therefore, could not be restrained. Their conclusion usually was that this aggressiveness made it incumbent upon the Soviet Union to play an active role abroad, to counter the enemy and promote a change in the 'correlation of forces' in the world. Where the opponents and advocates of détente occasionally agreed was on the point that Third World regimes and movements, whatever their claims to the contrary, could hardly be considered genuinely socialist. Once again, however, the conclusions for Soviet policy differed: for the pro-détentist, Soviet-Union-first school, this was all the more reason for restraint and realism with regard to Soviet involvement. Deputy head of the Central Committee's International Department, Karen Brutents, for example, drew such a conclusion. For the more conservative thinkers, usually anti-détentists such as Petr Fedoseev, head of the Central Committee Ideological Department's Institute of Marxism-Leninism, the same set of facts constituted a further incentive for direct Soviet involvement to ensure progress in the direction of socialism. This position was apparently attractive for those, such as CPSU ideological chief Suslov, who opposed détente on purely ideological grounds. Their opposition derived from a belief that foreign policy should be motivated solely by the principle of class struggle which meant, mainly, no association with capitalists and only by implication involvement to promote revolution even in the backward Third World. Others who opposed détente on ideological grounds were more concerned with the domestic indoctrinational and security problems posed by it; they were not necessarily interested in involvement abroad.

Refinements of each position could be described in abundance; there were also inconsistencies and changes both within each position and among those espousing the various positions. The differing, even conflicting views may have affected policy to the point of creating contradictions, shifts, reversals and inconsistencies in the eye of the observer if not in actual fact. Certain overall tendencies were apparent, however, following the post-Khrushchev deliberations on Soviet Third World policy in the late 1960s. Chronologically, the Soviet-

Union-first attitude was the most important change to emerge from this debate, presumably playing a role in the change in economic policy in the Third World as well as in the adoption of détente. This view was reflected in the speeches by Brezhnev and Gromyko at the 1971 CPSU Congress. Yet, at the same time, Brezhnev struck a relatively optimistic note regarding the potential for socialism in the Third World. This line was reinforced when, obviously in response to concerns expressed by Castro during a 1972 visit, Brezhnev introduced the divisibility of détente idea. As we have already seen, it was followed by the more ideologically dictated tactic of creating revolutionary vanguard parties to ensure the socialist orientation of Third World allies. This position became explicit at the 1976 CPSU Congress, when Brezhnev, declaring that détente and revolutionary activity were not contradictory, promised every kind of Soviet assistance for Third World struggles. Virtually all Soviet officials, with the exception of Andropov, echoed this more enthusiastic attitude. Indeed it was translated into action by greater Soviet involvement and even military intervention in the Third World.

The twenty-sixth CPSU Congress of 1981 marked the peak of Brezhnev's interest in the Third World. He expressed a strong interventionist position, to block the West in what was now a post-détente world. Yet, he was decidedly less enthusiastic about the Third World's potential for socialism, reflecting perhaps reservations long expressed by many Soviet academic and even party theoreticians such as Karen Brutents. This emerged shortly thereafter as the beginning of a broader policy change, when Brezhnev proposed that the superpowers adopt 'rules of conduct' in the Third World. A year later, in September 1982, the Soviet leader retreated still more from the interventionist position, calling upon both NATO and the Warsaw Pact to refrain from activity in the Third World. This was followed in October by a talk with his military commanders, in which Brezhnev outlined the country's economic problems, the implication being the need for a more restrained, less ambitious military policy.

This new position was most likely the result of the Soviet economic crisis and costly Soviet failures in the Third World, including the involvement in Afghanistan, as well as the more dangerous post-détente atmosphere and what Moscow perceived as a hostile American administration under Reagan. Yet it had been discussed and advocated by various elements even within the Soviet leadership well before these problems, reflecting a different set of foreign-policy principles and goals. It was these which became the dominant and explicit basis for policy in the subsequent regime of Andropov and, especially, Gorbachev.

It is not entirely clear that Soviet policy in the Middle East directly followed the overall gyrations of Third World policy and the same shades of differing opinions which guided policies toward the Third World. For example, the Soviet-Union-first attitude, at least in economic policy, was applied in the early 1970s to the Middle East, but the more interventionist-divisibility of détente idea was evident in Soviet Middle East policy well before this and particularly in the early 1970s. The rise in importance of economic considerations may, however, have contributed to the slight reduction in the relative importance of strategic considerations in the late 1970s and early 1980s in the Middle East, in keeping with overall policy for the Third World. Conversely, the more militant shift towards ideologically bound regimes based on revolutionary vanguard parties, born actually of Soviet setbacks in the Middle East itself, was not fully applied, if at all, in this region. Yet its counterpart in the Middle East may have been the greater emphasis on anti-American political efforts even when détente was still being pursued at the super-power level.

It has been argued that conflicting views within the Kremlin lay behind the apparent contradictions and dualism in Soviet Middle East policies themselves, for example, with regard to the degree of Soviet involvement in the Arab–Israeli conflict. Elements of the Soviet military, for example anti-détentist Defence Minister Grechko, reportedly argued for greater Soviet military aid to Egypt and Syria, particularly during the Yom Kippur War, along with Gorshkov, who had an obvious interest in securing facilities for the power-projection role he had designed for the Soviet fleet. Against this, there were apparently those like Kosygin, and apparently Brezhnev himself, who were concerned about the negative effect of such involvement with regard to détente. There may even have been some in the military who did not share Gorshkov's interest in involvement, and who were concerned rather with the dangers of confrontation with the Americans and, perhaps, potential losses of equipment and military secrets. The attitude of Soviet Chief of Staff Ogarkov, for example, was not wholly clear. He was reported to be a supporter of increased aid to the Arabs, yet he may actually have been an opponent to more direct Soviet involvement given his preference for concentration on European theatre warfare. Grechko's successor as Defence Minister, Dmitrii Ustinov, in the later Brezhnev period, may also have been such an opponent in view of his concern over the risks of escalation and global war.

There may also have been finer points distinguishing those who favoured greater and those who favoured less involvement. For example, Shelepin, as Soviet Trade Union chief and Politburo member, was associated with the idea of greater Soviet involvement, but in the form not of aid to the states of the Middle East but, rather, support for the Palestinian movement. Ponomarev and Podgornyi appear to have shared this interest in the Palestinians (Ponomarev presumably because of the ID's responsibility for relations with national liberation movements). Russian nationalists, generally unidentifiable, also tended to a more aggressive position, at least against Israel if not for the Palestinians, presumably because of anti-Semitic tendencies. Yet, as distinct from Shelepin and Ponomarev, for example, chief ideologist Suslov as well as other Politburo members such as Kirilenko, Andropov and apparently Brezhnev himself were far less interested in the Palestinians. Suslov, for example, reportedly found them ideologically suspect, rejecting them as extremist nationalists. In the eyes of Andropov and Brezhnev, apparently, the Palestinians' intransigence and irresponsibility was deemed counterproductive and dangerous to East–West relations.

Nevertheless, it appears most likely that the apparent contradictions within Soviet Middle East policies or discrepancies with Third World policy more generally may have been due to the fact that the Middle East held important interests for the Soviet Union directly connected with its super-power competition with the United States. While this was ultimately true of Soviet policies everywhere in the Third World, the direct involvement of both super-powers in the Eastern Mediterranean, in the Arab–Israeli conflict and, later, in the Persian Gulf raised both the stakes and the risks connected with Soviet policies in the region, according far higher priority to super-power considerations as factors determining these policies. Only in the very last months of Brezhnev's rule and in the post-Brezhnev period did the Soviet Middle Eastern, Third World, and super-power policies draw closer together as Gorbachev gradually adopted the theory of linkage, or what he called interdependence, as the basis for a non-ideological foreign policy.

2 The immediate post-war period: Iran–Turkey–Palestine

The Soviet Union had two basic objectives with regard to the Middle East in the immediate post-World War Two period. They were, first, to ensure some sort of Soviet presence in the region to the south of its border. This might be in the form of a physical presence by means of expansion on its periphery, as exemplified by Soviet moves regarding Iran and Turkey. It might also be in the form of a political presence, by means of participation in international agreements related to the region and recognition of the Soviet Union as an interested party – and power – in the region. The second, more general, objective was to weaken if not eliminate altogether the western, principally at the time British, presence in the region. Evidence of this interest was clear in Molotov's proposal at the September 1945 Foreign Ministers' meeting in London suggesting that Soviet troops pull out of Iran, despite that country's proximity to the Soviet Union, in exchange for British withdrawal from Egypt and Palestine. It seems unlikely that the Soviets believed that they could obtain British compliance, but the proposal was indicative of Moscow's relative priorities within the region at the time.

The Soviet refusal to remove its troops from the areas of northern Iran entered during the war was perhaps the first sign that Stalin intended to pursue Soviet Middle East interests in an aggressive and expansionist manner. That Moscow had ambitions regarding Iran had been clear from the Molotov–Ribbentrop Pact, in which the Soviets had demanded that Iran be in the sphere of Soviet influence. Until the war the Soviet–Iranian relationship had been based on the 1921 treaty between the two states which carried clauses permitting Moscow to introduce troops should a third-country threat arise to Russia through Iran or hostile activities be undertaken on its soil. These rights could, conceivably, be defined defensively, and they were in fact invoked only in 1941 when, together with Britain moving from the south, the Allies sought to prevent Iran from joining the German war effort.

While the World War Two occupation served traditional Russian (and British) interests, it was also designed to protect Iran's oilfields and transit routes for western supplies to the Soviets.

Even at this early date, however, there were signs that the Soviet demands put to the Germans had not been abandoned. In 1941 the Communist Party (Tudeh) was founded in Iran, and covert political organization was undertaken, particularly in the areas adjacent to the Soviet Union. The minorities in this area, namely the Azeris and the Kurds, were apparently provided with Soviet support and encouragement. In September 1944, the Soviets pressed Tehran for oil concessions in the five northern provinces which they occupied. The Iranians, with American backing, refused, prompting a Communist-led campaign against the Iranian Prime Minister who was, eventually, forced to resign. A little less than a year later, in October 1945, Moscow augmented its occupation force, despite the fact that allied troops were scheduled to withdraw within six months of the end of the war. In the autumn of 1945, and in the presence of Soviet troops, ethnic disturbances broke out in the Azerbaijani area of Iran as the Red Army virtually prevented the reestablishment of Iranian government control. On 12 December 1945, with the help of local Communists, the Autonomous Republic of Azerbaijan was created and, one month later, an Autonomous Kurdish Republic of Azerbaijan was established. The Soviet Union declared them to be under the protection of its occupation force, preventing the entry of Iranian government forces.

While it was not entirely certain that this was an attempt by Stalin to take over Iran, it was clearly an effort to expand Soviet influence on its periphery. Iran took the issue to the United Nations, demanding the withdrawal of Soviet troops. Apparently despairing of UN action, the new Iranian Prime Minister Qavam went to Moscow in February and March 1946, where he was told by Stalin that Soviet troops would withdraw from only certain areas of Iran. Both the United States and Britain protested to Moscow, which did in the end agree to remove all its troops by early May 1946. In exchange, Qavam conceded to the creation of a joint Soviet–Iranian oil company (with majority Soviet interests) and to honour Kurdish and Azerbaijani rights, although both governments denied that any deal had been made.

Thus the Soviets achieved a significant political and economic position in the northern area bordering the Soviet Union. Perhaps believing this would secure their interests, or perhaps because no Iranian parliament could be elected (and ratify the oil agreement) so long as foreign troops remained, the Soviets withdrew their army on 9 May as promised. A few months later Qavam brought three Communists into the government. Whether this was also part of the agreement reached between the two countries or simply a response to pressures from Tudeh-inspired disturbances in the south, it did appear to give Moscow a foothold in the central government itself. In 1946 this was the way in which Stalin prepared many of his takeovers in Western Europe, suggesting that he was after more than the influence gained in the north.

In time, however, Qavam, who was pressured or perhaps fortified by anti-Communist agitation in the south, reneged on his part of the bargain. He dismissed the Tudeh ministers and sent the army into Azerbaijan, leading to the collapse of both of the Soviet-inspired autonomous republics in December 1946. Without a commitment on his part, the new Iranian parliament rejected the oil agreement almost unanimously in the autumn of 1947, and Soviet–Iranian relations settled into a period of hostility and tension. Indeed, by the end of the 1940s there were frequent border clashes between the two countries, a Soviet economic boycott of Iran, Iranian suppression of the Tudeh, and a virtual break in relations between Moscow and Tehran.

It is not entirely clear as to why Stalin accepted Tehran's reversal, especially the reneging on the agreement reached with Qavam, without more than verbal efforts to maintain the Soviet gains, at least in northern Iran. The year 1946, even much of 1947, was a transition period in Soviet foreign policy. It was a period of relative flexibility in which local coalitions and infiltration were set in place for gradual takeover, rather than one of active revolution or direct military action such as marked the post–1947 Zhdanovist period. It may also have been the case that the Middle East, even that part of it directly bordering the Soviet Union, took second, even third place to higher priority Soviet interests in Europe and Asia. The factor which apparently tipped the scales against precipitous Soviet action, however, was the importance of Iran to the West. During the 1946 disturbances in the traditionally pro-British southern parts of Iran, London dispatched forces to the Iraqi port of Basra, just opposite Abadan where the Tudeh was stirring up trouble. In addition to this demonstration of British interest, the Americans became involved. During the United Nations discussions of the issue of the Soviet military withdrawal, the United States took a forceful stand, and the American ambassador to Tehran, George Allen apparently played an influential role in the decisions taken subsequently by Qavam. American policy under Secretary of

State Byrnes was indeed increasingly decisive in its opposition to
Soviet encroachments; by the time the Iranian parliament rejected the
oil agreement, the United States had already declared the Truman
Doctrine against the spread of Communism and entered a number of
agreements with the government in Tehran.

The Soviets' moves into Iran appear to have been part of Stalin's
efforts to take advantage of the fluidity of the wartime and immediate
post-war international situation by tentatives just beyond Soviet
borders. Turkey too was a target of these tentatives, as Stalin sought to
improve upon the Soviet Union's pre-war position and further secure
Moscow's interests. Specifically this meant demands regarding
control of the Turkish Straits and certain territorial questions. As in the
case of Iran, the Soviets had already raised these demands at least
generally when discussing the division of influence with Nazi
Germany. Subsequently allied with the West, the Soviets brought
their demands to the Yalta and Potsdam conferences in 1945. In March
1945 they announced that they would not renew their 1921 Friendship
Treaty with Turkey (which had been renegotiated as a Friendship and
Non-aggression Treaty and renewed for twenty years in 1925);
instead, the Soviets pressed their new demands directly with Turkey.

Soviet territorial demands called for a return to the Soviet Union of
the Eastern Anatolian provinces of Kars and Ardahan, wrested from
the Ottoman Empire in the nineteenth century and returned to Turkey
by the 1920 Treaty of Alexandropol, confirmed by the 1921 Friendship
Treaty which was negotiated during the revolutionary friendship
between Moscow and Attaturk. In addition, there were hints that the
territorial demands would include a large area (13,500 square miles) on
the Black Sea coast southwest of Batum, including the important port
of Trebizond.

Equally serious for Turkey, and perhaps more important for the
Soviet Union, were the demands regarding the Dardanelles and the
Bosphorus. These Straits had been governed since 1936 by the Montreux Convention which had given Turkey, rather than any international body, ultimate control over the Straits. At the time of its
negotiation, a period of close Soviet–Turkish relations, Moscow had
been relatively satisfied with this situation and the limitations placed
by the Convention on the passage of non-Black Sea navies. Nonetheless, ideally the Soviets preferred not to be dependent upon any
nation for access to and from the Black Sea, and Stalin placed demands
which would provide at least joint if not total Soviet power over the
Straits. At the Potsdam Conference the Soviets demanded the right to

Soviet bases in the Straits, specifically a naval base in the Sea of Mamora which connected the two Straits, as well as revision of the regulations governing passage through the Straits. The proposed regulations, presented by Moscow in August 1946, called for control of the Straits to be in the hands of Turkey and 'other Black Sea powers', with Turkey and the Soviet Union sharing joint defence of the waterways. Moscow also reiterated conditions already generously conceded by the West after Potsdam. These allowed for the passage at all times of warships belonging to the Black Sea powers subject to the specific consent of the Black Sea powers (except when acting under the authority of the United Nations).

Britain and the United States were totally unwilling to accept the Soviet-proposed regulations, proposing instead an international conference on the subject. They fully backed Turkey in its rejection of both these and the Soviets' territorial demands. The Soviet Union, however, had backed up its demands by massing troops on the Turkish border – mainly with already Soviet-dominated Bulgaria – and mounting a strident propaganda campaign against Ankara. This included agitation of the Armenians in Turkey, for whom the Soviets conducted a campaign (throughout the Middle East) for 'repatriation' to Soviet Armenia. Turkey responded to the growing tensions with Moscow by declaring a state of martial law and suppressing both socialist parties in Turkey with accusations of Communist subversion. By the spring of 1947 Ankara genuinely feared a Soviet invasion.

The United States too viewed the situation with growing alarm, particularly because of Soviet activities in Eastern Europe and the civil war in Greece (which Washington attributed to Moscow), and what was emerging as a cold war between the West and the Soviet Union. In September 1946, shortly after Moscow presented its demands regarding the Straits, the United States announced its intention to maintain a permanent naval presence in the Mediterranean. As the crises in Turkey and Greece mounted, Washington announced its Truman Doctrine, designed explicitly to contain Soviet expansionism and help Turkey and Greece secure their regimes. While this did not end the tension between Moscow and Ankara, it did appear to halt any further plans Stalin may have had for action.

Turkey, however, thoroughly alarmed by the Soviet actions, reverted to its historic animosity for its Russian neighbour and sought protection from the West. It requested membership of NATO following the creation of that alliance in 1949, and was accepted in 1952. It became the site of American military bases and the cornerstone of the western alliance in the Middle East. The Soviets protested verbally, even warning that they could not tolerate this kind of hostile presence on its border. But it was in fact Stalin's attempted expansionism which brought about the very situation he was seeking to avoid: a major American commitment to and military presence in the Mediterranean and in a country on the Soviet border. Both Turkish and Iranian dependence upon western protection were in fact the direct result of Stalin's policies, not easily undone even after Stalin's death.

If Stalin's policies with regard to the northern tier of the region were dictated by the objective of securing a presence to the south of the Soviet border at the expense of the western powers, his objectives with regard to the Palestine question were somewhat less clear. There was a Soviet interest in the internationalization of the issue of Palestine in the 1940s, so as to obtain some role for Moscow in the necessary decisions. Thus the Soviets supported the idea of an international trusteeship or, if Britain rejected this idea, the submission of the issue to the United Nations for settlement. Similarly they (unsuccessfully) sought super-power participation in the United Nations' Special Committee on Palestine (UNSCOP) to settle the future of the mandate and the conflicting Jewish and Arab demands.

Beyond that, however, the Soviets appeared reluctant to choose sides or express anything but ambiguity concerning, for example, the Jewish demands for their own state, presumably so as to avoid antagonizing the Arabs. Indeed, the United States may have been interested in Soviet involvement in the issue simply to force Moscow to take a position – and in so doing cease enjoying the favour of both sides. The British did not share this view, seeking American–British cooperation in favour of the Arabs on the grounds that the Soviets would, in fact, be the beneficiaries if Jewish demands were met. The argument in London was that British acquiescence to the creation of a Jewish state would open the door to Soviet expansion and influence both because of a weakening of the western defence in the area and the alleged Marxist leanings of the Jews.

The Soviets, indeed, had little to gain at this time from favouring the Arab position, against the Jews, in view of the pro-British orientation of the Arab regimes. For this reason, Soviet policy in the Arab world had been one of support for dissatisfied minorities or political groupings and fomenting trouble for the regimes, as well as encouraging nationalist opposition to the British. Thus, as pointed out by the Israeli expert on Soviet Middle East policy, Ya'acov Ro'i, there were short-term versus long-term interests at play in Soviet considerations on the

Palestine question. In the short-term, a pro-Jewish policy would serve to eject the British from Palestine, while support for the Arabs would only strengthen the British presence. A long-term goal, however, sought to eject the British altogether from the region, and that necessitated some consideration for Arab interests in hopes of engaging them for this task. Thus, the long-term objective meant that the Arabs could not be ignored even as Moscow sought to achieve its short-term goal.

An effort to reconcile these short-term and long-term objectives was evident in the speech made by the Soviet representative to the United Nations, Andrei Gromyko, to the special session of the General Assembly on 14 May 1947. Gromyko spoke of the failure of the British mandate which had led to deterioration of the situation in Palestine to the point that the country resembled two armed camps. He also spoke almost emotionally of the horrors of World War Two and the plight of the Jews, whose right to their own state after such ordeals could not be denied. He then posed four possible solutions to the Palestine issue: a single Arab–Jewish state; partition into two independent states; an Arab state; a Jewish state. Rejecting each of the last two on the grounds that a choice of either would deny the legitimate right of the other, Gromyko expressed the Soviet preference for a bi-national or federated state of Jews and Arabs in Palestine.

This solution was known to be unacceptable to the vast majority of Jews and Arabs alike, and as such it certainly could not be considered a pro-Jewish position, especially since a bi-national state in all of mandated Palestine would have an Arab majority. In the midst of support for the bi-national idea, however, was one sentence allowing that if this solution were not possible, because of the deterioration of the situation in Palestine, partition should be considered. Inasmuch as Gromyko had just spoken of the months of animosity and hostile actions between the Jews and the Arabs (provoked, he claimed, by the British as a pretext for remaining), one might deduce that the Soviet Union was in fact supporting the Jewish-preferred option at the time: partition. By not saying so directly, though, the Soviets could benefit from the appearance of impartiality.

It is possible that Moscow was still genuinely undecided. The Jews of Palestine were 'progressive' by Soviet standards, and they could not be described as anti-Soviet. Nonetheless, the economy of the Jewish community in Palestine (the *Yishuv*) was not fully socialist, and it certainly did not follow a Marxist design. Nor was the vast majority of the Zionist movement sympathetic to Communism. Moreover, the

Jews clearly were to have close links with the American Jewish
community and possibly dependence upon American economic
assistance with which the Soviets could not realistically hope to
compete. In addition, at that time Egypt was in the process of
demanding abrogation of the Anglo–Egyptian Treaty of 1926, and
anti-British sentiment in that country was growing. This then was a
potential asset not worth jeopardizing. Such ambivalence may explain
Gromyko's attempt to appear sympathetic to both sides, registering
for future reference what was officially a virtually neutral position,
even if adorned by legitimization of the Jewish demands for self-
determination.

In the autumn of 1947, Soviet ambivalence receded. By this time the
Egyptian efforts regarding the Treaty had failed to pass the Security
Council. More to the point, perhaps, UNSCOP had submitted its
recommendations, the British had announced their intention to withdraw from Palestine, and the General Assembly was now forced to
decide the issue. The Soviets were compelled to take a position, and
they came out for partition. Their previous ambiguity, and the
pro-Jewish nature of the new position, were attested to by the
surprised as well as disappointed response of the Arabs.

The reason for the Soviet position was most likely that, despite
uncertainty over the future orientation of the Jews, and despite the
long-term interest in avoiding alienation of the Arabs, the short-term
Soviet objective would be served by a Jewish victory. A bi-national
state in all of Palestine (up to Trans-Jordan) would be Arab-dominated
and, therefore, pro-British. Partition was not only the sole feasible
solution given the hostility between the two local communities, but
also the desirable one from the Soviets' point of view. This did not
mean that Moscow saw its own role as terminated. By having the
Security Council involved in the period of transition, Moscow could
obtain at least some participation in ensuring the withdrawal of the
British. The Americans and British preferred British rather than
United Nations supervision of the transition period. Thus it was the
prospect of Soviet participation which prompted the United States to
favour speedy implementation of the partition, and a compromise was
worked out whereby a UN committee, responsible to the Security
Council but composed only of small states, would supervise the
transition.

Nor did Soviet support for the partition of Palestine mean abandonment of all interest in the Arabs. Even as Moscow expressed
support for the Jews, its propaganda and official spokesmen were

conciliatory towards the Arabs, arguing that the UN partition decision was in the national interests of both peoples. Moscow defined the decision as an opportunity to create *two* states, including an Arab state, and to achieve independence from the British. During the 1948 war, following the attack by the Arab states on the newly declared State of Israel, Soviet propaganda attributed Arab hostility to British provocation designed to thwart partition and provide a pretext for the British to remain. The British were said to be aiding Arab reactionaries against the creation of an independent Arab state despite the fact, according to Soviet propaganda, that such a state was in the interests of the Arab peoples and the Arabs of Palestine. Partition, as portrayed by the Soviet Union, was to mean the end of British imperialist exploitation of the Arabs.

Despite this effort not to alienate the Arabs, the Soviet Union significantly assisted the defence of the new Jewish state. The Soviets were the first to accord Israel *de jure* recognition, on 18 May 1948, just three days after the declaration of the state. On the practical side, the Soviets permitted the emigration of some 200,000 Eastern European Jews, not only within the framework of settling displaced persons but even to the point of permitting Zionist groups to organize the preparations of prospective emigrants. These preparations occasionally included military training, as Israelis themselves were permitted to train and conduct training in Eastern Europe. Arms and equipment for the war were also supplied by Eastern European countries under Soviet control beginning with some 10,000 rifles and 450 machine guns in early 1948. These were provided mainly by Czechoslovakia, with Soviet permission, about the same time as the British arming of Iraq, Egypt and Trans-Jordan on the grounds that Britain had defence pacts with these countries. Although an Egyptian request for Czech arms was turned down, Czechoslovakia did sell Syria a consignment of $11 million worth of arms. These fell into the hands of the Israelis en route to Syria (possibly with Yugoslav collusion) and no further Soviet-bloc arms sales were made to the Arabs.

The period of Soviet assistance to Israel was, however, short-lived. By the end of 1948, problems began to develop in the granting of permission to Jews to emigrate. Emigration had in fact never been directly from the Soviet Union but rather from Eastern Europe or repatriation of Jews to Eastern Europe from the Soviet Union and from there to Palestine, later Israel. In December 1948, Rumania began to place obstacles in the way of the Jewish emigration; the Soviets merely responded that they could not interfere in the affairs of another state. This was to become a pattern. The arms deliveries (and with them training) suffered a similar fate, tapering off to a near halt also at the end of 1948. Contacts between Israeli diplomats and Soviet Jews were greatly restricted; commercial relations drew to a halt; and cultural relations, in any case only minimal, were nipped in the bud. In addition to all these signs, as pointed out by Ro'i, the term Zionist began to find its way back into Soviet publications. This was not outright criticism of Israel, but the term Zionist itself carried with it the Soviet-bestowed connotation of bourgeois nationalism, traditionally condemned by Marxism-Leninism. Rather than redefine the term during the period of Soviet–Israeli cooperation, the Soviet media had simply refrained from using it. Its return, even if only in an isolated instance, was the harbinger of a change in policy.

The reasons for the Soviet change of heart are not easily determined, but they may be instructive as to the real motive behind Soviet support for the Jewish state in the first place. There are a number of hypotheses as to why the Soviets abandoned their support, the most commonly accepted being that

(1) Israel was not Marxist enough, or
(2) Israel became pro-American.

Other hypotheses attribute the change to
(1) a turn towards the Arabs in Soviet foreign policy;
(2) a national revival of Soviet Jews;
(3) Zhdanovism or
(4) British withdrawal from Palestine.

According to the first hypothesis, the Soviets originally believed that the progressive nature of the *Yishuv* would make it fertile ground for Marxist development; indeed for many Communists – in Israel and elsewhere – this was the only feasible explanation for Soviet support. Moscow, as this explanation goes, was subsequently disappointed, mainly when the pro-Soviet left-wing Israeli party MAPAM was excluded from Israel's first elected coalition in March 1949. Yet, there had been Soviet comments all along, in 1946 and 1947, to the effect that the *Yishuv* was not Marxist, and they could have had few illusions about the relative strengths of the centre, left, and extreme left parties in Israel. Further, if the Soviets were indeed hopeful about Marxist political influence they would most likely have waited to see the results of the January 1949 elections and the eventual fate of MAPAM in connection with the creation of a coalition government. As it was, the deterioration in Soviet–Israeli relations came at the end of 1948 – before the Israeli elections and before the exclusion of MAPAM from the coalition. In fact, the Soviets allocated very little coverage to internal Israeli politics, condemning the elections *beforehand* on the grounds that the electorate excluded a large part of the population. The Soviets, therefore, did not wait to be 'disappointed', suggesting that they had had few expectations to begin with.

A similar retort may be given to the hypothesis claiming disappointment over an Israeli turn to the West, purportedly evidenced by the granting of a $100 million United States loan. While the Soviets must not have appreciated the American loan, it cannot have come as a surprise, given Soviet comments previously regarding the likelihood of Israeli economic links with the United States. The Soviets themselves subsequently turned down an Israeli request for a similar loan from Moscow. Moreover, as in the case of the elections, the US loan post-dated the change in Soviet–Israeli relations. A decidedly pro-American orientation on the part of Israel did not actually occur until 1950 and the Korean War, when Israel answered America's call for support in the United Nations. It seems unlikely, therefore, that a policy evident in December 1948 could have been the result of Soviet concern over a purported pro-American shift by Israel.

If the answer does not lie with Soviet disappointment over Israeli policies, be they domestic or foreign, the explanation may be found with the Soviet Union itself, specifically the hypothesis that Moscow shifted to a pro-Arab position, abandoning Israel in the wake. It is true that the Soviet Union, in 1949, was showing signs of interest in anti-imperialist groups in the Arab world, just as it had at various times in the past. It is also true, however, that there was no real change in actual policy towards the Arab states. In 1950, for example, Moscow lumped Israel and the Arab states together in its condemnation of the western Tripartite Declaration on the Middle East and the Arabs' response to it. Indeed it was only in 1951, during the Korean War, that the Soviets had some contacts with the Arabs, but even then no real change occurred in policy, until after Stalin's death. Indeed, even as Moscow became cooler towards Israel, it did not support the Arab side in the various disputes which arose in the Arab–Israeli context, as we shall see below.

There were, however, a number of developments within the Soviet Union which may have influenced policy towards Israel. The response of Soviet Jewry to the creation of the Jewish state may well have surprised and alarmed the Soviet leadership. The arrival in Moscow of Israel's first official envoy, Golda Meier and, particularly, her appearance at the Moscow synagogue for the holy day observances in September 1948, drew unprecedented crowds of Jews enthusiastically expressing their identification with Israel. The resurgence of Jewish nationalism promised to create internal problems for the Soviets, sensitive as they were both to the centrifugal forces of the various nationalities within the Soviet federal structure and to the attractions of emigration the new state might hold for the nearly three million strong, highly educated Soviet Jewish community. It was in fact at this point, on 21 September 1948, that a mild attack on Zionism was published in *Pravda*, warning the Jews – and perhaps signalling Soviet reconsideration of its pro-Israeli policies.

Yet, domestic Soviet steps of an anti-Semitic nature actually had begun before these events, indeed even before the State of Israel was founded in May 1948. An anti-Jewish campaign begun in 1947 did, in fact, worsen after Golda Meier's appearances in Moscow, but it would appear to have been more directly a part of Zhdanovism, introduced in 1947 in Soviet domestic as well as foreign policy. Domestically, Zhdanovism meant a general tightening up, bringing with it purges and punitive measures, some with clearly anti-Jewish as well as generally anti-nationalist overtones not necessarily planned by Zhdanov. Even after Zhdanov's death these policies linked to his name became particularly evident in the trials and purges conducted in Eastern Europe, following the Soviet break with Tito, the intensification of the Cold War with the Berlin crisis, and charges against Jews of 'cosmopolitanism', that is, contacts with the outside world, as well as bourgeois nationalism.

It has been claimed by some analysts of the East European trials, notably the Czech reform historian Karel Kaplan, that the anti-Semitic nature of at least the Czechoslovak trials was dictated by the Soviets' shift to a pro-Arab foreign policy. Ya'acov Ro'i has pointed out, however, that if the anti-Jewish accusations were indeed intended to please the Arabs, it is strange that Soviet propaganda to the Arab world at the time never even mentioned the trials or these accusations. In any case, Zhdanovism was a policy pre-dating the deterioration of relations with Israel; it was dictated by a different set of considerations. Yet, its implementation in 1948 may have been a contributing factor to this deterioration, together with the Soviet Jewish response to the creation of Israel.

The single factor which more than any other fits the timing and probably explains the change in Soviet behaviour is probably also the simplest one. Support for Israel ceased to be expedient. Israel's War of Independence was over, partition was achieved; the Jewish state was a fact and, most important, the British were out. The short-term objective, expulsion of the British from at least part of Palestine, had been achieved. It may not have been time yet to proceed to the longer term objective, but the need for the Jews was terminated. It is entirely possible that if the Jewish state had been a Marxist pro-Soviet state, Moscow would have continued its support, domestic Soviet policies notwithstanding. But inasmuch as there was apparently little reason, from the point of view of the Soviet leadership, to believe that this would be the case, the factors mitigating against continued support – the traditional as well as Zhdanovism–related anti-Semitism, anti-Zionism, anti-nationalism – far outweighed the one, temporary factor which had dictated support: expulsion of the British.

The Soviet Union did not set out immediately, or at least not directly, in pursuit of its longer term objective. The 1949–53 period of continued but decreasingly cordial Soviet–Israeli relations did not witness a Soviet shift to the Arabs' positions in the Arab–Israeli context. Nor did failure to support Israel in the dispute lead to support for Arab positions. Rather the Soviets became less involved, abstaining from taking any position, preferring neutrality to identification with either side. The reasons for such a policy were probably threefold. First, the Arab states were still decidedly pro-British; secondly, Moscow was too weak seriously to compete with or challenge the West in the Arab world. Thirdly, the remnants of Zhdanovism, the two-camp view of the world, combined with the above factors, may have prevented Stalin from seeking opportunities in the Arab world.

Soviet neutrality in the Arab–Israeli context might be viewed as a freeing of Moscow from its pro-Israeli identification so as to prepare an effort to win over the Arabs from Britain. In fact, however, Moscow's positions on specific issues of the Arab–Israeli conflict were not necessarily those designed to find favour in the eyes of the Arabs. On one of the central issues, for example, that of Israel's demand for direct negotiations, Moscow came out in favour, until 1952. Soviet and Israeli motivations were quite different, however: Israel was seeking recognition and acceptance of its existence from the Arabs; the Soviet Union was, rather, simply desirous of excluding the western powers from playing a role. The net result was a less than pro-Arab position.

The Soviets were more direct in their opposition to Jordan, because of King Abdullah's close association with the British. Thus, Moscow opposed the Jordanian annexation of the West Bank, championing, at least until the autumn of 1949, the creation of an independent Arab state (in accord with the partition plan) so as to thwart the Jordanian takeover of these territories. For the same reason, Moscow continued for some time to advocate the internationalization of Jerusalem, not as an anti-Israel position but, as explained to Israel, because of opposition to Jordanian annexation of East Jerusalem. Once this was accomplished, and both Israel and Jordan opposed internationalization, the Soviets began in early 1950 to speak of finding a solution acceptable to both 'sections' of the city. This was a *de facto* acceptance of the division of Jerusalem. As early as 1949 the Soviets attended the opening of the Israeli Knesset in Jerusalem, together with Holland constituting the only foreign state to thus accept Israel's seat of government in the city (although the Soviet diplomatic mission was established and remained in Tel Aviv).

On the refugee issue, Moscow tended to ignore any Israeli role or culpability. It placed the blame for the problem fully upon the British, claiming that the British created the issue by urging the Arabs to flee, even before the end of the Mandate, so as to generate a problem within the Arab states. According to this argument, the refugee problem would provide Britain with a pretext for assistance to and continued involvement with the Arab states. For example, the Soviets claimed that the creation of UNRWA was intended to set up a vehicle for western penetration of the area. The Soviets ascribed to the 1949 UN resolution on the refugee issue which called for the return of those Arab refugees willing to live in peace with their neighbours (a not particularly anti-Israeli formulation) or compensation.

On the issue of border skirmishes, the Soviets generally abstained from taking any position, occasionally claiming that the United States was pushing Israel to take certain actions. Altogether Soviet behaviour in the United Nations on issues connected with the conflict was one of abstention rather than support for the Arabs. This was the case, for example, with the resolution before the Security Council in 1951 on freedom of navigation in the Suez Canal, intended to halt Egyptian interference with Israeli use of the Canal.

At this point, the deterioration in Soviet–Israeli relations was also extended to Eastern Europe's relations with Israel. (According to Israeli expert Uri Bialer most of Moscow's new satellites in Eastern Europe had, surprisingly, continued commercial relations with Israel and permitted diminished but significant Jewish emigration even after

1948). Moscow's own relations with Jerusalem gradually deteriorated until they reached the breaking point in February 1953. Stalin's moves against Jews for what he called the 'Doctors' Plot' provoked the placement of a bomb on the grounds of the Soviet legation in Tel Aviv, which in turn provoked the Soviets to sever relations with Israel. At this lowest point in Soviet–Israeli relations, however, the Soviets were still condemning the new Nagib regime in Egypt and expressing their usual opposition to the other regimes in the Arab world. Only after Stalin's death in March 1953 did a change occur in Soviet Middle East policy.

By the summer of 1953, diplomatic relations with Israel were resumed, with Israel also agreeing to abstain from any anti-Soviet alliances. There was also an easing of the anti-Jewish measures characteristic of the last years of Stalin's life, and a small number of Jews were permitted to emigrate in family reunification plans. The Soviets raised their legation to embassy level, and they abstained from what was an almost unanimous condemnation at the Security Council of an Israeli reprisal raid against Jordan. Trade relations were also undertaken, with Moscow supplying Israel with a significant portion of its oil exports in exchange for citrus fruits. Far from presaging a shift back to Israel, however, this new; post-Stalin policy also encompassed, finally, overtures to the Arab states culminating in full support in the Arab–Israeli context.

The reasons for these changes were to be found in the policy reappraisal in the wake of Stalin's death and the new line introduced by Malenkov, as we have already seen. Renewal of relations with Israel was merely part of the overall thaw and moderation pursued by Malenkov. It is possible that the new Soviet leader hoped to deal with both sides to the conflict, as a power in the region. Yet, the Arab–Israeli conflict offered a vehicle to reach the Arabs and certain leverage over them and, with this, perhaps a chance for greater influence in the region. Unencumbered by the Stalinist objections to cooperation with non-aligned bourgeois-nationalist regimes, the post-Stalinist leadership was free to assume pro-Arab positions and, thereby, utilize the conflict to its own super-power ends.

3 The Soviet–Egyptian relationship

As we have seen, the deterioration in Soviet–Israeli relations preceded any Soviet turn towards the Arabs, with Moscow shifting from a pro-Israeli to a neutral position on issues of the Arab–Israeli conflict. The July 1952 revolution in Egypt brought no change in this general Soviet indifference. Indeed the Free Officers were dismissed in Soviet statements as 'reactionary officers . . . linked with the USA', a charge repeated continuously even as late as the spring of 1953. In December 1952 the Soviets changed their position on direct Arab–Israeli negotiations, voting against the proposal in the UN General Assembly. Yet, the actual change in Soviet attitude and behaviour towards Egypt came only later. In late 1953 and 1954, the Soviets supported Egypt's anti-British positions, and in January 1954 the Egyptian deputy Defence Minister made a prolonged visit to the USSR. Also in January the Soviets supported the Arab stand in the Security Council on the diversion of the Jordan River, and in March 1954 they used their veto, for the first time in the Arab–Israeli context, to block a resolution which would have permitted Israeli use of the Suez Canal (the same resolution they had merely abstained on in 1951). All of this was accompanied by a gradual reappraisal of the Egyptian regime and culminated in the Czechoslovak–Egyptian arms deal of September 1955.

A number of factors explain this clear shift in Soviet policy. Stalin's death was the catalyst for a rethinking of Soviet foreign policy towards the Third World. The new willingness to deal with and support bourgeois nationalist regimes and their non-alignment policies placed relations with the Arab world in an entirely new light. Moreover, Khrushchev's policy of peaceful coexistence which also formed part of the post-Stalin foreign policy, dictated competition, albeit of a peaceful kind, with the West. To compete with the West entailed offering an alternative attraction to the Arabs, and that attraction could be a more active, clearly pro-Arab position in the Arab–Israeli conflict. A second factor accounting for the change was the fact that Egypt was on the verge of ejecting the British. In a sense, the Egyptians were now at the point the Jews had been in 1947. Thus, a deterioration in Egyptian relations with the West could be exploited to further Moscow's unchanged interest in eliminating the western presence and influence in the region.

A facilitating factor, though not necessarily the cause of the shift in Soviet policy, was the leadership struggle occurring within the Arab world. Moscow was able to exploit the heated competition between Egypt and its arch-rival Iraq. Not only was Egypt the larger, more populous, economically advanced and politically influential state; it was also espousing neutralism, while Iraq was associated with the West. Of greater significance, and urgency, for the Soviet Union, however, was the form this association was taking. The United States, with the help of Britain, was striving to establish a network of regional alliances surrounding the Soviet Union. In the Middle East, the first of these was to be the Baghdad Pact, a regional pact based to a large degree on Iraq – and designed to contain Soviet expansion.

In summary, then, the reasons for the change in Soviet policy towards Egypt, and towards the Arab cause were:

(1) The post-Stalin reassessment in Soviet foreign policy;
(2) openings within the region itself; and
(3) the need to combat what was perceived as American inroads into the region.

The $250 million Czechoslovak–Egyptian arms deal of September 1955 was dramatic evidence of the new policy and the new relationship. For the Egyptians, the deal with Moscow may have been perceived as a counter-weight to the American backing of Iraq, as well as added weight in their struggle against the British. Nasser may actually have intended to use it in his bargaining with the West, particularly in response to the US refusal to meet Egyptian arms requests unconditionally. Moreover, the United States was uninterested in the Arabs' demands in the Arab–Israeli conflict; it viewed the spread of Communism as the central danger in the region, while Egypt saw only the conflict with Israel. The Soviet Union had the added advantage of the absence of any imperial history in the Arab world, its anti-imperialist positions suiting well the anti-colonial struggle of the non-aligned forces coalescing around Nasser, Nehru, and Tito.

There is some ambiguity over the more immediate Egyptian reasons for the arms deal. It has been claimed that the February 1955 Israeli retaliation raid on Egyptian army headquarters in Gaza was the trigger which led Nasser to this step. Yet, it appears likely that the possibility of such a move formed at least part of the discussions which took place during the Egyptian deputy Defence Minister's prolonged visit to Moscow in January 1954, almost a year before the Gaza raid. The arms agreement may well have been worked out in the ensuing months, particularly during the visit to Egypt by a Soviet military delegation in January 1955, one month before the raid. Whether the Israeli action was the immediate reason or merely a pretext, the convergence of underlying trends and interests in both Soviet and Egyptian policy basically accounted for the new relationship expressed by the September 1955 arms deal.

The Soviets and Egyptians by no means agreed upon every issue, whatever the coincidence of interests. Soviet behaviour in the world arena, specifically the United Nations, did shift to support for the Arabs at the expense of Israel. And Soviet propaganda gradually broadened to include the Arab–Israeli conflict. Yet, in Moscow's first official policy statement on the conflict certain discrepancies could be noted between the declared Soviet policy and that pursued by the Egyptians. The statement issued by the Soviet Foreign Ministry on 17 April 1956 was an extremely moderate one. The moderate tone may have been dictated by the then forthcoming visit of the Soviet leader to Britain, and the pursuit of peaceful coexistence. Yet, the statement was noteworthy for its placement of the blame for the conflict on the West, specifically the attempts to create a regional alliance 'to serve the aims of the colonialists'. Not only did this highlight Moscow's continued perception of the issues in a global context, in contrast to Egypt's quite different delineation of the principal culprit, that is Israel. It also presaged two areas of future if not actual dispute between the two countries.

One of these could be found in the statement's position that a settlement of the conflict be based on respect for the just national interests of all states concerned, including by implication Israel, for the statement listed Israel (albeit last) among those states such as Egypt, Saudi Arabia, Syria, Lebanon, and others whose 'efforts . . . at establishing and consolidating state independence [are] regarded with sympathy and warmly supported' by the Soviet Union. The second area of difference was that of peaceful versus military solution. The statement extensively condemned armed conflict, warned against being provoked in to fighting, and urged 'the parties concerned to abstain from any actions which might aggravate the situation' along the armistice lines. Both these issues – continued Soviet recognition of Israel and its right to exist plus Soviet opposition to a military solution – do not appear to have been explicitly disputed at this early stage of Soviet–Egyptian relations, but they were expressed from the very beginning and destined to become serious obstacles to Soviet–Egyptian understanding.

If in some way American reluctance to arm Egypt in 1955 contributed to the formation of the Egyptian–Soviet link, the American (and western) refusal to authorize the financing of the Aswan Dam project in 1956 may be said to have helped seal the budding Egyptian–Soviet friendship. The Soviets did not immediately offer to provide what the West had refused, but Nasser's disappointment with the West did lead to his decision to nationalize the Suez Canal and to a series of events which more clearly than ever placed Egypt in the anti-western camp. The Suez crisis was the first crisis to arise in the new Soviet–Egyptian relationship – serving to some degree as a test of the new friendship as well as setting something of a pattern for Soviet behaviour in future crises in the area.

The two major considerations which guided Soviet policy during the Suez crisis were: (a) the possibility to utilize the crisis as an opportunity to improve Moscow's own position in the area *vis-à-vis* its Arab clients and against western interests; and (b) the necessity of avoiding direct confrontation with the United States, which had clear strategic-nuclear superiority at the time as well as regional superiority in the form of the US Sixth Fleet in the Mediterranean. At the time, the Soviets were also operating under Khrushchev's doctrinal tenet that local wars inevitably would escalate to global, nuclear proportions. Moreover, Moscow tended to an exaggerated estimate of Washington's power over its allies, particularly Israel, but also Britain and France. There was, therefore, a Soviet tendency to believe either American collusion or at the very least greater American loyalty to its allies than claimed by Washington. Because of this estimate, Soviet policy-makers had to contend with what they viewed as uncertainty regarding American moves and responses.

At the same time, however, the crisis presented an excellent opportunity to accelerate the end of British influence in the area and to discredit the West in general, including the United States. In fact, Soviet propaganda against the United States varied between two lines: claims that the United States was as directly involved as its allies Britain and France, or claims that the US hoped to replace Britain and

France as the major power in the Middle East and, therefore, was happy to encourage a conflict which would discredit the other two powers.

In terms of actual behaviour, Moscow was slow to respond to the Egyptians' nationalization announcement and, also, to the outbreak of hostilities in October 1956. In the pre-war period of negotiations regarding the Canal, the Soviets championed Egyptian rights and actions, making propaganda profit of the anti-colonial nature of the action. Moscow may have calculated, as the Egyptians claimed, that Egypt would have the Canal running and that the crisis would subside before the use of force could be prepared by Britain and France. Operating on this estimate, the Soviets presumably sought to prolong the negotiation period, while dispatching assistance to Cairo in the form of navigation pilots (and grain, for Egyptian currency, once Britain froze Egyptian accounts in British banks). The Soviets may also have been concerned, however, that France and Britain would strike some compromise deal with Egypt. For this reason, among others, the Soviets sought to be a party to any negotiations taking place. Moscow also had an interest in the protection of freedom of navigation, preferring an international forum even as it asserted Egyptian sovereignty and rights over the Canal.

The Soviets did send letters of concern and warning to the British and the French, referring to the dangers of escalation as well as to Soviet interests in the region. These communications were not in the form of a threat or commitment; nor were they particularly strongly worded. Nor was there apparently any Soviet–Egyptian coordination of actions at this time. Cairo may have been encouraged by the informal comment regarding the possibility of Soviet volunteers made by Khrushchev at a Rumanian reception in Moscow in August. This remark was published by the Egyptian press but not by that of the Soviet Union. In fact, according to Nasser's confidante, Egyptian editor Mohammed Heikal, Nasser actually cancelled a trip to Moscow planned for August, because of the crisis. Far from seeking coordination, Heikal has claimed, Nasser purposely avoided such consultation for fear of Soviet over-cautiousness and restraint. While it seems unlikely that the Soviets would have urged Cairo to back down, Moscow did become increasingly cautious as the crisis augmented, rather than abated, and the actual use of force by Britain and France became a more immediate possibility.

On 29 October Israeli forces attacked Egypt and the following day, as prearranged, Britain and France delivered an ultimatum calling upon both sides to withdraw; in this way a threat to the Canal was presented as a pretext for British and French intervention. This began on 31 October when the British moved on Port Said, followed by French and British air attacks on Egypt. With the outbreak of the fighting, the Soviets took several steps – none of which indicated an intention of becoming involved. The forty-five Ilushin-28 aircraft previously provided for Egypt, with their Soviet instructors, were transferred to Luxor in Upper Egypt, for further removal to Syria. Thus, the Soviets obviously sought to avoid the destruction or capture of these aircraft, as well as to avoid their possible involvement in the conflict. In so doing, however, Moscow was in effect removing Egypt's striker-bomber offensive air capability. Then, after the beginning of the British and French air attacks, the Soviets transferred their approximately 380 Soviet and Czechoslovak advisers out of Egypt to the Sudan, for eventual evacuation from the region. This move followed orders issued earlier to the advisers to refrain from any involvement in the fighting. This was particularly significant inasmuch as these advisers included the instructor-crews for some two hundred Soviet tanks (which the British had apparently believed they would have to fight).

On 31 October, the day after the British and French ultimatum, the Soviet Union proposed that the crisis be referred to the Security Council and, on the next day, it urged India and Indonesia to activate the Bandung Conference nations. Thus, neither politically nor militarily were the Soviets prepared to take a direct role. Moreover, when asked directly for assistance, on 1 November, by Syrian President Kuwatly visiting in Moscow, the Soviet leadership was almost contemptuous in its reply. Marshal Zhukov is reported to have pulled out a map and demanded to know how Moscow could in fact intervene. The Soviets' offer at this point reportedly was limited to political support, particularly through the UN. A similar message was conveyed to the Egyptian ambassador in Moscow on 2 November, that is, that the Soviets would not provide military assistance but would mobilize world opinion. (Nasser later claimed that the Soviet Union did offer to supply tanks and technicians but that the offer was rejected because Egypt did not require such aid. In light of the evacuation of the Soviet tank crews already in Egypt, it is unlikely that such an offer was actually made or that it was meant – or taken – seriously.)

Until 5 November, the picture was one of Soviet caution, both in the messages conveyed to the Arabs and in the responses to such measures as closure of the eastern Mediterranean and the northern Red Sea, as well as to the alert of the US Strategic Air Command (Soviet forces had already been on the alert since the beginning of the Polish and Hungarian crises in mid-October). Soviet political measures were indirect, even to the point of supporting an American resolution at the UN. A direct, and strong, Soviet move came only on the night of 5 November in the form of an ultimatum. The ultimatum was contained in five letters, and included

(1) to Britain and France, the threat of 'rocket attack';
(2) to Israel, the possibility of 'placing the existence of the State of Israel' in question;
(3) to the Security Council, a twelve-hour deadline for cessation of the hostilities; and
(4) to the United States, a proposal for a joint force including the American Sixth Fleet.

The delay in the Soviets' response, until the night of the fifth of November, has been explained by their involvement in Hungary. It was indeed true that Moscow was occupied with the Hungarian revolution, especially and acutely from the time of its first military intervention in Hungary on the night of 23–24 October, through the second intervention on 4 November. It may be, however, that the delay was due to another reason. The Soviet Union most likely awaited the American response to the Middle East crisis, acting only when relatively certain that there would be no risk of confrontation with the United States. The Soviets also awaited the passage of the critical point in the fighting in the field, when they could be relatively certain that there would be little likelihood of any necessity to carry out their threatened actions. That is, they waited until the crisis had passed its peak militarily and diplomatically, resolution was in sight, and the US was likely to support the end of the conflict (that is, restrain its allies).

Thus, the timing of the threats was dependent upon the Soviets' own risk-taking propensity, rather than the Arabs' needs or plight. The threats added another political objective, aimed, for example, at audiences in the Third World beyond the actual combatants, promising propaganda-political benefits with no need actually to implement the threats. From the Arabs' point of view the more effective time for the Soviet threat would have been immediately after the British–French ultimatum of 30 October or the attacks of 31 October, but at this time there was no certainty on the Soviets' part that the US would not support its allies' action. The crisis had then been at its peak, and risk-taking high. Indeed the delay in the Soviet action indicated the priority of the second Soviet objective in the war, avoidance of confrontation with the United States, over the first objective which was an improvement of Soviet positions in the Arab world. By the evening of 5 November, the peak of the crisis had passed: the Egyptian air force was destroyed or crippled, Egyptian forces in Sinai were routed, a cease-fire had already been attempted in Port Said, and, most important, the United States was involved in trying to stop the British and the French.

Another interesting aspect of the threats, pointed out by American analyst Francis Fukuyama, was their actual wording. The language was merely conditional: the terms 'could', not 'would', were used in relation to threatened actions. And joint action was sought with the United States, against America's allies and client. This was a proposal which the Soviets knew could not be accepted. Chester Bohlen, US Ambassador to Moscow at the time, later wrote that he could not believe that Moscow actually expected him to deliver such a proposal when it was handed to him. This part of the threat was also politically dictated, designed to embarrass the United States, at least in the eyes of the Third World, and even portray Washington as colluding with the British and French.

Nor were there any military moves to provide credibility to the Soviet ultimatum. In fact, the military element was the least credible part of the threats in view of the Soviets' strategic capabilities at the time. They had only a fraction of the American missile capability, and what little they did have, according to military expert John Ericson, were first generation rockets, that is, modified V-2s with the limited range of 400 to 450 miles. Ericson has concluded that they could have used these only in a sporadic, uncoordinated way, and then only from launching points in the western part of Eastern Europe – at a time when Eastern Europe was in turmoil. With regard to actual intervention – which was not in fact threatened (the Soviets spoke publicly of volunteers only after the crisis, on 10 November) – there was little possibility as well. There were no Soviet airborne divisions until the late 1960s and no large transport planes to bring sizeable numbers even of volunteers. There were long-range bombers capable of hitting the British, for example at their Cyprus staging positions, but there were no signs of preparations or intention to deploy them. And the Soviets had virtually no marines, nor Mediterranean naval presence (except port facilities in Albania) at the time.

This over-all lack of capability is one of the reasons that the standard argument that Moscow was simply preoccupied with Hungary does not fully explain the delay in the Soviet threat. The delay until after the second intervention in Hungary might conceivably have accorded Soviet threats greater credibility, that is, Moscow could then, theoretically, have been believed to be free to act militarily elsewhere. But it is unlikely that involvement in Hungary actually prevented an earlier threat inasmuch as this kind of empty, purely symbolic or verbal threat could have been made at any time. There was neither more nor less ability to back it up during or after the Hungarian crisis. What was different and significant for the timing, was the US factor, and the progress of the Suez crisis itself.

One interpretation of the outcome of the crisis, an interpretation nurtured by Moscow, has been that the Soviet Union was the major beneficiary of the 1956 war. Britian and France were discredited and their influence in the region virtually ended. The United States was to some degree linked to its allies' aggression or, on the contrary, perceived as having behaved as a poor ally to them; the Soviet Union, however, had saved the day, brought about the end to the hostilities and emerged as the champion of the Third World in general, and the Arabs in particular. In fact, however, several elements of dissonance entered, or became apparent, in Soviet–Arab relations as a result of Soviet behaviour.

First, the Egyptians resented the Soviet attempt to take credit for the political defeat of the West. The Egyptian attitude was evident in its media emphasis and careful insistence upon the exclusive Arab role in the crisis. The Egyptian press did not even comment beyond reporting the Soviet threats; nor did it express any gratitude to Moscow. Nasser actually credited other outside factors (including the efforts of President Eisenhower) equally with those of the Soviet Union. Secondly, the Egyptians resented the Soviet delay and inaction during the crisis. Nasser made several public statements which clearly referred to this, saying for example, that the Soviets had waited nine days to make up their mind. His eventual successor Anwar Sadat later said that his own disillusionment with Moscow began at this time (and he credited the Americans with the major role in ending the crisis). Heikal later reported the same, claiming on one occasion that this was the beginning of the deterioration which was to come to a head in the Soviet–Egyptian rift at the end of the 1950s.

Thirdly, the Arabs now became aware of Soviet priorities, that is, the elevation of Soviet interests above those of their clients, inasmuch as the concern over war with the United States was coupled with if not dictated by American strategic superiority. It was clear to the Arabs that all else was secondary to this concern, and that the Soviets were willing to do little more than engage in symbolic, propagandistic actions, while exploiting the crisis to their own political benefit.

Conversely, it may be that the Soviets, for their part, became aware of the poor performance of the Arabs militarily, even with some of the recently supplied Soviet arms. This may have strengthened those within the Kremlin who argued for the provision of newer and better equipment and training for the Arab armies, but by the same token, it may have fortified those who opposed the involvement altogether – creating if not continuing a difference of opinions on the issue in the Soviet leadership. Neither group, if indeed there were groups, can have concluded, however, that Arab–Israeli war in the near future would be a positive option. Opposition to such an option would have been based on the Soviets' unwillingness directly to intervene in such a war, highlighting what was probably the major lesson to both sides: the importance of the global factor, that is, the centrality of the response of and risks emanating from American military strength and the possibility of super-power confrontation.

Although the Suez crisis may have augmented Soviet prestige in the eyes of some in the region, another result of the war was the Eisenhower Doctrine, which constituted a stronger American commitment to the area. While this was a negative phenomenon for the Soviet Union, Moscow's reaction was not necessarily the one the Egyptians might have chosen. Rather the response was a Soviet proposal, in February 1957, for a Soviet–American cooperative approach to the region, including an arms embargo and a peaceful solution to the Arab–Israeli conflict. These were just two points which were to become serious bones of contention in the subsequent Soviet–Egyptian relationship. On the first point, the Soviets were reluctant to deliver everything in the way of arms and equipment requested by Cairo. In a 1981 Soviet retrospective of the Suez crisis, it was even stated that one of the lessons of the war had been that a state did not need military superiority and that hardware was not the most important factor in a conflict. On the second point, there was Soviet reluctance to support the war option, that is, there was a preference for political means over military, because of the concern over Soviet–US confrontation.

Despite the differences in Soviet and Egyptian positions and Egyptian disappointment with Moscow's behaviour regarding the Suez crisis, relations between the two countries remained warm for another two years. In January 1958, Moscow even accorded Egypt a $175 million loan, the largest it had yet granted to a Third World state, as well as $100 million for the Aswan Dam. Nasser made two trips to the Soviet Union in 1958, and Soviet arms flowed to Egypt. The year 1958, nonetheless, brought with it a serious crisis in Soviet–Egyptian relations. A number of factors accounted for the deterioration which ensued, including problems connected with the Egyptian–Syrian union, local Communists, Iraq, and changes in Soviet ideological considerations.

The Egyptian–Syrian unification, creating the United Arab Republic (UAR) was viewed with alarm in Moscow, even though Soviet propaganda was initially favourable. Soviet–Syrian relations had been quite close for some years, and the Soviets were fearful that the union of the two Arab states might interfere with Soviet influence in Damascus. Indeed, one of the Syrian motives for joining with Cairo was said to have been a desire to curb just this influence, particularly as it was connected with the Syrian Communists. Nasser claimed that the Communists were in fact planning a takeover in Syria; at the very least there was genuine concern over the strength of the Communists in the usually politically influential Syrian armed forces. The unification carried with it imposition of the Egyptian political system upon Syria, that is, abolition of all political parties with the exception of Nasser's Arab Socialist Union. Together with this came suppression of the Syrian Communist Party which for obvious reasons opposed the creation of the UAR. Syrian Communist leader Bakdesh fled to the Soviet Union, but the Communist opposition to the UAR in turn led to violent Egyptian suppression of its own Communists at the end of 1958.

The unification carried with it the additional problem for the Soviets of contributing to the aggrandizement of Nasser. This meant not only increased Egyptian independence, but also further power for Nasser's brand of Arab nationalism. Moscow anticipated that this would work against outside, non-Arab influences and was even called 'racism' by Khrushchev. The July 1958 revolution in Iraq also played a role, for Moscow drew close to the new Iraqi regime, which itself opposed Nasser's apparent expansionism. The Soviets probably shared the Iraqi concern that the union with Syria was but a first step in Egyptian plans to promulgate Nasserism throughout the region. For his part, Nasser was angry over the Iraqi Communists' support for Iraq's anti-Nasser positions and opposition to the Egyptian–Syrian unification. To Nasser it appeared that Moscow was shifting significantly towards Egypt's arch-rivals in Baghdad.

The result of all this was not only the bloody suppression of Egyptian Communists, but Egyptian polemics against the Soviet Union and a decided cooling in Soviet–Egyptian relations in 1959–61. Official Soviet acknowledgement of the problem could be discerned in Khrushchev's comment to the twenty-first CPSU Congress in 1959 to the effect that Moscow would continue supporting Egypt, which as an ex-colony, deserved such support 'despite differences'. Indeed trade relations did remain the same, Moscow fulfilling its promise of aid for the Aswan Dam and even providing Cairo with a small nuclear reactor.

Nevertheless, polemics between the two were mutual. Moscow was unwilling to accept what it viewed as Nasser's power play in Syria nor could it totally ignore the persecution of local Communists on such a large scale. It is possible that, as Nasser feared, Moscow was harbouring higher hopes for the ideological tendencies of the new regime in Iraq. This was a period (1959–60) of the emerging Sino-Soviet dispute with something of a showdown anticipated for the 1960 international meeting of Communist parties. In preparation for this conference, the Soviet Union assumed more ideologically-orientated positions, in order to counter Chinese accusations of Soviet revisionism and 'sell-out' to the concept of peaceful coexistence. The Soviets sought to demonstrate their loyalty to ideological purity by adopting more stringent demands regarding the role of the Communists in Third World countries and a more critical attitude towards non-Marxist ideologies such as 'Arab socialism'.

The impasse in Soviet–Egyptian relations was broken only in 1961. For the Soviets, circumstances had changed by this time. The most important factor for improvement of relations was the failure and split, in 1961, of the Egyptian–Syrian union. This in itself removed one of the most serious irritants in Soviet relations with Nasser. In fact, Moscow was relatively isolated in the Arab world, for the Kassem regime in Iraq had turned out to be a disappointment, turning against its local Communists once they were no longer essential to the new regime. It is also possible that the Soviets' loss of their only Mediterranean sea facility, the port in Albania, provided added incentive for the restoration of the relationship with Egypt. By 1962, the ideological atmosphere was a bit better for such a move, inasmuch as following the harder Soviet position in 1959–60, the Soviets were now swinging back to greater tolerance of bourgeois regimes.

Nasser too appeared interested in improved relations; he desisted from further persecution of the Communists and gradually, though with restrictions, released most of those who had been incarcerated. In 1962, Nasser was seeking Soviet support and even concrete assistance for the Egyptian intervention in the Yemen civil war. Egypt had some 60,000 troops there aiding the republicans against Yemeni royalists, who enjoyed western as well as Saudi Arabian and Jordanian support. Indeed, at this point Nasser's power in the Arab world was on the wane, and in subsequent years his importance as a leader of the non-aligned movement was reduced as the movement itself lost its luminaries (Ben Bella, Nehru and Sukarno in 1965, and Nkrumah in 1966). Domestically Nasser was faced with growing economic problems, which he answered with nationalization and other socialist measures, steps which also facilitated the rapprochement with Moscow, if not actually drew the two states closer. At the same time Egypt had less to fear regarding the threat of Soviet-Communist penetration of the region given the anti-Communist nature of the regime in Damascus and, once again, in Baghdad.

Against this background of renewed interest on both sides and the removal of most of the past irritants, Soviet–Egyptian relations began once again steadily to improve. The brief episode of mutual recrimination may have suggested to both the vulnerability of their relationship, but growing needs on the part of both states generated a closer alliance than either side may have anticipated. As Moscow's plans for an expanded fleet progressed, with the opening of the Mediterranean Squadron in 1964, Soviet interest in Egypt grew in importance. Khrushchev's visit to Egypt in that year sealed the re-found friendship; it was followed by visits by Navy Commander Gorshkov carrying requests for naval facilities. These were accompanied by steadily increasing supplies of arms, and cancellation of a large portion of the Egyptians' military debt to the Soviet Union. This was rewarded in 1966 by the granting of rights to the Soviet Union in Egyptian ports and airfields.

Although a change in leadership occurred in Moscow with the removal of Khrushchev in October 1964, Soviet interests dictated continuation of the policy towards Egypt undertaken by Khrushchev. Whatever concern there may have been over Khrushchev's adventurist policies or commitments in the Third World, the Soviets by no means reversed the trend with regard to Egypt, or the Middle East. In 1965, whether upon decision from Moscow or on its own initiative, the Egyptian Communist Party decided to disband, many of its members joining the ruling Arab Socialist Union. The Soviet Union referred to Egypt as a country building 'socialism', and it sent Soviet pilots to assist Egyptian forces in Yemen. The stability of the Egyptian regime, particularly in contrast to the continuous upheavals and coups in Iraq and Syria, was a significant factor which, combined with Moscow's interest in military facilities in the country, heightened the Soviets' view of Egypt as the cornerstone of their policy in the region.

4   The Six-Day War, 1967

The major Soviet interest in the Middle East in the 1960s was acquisition of naval facilities and bases, including air bases, and in this effort Egypt was the focal point. While some facilities were obtained prior to 1967, the Six-Day War of June 1967 proved to be a turning point for the Soviet military as well as political presence. Indeed, inasmuch as this major achievement was a result of the war, it may have been argued that the Soviets actually encouraged the war with the intention of gaining Arab or, at least, Egyptian dependence upon Moscow and thus the desired facilities. This somewhat Machiavellian view was in fact prompted by the somewhat contradictory role played by Moscow in the events leading up to the war. For this reason, an examination of this role may well shed some light on Soviet motivations and policy in connection with the war altogether.

For over a year prior to the war, Soviet propaganda had generally echoed the bellicose statements made by the Syrian regime regarding Israel. Soviet media even spoke of Israeli intentions to attack Syria, be it in retaliation for Palestinian raids across Israel's border or in relation to the ongoing Israeli–Syrian water dispute. These comments became more than propaganda, however, when on 11 May 1967 Soviet President Podgornyi told a visiting Egyptian parliamentary delegation (led by Anwar Sadat) that Israel was concentrating forces on its border with Syria and planned to attack between 18 and 22 May 1967.

There had been Israeli troop concentrations in that area earlier in the spring, but at the time of the Soviet report the information was false. Soviet Ambassador to Israel Chuvakhin refused an Israeli invitation to visit the border area and see this for himself. Nasser, however, apparently asked for and received Soviet confirmation of Podgornyi's claim, but on 14 May he sent Egyptian chief of staff General Mohamed Fawzi to Syria to investigate and received the report that there were in fact no Israeli concentrations. Thus Nasser knew that the Soviets' information was false. He may, therefore, have interpreted the report to mean Soviet encouragement of an Egyptian move against Israel.

Nasser ordered his troops into Sinai on 14 May and on 16 May asked the UN to withdraw its emergency force (UNEF) from Sinai, extending this on 18 May to include UNEF evacuation of Sharm-el-Sheikh and the Gaza Strip. Soviet media supported these moves and Moscow refused to cooperate with American efforts for the return of the UN forces. The Soviet Ambassador to Israel also rejected an Israeli proposal on 19 May, for demobilization on both sides of the Egyptian–Israeli border. On 22 May, Nasser announced the blockade of Israeli shipping through the Straits of Tiran, thus closing off access to Israel's only southern port and exit to the Red Sea. In continuation of what appeared to be Soviet encouragement of these bellicose acts, Soviet Defence Minister Grechko told visiting Egyptian War Minister Badran on 28 May, when the crisis was in full bloom, that the Soviet Union would dispatch its fleet if needed. Cairo radio quoted Grechko as saying that the Soviet armed forces 'will stand by you', while Soviet Premier Kosygin told Badran that the Soviet Union would stand by Egypt in battle. Moscow also informed the Turkish government that ten Soviet warships would be traversing the Dardanelles en route to the Mediterranean. And, according to Lyndon Johnson, the Soviets sent him a note on 28 May saying that if Israel attacked, the Soviet Union would help the attacked (although other sources claim this note was sent on 27 May informing Washington that Moscow had information that Israel was planning an attack).

Yet there was another side to these moves which suggests a different interpretation. During the war itself, the Soviets amplified on Grechko's comments, explaining that what had been meant was only that Moscow would act if the United States intervened, and indeed Kosygin's remarks to Badran were apparently qualified as Soviet aid to prevent American involvement. Even these caveats were open to misinterpretation, however, for they could be seen, on the one hand, as encouragement: the Soviets would not permit the Americans to intervene against Egypt, leaving Egypt free to act. On the other hand, they could be seen as warnings not to expect any Soviet assistance, the Soviet role, if any, being limited to the case of American involvement should it occur.

The second interpretation is suggested by the fact that Kosygin's comments to the Egyptians reportedly came in response to a request by Nasser through Badran for a Soviet airlift of material aid. The answer, therefore, that he received was negative, promising only generally to stand by Egypt in battle. Moreover, according to Heikal, Kosygin on 24 May also told Badran that Egypt had achieved its goals by its actions in Sinai and that all it had now to do was to 'cool things down' so as not to trigger a military conflict. Gromyko and Grechko were said to have conveyed a similar message of constraint, and the Egyptian Ambassador to Moscow warned Nasser that Grechko's more encouraging remarks to Badran, apparently made informally at the airport just prior to Badran's departure, should not be taken at face value (a warning which, according to Heikal, did not reach Nasser until after the war began).

Earlier, an Egyptian request for Soviet intelligence estimates of Israeli strength on the Syrian border, according to Heikal, was answered by Moscow sometime after 15 May to the effect that there was no way to determine if Israeli troops were a deliberate provocation or merely a precautionary act by Israel in case Syria had been planning an attack on Israel's Independence Day, 15 May. Heikal interpreted this as one of a number of Soviet signals for restraint. In fact the official Soviet statement issued on 23 May, the day after Nasser announced the blockade of the Straits of Tiran, was quite restrained. Supporting Egypt's moves in Sinai, without, however, mentioning the Straits of Tiran, it contained no real threat to Israel. It warned only that attack would be met by 'strong opposition to oppression from the Soviet Union and all peace-loving countries', and basically called on all sides to back down. Indeed, even as Badran was in Moscow, Nasser received a note from the Soviet government, on 27 May, urging restraint, and when Syrian Premier Nureddin Atassi arrived in Moscow on 29 May, he reportedly received the same message. A Soviet note to Israeli Premier Levi Eshkol at the end of May was similarly devoid of threats.

Militarily, the Soviet moves taken were precautionary. Not all of the ten announced ships traversing the Dardanelles, from 30 May to 5 June, were in fact warships; they were mainly small, auxiliary vessels, brought through unobtrusively. The largest warship was a destroyer, and it was brought through only on 4 June. More importantly, the Soviet reinforcements were placed off the island of Crete where they joined the rest of the Soviet fleet (some fifteen ships) which had been moved westward, even further away (some 500 miles) from the crisis area than the American fleet. Far inferior in size and numbers to the US Sixth Fleet, the Soviets were said by US Admiral J. C. Wylie, deputy Commander in Chief of US Naval Forces in Europe, to be 'even less anxious than the United States to have any of their forces involved' in the crisis. Thus the naval profile was kept low, while Soviet aircraft were removed from Egypt, as in 1956. No Soviet naval activity was evident in the Red Sea area, despite discussion in the West of a trial sail through the Straits.

As noted in western analyses of Soviet military behaviour, notably in Stephen Kaplan's *Diplomacy of Power*, both the deployment and quality of reinforcements for the Soviets' Mediterranean Squadron clearly signalled the United States that the Soviets had no intention of intervening or becoming directly involved. Indeed they may also have been seeking, at this stage, *not* to encourage the Arabs to move, although the deterrent to Israel was not voiced in particularly strong terms. By the time of the Soviets' note to Israel, however, the Soviet Union may have believed that de-escalation had been achieved. On 31 May the Soviet leadership left Moscow, Brezhnev, Kosygin, and Grechko going off to Murmansk to watch Soviet military exercises, Podgornyi departing for a scheduled tour of Asia. Moscow, like many other capitals, was surprised by the outbreak of hostilities on 5 June.

However restraining the Soviets became as the crisis developed, it is undeniable that they did emit provocative comments and clearly did play a role in the creation of the crisis. Their bellicose statements and, in particular, their false report to Egypt of Israeli troop concentrations clearly warranted an explanation. The first and most compelling explanation may be that Moscow was acting in the interest of bolstering the left-wing Ba'ath regime of Atassi which had come to power in Syria in 1966. The Soviet Union had been supportive of this regime's use of an outside, Israeli, threat as a means of consolidaating the government's position domestically. In the spring of 1967 this had become particularly critical in view of renewed opposition to Atassi within Syria. This had been triggered by an anti-religious article published in Damascus on 25 April 1967, the public response to which was religious demonstrations and a degree of popular unrest. Thus, Soviet efforts may have been designed to help Atassi contain the situation by diverting attention to an outside threat.

The Soviets may also have hoped to strengthen the Atassi regime by prompting Egyptian support and activating the 1966 Egyptian–Syrian defence pact. Bringing Egypt into the picture may have been designed not only to bolster Atassi but to provide a deterrent to any Israeli reprisals against Syria in response to Syrian artillery shelling on Israeli border farms and Palestinian (Fatah) raids which had been taking place across the Syrian–Israeli border. Particularly after a major air battle on 7 April in which Israel downed six Syrian MIG-21s, Moscow sought a means of deterring further Israeli reprisals. Thus Israel would be warned that further or more serious actions against Syria might involve Israel in a two-front war.

A by-product might also be the withdrawal of Egyptian troops from Yemen (for transfer to the Arab/Israeli front, according to another interpretation, leaving the way open to greater Soviet influence in Yemen). The activation of the Egyptian–Syrian alliance in an atmosphere of increased tension would further serve to consolidate a radical, pro-Soviet camp in the Arab world. The pro-western (pro-American) conservative states could be discredited, as America was singled out as the primary supporter of Israel and, according to Soviet propaganda, the prime mover in the 'aggressive plans' of Israel.

All of these objectives, mainly political rather than military in nature, were most likely based on the assumption of low-risk, that is, that Israel would not in fact respond by going to war. A number of factors may have led Moscow to such an assumption. First, the Soviets' may have calculated that their own military aid over the years to Egypt and more recently Syria, combined with their political support for the Arabs would act as a deterrent to an Israeli attack. Secondly, Arab unity, in particular the Egyptian–Syrian defence pact posing the threat of a two-front war, would also deter the Israelis. A third assumption may have been that the United States would restrain Israel, in part at least because of American preoccupation with Vietnam and, therefore, reluctance to condone a conflict elsewhere. Such an assumption, even if valid, further presumed a degree of American control over Israel which the Soviets' often over-estimated.

Finally, the Soviets may also have assumed that in addition to the various external deterrents and restraints facing Israel, domestic Israeli factors would also militate against the war option. The Israeli economy was experiencing a recession, Jewish immigration was low while emigration from the country was growing, and morale within the country was at an all-time low. (A popular joke at the time in Israel was the remark 'The last person to leave should turn out the lights at Lod airport.') Israeli Premier Eshkol was an uncharismatic figure, perceived domestically and perhaps also in Moscow, as indecisive and weak. Thus, there were good reasons for observers to conclude that conditions were not conducive to an Israeli decision to launch a war at this time.

It is entirely possible, indeed likely, that the Soviets were totally unprepared for the escalation which ensued, in part from their own statements. There is no evidence of any foreknowledge or collusion regarding Nasser's request for UNEF to leave, nor any foreknowledge or role in the United Nations' acquiescence. The Soviets did not criticize these moves, but they may not have shared (nor even have been aware of) Egyptian intelligence estimates supplied to Nasser some months earlier to the effect that the removal of UNEF would lead to war.

The Soviets became alarmed only with the closing of the Straits of Tiran. This was a step opposed by Moscow both because it was a clear *casus belli* in the eyes of Israel and because freedom of navigation was an issue of particular importance to the Soviet Union. Moscow may also have feared an American response to the blockade. Even then, however, it would appear that the Soviets did not believe that Israel would respond militarily. Rather they seemed to accept each new step as a new *status quo* which could be contained. And on this basis they reportedly assured Nasser as late as 3 or 4 June that there was no need to anticipate any Israeli attack. They thereby drew upon themselves subsequent accusations that Moscow had prevented an Egyptian move and caused Nasser to be taken by surprise when Israel launched its pre-emptive strike in the early hours of 5 June 1967.

Shortly after the outbreak of war, which began with the destruction by Israel of the Egyptian and Syrian air forces on the ground, the US contacted Moscow and was answered by Kosygin on the 'hot line'. This was the first time this line had been used in a crisis situation. Kosygin sought US cooperation for a cease-fire and withdrawal of Israeli forces. There was no movement of Soviet naval forces in the direction of the conflict, suggesting that Moscow was careful not to alarm Washington about Kremlin intentions. The Soviet objective was apparently to minimize Arab losses, and any risk of super-power clashes by achieving an early cease-fire through collaborative efforts with Washington. Thus when by the next day it was clear that Israel, and the US, were unwilling to accept a cease-fire with withdrawal, Moscow agreed to a UN resolution for a cease-fire 'in place'. Although the Soviets said that withdrawal should be discussed, the Arab states categorically rejected any cease-fire which did not include immediate withdrawal.

On 7 June the defeat of the Egyptian army in Sinai turned into a rout. The Soviets sent a warning to Israel that failure to observe the cease-fire – which had not been accepted by Egypt – might result in Moscow's severing diplomatic relations and the consideration of 'other necessary measures'. Yet on the same day, Moscow refused a request to send Egypt aid, on the grounds that there was no place to land aircraft and, according to Egyptian intelligence sources, the Soviet Union also refused to send aid via Iraq or Sudan. By the evening of 8 June both Jordan and Egypt had agreed to the cease-fire following a day in which there had been more strident Soviet calls for Israel to observe the cease-fire and withdraw, as well as some minor Soviet harassment of the American fleet. On 9 June Israeli forces broke through into Syrian territory and Syria agreed to the cease-fire. Israel continued to fight on the Syrian front and on 10 June held most of the Golan Heights. At this point Moscow showed signs of anxiety lest Damascus be taken or sufficiently threatened that the Atassi government would fall.

The Soviet response was two-fold, in the form of what were the first genuine threats of the war. One was a government note to Israel severing diplomatic relations and threatening sanctions if the hostilities against Syria were not immediately halted. Although Moscow had threatened the severance of relations during the war, the actual decision was initiated by Tito, close ally of Nasser in the non-aligned movement. On the night of 8 June, the eve of a Warsaw Pact meeting, the Yugoslav proposal was conveyed to the various Soviet bloc states, all of which agreed to the idea, with the exception of Rumania, at the Pact meeting on 9 June. This decision was conveyed to Israel on 10 June together with the sanction threat. The threat itself did not, however, speak of military action. Indeed, compared with the 1956 note to Ben Gurion, it was relatively mild.

A second message, however, of a more threatening nature had already been dispatched the same day to the White House via the 'hot line'. According to Lyndon Johnson's memoirs, Soviet Premier Kosygin said that 'a very crucial moment' had arrived; he spoke of the possibility of an 'independent decision' by Moscow, and he said that he foresaw the risk of 'grave catastrophe' unless Israel halted operations within the next few hours. If not, the Soviet Union would take the 'necessary actions including military'. The more explicit nature of the message to Washington may have been an indication of just how much the Soviet Union believed that the American President could control Jerusalem. In fact, the Americans themselves had counselled Israel not to take Damascus – which Jerusalem in any case had had no intention of doing. Nonetheless, the Americans moved their fleet towards Syrian waters, presumably to convey to Moscow that they would not tolerate Soviet intervention. Moscow made no response to counter this move. Nor did it undertake any military moves to back up its verbal threat, although there was one unconfirmed report that it had placed its only recently formed airborne divisions on alert.

In fact, however, the fighting on the ground was virtually finished when Moscow issued its threats, combat having already ceased on all but the Syrian front, and there too Israel was already in the process of proclaiming victory. While the Soviets may have been genuinely fearful that Damascus and/or the Atassi regime would fall, it is unlikely that they had contemplated more than verbal intervention. Whatever the capabilities of the Soviets' new airborne divisions, there was no chance of introducing them into battle before Israeli forces took Damascus, if indeed Israel had tried to take it. More to the point, the American naval presence and active political role during the war meant, from the Soviet point of view, that intervention might well result in super-power confrontation. There was no sign that the Soviets were willing to take that kind of risk for their Arab friends.

Indeed, according to an Egyptian account, Nasser accepted the cease-fire on 8 June because the Russians had been frozen into immobility because of the fear of involvement with the American fleet, and the Israeli air force. Cairo and other Arab capitals were in fact quite angry – then and in retrospective accounts – over the absence of any significant Soviet action or assistance even in the way of emergency supplies. The Soviet severing of relations with Israel was a belated gesture, probably intended to dissipate some of the Arab resentment and, as in 1956, the Soviets subsequently strove to credit their threats with bringing the war to an end.

There were signs that some Soviet officials disagreed with this relative inaction. A former Israeli intelligence source has claimed the KGB and military elements favoured a more active Soviet role and assistance to the Egyptians and, especially, the Syrians. All that is known (in the public domain) is that the Moscow party first secretary, Nikolai Yegorychev was replaced at the end of June 1967, reportedly for having criticized the lack of decisive support for the Arabs. He in turn was associated with Central Committee secretary Aleksandr Shelepin whose gradual decline from leadership circles began with his demotion from the party Secretariat in July 1967. Shelepin had been close to the Egyptians and, reportedly, even more so to the Syrian Ba'athists. French journalist Michel Tatu has associated both Shelepin and Vladimir Semichastny (removed as KGB chief on 17 May 1967) with a strong pro-Ba'athist, militantly anti-Zionist position which may have prompted them to urge greater Soviet involvement on behalf of the Arabs. To what degree these men were demoted because of their criticism of Soviet inaction or because they had advocated and encouraged the provocative Soviet behaviour prior to the war, is difficult to know (if in fact their demotions were in any way connected with Middle East affairs).

What does appear more certain is that the Soviets made a number of incorrect intelligence estimates and decisions, from their 14 May false reports of Israeli troop concentrations right up to and possibly during the war itself. They appear to have misjudged the volatility of the Arab–Israeli conflict, with the propensity for escalation on both sides. They may have overestimated their own ability to control events, and their clients, while they appear to have been ignorant of Nasser's plans regarding the removal of UNEF from Sinai and the closing of the Straits of Tiran. Moscow equally misjudged Israel, for it overestimated the degree of Israeli tolerance of continued terrorism from Palestinians based in Syria; it overestimated the demoralizing effects of the domestic Israeli situation, particularly on Israel's will and ability to fight; it overestimated the deterrent value of the Soviets' relationship with the Arabs and of the prospect of fighting a two-front war; and it overestimated the ability (or perhaps interest) of the United States to restrain Israel.

With regard to the war itself, one may assume that Moscow misjudged the Arabs' ability to fight. While there may not have been any expectation of an Arab victory, there reportedly were Soviet estimates that the Arab armies could pursue a protracted war. An Arab military victory carried the risk of American intervention, a most undesirable eventuality from the Soviet point of view, but protracted war might weaken Israel (through prolonged mobilization and exhaustion of resources) while discrediting the United States politically, until a cease-fire could be gradually achieved. Even protracted war, however, carried with it the danger of escalation and superpower confrontation.

Yet it is by no means certain that the Soviet Union foresaw or actually wanted the war to break out at all. Posing the Machiavellian hypothesis that the Soviets wanted an Arab defeat so as to create Arab dependence, one must nonetheless ask how the Soviets hoped to explain their lack of assistance, as well as the poor performance of their arms and training. Arab defeat would also discredit the Soviets generally, in the Third World, while it ran the risk of toppling Moscow's allies in Cairo and Damascus. This in turn would not only eliminate the pro-Soviet regimes Moscow had been cultivating but also destroy the chance to achieve the bases and facilities that dependency was supposed to bring. Gambling on Arab defeat was indeed a risky, highly costly venture.

One might posit, on the other hand, the hypothesis that the Soviets wanted a victorious Arab war, in order, for example, to draw Egyptian troops out of Yemen and/or simply to bolster the pro-Soviet Arab regimes while discrediting the United States. Here too the risks were enormous and Soviet behaviour difficult to explain. If the Soviets actually wanted an Arab victory in a war Moscow had encouraged them to initiate, how were they to explain the Soviet refusal to send any kind of aid (especially when the Egyptians claimed that the United States was directly assisting Israel)? Aside from the very grave risk that Moscow's carefully cultivated allies might not win and, therefore, might fall from power, there was the even more serious possibility of American intervention to help a losing Israel – and with this even greater possibility of Soviet–American conflict.

One cannot say with any certainty that there were no members of the Soviet leadership who were willing to take such risks. Yet, Soviet efforts to restrain Nasser in the days preceding the war, the refusal to help once the war broke out and, instead, the pursuit of a collaborative effort with the United States for an early cease-fire even against Arab wishes and terms, all strongly suggest that the Soviet Union had few illusions about an Arab victory. It would appear, rather, that the Soviets' provocative behaviour in May 1967 was politically motivated, to strengthen the Atassi regime , without accurately anticipating the escalatory direction events would take and/or their own inability to control the situation.

5 The inter-war period, 1967–1973

The Six-Day War of June 1967 had demonstrated a number of problems for the Soviet presence in the Middle East: the instability of Moscow's own clients and the lack of Soviet control; the instability of the area itself and the risks of war including (and especially) the danger of escalation and super-power confrontation. There were also the standard problems of the economic cost of supplying, and resupplying, the Arabs. And there was the at least theoretical possibility that the Arab states in certain circumstances might alter their pro-Soviet orientations. More specifically, the war had served a blow to Soviet prestige and credibility, tarnishing the Soviets' reputation both with regard to the quality of their arms and training and to Soviet willingness to assist a Third World client in a crisis situation. Further, it also led to renewed American interest and involvement in the Arab–Israeli conflict.

There may have been those in the Kremlin who noted all of these negative elements of the Soviet involvement with the Arabs, recommending perhaps withdrawal or at the least reassessment. The demotion of persons believed to be connected with the more militant policy (favouring deeper Soviet involvement) suggested such a reassessment. Yet, on the other side of the ledger, the Soviets may have hoped to derive very significant benefits from this temporarily embarrassing situation. Aside from a direct political role *vis-à-vis* the Americans in the Arab–Israeli context, the Soviets could now consolidate and expand their Mediterranean presence by exploiting the Arabs' need for refurbishing and rebuilding their armed forces. The bases, naval and air facilities sought before the war could now be obtained. The Soviets' Mediterranean presence, now secured, enabled Moscow to maintain and strengthen its naval challenge to western naval dominance of the Mediterranean, to engage in defensive action – so far as this was possible – against the Polaris threat to Soviet industrial centres, and to intervene in local crises. This presence, which might psychologically if not militarily affect vulnerable NATO states such as Turkey and Greece, could also assist the Soviet Union in its efforts to radicalize the Arab world and, possibly, whittle away western influence in the oil-producing states. In broader terms it might strengthen Soviet efforts further south, in Sudan and the Horn of Africa.

Apparently these strategic interests, despite the uncertainties and problems which accompanied them, won the day in Soviet thinking. Moscow dispatched President Podgornyi to Egypt one week after the war's end and, opting to continue their Middle East involvement, the Soviets undertook a number of steps to meet the situation. They initiated a propaganda drive which placed the blame for the Arab military debacle on the shoulders of the Arab forces themselves rather than their Soviet-made arms. This also served as a pretext for the social and ideological restructuring of the Egyptian army which the Soviets undertook. To improve their own tarnished image, the Soviets also mounted an immediate and massive resupply effort while ostentatiously augmenting their own fleet. Soviet military advisers were sent, reaching approximately 4000 in Egypt by the end of the year. And, presumably to solve the problem of control, Moscow used advisers, sympathizers, and others to penetrate the Egyptian (probably also the Syrian) army, police, security services, political and governmental bodies.

Yet the Soviet Union also put some limits on its support. Militarily it turned down Nasser's request for a formal treaty, which would have provided for Soviet responsibility for the air defence of Egypt. Politically it undertook a quest for some sort of negotiated settlement of the Arab–Israeli conflict. Thus the message Moscow conveyed to its two allies, at this time and throughout the inter-war period, was that the supply of arms, which in itself would have some qualitative limitations, did not mean that the Soviet Union believed that the military option was a viable or a desirable one. Translated operatively, the Soviet position meant urging the Arabs to recognize Israel's existence, in exchange for the return of the territories lost in June 1967, that is, acceptance (temporary or permanent was not clear) of Israel in its 1949 borders. This position was most likely dictated not only by an estimate of Israeli military superiority (including a nuclear potential) but also by Soviet concern over the escalation of military conflict to the super-power level.

It is difficult to determine the degree of genuineness or seriousness of the Soviets' pursuit of a negotiated settlement at this time. They had to face the problem of justifying their continued and increasing military presence if a settlement were achieved. Moreover, too great Soviet pressure on the Arabs, at this early stage of Soviet penetration, could be harmful to Soviet interests. Indeed signs of friction between Cairo and Moscow had already reappeared because of Soviet positions. It may be, therefore, that the more operative Soviet objective at this time was to reduce the Arab–Israeli conflict to minimum volatility, presumably something in the nature of the pre-1967 *status quo*, or possibly even an end to the state of belligerency in exchange for a Soviet engineered return of territories lost in the 1967 war. What does appear relatively certain and consistent was the Soviets' opposition to the renewal of hostilities.

Moscow obviously favoured international negotiations, be they between the two super-powers, additional powers, or at the United Nations, as distinct from direct talks between Israel and the Arab states. For only in a multilateral framework could the USSR itself play a role. Having achieved the status of spokesman for at least Egypt if not all the Arab parties to the conflict, the other important ingredient was a modicum of cooperation with Washington. Following the 23–25 June Glassboro meeting between President Johnson and Premier Kosygin, the Soviets and Americans prepared the draft of a joint resolution for the UN General Assembly. This proposal, which was rejected by Israel and the Arabs alike, called for Israeli withdrawal, recognition of Israel, end of belligerency, and efforts to solve the conflict through the United Nations.

The Arab response was the 'three nos' of the Khartoum Arab summit (no peace, no recognition, no negotiations). Moscow chose to ignore this part of the Khartoum decisions. Instead it seized upon the summit's agreement to coordinate Arab political efforts to end the 'effects of aggression', hailing this as a decision to pursue a political solution rather than the war option. The Arabs themselves, however, were far from united at the Khartoum conference, Syria refusing to attend altogether, and the PLO (still under Ahmad Shukeiry) walking out before its conclusion, while the attending Arab states disagreed on the path to be taken. The Soviet Union presumably believed that it could go on several weeks later with a slightly revised version of the resolution it had worked out with the United States. This became resolution 242 passed by the Security Council on 22 November 1967 and accepted by Egypt, Jordan and Israel though not by Syria (or the PLO).

Resolution 242 contained the essential elements agreed upon by Washington and Moscow: Israeli withdrawal ('from territories occupied in the recent conflict'), recognition of Israel ('respect for and acknowledgement of the sovereignty, territorial integrity and political independence of every state in the area and their right to live in peace within secure and recognized borders free from the threat of force'), end of the state of belligerency and the appointment of a UN representative to mediate a peace agreement. It also called for freedom of navigation, just settlement of the refugee problem, and demilitarized zones. The major areas of Soviet–American disagreement were left vague: (1) how much of the territory was to be evacuated – the Americans preferring 'minor adjustments' of the pre-June border, Moscow championing the Arab demand for withdrawal from 'all the' territories taken in 1967; (2) the timing or sequence of the steps – the Soviet Union demanding a staged Israeli withdrawal prior to the achievement of an agreement, the US calling for an agreement before withdrawal. These Soviet positions, in addition to the points in resolution 242, were spelled out in their own peace plan published in *Pravda*, 25 January 1968.

Moscow sought to persuade the Arabs, particularly Egypt, to accept this plan rather than prepare for military action. Egyptian sources have claimed that this issue was the source of serious dispute during Nasser's July 1968 visit to Moscow, while western sources have claimed that Brezhnev conceded to Nasser that he could at least place a time limit on the effort to reach a political solution rather than a military one. It would appear that the Soviets were now involved in what became a perpetual dilemma for them: how to arm and prepare the Arabs for war and yet limit them to purely political action.

With the failure of UN mediation through Gunnar Jarring, Soviet Foreign Minister Gromyko made a trip to Cairo in December 1968. A new Soviet peace plan was announced, but it differed little from the previous plans. A negotiating process did follow, however, at the level of two-power (Soviet–American) and four-power (the addition of France and Britain) talks throughout 1969. This activity, accompanied by resumption of the Jarring mission, was less a Soviet initiative than, apparently, the work of the new administration in Washington of Richard Nixon and his national security adviser Henry Kissinger.

Yet there are indications, from Kissinger himself, that the Soviets were actually more flexible in their positions and more interested in reaching an agreement than were the Americans. The latter, it has been implied by Kissinger, sought prolongation of the *status quo* on the assumption that Soviet–Egyptian relations would eventually deteriorate in the absence of a settlement, so that there was in fact no incentive for the US to agree to an early accord at least on the Egyptian front. The United States was also trying to establish some linkage between the Arab–Israeli conflict and the war in Vietnam, implying if not actually stating that Washington would be more responsive to Soviet positions in the Middle East if Moscow were more helpful in resolving the Vietnam conflict.

The Soviet position at this time in fact exhibited what would appear to be contradictions, inconsistencies or simply fluctuation. Despite their opposition to an all-out resumption of hostilities, the Soviets did not oppose the Egyptian commando raids which, by the spring of 1969, grew into what became known as the War of Attrition between Israel and Egypt. In fact they apparently provided certain supplies, including SAM-7s, necessary for these actions, reportedly requesting Cairo to limit its actions to the northern area of the Canal zone, within the range of the Soviet fleet (believed to provide a deterrent to Israeli response). Nonetheless, in May the Soviets sought to restrain Nasser, urging him to cease hostilities. Nasser ignored these demands, which had been prompted by the strong Israeli retaliation. Instead he apparently accused Moscow of capitulating to the Americans and, in September 1969, he temporarily placed the pro-Soviet Egyptian Vice-President Ali Sabry under house arrest. This apparent deterioration in Soviet–Egyptian relations did not, however, lead to a slackening of Soviet aid. On the contrary, possibly to mend fences with Egypt, possibly in response to the deadlock reached in Soviet–American talks over the summer, Soviet positions became more militant, including a warning to Israel and propaganda which spoke of direct American involvement in the War of Attrition.

The stalemate in Soviet–American talks led the United States to propose a new peace plan, named for US Secretary of State William Rogers. The outline of this plan had already been discussed with Moscow, but cooperation between the two super-powers had broken down before its completion. It was conveyed to the Soviets at the end of October before its publication in December 1969. The Soviet response, at least publicly, was still harsher criticism of both the United States and Israel, although Israel itself as well as Egypt rejected the plan. Substantively the Rogers Plan reiterated resolution 242 and deviated little from Moscow's own position regarding Israeli withdrawal from virtually all the territories occupied in 1967. Moscow's objections could be attributed not so much to substantive issues but rather to the fact that the Rogers Plan had become a unilateral American initiative.

Despite, possibly even because, of the Rogers Plan, matters were clearly taking a turn for the worse in the Middle East. The War of Attrition had been stepped up (Sadat was in Moscow seeking fighter-bombers and more arms when the Rogers Plan was announced). Israel had stepped up its own response and, early in January, expanded the war beyond the Canal zone by means of deep penetration bombing west of the Canal. This was the background for an extraordinary move by Moscow, a decision which was virtually unprecedented for the Soviet leadership and one which Nasser had been seeking since the 1967 defeat.

In January 1970, following a secret trip to Moscow by Nasser, the Soviets decided to assume responsibility for the air defence of Egypt. To implement this they were to send some 15,000–20,000 military advisers including personnel to handle a SAM-3 air defence system and Soviet pilots who would actually man Soviet aircraft in the Egyptian air force. Although Soviet pilots had been used previously, in Korea and in Yemen, such numbers of Soviet military personnel had never before been dispatched to a non-Communist, let alone a non-Marxist country. Moreover SAM-3 missiles had never before been placed outside the Soviet bloc (and then only most selectively in Eastern Europe). Brezhnev himself, according to Heikal (who accompanied Nasser on the trip), acknowledged the magnitude of this decision when he reportedly said 'the Soviet Union has today taken a decision fraught with grave consequences. It is a decision unlike any we have ever taken before.' Also according to Heikal, the Soviet decision was not an easy one. The Politburo was reportedly consulted, and indeed there was much evidence in subsequent months of differences of opinion within the Soviet bureaucracy regarding this decision.

The reasons for this extraordinary Soviet step may be speculated. The central one must have been Soviet concern over the very survival of Nasser's government. The Israeli deep penetration bombing, although aimed at military targets, was clearly designed to discredit and weaken Nasser. Nasser himself indicated the precariousness of his position should the attacks go unchecked. In this sense Soviet credibility was also at stake. The United States had provided Israel with Phantom aircraft some months earlier and appeared to be supporting Israel's actions. From the Soviet point of view, the situation was further complicated by the fact that the two-power and four-power talks had led nowhere, and the Americans were striking out on their own by presenting a purely American peace proposal, the Rogers Plan.

Just which elements or persons in the Soviet leadership opposed the decision is difficult to ascertain. The military, however, may well have been concerned over the risks involved. The Israeli army had already captured and physically transferred from Egypt a fully equipped, Russian-built radar station, so that the presence in Egypt of highly advanced Soviet systems could not have been relished. The presence of such large numbers of Soviet military personnel, the risks of war, and the possibility of confrontation (of the type which did in fact materialize later between Soviet and Israeli pilots, to the loss of five Soviet aircraft) cannot have been taken lightly. Moscow was careful to place its missiles, together with the SAM-2s already present in Egypt, in the areas around Cairo, Alexandria and the Aswan Dam, so as to confine the fighting to the Canal zone – to no avail. In addition to these military precautions, Brezhnev and Kosygin also admonished Nasser to exercise restraint. There was also a message from Kosygin to President Nixon urging Washington to restrain Israel, threatening increased Soviet military aid should the Israeli bombing continue. Perhaps more significantly, these Soviet moves were accompanied by a shift in the Soviet political position – in the direction of moderation.

The first sign of this shift came in an article by a relatively unknown Soviet journalist, Viktor Laptev, in the weekly *Novoe vremia*, which is also published in several languages for propaganda purposes abroad. Discussing resolution 242 and the matter of secure borders, Laptev said:

> The Soviet Union proposes formalizing the lines that existed on June 5, 1967 as the permanent and recognized frontiers between Israel and the neighboring Arab states party to the June conflict. The Arab states agree to this, though it means a certain concession on their part. For it is known that the June 5, 1967 frontiers are more favorable for Israel than those defined by the UN decision on the creation of Israel in 1947.

Those frontiers of the 1947 Partition Plan were in fact the only border of Israel ever officially accepted by the Soviet Union, Soviet maps and documents having consistently acknowledged only the additional 'armistice lines of 1949' and the 'cease-fire lines' of 10 June 1967. Such an important Soviet concession, that is, recognition of Israel's 1949–67 border, would constitute a significant conciliatory gesture towards Israel. That Moscow was indeed preparing the ground for such a gesture was further evidenced by an article by a much better known Soviet Middle East specialist Igor Beliaev in an article in the March 1970 issue of *Mezhdunarodnye zhizn'*. Here Beliaev not only repeated the new border position but also added another new element to the Soviet position. According to the peace plan outlined by Beliaev, the peace agreement achieved between Israel and the Arab states would precede the beginning of Israeli withdrawal. This significant reversal of the Soviets' insistence that withdrawal commence prior to the achievement of an agreement brought the Soviet plan significantly closer to the American and, to some degree, even the Israeli position.

Both of these innovations – on the borders and on withdrawal following a peace agreement – signalled by these articles were finally and officially stipulated in the Soviet peace proposal conveyed to the Americans in July 1970. The contents of this plan were revealed by Moscow's senior Middle East specialist Evgenii Primakov in an article in the authoritative *Pravda* on 15 October 1970. The plan included the conclusion of a negotiated settlement prior to withdrawal (to go into effect after the first of a two-phased withdrawal) as well as the idea that the 1949–67 border prior to the June war would be the officially recognized border of Israel. Thus even as the Soviets were implementing their most forthcoming and risky military assistance to Egypt, they adopted what was their most moderate ever, negotiating position. Their objective, apparently, was to bolster the faltering Egyptian government in the face of the military failure of its War of Attrition against Israel, while nonetheless taking steps to break the deadlock in the negotiating process, counter American initiatives, and encourage Israel to make territorial concessions as well as cease fighting.

Just prior to the presentation to the Americans of the new Soviet peace plan, an important event took place. In June, Secretary of State Rogers presented what became known as the Roger's Initiative calling for a cease-fire at the Canal and the beginning of negotiations. The Soviet response to this, as conveyed in the four-power talks at the end of June, was positive, exhibiting the more flexible position outlined in the Beliaev article. A few days later, Nasser began an unusually long visit (from 29 June to 17 July) to Moscow during which the cease-fire was discussed.

According to Egyptian accounts, the very difficult talks in Moscow ended with Nasser angrily proclaiming that he would accept the American proposed cease-fire out of despair over the Soviet position. From this it would appear that the Soviets were opposed to a cease-fire, but it is more likely that the Soviets actually did favour an end to the War of Attrition. The issue between the two, as in the past, was not the cease-fire as such but the military *versus* the political option. As both Sadat and Heikal later indicated, Brezhnev refused to provide new or additional weaponry to take the battle beyond defence. It was, therefore, out of frustration and despair over receiving Soviet support for offensive action (specifically an Egyptian crossing of the Canal) that Nasser threatened to accept the American plan. Judging from Brezhnev's comments and the final communique, Moscow had pressed Nasser to agree to the political option, which at this point meant accepting a cease-fire, even if, from the Soviets' point of view, this was connected with an American initiative. Presentation to Washington of the new Soviet peace plan a few days later was designed to bring Moscow back into the picture, allowing the Soviets also to share in the credit for the cease-fire achieved on 7 August. The Soviets proclaimed that only their insistence on a political solution had brought about the end of the War of Attrition.

While the cease-fire was basically an American accomplishment, the Soviets did have reason to be interested in it at this time. The Egyptian position had been improved by the Soviet military assistance, but Israeli action had not been halted. The risk of escalation was ever present, from both sides, and Soviet pilots had even been lost in direct clashes with the Israeli air force. The Soviets' own interests in the area, particularly its new bases, could best be served by quiet and relative stability, which might be obtainable now that Nasser's position was reassured and the Americans actively seeking a cease-fire which Israel too would welcome.

Continued Soviet supplies to Egypt and probably a promise to advance the SAM-3 system (in violation of the cease-fire accord) were meant to placate Nasser. At the same time, if the purpose was to encourage the political over the military option, the Soviets needed to present an incentive in order to interest the Americans and the Israelis in cooperating. This incentive presumably was the Soviet peace plan presented in July, with its official concessions (revealed unofficially some months earlier) on the crucial issues of the timing of the Israeli withdrawal and recognition of Israel's borders. From the Soviet point of view, these were significant concessions, bringing Soviet–US positions decidedly closer, though still unacceptable to Israel.

In any case, events were to take a turn in another direction. Within weeks of the cease-fire civil war broke out in Jordan between the Jordanian army and the PLO, with intervention by the Syrian army. When it became apparent that Israel, possibly with American assistance, might intervene, the Soviets pressured Syria to withdraw. On 28 September 1970 Nasser died. Soviet Premier Kosygin attended Nasser's funeral, followed by the Soviet party's International Department chief Boris Ponomarev visiting Egypt in December. A high-level Egyptian delegation went to Moscow and President Podgornyi attended the opening ceremonies of the Aswan Dam in January 1971, followed by a visit to Moscow in March by the new Egyptian President Sadat. These contacts culminated in a second trip by Podgornyi in May during which the Soviet–Egyptian Treaty of Friendship and Cooperation was signed.

To many outside observers all this indicated a deepening of the bonds between Moscow and Cairo. The treaty repeatedly sought by Nasser had finally become a reality, and Moscow's commitment to Egypt was now ensured by formal alliance akin, some believed, to the Warsaw Pact alliances (and therefore subject to the 'Brezhnev Doctrine' justifying Soviet military intervention to preserve socialist regimes). In fact, however, just the opposite was true. The Treaty was a Soviet initiative in the spring of 1971, and it was sought by Moscow primarily because of Soviet uncertainty regarding Nasser's successor, Sadat.

Soviet concern, possibly even alarm, regarding Sadat was prompted by measures undertaken by the new leader in a number of spheres. Domestically Sadat began a gradual de-Nasserization of much of the Egyptian economy, starting with certain reforms in December 1970. He also moved against some of Nasser's leading, leftist political supporters and, most notably, arrested the pro-Soviet Vice-President Ali Sabry on charges of planning a coup. This was followed by a major purge in the Egyptian government and ruling party.

In the international arena contacts were made with Washington. Sadat's own proposals for an interim agreement in the Canal zone had been rejected by Israel in February, but Sadat agreed to American mediation of the same issue through the US Assistant Secretary of State Joseph Sisco, who visited Cairo in March. Secretary of State Rogers himself visited Egypt in May. At the same time that these, for the Russians distressing, steps were being taken domestically and internationally, there were actual arguments – and possibly Soviet concern over their lack of control – regarding Sadat's plans in the Arab–Israeli context. On 7 March Sadat announced his refusal to extend the cease-fire at the Canal, having declared 1971 a 'year of decision'. Pressing for renewal of armed action, Sadat sought – in vain – offensive weapons from the Soviets, specifically surface-to-surface SCUD missiles and MIG-23 and MIG-25 aircraft. Thus just as Soviet–American détente was getting underway, Sadat was confronting the Soviets with the implicit ultimatum of supporting him in a move towards war or losing Egypt to American mediation. Unwilling to risk either alternative, the Soviets sought to protect their interests (and bases) in Egypt by means of the formal treaty.

The idea of such a treaty with a non-Communist state was a departure for Soviet tactics in the Third World under Brezhnev. The fact that subsequently, over the next fifteen years, such treaties were sought with some twenty-odd Third World states suggests that this was the new Soviet tactic designed to provide formalization of relations and, in many instances, a formal framework for Soviet bases, facilities or rights. Given the timing of the treaty with the first of these signatories, Egypt, and in view of Sadat's claim that Podgornyi suddenly produced the idea and pressed for Egyptian agreement during his May visit, it would appear that Moscow introduced this tactical change somewhat precipitously, in response to events in Egypt. The much heralded Soviet–Egyptian Treaty was not, therefore, a sign of increased Soviet influence but rather a Soviet effort to salvage something from a faltering relationship. Moreover, it did not imply greater Soviet commitment for, unlike the Warsaw Pact alliance treaties, this and subsequent Soviet treaties in the Third World did not promise mutual defence in the case of attack, but only 'contact with each other without delay in order to concert their positions'.

The Treaty did not, however, achieve its purpose for the Soviet Union. In July 1972, Sadat expelled the nearly 20,000 Soviet military advisers, and Soviet–Egyptian relations were virtually frozen. The reasons for this action may be found in three major related areas of disagreement between the Soviet Union and Sadat: Soviet arms supplies, the renewal of war against Israel, and super-power détente. Other issues contributed to tensions, for example, the haughty attitude and behaviour of Soviet personnel in Egypt, including involvement in gold-smuggling activities, and the Communist support for the coup attempt against Egypt's ally Numeri in neighbouring Sudan in the summer of 1971.

Sadat, however, was later to chronicle his growing frustration with Moscow. He cited the Soviet refusal to deliver the requested missiles and aircraft, due to the Soviets' continued opposition to Sadat's plans for military action across the Canal, opposition presumed by Sadat to be dictated by the Soviet interest in détente. According to the Egyptian President, he argued with the Soviet leaders over these issues during his March 1971 visit but did receive certain promises regarding the offensive weapons and planes. When Podgornyi elicited the Treaty from Sadat in May, the Soviet President reportedly claimed that the requested equipment was on its way but, by October 1971, when Sadat was invited to Moscow, it had not yet arrived. Furious over this, Sadat, according to his own accounts, again obtained Soviet promises.

Then, in December, the last month of the 'year of decision', the Indo-Pakistani war broke out, and Moscow dispatched weapons from Egypt to India. Sadat requested a meeting to rearrange his 'year of decision' plans for battle, but he was put off until February. During his February 1972 trip he was again given promises, although he now believed that the Soviets would postpone any action until after the Nixon–Brezhnev summit scheduled for May. At the end of April, Defence Minister Grechko visited Cairo, and there was a fly-over of four MIG-23 aircraft during the May Day celebrations, but the planes had not been delivered to Egypt and were merely used on this occasion, according to Sadat, to impress the outside world, in particular the Americans. He had a similar interpretation for an invitation he received for a twenty-four-hour visit to Moscow at the end of April, prior to Nixon's trip to Moscow, but he used this opportunity once again to press for military action. According to Sadat, the Soviets 'had only peace on their mind'.

He believed, however, that he had persuaded them to agree to a battle, to commence after the US elections in November, with the requested Soviet equipment to be sent during the interim so that Egypt would be ready for battle, or at least prepared to negotiate from a position of strength. Then came the Nixon–Brezhnev communique which called for military relaxation in the Middle East, interpreted angrily by Sadat as perpetuation of the 'no war, no peace' *status quo*. Only some six weeks after the summit did the Soviets send Egypt their (positive) analysis of the Brezhnev–Nixon meeting, with no mention of either the promised arms or the plans for battle. It was then, on 8 July 1972, that Sadat took the decision – announced publicly on 18 July – to expel the Soviet military advisers. He asked them to leave within one week, taking their equipment with them or selling it to Egypt.

The Soviets complied, indeed over-complied, immediately, withdrawing personnel beyond the advisers sent with the air-defence system in 1970, so that even Soviet instructors working in Egyptian military institutions were withdrawn. They took with them all their SAM equipment and refused to sell any of the systems to Egypt. In addition, they refused to cooperate with Egyptian Premier Sidki sent by Sadat to Moscow to work out a joint announcement which might permit the Soviets some face-saving. They also recalled their Ambassador from Cairo.

This Soviet response could be interpreted in various ways. It was so surprising that some even claimed it was disinformation intended to induce Israel to lower its guard in the belief that Egypt could not go to war without the Soviet Union. Others claimed that Soviet compliance was a sign that Moscow had actually welcomed the opportunity to reduce its involvement in Egypt, the better to concentrate on the Persian Gulf–Indian Ocean area which had risen in importance for the Soviet Union. This may well have been the case, although one might argue that the Soviets could have found a more positive way to withdraw their personnel than by expulsion. Moreover, there was no sign that the Soviets had lost all interest in Egypt, however much they might have sought reduction of their involvement or concentration on other parts of the region. Indeed the Soviets' effort to bolster their positions with Syria and even the PLO after the expulsion were indicative of their continued interest in this part of the Middle East.

Rather one must understand the Soviet response as a choice between very few alternatives. Once asked to leave, the Soviets had almost no option but to comply. To attempt to stay by force would have been difficult logistically, counter-productive politically, and even risky militarily. Soviet interests elsewhere in the region and the Third World, as well as in détente, would have been harmed by such a move. The Americans might have responded with their fleet or other military moves, leading to super-power confrontation. There may also have been divisions within the Kremlin over the issue. All of these possibilities argued against such a drastic, unprecedented move regarding a non-Marxist, non-contiguous Third World state. The way in which the Soviets left may well have been tactical, designed to demonstrate to Sadat that he could not expect to dictate to Moscow nor have what he wanted easily. Mainly they may have sought to prove to him just how much Egypt was indeed dependent upon Moscow militarily.

Yet, the Soviets were shocked by Sadat's move. Permitted to keep most of their own naval facilities or privileges, they viewed the setback more in political than military terms. The Soviet Union ostentatiously provided increased support to Syria, Iraq, and the PLO not only to preserve its presence in the area, but as a means of minimizing the political damage. At home, however, a thorough re-examination of Soviet policies towards Egypt led to a rethinking of Soviet Third World policy altogether. The more militant, ideologically based approach of the mid- to late 1970s could be traced to this rethinking, precipitated by the crisis with Cairo. The results were demands to Third World clients for greater ideological affinity, socialist orientation, and the creation of a strong organizational base through Marxist-Leninist parties or, at the very least, the forging of radical blocs at the regional level. This new policy was never to constitute the entire Soviet position regarding the Third World or the Middle East; nor did it affect Moscow's attitude towards the Arab–Israeli conflict. In this sense, the crisis with Egypt had even greater impact upon Soviet Third World policy in general than on Soviet Middle East policy in particular, its repercussions emerging only gradually over the ensuing years.

6   The Yom Kippur War, 1973

Egyptian preparations for the October 1973 (Yom Kippur) War can be traced to the period of Sadat's dispute with the Soviet Union over offensive weapons and the very idea of an armed action. The expulsion of the Soviet military advisers was not only a sign of Sadat's exasperation and anger over Soviet recalcitrance but, as he himself later proclaimed, an act to free Egypt from Soviet restraints so as to move towards the long-awaited battle. This did not mean, obviously, that Moscow was to play no role whatsoever in either the preparations or the war itself. But this role was a complex, often contradictory one clearly influenced by the conflict which had arisen between the two countries.

With the expulsion of the Soviet military advisers, a period ensued of what Sadat called a 'freeze' in Soviet–Egyptian relations. Syrian President Assad sought to mediate between the two during a trip to Moscow in September 1972. In response to this Sadat sent Premier Sidki to the Soviet Union with the message that he still opposed a political solution but might be better inclined to talks were he to have the long-sought weapons. The Soviets responded by returning the SAM-6s to Egypt along with a few hundred advisers and the Soviet Ambassador Vinogradov. This, together with the replacement in November of Egyptian War Minister Sadek – a person known to be relatively anti-Soviet – led to rumours of Soviet–Egyptian rapprochement. In fact, as Sadat made quite clear, the 'freeze' in relations continued until February 1973. (Although in December Sadat renewed the Soviets' naval rights for another five-year period.) The replacement of Sadek was not, as then interpreted, a sign of improving Soviet–Egyptian relations, however. Rather, it was a move by Sadat to begin military preparations for war. Sadek had earlier been ordered to make such preparations, but had failed to do so in the belief, according to Sadat, that without the unobtainable Soviet equipment (MIG-23s and SCUDs) an Egyptian offensive was out of the question. Angry that nothing had been done to prepare what Sadat had hoped would be a military action after the US elections of November, Sadat named Ahmad Ismail War Minister with orders to build the necessary embankments on the Egyptian side of the Suez Canal in preparation for war.

This was accomplished by January, and in February Sadat picked four possible dates for the action: end of May, August, September or October 1973. In April operative plans were set in a joint meeting with the Syrians, the offensive to begin with what were to appear as military exercises. Such manoeuvres did in fact take place at the end of May, leading to a partial Israeli mobilization in anticipation of Egyptian attack. This mobilization may indeed have been the reason Cairo called off the offensive, although a number of additional reasons have been offered by Sadat and others. These reasons included the continued delay in Soviet arms deliveries, urgings by King Feisal to seek a solution through the Americans, and the scheduling of the Washington summit for June.

Just how much the Soviets knew of all these plans remains unclear. There reportedly was a Soviet reassessment of policy towards Egypt in December, and in January there were some signs, such as a reference in a *New Times* editorial to Israeli plans for war in 1973, suggesting that Moscow expected Sadat to act in 1973. The Soviets were not, however, directly informed by Cairo, learning of the plans apparently from their own sources in Egypt and, later, Syria. Nonetheless, a decision was taken in Moscow fully to resume arms supplies to Egypt, most likely in full knowledge that an offensive was being planned. Thus a trip to Moscow in February by Sadat's security adviser, Hafiz Ismail was followed immediately by that of an Egyptian military delegation under Ahmad Ismail negotiating the resumption of arms deliveries. These included SCUDs but not MIG-23s, and the return of approximately 1500–2000 military advisers to Egypt.

The reasons for the Soviet decision to resume arms supplies to Egypt, thereby apparently revising the Kremlin's opposition to military action, can only be speculated upon. The Soviet move may have been merely tactical, designed to avoid further deterioration of its position in the Middle East, particularly in view of Sadat's developing cooperation with Saudi Arabia and the then anti-Soviet Libya, as well as the ever-present possibility of an Egyptian turn to the United States. Probably aware of Sadat's decision to go to war even without further Soviet arms supplies, Moscow may have decided that it stood to lose too much in the region if it persisted in its uncooperative attitude. The withholding of arms had not only failed to deter Sadat from the military option, but promised to further jeopardize Soviet aspirations in the region. In this sense the calculation may simply have been that it was preferable to be in, rather than out, inasmuch as Sadat was determined to act in any case. Moreover, it is possible the Soviets hoped that they might still be able to dissuade Sadat or at least be in a better position to restrain him were they to return to Egypt even partially. Maintaining direct control of the SCUDs and continuing to withhold some of the promised equipment may have been designed to achieve such influence. On the other hand, it is also possible that Moscow, like other capitals in the world, did not take Sadat's threats seriously. He had been talking so long about the 'year of decision' and, yet, done so little, that there was good reason to be skeptical. Payment in hard currency, now demanded by the Soviets, presumably also enhanced the attractiveness of the decision, but it does not seem likely that this shift in Soviet policy, with all its implications and risks regarding war, was determined primarily by economic considerations. Nor is it certain that the Soviet leadership was unanimous in its decision. Those most concerned about the risks of war, and potential damage to détente, were probably somewhat hesitant, joined perhaps by the ideologists who were already justifiably doubtful of Sadat's loyalty as an ally.

As critical as the Soviets' decision to resume arms supplies to Egypt was, it did not in fact signify a reversal of Moscow's opposition to Sadat's intention to go to war. This was misunderstood even by Sadat, who said in a 1 April 1974 speech:

some of the [arms] deal began reaching us after the Field Marshal's [Ahmad Ismail] return in February. We were happy that our relations would return to normal. But the USSR persisted in the view that a military battle must be ruled out and that the question must await a peaceful solution.

Other comments by Sadat and the Egyptian press, as well as other Arab sources including pro-Soviet ones, both before and after the war, clearly indicate that Moscow sought to dissuade Sadat from going to war. Similar pressures were brought to bear on Assad as well, both during the Syrian leader's secret visit to Moscow in May and during Soviet politburo member Kirilenko's visit to Syria in July. In fact, open arguments and a decided strain developed in the relations between the two Arab states on the one hand and Moscow, on the other hand. The Arab leaders' complaints and post-war criticism related to problems with arms deliveries as well, suggesting that the Soviets combined their arguments with some foot-dragging in the actual preparations for the war. In this sense Soviet policy was dualistic, not unlike the preceding years, providing the wherewithal for hostilities while nonetheless urging the Arabs to forego their war plans in favour of political means. Thus Moscow had good cause to warn the Americans at the June 1973 summit that another Arab–Israeli war would result if some breakthrough were not achieved in the political sphere.

The Arabs later claimed that the Soviets were not made privy to the actual war plans nor, especially, to the various dates set, lest they try to interfere or jeopardize the element of surprise critical to the Arab attack. There are signs that Moscow (as well as Washington) was concerned that something was about to occur; both countries sent up observer satellites in September, and the Soviet Ambassador to Cairo apparently sought information from Sadat. Vinogradov was directly informed, however, only on 3 October when Sadat told him that hostilities were imminent. During the following two days the Soviets openly air-lifted their civilian personnel out of Egypt (to the distress of the Egyptian high command, which feared that Israel would thus be alerted – which it was – and the element of surprise lost). They also moved their ships out of Egyptian and Syrian ports, transferring them to a point westward, off the island of Crete. On 4 October the Syrians informed the Soviets of the exact time for the attack.

With the outbreak of hostilities the Soviet leadership most likely perceived two objectives which were to guide their ensuing actions. The first was to attempt not simply to retain but, due to the pre-war tensions, actually redeem some of the Soviet position and prestige in the Arab world by providing assistance. The second, potentially contradictory objective, was to avoid confrontation with the United States and, secondarily, limit damage to détente, by preventing escalation of the conflict. Neither objective was easily attainable; achievement of both simultaneously was to prove impossible. Moreover there may even have been those in the Kremlin who preferred one over the other, for example, pro-détentists may have advocated caution and restraint. Evidence of such differences could be seen in the different characterizations of the war by Brezhnev, for example, who spoke (on 8 October) of the war as an exception to the successful reduction of tensions achieved by détente, and by Defence Minister Grechko who, on the same day, cited the war as proof of the aggressive nature of imperialism. In any case, whether because of the potentially contradictory nature of the objectives or the perhaps less likely possibility of internal conflict in the Soviet leadership, or both,

Soviet policy even during the war continued to be characterized by a certain dualism.

Acting on the basis of the second, escalation prevention objective, Moscow's first act during the war was to seek an immediate cease-fire. Disregarding events in the field, indeed acting before the results of the Arab offensive could have been known, Vinogradov immediately requested an appointment with Sadat, succeeding in seeing him six hours after the opening of hostilities. This was to be the first of a series of attempts by the Soviets to elicit Sadat's agreement to a cease-fire. In reply to Sadat's angry refusal, the Soviet Ambassador claimed that Moscow had obtained Syrian agreement. Vinogradov subsequently explained that Assad had not actually agreed to a cease-fire on the first day but that prior to the war he had arranged with the Soviets that they would seek a cease-fire forty-eight hours after the initial attacks. Assad denied any agreement to a cease-fire, and Sadat accused Vinogradov of lying when the Soviet Ambassador returned to press his bid for a cease-fire once again on 7 October.

The Soviet interest in an early cease-fire was consistent with both Soviet behaviour prior to the war and Moscow's concern over escalation or expansion of the war. Prolongation of the hostilities ran counter to Soviet interests whatever the estimate of the combatants' capabilities. On the one hand, reversals of the Arabs' early victories might lead to defeat and the need or call for Soviet intervention with all the attendant risks. On the other hand, continued progress of the Arab armies and Israeli distress might precipitate American intervention with similar risks of super-power confrontation. Even short of these eventualities, continued fighting polarized the international scene, endangering détente and placing the Soviets in the difficult position of having to prove their loyalty to their Third World clients while facing the first genuine test of the new relationship with the United States. For these reasons, it is not surprising that the Soviets sought a cease-fire even before knowing of the Arabs' progress in the field, and that they persisted in this effort throughout the changes – known or unknown to Moscow – in the Arabs' battle plans. Nonetheless the other Soviet objective, that of improving and maintaining relations with Egypt and Syria, was respected insofar as Moscow did not seek to impose a cease-fire, for example, through cooperative moves with the United States, against the wishes of Sadat.

The Soviets also undertook two moves which appeared to encourage or facilitate the prolongation of the war. The first of these was a call for Arab solidarity, aid and support so that Egypt and Syria would not stand alone in their battle. Contained in letters to various Arab leaders, this appeal appeared to be a Soviet attempt to expand the conflict and thereby also prolong the war. Yet the appeal may not have been a Soviet initiative. It was in fact a response to a query from Algerian President Boumedienne, who had urged Moscow to provide full support. Probably not intended for publication (which was provided by the Algerians on 5 October) the Soviet call for Arab support may in fact have been a way of obtaining the kind of direct aid Moscow was itself hesitant to supply. Alternatively, it may have been somewhat defensive, implying that it was the duty of the Arabs, before all others, to help Egypt and Syria. Both of these interpretations are strengthened by the fact that in the note to Boumedienne the Soviets referred to the 'complexities' of the situation which, they said, Algeria understood – implying that Algiers knew that, as a super power, Moscow could not take certain risks. The Soviet leadership did meet with the Iraqi Foreign Minister in Moscow, ordering the transfer of Soviet tanks from Iraq to Syria and, possibly, urging the dispatch of some Iraqi troops to fight with the Syrians. Yet Moscow made no other contacts, attempts or even propaganda appeals to engage the Arab states in the war. Dealings with Iraq and other Arab states may in fact have focused more on nationalization of western oil companies and the emergent oil embargo. A step which was much more clearly designed to assist Egypt and Syria was the air and sea lift of arms begun by Moscow on 9–10 October. One of the most controversial Soviet acts of the war, it represented Soviet intervention which, the Soviet leadership must have calculated, would invite similar American action, endanger détente, prolong the war and increase the risks of super-power confrontation. Boumedienne claimed that in fact the Soviets sent only medical and non-military supplies until he himself travelled to Moscow on 14 October and provided hard-currency payments, thereby persuading the Soviets to ship arms and equipment. Sadat too complained that the Soviets did not send badly needed military equipment (Yugoslavia, he said, supplied tanks via Libya), sending only items which had been previously ordered. He further claimed that the Soviets not only demanded cash payments but refused shipment until the interest on past deliveries was paid. Egypt did obtain a $100 million loan from Abu Dhabi presumably for this purpose.

Sadat's complaints not withstanding, the Soviet decision to resupply Egypt and Syria during the war was widely viewed as a Soviet commitment to assist the Arabs in pursuing broadened war objectives.

Egyptian forces had not only successfully crossed the Suez Canal, destroying the Israeli fortifications known as the Bar-Lev line, but they had also impressively repelled an Israeli counter-attack on 8 October. On the Syrian front, however, the earlier victories had already been reversed by 9 October, with the Israeli air force bombing Damascus that day. This attack included a hit on the Soviet cultural centre which took the life of at least one Soviet citizen. The Soviet resupply effort began that day, presumably in response to these same problems on the Syrian front. With regard to Egypt, the air lift tripled in size after 15 October, that is, after Egyptian forces finally suffered a reversal in the Sinai (and after Boumedienne brought a hard-currency payment to Moscow). Thus, it may be the case that the Soviet resupply operation was intended not so much to prolong or extend the war but rather to shore up the Arab armies and prevent their defeat, until a cease-fire could be achieved. Given Arab resentment of Soviet inactivity during the 1967 war, Moscow presumably did not want to suffer a similar blow either to its prestige or credibility as an ally. Even as the resupply effort was getting underway, the Soviets were in contact with both the United States and, once again, Sadat for the purpose of arranging a cease-fire. On 10 October and again on 13 October Sadat angrily rejected the Soviet cease-fire proposals, including a joint Soviet–American proposal, agreed to by Israel and transmitted by the British early 13 October. At this time the Egyptians were still in ascendancy in Sinai although the Syrians had lost the Golan once again and were in retreat.

On 12 October, the day before the renewed bid for a cease-fire, Moscow issued its first official warning of the war to Israel. Aside from the trouble the Syrians were having, there was no obvious immediate reason for this warning. Soviet personnel had been killed on 9 October, but the statement referring to these losses came only three days later. Western sources believed the warning came to protect the Soviets in the eyes of the Arabs because of the unpopular moves with the Americans to achieve the cease-fire. A more likely reason for the warning at this time may have been the Israeli sinking of a Soviet merchant ship in the Syrian port of Tartus. The warning demanded Israeli observance of international law, specifying the freedom of navigation. This would suggest a particular Soviet sensitivity on this matter, demonstrated by the dispatch of a Soviet destroyer northeast of Cyprus to protect Soviet merchant vessels en route to Syria. Primarily, however, there was serious concern about the future of Damascus in the face of Israeli victories on the Syrian front. For this reason Moscow informed the United States of its airborne alert for the defence of Damascus and reportedly sent advance staff of this division to Syrian military headquarters near Damascus. All of this occurred simultaneously with the cease-fire bid rejected by Sadat on 13 October. The following day the largest tank battle in history was fought in the Sinai ending in an Israeli victory. With the tide turned in their favour, Israeli forces began to cross the Canal on the night of 15 October. The following morning Soviet Premier Kosygin cancelled a scheduled meeting with visiting Danish Premier Jorgensen and flew to Cairo.

This was Moscow's final attempt to persuade Sadat to accept a cease-fire, and the Soviets (reportedly together with the Americans) enlisted Yugoslav Foreign Minister Minic to help them in this effort. According to the Yugoslavs, Kosygin brought the draft of a peace plan which called for a cease-fire to be followed by negotiations for an Israeli withdrawal to the 1967 lines, with small corrections, and super-power guarantees of a peace treaty. It seems unlikely that Kosygin discussed this plan at any length with Sadat. The Egyptian leader angrily delayed a meeting with Kosygin, who spent most of his two days in Cairo in the Soviet Embassy. Kosygin may not even have had Sadat's agreement to a cease-fire when he returned to Moscow in the morning of 19 October, for Sadat later gave different times as to his own agreement on the nineteenth to end the war. Transmitted before or after Kosygin's departure, Egyptian acquiescence opened the way for Moscow to contact Washington for an urgent meeting finally to bring about a cessation of hostilities. With Israeli forces on the western side of the Canal and on the offensive, time became of the essence. Brezhnev insisted upon meeting with Kissinger immediately upon the arrival in Moscow of the US Secretary of State and, within hours, the Soviets abandoned their demand for Israeli withdrawal to the 1967 lines, accepting a cease-fire in place. The joint Soviet–American proposal brought to the UN, becoming Security Council resolution 338, called for a cease-fire as of 22 October, the implementation of resolution 242, and the beginning of peace negotiations 'under appropriate auspices'.

These activities, including the cease-fire, did not please Moscow's Arab clients. Both Sadat and Assad would have preferred clarification of Israel's withdrawal rather than a cease fire in place. Worse still was the linking of the cease-fire to resolution 242, a vague formulation never accepted by Syria. Syria had further complaints, for Assad claimed that he had not been consulted at every stage and learned of the final proposal only when it was brought to the UN. He claimed that with Iraqi help he had actually been planning a counter-offensive and was therefore not only surprised but opposed to the cease-fire. He was, nonetheless, persuaded to honour it a few days later, marking Syria's first albeit indirect acceptance of resolution 242. Iraq, Algeria, the PLO, Kuwait and Libya all joined Syria in criticizing the cease-fire, not only because of the link with resolution 242, the ignoring of the territorial question, and of the Palestinian issue, but also because it was perceived as Soviet–American collusion to impose their will on the Arab world. The Chinese too, ever anxious to exploit any crisis for use in their own dispute with Moscow, fanned this criticism with comments that Moscow had sold out its friends in the interests of détente and super-power hegemony.

Because of these responses Moscow was particularly sensitive to the subsequent breakdown of the cease-fire and the increasing Israeli threat to Egypt, for which Moscow could now be held at least theoretically, if indirectly responsible. On 23 October the Security Council voted to send observers to enforce the cease-fire, but by 24 October Israeli forces had virtually occupied the town of Suez, surrounded the 20,000-strong Egyptian Third Army left on the East bank of the Canal and, from the Egyptian point of view, had an open road to Cairo. Sadat urgently requested the Soviets and the Americans to send in their own forces to ensure the cease-fire, a request rejected by Washington but supported by Moscow in talks with Kissinger during the late afternoon and the evening of 24 October. At 9.35p.m. a note from Brezhnev to Nixon arrived at the White House and at 3 a.m. America declared a Defcon III alert. Having succeeded only in raising the ire of the Arabs, the Soviets were now faced with the super-power confrontation they had so assiduously sought to avert.

Just what Soviet steps and intentions precipitated this confrontation are not entirely clear. Two days earlier a Soviet ship emitting signals which indicated the presence of nuclear material aboard passed through the Bosphorus. Washington received this information only three days later, some hours after the activation of Defcon III, although many were subsequently to connect the nuclear material with the alert itself. Why the Soviets dispatched nuclear material to a war zone at this time remains unclear. There was speculation that the ships contained nuclear warheads for the SCUDs supplied to Egypt earlier, but it is most unlikely that Moscow was in fact willing to supply a non-bloc, erstwhile ally such as Egypt with nuclear warheads. And, if they had intended to provide nuclear warheads for the present emergency, they probably would not have done so via a three-to-four-day sea passage through the closely monitored Turkish Straits. It is more likely that the nuclear material was intended for the Soviet fleet in the Mediterranean but, even so, the dispatch of such material through the Straits at this time could not but provoke alarm. Therefore, one cannot rule out the possibility that this was part of a deliberate Soviet show-of-force decision. Inasmuch as the Soviets appeared to believe, as did the Americans, that the war could be winding down (Soviet media also exhibited this attitude), this may have been intended as a signal of Soviet commitment to ensure implementation of the cease-fire. This would be an extremely strong and risky signal in the circumstances but undeniably convincing, particularly when linked to the further alert in the Soviet airborne divisions initiated the next day, 23 October. This alert, in response to the violations of the cease-fire in the Suez area, was accompanied by the transfer towards Egypt of two amphibious Soviet ships anchored off the coast of Syria. Also flights of Soviet transport aircraft to Egypt were almost totally halted, meaning that these aircraft were now free to transport the alerted airborne divisions, if the troops were planning to act unilaterally.

In the political sphere there were complaints conveyed by Dobrynin to Kissinger over Israel's violation of the cease-fire as well as an official warning issued to Israel on 23 October. Domestically, however, there was no propaganda preparation for a Soviet intervention; the Soviet media on 24 October optimistically claimed that the cease-fire had taken hold. On the day of this announcement, however, when Israeli forces cut off the Egyptian Third Army from behind, the Soviets established an inflight airborne command post in southern Russia and, according to some reports, issued special military orders associated with intervention. Also detected en route to Egypt were twelve Soviet transport planes, despite the cessation of such flights from the previous day. It later became clear that these planes did not carry troops. Late on 24 October a Soviet helicopter carrier and two destroyers left their positions off Crete and relieved the anti-carrier group covering the USS Independence – the group nearest the war zone. While this could have been routine, the timing – almost coincident with Brezhnev's note to Nixon – suggested an effort to counter movement of the US Sixth Fleet towards Egypt and thus protect Soviet sea and air lines in time of airborne intervention. Dobrynin again met with Kissinger late on the afternoon of 24 October, in a conciliatory manner, indicating that Moscow rejected Sadat's appeal for US–Soviet troops to enforce the cease-fire (which Washington had publicly turned down an hour earlier). The two then proceeded to discuss the convening of the Geneva Peace Conference. Later, however, at 7.05 p.m. Washington time, Dobrynin called to say that the Soviet Union would support Sadat's appeal at that evening's Security Council session. A few hours later, when no US response had been received, Dobrynin delivered the message from Brezhnev to Nixon inviting the United States to join with the Soviet Union to ensure observance of the cease-fire, adding the threat:

I will say it straight that if you find it impossible to act jointly with us in this matter, we should be faced with the necessity urgently to consider the question of taking appropriate steps unilaterally. We cannot allow arbitrariness on the part of Israel.

The US response was the Defcon III alert. They were also successful in applying pressure on Israel – just before the alert – to permit the passage of vital supplies to the Egyptian Third Army, in effect saving the 20,000 strong Egyptian force.

Did the Soviets intend to intervene militarily? Reportedly even Kissinger did not anticipate massive Soviet intervention to battle with the Israelis. The concern was over a symbolic display of Soviet force, such as the landing of a contingent to 'protect' Cario airport or a small 'peace-keeping' force to bring supplies to the Third Army. The assessment of some in Washington was of 'high probability' that the Soviets would dispatch airborne troops, perhaps as many as 5,000 per day, which alone would be a potentially explosive measure. The Soviet capability for actually joining battle rapidly was, however, questionable. It seems more likely that Moscow did not intend actual battlefield intervention, but rather the threat of intervention – using the above-mentioned steps as signals, with the outside possibility, if the threat failed, of the landing of some forces, limited to Cairo, in the unlikely event that the capital was actually threatened. Such a contingent, even small, ran the risk of battle with Israeli forces as well as confrontation with the United States. While there may have been some in the Kremlin willing to run such risks, it seems much more likely that the estimate was that a threat (made credible by the various alerts, fleet movements, and airborne command) would be sufficient to persuade the Americans, and assist them, to pressure Israel. In this sense the threat was somewhat similar to those issued in the 1956 and 1967 wars, that is, issued after the major fighting on the ground was virtually finished and the actual need to implement the threat was most unlikely. While providing greater credibility than the earlier threats, it too was couched in conditional terms; it also proposed the clearly impossible-to-achieve suggestion of joint Soviet–American military action and, as in past threats, it was intended for political, though also military, purposes.

The Soviet moves, however, did jeopardize Soviet–American relations and détente, even risking, if unintentionally, US–Soviet confrontation. One explanation may be that the Soviets simply misjudged the Americans' likely response. Soviet naval action may have been predicated on the expectation that the US would respond merely by moving its fleet (and pressuring Israel) rather than by declaring a Defcon III alert (and pressuring Israel). Even so, the Soviet leadership cannot have been unaware of the risks, at the very least to détente. Whatever their estimates as to the possibility of quickly recouping such losses to détente, their willingness to run the risks of an intervention threat indicated the seriousness with which they viewed Sadat's call for help. While in other circumstances Moscow might welcome Sadat's failure and fall from power, a new Egyptian leader promised to be even more anti-Soviet than Sadat if the change were to occur under these circumstances of military defeat. There was also the damage to Soviet credibility and authority, particularly in the Arab world, for Moscow had negotiated the cease-fire and was partially responsible for ensuring that it aided, not further endangered, the Arabs. Breakdown of the cease-fire and subsequent failure to act would not only strengthen those (including the Chinese) who had argued throughout for greater Soviet action and against a cease-fire, but it would fortify those within the Kremlin who opposed détente. Thus, almost paradoxically, Brezhnev had to risk a blow to détente in part in order to save the policy. Post-war comments clearly reflected this dilemma. Pro-détentists such as Brezhnev and Kosygin emphasized the role of détente in bringing about super-power cooperation which prevented world catastrophe, while Grechko and other military figures presumed to be anti-détentists referred to the war as the work of the imperialists behind Israel and the need for vigilance.

From the Soviet point of view, the dualistic policy pursued during the war failed entirely, as Moscow's main objectives proved contradictory and unobtainable. The efforts to maintain détente and, more importantly, avoid Soviet–American confrontation dictated a degree of cooperation with the Americans and even a compromise in order to obtain a cease-fire. This in turn angered the Arabs, jeopardizing the objective of improving and maintaining relations with Egypt and Syria. Pursuit of this objective, in the form of material assistance during the war and the intervention threat, was apparently insufficient to placate the Arabs while it significantly endangered détente and did in fact lead to Soviet–American alerts and near military confrontation. It could be argued that the contradictory, dualistic policy was the result of countervailing forces and arguments within the Soviet leadership. It is more likely, however, that Moscow believed that actions of both types were integrally connected and necessary to each other: material aid to the Arabs in order to prevent the need to intervene, with its incumbent threat to super-power confrontation. Whatever the Soviet calculations, the net result was that the end of the war saw a new period of sharp deterioration in Soviet–Egyptian relations, which culminated in Egyptian abrogation of the Friendship Treaty in 1976, and a period of broadened, successful American involvement in the Middle East. At the same time détente suffered a blow, of perhaps less serious proportions than that dealt Soviet–Arab relations but nonetheless costly at least in American public opinion, which further enhanced the ability of Washington to exclude Moscow from the sphere of the Arab–Israeli conflict.

7 Settlement of the Arab–Israeli conflict

It may be argued that the ongoing Arab–Israeli conflict has served Soviet interests in the Middle East. Therefore Moscow's participation in the inter-war two-power and four-power talks was disingenuous, intended at best to prevent open hostilities but designed to maintain the conflict on a low flame. Following this line of thinking, without an ongoing conflict there would be no Arab need for nor dependence upon the Soviets. No longer in need of significant arms supplies, the Arabs would no longer be dependent upon Soviet promises and deliveries. Similarly they would no longer be in need of Soviet military advisers; indeed they would no longer even be in need of Moscow as political champion in the world arena, for America's backing of Israel would no longer be of vital concern to the Arabs. Without the conflict, then, Moscow would lose its foothold in that part of the region and with it the bases, facilities, influence and benefits derived from that foothold. The basic assumption of this conventional wisdom is that crises are beneficial to the spread and maintenance of Soviet influence. And, indeed, this crisis has been beneficial in the past. It provided the vehicle for Soviet entry to the area in the 1950s and for the massive military move into the region in the 1960s, furthering Moscow's military as well as political interests at the regional and even global level.

It may be the case, however, that the Soviets became doubtful about these benefits and the advantages of this crisis following the 1973 War. Such second thoughts may even have been operative before the war, as a result of the reassessment in the wake of the expulsion of the Soviet advisers from Egypt or possibly even earlier, in the late 1960s. There were clearly signs after the war that the Soviets were beginning to view the costs or risks of this conflict as greater than the benefits. A book on international crises was published in 1972 by Primakov and international affairs specialist V. V. Zhurkin that warned against certain regional crises which might lead to global crisis. The Arab–

Israeli conflict was cited as one of these crises, the resolution of which was critical to world peace. The US Defcon III and the near collision of the super-powers in the October War was a clear demonstration of the validity of this claim. At least this was the way Brezhnev and others were to characterize the war.

A central factor accounting for this characterization was the lack of Soviet control over this conflict, which had in fact become increasingly volatile. The lack of control had become quite evident with the Six-Day War, and the subsequent massive Soviet penetration, particularly of Egypt, had been designed to remedy this. Nonetheless, Moscow was not able to achieve sufficient control or influence, particularly after Sadat came to power, to deter Egypt or Syria from going to war. Sadat was determined to go through with his decision with or without Soviet approval, and the Soviets were unable or unwilling to take advantage of their positions physically to prevent the outbreak of war, presumably because of the risks involved and the damage this would entail for future relations.

The manipulation of arms supplies and, finally, the suspension of arms deliveries were of no avail. Use of the arms weapon may have influenced the type of battle to be undertaken, but Sadat's decision to go to war even without the long-sought weapons completely undermined whatever leverage the Soviets believed they had. Indeed the failure of this arms embargo casts some doubt on the whole idea of arms dependency and the supply of arms as an instrument of control. This was not the only occasion upon which the suspension of Soviet arms deliveries failed to produce the desired policy change on the part of a Soviet Third World client, for example in the case of Soviet opposition to the 1976 Syrian invasion of Lebanon, as we shall see below. Even as a more subtle long-range instrument deriving from the Soviets' status as sole arms supplier, the arms weapon was ineffective. While conversion to western weapons systems would be a lengthy process, Sadat, for example, proved willing to undertake this ten-year conversion, finding means of accommodation in the interim. Moreover, ineffective as it proved to be, the arms weapon had even less efficacy once the Soviets began to demand hard-currency payments for their supplies.

The independence of the Arab leaders had long been an impediment to Soviet control and influence. Even Nasser, but particularly Sadat and Assad, had assiduously guarded their freedom of action. Such independence in the political sphere was exemplified by Assad's persistent refusal to enter into the Treaty of Friendship and Cooperation sought by Moscow. Ideology was more an obstacle to influence than a factor for adhesion. And economic independence was enhanced by the world energy crisis, during which the oil-rich states shared some of their petro-dollars with Egypt and Syria. Indeed Arab independence of Moscow was generally strengthened by the power accrued to and through the oil-producing states.

A second disturbing factor for the Soviets in this ongoing conflict was the increasing involvement of the United States. This involvement raised the risks of what was already a crisis of potentially global proportions. The creation of the American Rapid Deployment Force, coordinated with Egypt, augmented the possibility of super-power clashes, as did the expanded strategic cooperation between the United States and Israel, which included Sixth Fleet visits to Israeli ports and the rumoured (though unfounded) storage of US missiles in Israel. Growing American involvement not only raised the risks, however. It also proceeded at the expense of the Soviet Union or at the very least simultaneously with a decline in Soviet prestige and power in the area. In fact the 1970s saw a deterioration in the Soviets' position in the area, with relations with Egypt declining to the point of Sadat's abrogation of his Treaty with Moscow, the loss of the various military rights in that country, continued Syrian obstinance regarding a Treaty and some flirtation with Washington particularly during the Lebanon Civil War, which saw a sharp deterioration in Soviet–Syrian relations. These setbacks were accompanied by a serious rift with Saddam Hussein's regime in Iraq in 1978.

Thus the foothold the Soviets theoretically might lose if the conflict came to an end was somewhat dubious to begin with, Moscow's declining position possibly even providing further motivation for seeking a settlement, for reasons we shall examine below. The Soviets appeared unwilling, however, to make what seemed to be the necessary concessions to reverse this trend of deterioration, such as agreement to reschedule the Egyptian arms debt or support for the Syrian military effort in Lebanon. Although there were specific reasons in each case, such reticence may have been more generally explained by the fact that Soviet priorities in the region had shifted to the Indian Ocean area, especially the Horn of Africa and the Persian Gulf. This shift may have prompted them to seek stability in the area of the Arab–Israeli context. At the very least it made them less willing to run the risks of such a conflict. To these risks must be added the possible Soviet concern over the nuclearization of the conflict, mentioned from time to time by Soviet commentators and by Brezhnev as a serious danger. Propaganda aside, Soviet policy did oppose the proliferation of nuclear weapons, and the growing conviction that Israel possessed such weapons not only increased the risks of the conflict but also created pressures upon Moscow to provide its Arab clients with parity.

On balance the Arab–Israeli conflict had become a far less positive vehicle for Soviet interests, possibly even counter-productive and certainly risky. There might, therefore, actually be greater benefits than costs to a settlement, under the circumstances which developed in the 1970s. Provided that the Soviet Union were a party to such a settlement, Moscow might thus obtain formal, international recognition of the legitimacy of its interests and presence in the area. The quest for formal accords and legitimacy has historically been part of Soviet foreign policy. One need only look at the example of the Helsinki Conference of 1975, sought for over twenty years by Soviet leaders for one thing only: formal recognition of the status quo in Europe – meaning Communist rule in Eastern Europe. This, despite the fact that for over two decades the Communists had been ruling over Eastern Europe, with the help of Soviet invasions in 1956 and 1968, virtually unchallenged by the West. Formal, international recognition would, thus, appear to be of some importance to the Soviets, and such recognition of their more limited interests in the region to the south of their border was of some value to Moscow.

This took on greater importance in view of the successful challenge of the United States, whose policy was exclusion of the Soviet Union from the area. At the same time, such an international accord might provide greater stability and permanence to the Soviet presence than the already proven unreliable goodwill of the various Arab regimes in the region. As guarantors of a peace agreement between Israel and the Arabs, the Soviets would have a legitimate role and stable presence. This might even halt the advance of the Americans, and the forced retreat of the Soviets, without necessarily preventing competition within safer political limits. Similarly, arms limitations which might be part of such an agreement, would be more of a limitation on the Americans than the Soviets, the former being the larger merchant in the area. This might relieve some of the pressure on the Soviets to maintain the arms race in the region, and thus reduce the danger of nuclearization.

Settlement of the conflict may not have been the ideal policy for the Soviet Union had the Soviets been able to maintain control and limit American involvement. Given, however, the lack of control and the increasing risks, as well as changes in Soviet regional priorities and fortunes, the best way to cope with American gains may have been to seek a cooperative venture leading to joint guarantees of an Arab–Israeli peace, rather than continued unsuccessful competition. In fact the greatest threat to the Soviet presence in the area was the growing possibility of a *Pax America*, that is a US-mediated settlement which totally excluded the Soviet Union.

The first and foremost Soviet condition for a settlement of the Arab–Israeli conflict was, therefore, Soviet participation, both in the achievement of such a settlement and in its implementation. The Soviet demand was for multilateral negotiations for a complete settlement rather than a step by step or what they called a partial approach which might be conducted directly on a bilateral basis, or, with an American client, through US mediation, in either case excluding the USSR. The framework sought was an international conference, the first of which was held in Geneva in December 1973 (following the Yom Kippur War) under joint Soviet and US sponsorship, with invitations issued by the United Nations to the states directly involved in the conflict. Subsequently the Soviets called for the addition of France and Britain and, still later, for all the permanent Security Council members. They were also to demand Palestinian participation, often specifying this as PLO participation or a joint Palestinian–Jordanian delegation or other combinations to include the Palestinians. Participation in the implementation was left open; the Soviets spoke generally of joint Soviet–US or international guarantees for the borders to be worked out or for the settlement as a whole (presumably by means of air and sea surveillance, possibly by observers in the field, but actually never specified or clarified).

The Soviets had their positions regarding the contents of the settlement or at least what they termed the basic principles upon which the peace agreement should be based. These were similar to but more explicit than resolution 242 with regard to the need for Israeli withdrawal, usually stated as withdrawal from all the territories occupied in 1967 (and after). Just as in the peace plan presented to the Americans in 1970, the Soviet position presented in Gromyko's opening address to the Geneva Peace Conference called for recognition of Israel's borders as those which existed on 4 June 1967, that is the armistice lines of the 1948–9 War of Independence within which Israel had existed without official international (or Soviet) recognition until the 1967 war.

The second principle on which a settlement was to be based was fulfilment of the Palestinians' inalienable legitimate rights, in time changed to the Palestinians' national rights, and somewhat later still, the Palestinians' rights to an independent state on the West Bank and Gaza Strip. The third principle was recognition and guarantees for the independence, territorial integrity and security of all the states in the region, often specified explicitly to include Israel. This was the basic three-pronged Soviet position for a settlement, although occasional additions were made, such as a call for demilitarizations on both sides of the border, freedom of navigation, arms limitations, return of the Palestinian refugees, the inclusion of East Jerusalem in the territories to be formed as a Palestinian state, and the possibility of Palestinian confederation with Jordan.

The content of the settlement, the fine points of which will be discussed below, was actually of less importance to Moscow than Soviet participation in the peace process itself. For this reason the tactics employed were directed at achieving such participation and, short of this, preventing any negotiations which might exclude the Soviets. One tactic was to support the Arabs' demands including the more radical ones so as to prevent the Arabs from going to talks without Moscow. The Soviets could thus claim that only they supported all of the Arab demands as distinct from the Americans, who, they claimed, were interested only in partial solutions. Hoping to disprove Heikal's comment to Kissinger in the wake of the October War that the Soviets were necessary for war but only the Americans could bring peace, Moscow sought to prove its indispensibility to the Arabs for peace talks as well. Thus they argued that only Soviet support for the Arabs and Soviet pressure at the super-power level could bring about the necessary concessions from Israel. Without this pressure America would merely support Israel in all its positions, and no concessions would be forthcoming. Put slightly differently, the Arabs could achieve much more if they relied upon Soviet pressure on the Americans.

At the same time, the Soviets tried to build a bloc of the radical Arab states. This was in part a result of the change in Soviet Third World policy after the expulsion from Egypt, focusing on a more ideological approach in order to ensure greater loyalty. In the Arab-Israeli context this meant an effort to create a unified bloc which would resist American overtures. In so doing Moscow hoped not only to block the United States but also to force Washington to include the Soviet Union in the negotiating process. For the Soviets could claim to represent the Arabs and, more importantly, to control the war option. They could claim to the Americans that only Moscow, through its influence, could prevent the Arabs from going to war and bring them to the negotiating table. Increased tension on Israel's borders would presumably bring this point home, adding an element of urgency as well, but it is not entirely certain that the Soviets actually encouraged the tactic of increased tensions given the risks involved for escalation and outright war.

Another tactic employed to persuade the Americans was the invocation of détente. Brezhnev called for the extension of détente to the Middle East, citing super-power cooperation and joint crisis control under détente as an additional rationale for the inclusion of Moscow in Middle East negotiations. The Soviets did not, however, engage in linkage politics. They did not in any way condition progress in their bilateral, détente-related dealings with Washington upon progress or cooperation in the Middle East. In fact, the nadir of Soviet–American relations in the Middle East was reached when the US mediated the Israeli–Egyptian Interim Agreement in 1975, the same year as the Helsinki Conference, which was a high point of détente. Rather it was the Soviets who usually sought to dissociate détente from super-power behaviour in Angola and the Horn of Africa even as Moscow actively pursued arms negotiations and other détente-related policies.

If the Arabs had to be prevented from negotiating without Moscow, and the United States persuaded to let the Soviets in, Israel too had to agree to Soviet participation. The tactics employed towards Israel were presumably the same as those used regarding the United States, that is Soviet control of the war option and the claim to be the only power able to moderate the Arabs, as well, possibly, as the periodic heightening of tension on Israel's borders. Soviet tactics were also designed, however, to convince Israel that the Soviet Union could be a constructive factor in negotiations rather than an obstacle to the achievement of a settlement. Similarly, the Soviets had to prove to Jerusalem that they would not be a purely anti-Israeli force if included in the peace process.

Therefore, employing what may have been stick and carrot measures, the Soviets alternated between two tactics. Occasionally they hardened their positions, referring to the 1947 Partition Plan borders or adding specific demands to their three-pronged formula, such as the demand for the return of the refugees. Alternatively, they softened their positions, adding the specific reference to Israel in the three-pronged formula as one of the states whose independence, territorial integrity and security were to be guaranteed under a peace agreement. More significantly they occasionally emphasized their willingness officially to recognize Israel's 1949–67 borders. Sometimes they also hinted at a renewal of diplomatic relations in exchange for what they called progress in the peace process, later specifically linked to the convening of an international conference.

Quite logically the softer line appeared when there seemed to be some possibility for actually convening an international conference, the harder line emerging when Israel became more closely involved with the United States and American mediating efforts. This resembled the corollary between Soviet interest and advocacy of an international conference on the one hand, and American progress in the region on the other hand; the former increased with the latter, and declined when Washington appeared to be meeting with less success.

It cannot be ruled out that the shifting, occasionally contradictory lines regarding Israel and even an international conference were the result of conflicting opinions within the Kremlin. As in the pre-October War period, there were signs that some, such as Brezhnev himself, Kosygin and in time Andropov, were less enthusiastic about Soviet involvement in the Third World and particularly concerned about the risks of escalation as well as the threat to détente. There were also commentators and influential experts such as Primakov who advocated, or perhaps even represented leadership advocacy of, the more accommodating line regarding Israel. Others, such as Ponomarev or, among journalists, Kudryavtsev, clearly took the harder line, referring to the 1947 border lines and particularly championing the Palestinians' rights. How much of this was intentional manoeuvering and how much actual disagreement is almost impossible to determine, but there were less, and more, conciliatory positions emanating from Moscow at various times.

There were more than apparent contradictions and problems in Soviet tactics regarding a settlement. An inherent contradiction was that between Soviet support, on the one hand, for the radical Arab states (who, as rejectionists, actually opposed peace negotiations for a settlement) and, on the other hand, Soviet interest in convening a peace conference. Their substantive positions were also less moderate than those of Moscow, with a unified position being almost impossible to achieve. Moreover, by supporting the radicals' positions, and, by implication, the war option, the Soviets ran the risk of encouraging exactly the option which they hoped to avoid, that of armed conflict breaking out again. Further, Moscow did not oppose the partial settlements achieved over the years as such, inasmuch as they reduced the possibility of renewed war. But it did oppose the fact that American mediation, exclusively, was producing these agreements and therefore condemned most of them, particularly after Washington refused the Soviets even token participation from 1975 onward.

Another contradiction was that the positions closest to their own, both procedurally and substantively, favouring negotiations, compromise, recognition of Israel and so forth, were held by the Egyptians rather than the radicals. And it was just this moderation which made Egypt, for example, a candidate for cooperation with the Americans. Indeed, Soviet encouragement of a moderation of the Arabs' positions ran the risk of losing the Arabs to the Americans.

Some of these dilemmas for Soviet tactics became immediately apparent after the Yom Kippur War when Syria refused to attend the Geneva Peace Conference. The Soviets nonetheless went ahead with the conference, in fact pressing all sides to maintain this multilateral framework even symbolically once the bilateral disengagement talks began between Israel and Egypt, Israel and Syria. The Israeli–Egyptian disengagement talks were successfully completed only with the help of American mediation. Yet Moscow, interested in the defusion of the military situation which the agreement brought, hailed this success as the result of joint Soviet–American efforts. The signing of the agreement back in Geneva satisfied Moscow's desire to be a party to the accord and to keep at least the skeleton of the international forum in place. It was much harder to present the May 1974 Israeli–Syrian disengagement also as the result of super-power cooperation. Nonetheless, Gromyko travelled to Damascus as Kissinger was completing the agreement; he also met with Kissinger in Cyprus, and, thus, the façade of cooperation was maintained. Again the signing of the accord in Geneva helped Moscow to support it and present it as a joint venture, the positive product of the multi-lateral framework.

Nonetheless the Geneva Conference was indefinitely recessed, the reconvening for the purpose of working out a political settlement never having taken place. As the likelihood of reconvening diminished and American advances in the area progressed, at the expense of Moscow, the Soviets became increasingly critical of the United States. They became more supportive of the radical Arab positions, including support for the creation of a Palestinian state, and more belligerent towards Israel in their propaganda. There was a brief respite from this in the spring of 1975 when Kissinger's efforts to negotiate a second agreement between Israel and Egypt broke down and Washington announced a 'reassessment' of its relations with

Israel. Heartened by Kissinger's failure, the Soviets suddenly became less emphatic about the urgent need for a resumption of Geneva; they began to speak of the need for painstaking preparations.

It was at this time that the gulf between their own substantive positions and those of most of their Arab allies became acutely apparent. Meetings in Moscow with individual delegations from the Arab states and the PLO failed to produce a unified position. And Moscow made the limits of its own peace plan quite clear to the Arabs, presenting a moderate view regarding Israel's right to exist, within its pre-1967 borders, which should have pleased the Israelis. Whatever hopes Moscow may have nurtured for a unified policy with their own allies were dashed by subsequent events. In the summer of 1975, the Soviets were once again faced with an American success when Israel acceded to US demands and signed a significant second agreement with Egypt, the Interim Agreement. Not only was this accord mediated exclusively by Washington, but the Soviets were not even rendered symbolic participation. Further, the new accord provided for American military personnel to supervise the demilitarization and early warning systems of the area evacuated by Israel in the Sinai. Such on-the-spot guarantees were just the type of thing the Soviets might have welcomed were they to have been a part of them, but the unilateral nature of the American presence made the Interim Agreement all the more repugnant to Moscow.

The following year saw an even greater deterioration in Soviet fortunes in the Middle East. In 1976 not only did Egypt abrogate its already clearly defunct treaty with the Soviet Union, but a serious disruption occurred in Soviet–Syrian relations over the Civil War in Lebanon. These events, which carried the potential of both heightened danger of Syrian–Israeli war and of a Syrian move towards Washington, may have prompted Moscow once again to push for negotiations. In the spring, the Soviets presented a peace plan which spelled out to some degree the three principles already familiar to Soviet positions: Israeli withdrawal from the territories occupied in 1967, the creation of a Palestinian state, and guarantees for the independence of all states including Israel. It contained a proposal for the reconvening of Geneva on a two-stage basis, the first stage being organizational, the second to be substantive. It was stated that the PLO was the legitimate representative of the Palestinian people and that the Palestinians were to participate in both stages. Yet room for manoeuvre on this issue was left inasmuch as the Soviets refrained from specifying that this participation had to be 'from the beginning and on an equal footing', as their propaganda had been previously arguing.

That the Soviets had indeed intended this to be a moderate proposal became somewhat clearer some months later when a new administration in Washington took up the issue. The two-stage conference idea was seriously discussed with the Carter Administration, and in fact a great deal of progress was made in the spring of 1977 towards a reconvening of Geneva. At this time, Brezhnev announced a new Soviet peace plan. More comprehensive than past plans, this proposal spoke of a two-stage Israeli withdrawal to be followed by the creation of a Palestinian state, by implication in the territories evacuated by Israel. It added specific references to freedom of navigation, an issue of importance to Israel, and arms limitations, discussed in the context of the dangers of nuclearization. It also spoke of demilitarization and international guarantees, with super-power participation in a UN peace-keeping force.

Most significantly, Brezhnev made no mention of the PLO, nor of its participation in a reconvened conference. Indeed in the talks which followed between Moscow and Washington, the Soviets agreed that the issue of Palestinian participation could be settled during the first stage of the conference, while the idea of a joint Arab delegation or Palestinian participation on the delegations of the Arab states was mooted. At the same time Moscow exerted pressure upon the PLO to accept resolution 242, upon which the conference was based. And, to further facilitate the reconvening of Geneva, the Soviets dropped hints about the possibility of renewing diplomatic relations with Israel within the context of the conference.

A significant breakthrough seemed to have been made when the United States and the Soviet Union issued a joint statement on 1 October 1977 calling for the reconvening of the Geneva Conference. Coming as it did during the SALT II negotiations it was interpreted by some as a Soviet concession so as to obtain American agreement to the arms accord. There does not, however, appear to have been any linkage involved, for it was the Americans who made the concessions. Unlike his predecessor, Carter was willing to include the Soviets in the Middle East peace process. His National Security adviser, Zbigniew Brzezinski spoke of interlocking circles of parties to negotiations, the Soviet Union being in the outer, last circle to be involved. Nonetheless, Moscow was brought directly into the process by the joint statement with Washington. Moreover, this statement contained what was essentially a reiteration of the substance of resolution 242, with the addition of the recognition of the legitimate rights of the Palestinian people. This was not the national rights formula sought by the Palestinians (and was therefore initially rejected by the PLO), but it was the addition of Palestinian rights which, missing from resolution 242 itself, constituted an American concession sought by Moscow to accommodate the Palestinians. Palestinian representation at Geneva was also advocated, although in fact the intention appeared to be in the form of some kind of joint Arab delegation.

Israel immediately rejected the statement, alarmed both by America's inclusion of the Soviets and its concessions on the Palestinian issue. Israeli Foreign Minister Dayan travelled to Washington with a working paper which virtually voided the procedural and substantive proposals agreed to by Moscow and Washington. Egypt, too, rejected the joint Soviet–American initiative, despite the fact that it had appeared to have supported the reconvening of Geneva. Sadat's rejection, less explicit than that of Israel, was based on his growing opposition to any Soviet participation. Unbeknownst to Moscow, and apparently also to Washington, Egypt and Israel had for some months been engaged in contacts, through the mediation of Morocco and Rumania, aimed at achieving an Egyptian–Israeli settlement. With the adamant Israeli rejection of the Soviet–American proposal, and Washington's subsequent agreement to the Israeli working paper, which appeared to end the chances for a Geneva conference in any case, Sadat made his dramatic visit to Jerusalem in pursuit of a peace agreement.

Moscow did not immediately condemn Sadat's move, probably because it still harboured hopes of reconciliation with Egypt. It also did not want to appear to be opposed to peace. As it became increasingly clear, however, that the move was intended to exclude the Soviets and was to usher in a new round of American mediation, the Soviet media and leadership launched a virulent campaign against the Camp David talks and the accord which emerged from them. They castigated Sadat for agreeing to a separate peace rather than a comprehensive settlement, altering their own peace formulae to include a reference to East Jerusalem. This came partially in response to Sadat's having visited Jerusalem itself. More significantly, the Soviets officially recognized the PLO as the sole legitimate representative of the Palestinian people, in November 1978, by way of response to the Camp David accords just a few weeks earlier. Increased support for the Palestinians, the rejectionists, and Syria, as well as renewed efforts to forge a radical bloc and to prevent further defections to the

United States or emulation of Egypt ensued. Similarly anti-Israeli, anti-Zionist propaganda eventually became more virulent than at any time in the past, and Israel's full withdrawal from the occupied territories and, later, reduction of its relations with Washington gradually crept into Soviet demands regarding renewal of relations.

It is possible that the Soviets even lost all interest in a peace agreement at this stage, having perhaps concluded that it would be impossible to break the Americans' monopoly on the peace process. Yet even in this period, for all their condemnation of the Camp David accords, they did not encourage any kind of military action on the part of the Syrians, for example, or even suggest that Damascus refrain from its virtually automatic renewal of the UN peace-keeping force on the Syrian–Israeli disengagement lines. Moreover they continued to advocate the convening of an international conference, remaining adamant about the necessity for negotiations, at least in their discussions with the Palestinians.

Moscow's problem with the Camp David accords and the Egyptian–Israeli peace was not that they ended the danger of war between these two states, but that they had been achieved without – and intentionally excluded – the Soviet Union, to the benefit of the United States. Soviet demands for a comprehensive settlement rather than a step by step approach were born of their wish to be a participant and their fear that separate agreements could be reached without them. One might speculate that Soviet involvement in the Egyptian–Israeli accords would have made such accords acceptable to Moscow. The Soviets might have presented them,as they did the disengagement agreements, as a part of broader accords next on the agenda. Be that as it may, the Soviets could but advocate an international conference as the only legitimate form of negotiation. At the least, they were still urging negotiation, although events outside the region such as those in Poland and Afghanistan, the ailing Soviet leadership, and the dramatic end of détente all eclipsed and, to some degree, eliminated any Soviet effort towards a settlement of the Arab–Israeli conflict at the end of the 1970s, beginning of the 1980s.

The Brezhnev Plan, issued 15 September 1982, probably was more a response to the Americans' presentation of a new plan, the Reagan Initiative, than a serious Soviet effort to renew the peace process. Brezhnev's new plan in fact differed little from previous Soviet plans. It officially delineated the lines of the proposed Palestinian state by saying that such a state should be set up in the West Bank and Gaza, adding also East Jerusalem (lest Israel's official annexation of this part of the city go unchallenged). It also contained a stipulation regarding refugees, albeit far less than the demands of the Arabs in this regard. Positive reference was made to the Fez plan which had emerged from the Arab summit a few days earlier. Containing many fewer details than previous plans, the Brezhnev Plan posed no particular obstacles nor produced any new inducements to peace talks. As usual, it called for an international peace conference, the natural alternative to the Reagan Initiative.

It seems unlikely that the Soviets believed that the United States had any chance of successfully mediating a new agreement at this time. All parties concerned, including Israel, had immediately rejected the Initiative. And rejectionist sentiment, produced by Israel's invasion of Lebanon, had grown significantly. Yet Arab anger over Soviet inaction in the Lebanon War as well as America's successful organization of the peaceful evacuation of the PLO from Beirut may have prompted Moscow to counter any appeal the Americans might have. Thus the Soviets offered a political response to the Reagan Initiative, as well as new arms deliveries to the Syrians.

In a sense the Soviet leadership, in the closing days of the Brezhnev regime, would appear to have returned to a dualistic policy, if in fact this policy had ever been abandoned. It is difficult to determine if Brezhnev's immediate successors viewed the conflict any differently or accorded it any greater priority. They did, however, have to deal with new developments in the conflict, which dictated still another, somewhat different, Soviet peace proposal. These new developments were the rebellion within the PLO, the Syrian attempt to take over that organization, the tension-producing American involvement in Lebanon (with Syrian forces in Lebanon and Soviet advisers nearby), the renewed risk of Syrian–Israeli hostilities and, most importantly at the time, the increasingly apparent move towards Jordan on the part of Arafat in what promised to be a joint effort to pursue the Reagan Initiative.

It was to offset these developments, but particularly the last of these, that the Soviet Union, now under the rule of Chernenko, issued detailed proposals on 30 July 1984. This plan for the first time presented relatively detailed suggestions for the conduct of an international conference, suggesting that the Soviets were now seriously intent upon convening such a forum. According to this plan, the conference could be conducted in the form of working groups dealing with specific issues, including bilateral meetings to work out details on issues of only bilateral concern, with plenary sessions to endorse the agreements with the consent of all the conference participants. The components of the peace treaty to be achieved at the conference were the usual three-pronged Soviet formula, although in the first half of the Soviet proposal, in which principles for a settlement were put forth, much greater detail and some new elements were specified.

The new elements included a call for the dismantling of Israeli settlements set up after 1967 in the Arab territories, the return of East Jerusalem as 'an inalienable part of the Palestinian state', the possibility of the formation of a confederation (the intention being a confederation with Jordan as planned by Arafat and Hussein), as well as a reference to the refugees, and the respect by all, including Israel and the Palestinian state, for the 'sovereignty, independence and territorial integrity of each other'. It was also stipulated that the PLO should be an equal participant in the conference, along with the two super-powers and the Arab states having a common border with Israel. One might be able to argue that this did not rule out the earlier idea of postponing PLO participation to a later stage rather than from the outset, which formula was missing, but the thrust of the statement on PLO participation did not justify such an interpretation. Other states in the region or bordering on it might also be invited, although it was not clear just whom this meant.

Intended primarily to woo the Palestinians away from a Jordanian-guided move towards the Americans and the Reagan Initiative, the new Soviet proposal contained little that was new for inducing Israel to agree. If anything, it was more demanding than in the past with regard to Israel and to the potential benefit of the Palestinians. The most the Soviets could hope to accomplish with this proposal, therefore, was to initiate concrete consideration of an international framework as an alternative to the Arafat–Hussein plans. In this it failed, and no new Soviet proposal for or attitude towards a settlement appeared until the Gorbachev era.

8   The Palestinians and the PLO

The Soviet attitude towards the Palestinians and the PLO must be seen both within the context of the Arab–Israeli conflict and as part of Soviet behaviour with regard to national liberation movements. The latter has usually been dictated by tactical considerations, with Moscow viewing national liberation movements instrumentally, as a tactical option in the pursuit of more strategic, long-range objectives. Indeed the commencement of Soviet support for a movement has often indicated no more than a Soviet decision to cultivate an additional option or potential channel for the pursuit of broader interests in a particular country or region. This general approach has applied with regard to the PLO, with which Moscow's relationship has been a tactical one, determined by the broader Soviet–Arab and especially the Soviet–US relationships.

The Soviet Union apparently did not see even any tactical value in the PLO during the organization's first few years of existence (1964–8), for it generally rejected efforts by the PLO to make contact and gain Soviet support. Moscow viewed the Arab–Israeli conflict as a conflict between states and saw the Palestinian issue only in terms of a refugee problem (as stated in resolution 242). Thus the Soviets made no effort to compete with the Chinese, who did support the movement from its inception. This negative attitude began to change only late in 1968 and early 1969 following Arafat's inclusion in an Egyptian delegation, led by Nasser, to Moscow in the summer of 1968. At this time the Soviets began to refer to the Palestinians as a 'people', calling the PLO a 'national liberation movement' for the first time in 1969. They began to provide propaganda support and, by 1970, following another trip to Moscow by Arafat, they gave permission for indirect arms supplies.

The reason for this change may have been the personnel and organizational developments within the PLO, that is the ascendency of Fatah, under Arafat. The change may also have been due to the attention the PLO was now attracting in its terrorist operations inside

and outside Israel. The most likely reason, however, was the change
which had taken place in the attitude of the Arab states, most notably
Egypt, with regard to the PLO. As Egypt increasingly emphasized the
Palestinian issue, the Soviets provided the corresponding support, in
the form of contacts, arms, training, and greater political attention.

This support materialized, however, without any shift in the
Soviets' basic perception of the conflict as one principally between
states. In fact the Soviets still had serious reservations about fully
supporting the PLO. This was evidenced by the lack of any, even
propaganda support to the PLO during its armed conflict with King
Hussein, termed Black September by the Palestinians because of
Hussein's bloody attack upon and expulsion of the PLO. The Syrian
invasion of Jordan, ostensibly to assist the Palestinians, was not
apparently supported by the Soviets, who pressured Damascus to
withdraw when an Israeli, even Israeli–American military response
appeared likely. Further evidence of Soviet reservations regarding the
PLO was the reprimand delivered the Syrian Communist Party in 1971
for placing too much emphasis on the Palestinian question, a reprimand that contained criticism of almost every one of the PLO's
positions and policies at the time.

Somewhere around the time of the October War, in the year
preceding it and as it was drawing to a close, there were signs of a
Soviet reassessment of their attitude to the Palestinian issue (as well as
to the conflict itself, as we have already seen). The immediate cause
was most likely the expulsion of the Soviet advisers from Egypt and
the general deterioration in Soviet–Egyptian relations. Egypt had been
the cornerstone of Soviet policy in the Middle East – indeed to some
degree in the Third World. The failure there was a serious blow to
Soviet policy-makers and, as such, it occasioned a rethinking altogether. In the Arab–Israeli context, it led to an emphasis on the more
radical forces in the area and, with this, an increase in Soviet support
for the PLO. In the wake of the Yom Kippur War, if not prior to it, the
Soviets may well have come to the conclusion that the Americans were
becoming a more significant factor, and one which might well prove
effective in obtaining the return to the Arabs of their territories and
possibly even a peace agreement. The Palestinians, then, could
become the outstanding issue, the one which would provide the
Soviets an 'in', not only in any talks concerning Jordan (America's
client), but generally into the peace process. As events unfolded, and
particularly in the years which followed, the Palestinian issue, rather
than the return of the Arab states' territories, was the one on which the

Americans might be the most vulnerable, most restricted and most frustrated, as well as the one which, at least publicly, united the Arab world.

Inasmuch as this was also the period in which the Soviets exhibited greater interest in a settlement, it cannot be ruled out that the altered attitude towards the PLO was also prompted by a realization that the Palestinian issue was essential to a settlement, therefore demanding greater Soviet attention. This would explain Soviet queries to the three PLO leaders, Arafat, Habash and Hawatmeh at the end of October 1973, asking just what was meant by the demand for Palestinian 'national rights'. This was followed by public use of the term on the part of the Soviets, signalling a change in attitude which led to the explicit support for the creation of a Palestinian state pronounced by the Soviet President Podgornyi in September 1974.

This pronouncement was prompted by a number of immediate considerations. Coming as it did just prior to the Arab summit conference in Rabat, it would appear that the Soviets knew of the Arab leaders' decision to pass a resolution in favour of a Palestinian entity on the West Bank and Gaza, as had finally been agreed in principle earlier in the year by the Palestine National Council. The decision was a controversial one; George Habash, head of the Popular Front for the Liberation of Palestine (PFLP), disapproved of the idea of declaring for a state at that time. Because of his opposition to a mini-state on the West Bank and Gaza, Habash refused to participate in Rabat, just as he refused to go to Moscow with Arafat in the summer of 1974 because of his differences with Moscow on this and other issues. By supporting the idea of a Palestinian state, the Soviets most likely hoped to counter both the pro-American stance Egypt would be advocating at the Arab summit and the very real possibility of continued US progress in the region through a second Egyptian-Israeli agreement. More specifically, the Soviet leadership may have been hoping to forestall any progress in Kissinger's efforts to achieve a Jordanian–Israeli disengagement agreement on the West Bank.

Presumably with the same objectives in mind, the Soviets announced in the summer of 1974 their agreement to the opening of a PLO office in Moscow. The only other national liberation movement to be so accommodated until that time (and in fact until 1987) was the National Liberation Front of Vietnam. The Soviets approved a Palestinian representative and permitted the actual opening of the office only two years later, in an obvious compensatory gesture on the eve of a visit to Moscow by Jordanian King Hussein in June 1976. A temporary increase in support occurred in 1977 when the Soviets placed the return of the Palestinian refugees in their official slogan on a settlement. This was in direct response to a PLO request, but Soviet acquiescence probably came to counter what appeared to be a US approach to the PLO when President Carter spoke of the need for a 'homeland' for the Palestinians. This, together with Brezhnev's first publicized official meeting with Arafat in April 1977 may also have been designed to compensate the PLO for the concessions Moscow was in the process of making to the Americans with regard to the nature and timing of PLO participation in a reconvened Geneva conference.

More direct, and significant, was the official Soviet recognition of the PLO as the sole legitimate representative of the Palestinian people, immediately after and in obvious response to Camp David, in November 1978. In 1981 the PLO office was granted diplomatic status, possibly to soften Arafat's anger over Soviet refusal to provide all the material support he was seeking for his forces in Lebanon, but also, perhaps, to counter PLO–American contacts which resulted in a PLO–Israeli cease-fire on the Lebanese border. Moscow made its most explicit and forthcoming official statement regarding the PLO in its 1984 peace plan, when trying to deter Arafat from negotiating with Washington through the intermediary of Jordan. This concession having failed, the Soviets finally responded with a suspension of aid to Arafat, though not to the other components of the PLO, until the pro-American efforts were abandoned in 1986.

From this brief history of Soviet–PLO relations, it emerges that the Soviets used their stances on the Palestinian issue to enhance their position in the Arab world and increasingly to counter US inroads or potential successes in the region. Support for the PLO was part of Moscow's tactic of supporting the more radical Arab demands to prove Soviet usefulness in the eyes of the Arabs, and essentiality in the eyes of the United States and Israel with regard to the peace process. The PLO component of Moscow's tactics assumed ever-increasing importance as the Palestinian issue itself assumed the dimensions of an issue of super-power competition. Yet the tactical nature of the relationship remained. The Soviets did not let their support for the PLO overshadow or interfere with the pursuit of Soviet interests, such as reentry of Moscow into the Middle East peace process, or to change their basic positions on the nature of an Arab–Israeli settlement or other regional issues. In fact there were serious disagreements between the two on a number of substantive, procedural and organi-

zational issues. These disagreements do not appear to have affected
the Soviets' support, except when the issues became linked with the
possibility of a Palestinian shift in the direction of the Americans.

Disagreement or at least differences over substantive issues revolved around the existence of the state of Israel, the locale of a
Palestinian state (alongside or instead of Israel – either within the 1947
Partition Plan lines or the 1949–67 borders), and the relationship with
Jordan; the return of the refugees; possibly the issue of Jerusalem;
southern Lebanon; and the immigration of Jews from the Soviet
Union. There were also differences over Afghanistan, Eritrea, and
other inter-Arab subjects, though these were of somewhat less importance. Regarding the first set of issues, the Soviets consistently argued
with the Palestinians that it was unrealistic and therefore undesirable
to seek the destruction of Israel, either militarily or politically (by
creating a secular democratic state in all of Palestine) or even to try
drastically to reduce Israel to the 1947 Partition Plan lines. According
to the Soviets, from their earliest discussions of the subject, the only
objective worthy of pursuit, that is, one which stood a chance of
success without threatening war and super-power confrontation, was
the creation of a Palestinian state limited to the West Bank and Gaza.

This was the position implicitly accepted by the Palestine National
Council in 1974, but the PLO, Fatah and Arafat refused to go beyond
this explicitly because of strong opposition from certain quarters
within the PLO. Hawatmeh, as well as the Palestinian Communists,
did explicitly endorse this position, although Hawatmeh spoke of this
as a first step towards a state in all of Palestine. The Soviets were not
willing publicly to support the demand for a Palestinian state until
there was at least implicit agreement to the mini-state idea. They
preferred to make no positive reference to the secular democratic state
idea and deleted such references from their reports of Palestinian
statements, praising the PLO for having, according to Moscow,
gradually accepted the more moderate two-state option.

In this connection, the Soviets had no particular problem with the
idea of a Palestinian–Jordanian confederation, depending upon the
source or underlying purpose of such a proposal at any given time.
Moscow was pursuing its own improvement of relations with Jordan
in the late 1970s and 1980s. In fact the success of this effort was
demonstrated not only by Hussein's trips to Moscow but also by arms
agreements which provided for the dispatch of a Soviet SAM system
and even some Soviet advisers to Jordan. Nonetheless, when the
confederation idea appeared as part of Arafat's flirtation with the

Reagan Initiative in 1984–5, the Soviets became increasingly critical of the proposal, begrudgingly referring to it only as one possible option. Indeed, in this later period, they even became the great champions of the independent Palestinian state idea as distinct from a confederation, because this was explicitly ruled out by the Reagan Initiative.

The refugee issue was apparently much less important or pressing from the Soviet point of view, though there were indeed differences between the Soviet and the PLO approaches. Realizing perhaps that the PLO position favouring the return of all the Palestinian refugees, their descendants and families to their former homes in Israel could be viewed by Israel as tantamount to an attempt to destroy the Jewish state, the Soviet position (not often expressed in any case) called for 'return' of the refugees to the new Palestinian state when created or 'to their homes in accordance with the UN resolution'. The resolution in question, absent from the PLO formula, was UN General Assembly resolution 194 of 1948 which called for the return of those willing to live in peace with their neighbours. Mention of the refugees in the Brezhnev Plan of 1982 and in the Soviet peace plan of 1984 employed the same formula, speaking of the 'opportunity' rather than the 'right' to return or compensation as stipulated in the UN resolution.

Similarly the issue of Jerusalem was far less central for the Soviets than the PLO, appearing in Soviet statements only after Sadat's visit to that city and, more frequently, after Israel's formal annexation of East Jerusalem in 1980. Even then, however, Moscow called only for inclusion of East Jerusalem in the territory to be evacuated by Israel and formed into a Palestinian state. The PLO's reference more vaguely to Jerusalem as a whole, and as the capital of a Palestinian state found no echo in Soviet statements.

Both the refugee issue and Jerusalem were eventually if sparingly referred to by Moscow at the PLO's request, albeit in Moscow's own terms and at times of its choosing, usually in response to some particular event or American move. The Soviets were less accommodating regarding other Palestinian requests, such as the repeated PLO demand that Moscow cease Soviet Jewish emigration to Israel or that it withdraw its recognition of the state of Israel. In keeping with Moscow's efforts to moderate Palestinian demands regarding the creation of a Palestinian state in place of Israel, the Soviets not only resisted the Palestinian request regarding withdrawal of Soviet recognition, but they also urged the PLO to accept resolution 242 or opt for a mutual recognition resolution at the UN. While the Soviet leadership was willing to launch anti-Zionist campaigns, including the labelling of Zionism as racism, it was not willing to have its détente-related policy on emigration be altered by the demands of this local actor. Where broader Soviet interests were at stake, no accommodation could be expected.

This was also the case, for example, with regard to Moscow's assistance to Ethiopia's suppression of the Eritrean revolt, despite PLO aid to the Eritreans. Indeed, continued PLO aid to the Eritreans demonstrated the Palestinians' own independence from Moscow. Similar independence, of greater consequence for the Soviets, was exhibited by Arafat, though not Habash and Hawatmeh, with regard to the Soviet invasion of Afghanistan. While the PLO officially if unenthusiastically supported the Soviet move, Arafat himself did not provide the kind of public support solicited by Moscow, particularly in Muslim circles.

The Palestinian struggle in southern Lebanon, first against the Syrians and then against the Israelis, prior to the Israeli invasion of Lebanon, was also a source of dispute. The PLO, particularly Fatah, had long pressed the Soviets to take a more direct military role or, at the very least, provide more advanced weapons. The Soviets, for their part, had been relatively restrained out of concern that massive Israeli retaliation would lead to a new Arab–Israeli war, which is virtually what occurred in 1982. Thus, despite Soviet opposition to the Syrian invasion of Lebanon in June 1976, there was not significant aid to the PLO even during the bloody Syrian siege and attack on the Palestinian refugee camp Tel a-Zatar in Beirut. Arafat reportedly refrained from visiting Moscow in 1976 and again in 1980 because of this clash over Soviet aid. His second-in-command, Abu Iyyad, explicitly criticized the Soviet Union for its reticence, which became strikingly more significant with the outbreak of the Lebanon War (to be discussed in the next chapter).

Numerous issues of methods and tactics were also the source of controversy between the Soviet Union and the PLO. The most fundamental and important of these was the complex of issues connected with negotiations, resolution 242 as a basis for the Geneva framework, political versus armed struggle, and the use of terror. For some time the Soviets sought PLO acceptance of resolution 242, with its implied recognition of Israel, so as to secure PLO participation in a reconvened Geneva conference. Given PLO objection to the fact that resolution 242 viewed the Palestinian issue as one of refugees rather than one of national rights, the Soviets' own formulae added this national element. Presumably this was the purpose behind the

October 1977 joint statement with the United States, in which resolution 242 was not directly mentioned but rather paraphrased with the addition of a clause recognizing the 'legitimate rights of the Palestinian people'. After some initial hesitation, the PLO did unofficially accept this as a substitute for resolution 242. It was the Americans, however, who increasingly demanded acceptance of resolution 242 as a condition for the inclusion of the PLO in any talks. Therefore, with the Arab states' explicit rejection of resolution 242 at their 1981 summit, if not earlier, Moscow ceased referring specifically to this resolution and the Geneva conference which was based on it. Rather, it began to advocate a more general type of international conference.

More basic than the framework for negotiations was the question of negotiations or political methods versus armed struggle. The Soviets' position was similar to the one they had taken with Egypt, for even with national liberation movements, Moscow preferred political over military methods. Traceable perhaps to the Bolsheviks' preference for political struggle, through strikes, demonstrations, organizational and ideological work among the proletariat, the more pragmatic reason was concern over the escalation of local conflicts and the risk of super-power confrontation. These preferences were conveyed to the PLO and were the source of some of the problems over Soviet supplies to the movement in Lebanon. Recognizing, however, that national liberation movements themselves had and would continue to opt for armed struggle, regardless of Soviet advice, Moscow pressed for what it called a combination of the two means of struggle. Rather than remain on the sidelines or abandon the possibility of gaining influence over such movements, the Soviets provided the wherewithal for the use of both methods – within limits.

These limits were connected with Soviet preferences in the realm of armed struggle itself. Guerrilla warfare and conventional warfare (the use of regular forces) were the two types of armed struggle worthy of consideration by the Soviets. Sabotage and terror were considered offshoots of guerrilla warfare, the former acceptable and considered useful to some degree, the latter, terror, considered counter-productive and adventuristic. Indeed, even guerrilla warfare was viewed with some misgivings, acceptable basically only as a prelude to or adjunct of conventional war (perhaps because guerrilla warfare was associated with the countryside and peasants as distinct from proletarian struggle in the city).

Thus the Soviets were critical of the PLO's use of armed struggle including guerrilla, but they were particularly critical of the use of terror. Their public dispute with Habash in the mid-1970s was in part connected with this opposition to terrorism and was the source of tension between Moscow and other PLO leaders as well. The Soviets condemned most PLO terrorist operations, especially those of an international nature (a type of action to which the Soviets may have felt themselves vulnerable), or they depicted such operations as sabotage, rather than terror, directed against military targets and soldiers rather than civilians.

There is no doubt that Moscow and its allies provided arms and training for what they termed sabotage, clearly aware of the ultimate character of the operations for which these facilities were to be used. Even as they probably sought to manipulate and guide the uses to which their training and equipment would be put, they nevertheless continued to attempt to channel the actions of the PLO into the more acceptable lines of sabotage and even guerrilla warfare. Even this was secondary to the more significant Soviet effort to shift the armed activities of the PLO away from terror and guerrilla to conventional warfare by means of regular units. This effort, similar to Soviet policies in connection with other national liberation movements in the past, such as the Angolan MPLA, the PAIGC of Guinea-Bissau, and the ZAPU of Zimbabwe, was clearly evident from the documents confiscated by Israel in the Lebanon War. In fact the war itself demonstrated the folly of the Soviets' efforts, apparently supported by Arafat, to convert the PLO forces into a conventional army.

Still another problematic area in Soviet–PLO relations was connected with the lack of unity with the PLO. This lack of unity existed at all levels and in all dimensions, from purely organizational matters to ideological features and social composition. Thus, the Soviets were faced with the problem of a certain instability regarding leadership positions and decisions (and therefore greater difficulty in achieving a measure of outside control). They also had to contend with nationalist, even to some degree religious (and occasionally anti-Communist) rather than socialist orientations, as well as a predominantly bourgeois-class character. These problems were further complicated by the involvement of various, often rival Arab countries with specific member organizations. They frequently sought control of the movement, creating disorder and even fighting between the factions.

The Soviets were critical of all of these aspects of the PLO, although many of these problems were typical of national liberation movements in general and, as such, tolerated by Moscow. This is not to say that there were not some critics in the Soviet leadership who were unhappy, particularly over the ideological and social composition of this as well as other movements. There may even have been some rethinking of relations with such movements in the reassessment of Soviet Third World policies after the expulsion from Egypt. The PLO was in no way singled out, however, in this reassessment.

One dilemma for the Soviets was the existence of two Marxist organizations within the PLO, Nayif Hawatmeh's Democratic Front for the Liberation of Palestine (DFLP) and George Habash's Popular Front for the Liberation of Palestine (PFLP). While important politically, neither of them was ever militarily or numerically strong enough to rule the whole movement. Moreover, at least in the case of the PFLP, the group's totally rejectionist positions were often too radical and too negative to accommodate Soviet interests. Aside from early association with the Chinese and dedication to the use of terror, the PFLP polemicized with the Soviets in the 1970s over the issue of the two-state (mini-state) solution, recognition of Israel, negotiations, and resolution 242, as well as armed struggle. The mutual hostility only came to an end after the 1978 Camp David Accords, since which time Soviet–PFLP cooperation developed to significant proportions. Such cooperation notwithstanding, Habash's rejectionist position could not provide the Soviets any entrée into Middle East peace talks and hardly served to promote Moscow's main vehicle for participation: an international conference.

Nayif Hawatmeh was much closer to Moscow and to its positions. Indeed Hawatmeh, though not the Soviets, claimed that his organization was virtually a Soviet-type Communist party. Unlike the Soviets, however, his advocacy of a two-state solution was perceived and presented as merely a first step towards a Palestinian state in all of Palestine. He was also occasionally at odds with Moscow over the issue of terrorism. Whatever the degree of agreement or disagreement with Moscow on specific issues, neither Hawatmeh nor Habash, even together, commanded sufficient numbers within the PLO to provide an alternative leadership.

The one component which did possess sufficient strength, overwhelmingly in comparison with the other groups, was Fatah, under the leadership of Arafat. And Fatah was clearly a bourgeois nationalist organization, closely aligned with and supported by Saudi Arabia. It was not only (though perhaps mainly) its numerical strength which elicited the Soviets' support. Fatah was also relatively close to Moscow's positions, even if hesitant to espouse all of them officially and publicly. Arafat's preference for what was termed the political path, his flirtation with the Israeli left, his gradual evolution towards negotiations all made him more amenable from the Soviet point of view. Unfortunately for the Soviets, however, these were the very characteristics which promised to render him still more amenable to the Americans. And therein lay the risk from the Soviet point of view: there was no ideological or class bond with which to tie Fatah to Soviet patronage.

Indeed Arafat was even consistently resistant to Communist inroads into the PLO, seeking to preserve PLO independence. Every Soviet attempt to gain some control or influence over the PLO by means of the creation of its own organization met with failure. Al Ansar, set up by the Arab Communist parties in 1970, died a natural death in 1972 after failing to gain entry into the PLO executive. Palestinian sources claimed that Al Ansar was rejected because of its opposition to the idea of armed struggle and its acceptance of Israel's right to exist (resolution 242). According to Soviet accounts, the second Arab Communist creation was the Palestine National Front, founded on the West Bank in 1973 with non-Communists as well. It was destroyed by Israeli deportations, although it too had espoused the more moderate Soviet positions on a mini-state, Israel's existence and negotiations. (It was replaced by the more radical Palestine Guidance Committee, which was dominated by rejectionists and non-Communist supporters.)

Finally, the Palestine Communist Party was officially created in 1981, having grown out of the Palestine Communist Organization, which itself had been the West Bank branch of the Jordanian Communist Party. The creation of this party was not necessarily or primarily an attempt by the Soviets to gain an organizational foothold within the PLO. Rather, its independence from the Jordanian Communist Party was probably deemed expedient and ideologically necessary in view of the distinction being made between Jordan and what was proposed as a Palestinian state to be born on the West Bank and Gaza. Nonetheless, this party sought – and was refused – representation on the PLO executive, until the Soviet-mediated reunification of the PLO in 1987. Despite some strength in the West Bank, the Communists were not able to provide the Soviets with the kind of influence they undoubtedly sought within if not over the PLO.

The split which occurred in the PLO following the Lebanon War of 1982 did little to further Soviet interests even though it was not linked directly in any way to Soviet–PLO relations. It was the result of internal dissatisfaction with Arafat. The Israeli invasion had strengthened those forces within the PLO, the rejectionists as well as some in Fatah itself, who had opposed the diplomatic-political path pursued by Arafat. They could now argue that Israel's move had proven the futility of such a path when dealing with an enemy bent on the military option. Fatah moderates such as Issam Sartawi were to argue that the war had proven just the opposite theory. It had demonstrated the impossibility of defeating Israel militarily and, therefore, the need for political means. Nonetheless, the radical elements, joined by some who also opposed what they claimed were Arafat's dictatorial leadership methods, found support from Syria (long interested in taking over the PLO) and staged an armed revolt against the PLO leader. This revolt coincided with, indeed was partially prompted by Arafat's moves toward Hussein and the Reagan Initiative. The Soviet response, therefore, contained no small amount of ambivalence in an effort to cope with a new set of dilemmas and conflicting interests, connected not only with methodological issues and personalities, but regional and global actors as well.

One of the dilemmas was that the Soviets were faced with a confrontation between two allies, Syria and the PLO, but they could not simply choose the state over the movement as that side which would best serve Soviet interests. The reasons were numerous. Although the Soviets had increased their commitment to Syria in the wake of the Lebanon War, as we shall see below, they were not interested in augmenting Syrian independence. Syria, theoretically dependent upon Soviet arms, had repeatedly demonstrated in the past its unwillingness to subordinate itself to Moscow's orders or restrain its own ambitions at the Soviets' behest. No less than in the past, the Soviets ran the risk of Syria's provoking a war with Israel, involving the Soviets in a confrontation with the United States. Such a risk seemed all the more probable given the temporary presence of both American and Soviet military personnel in Lebanon, the former as part of the peace-keeping force after the war, the latter as advisers to the Syrian army.

Moscow, therefore, had little desire to see Syrian strength increased by a takeover of the PLO, and it was aware of the opposition within the Arab world to such a move. The Syrian battle against Arafat was fought in terms of opposition to Arafat's contacts with Egypt and Jordan – states with which Moscow sought improved relations at this time. In view of Syria's past record of independent, and risky, decision-making, as well as the instability and unpopularity of the Assad regime, the Soviets had begun to respond to Syria's isolation in the Arab world. It had done so not by bolstering the Damascus regime politically but, rather, by seeking allies elsewhere and broadening Soviet options in the area. Moreover, a Syrian takeover of the PLO would have virtually taken the organization out of the picture as an actor in the Middle East conflict, melting it into the rejectionist position of Syria itself, providing the Soviets with no entrée or independent levers in the evolving peace process.

By the same token, Soviet support for Arafat's opponents (which occasionally but not always included the DFLP and the PFLP) meant strengthening the rejectionist–armed struggle position over the more moderate substantive views. The latter were indeed quite close to those held by the Soviets themselves regarding a negotiated settlement through an international conference. Finally such support would only assist in splitting the PLO formally and irrevocably, spelling the end of the PLO as a factor – even a tactical one – in the Middle East conflict. A splintered, weakened PLO, two or more organizations competing to speak for the Palestinians, would be of little use to the Soviets or probably anyone else. As much as the Soviets were genuinely concerned over his flirtation with the West, Arafat's strength and independence, even his substantive positions, all ruled against supporting an attempt to replace him.

Yet the Syrians were the Soviets' only ally among the confrontation states and provided Moscow its strategic foothold in the region. They were opposing Arafat ostensibly on anti-western, anti-imperialist grounds. Syria, therefore, could not be totally rebuffed either. The rebels' points were clearly well taken insofar as they opposed any shift towards the Americans, even if the Soviets could not agree with the more fully rejectionist thrust of the rebels' position. Moreover, it was far from clear just how the internecine Arab and Palestinian struggle would come out, regardless of Soviet preferences or assistance. The result was a policy which sought to satisfy all but pleased none, a policy which sought to support no one but alienated all. It was probably the only policy the Soviets could pursue under the circumstances, designed to promote a unified PLO, under Arafat – in the absence of a viable substitute – but pressuring for an Arafat willing to work with the Syrians and, more importantly, willing to limit his political efforts to initiatives acceptable to the Soviet Union.

It was this policy which dictated Andropov's agreement to a statement in January 1983 expressing Soviet 'understanding of the position of the PLO leadership' favouring a confederation with Jordan. The mention of 'the leadership' already spelled a subtle Soviet distinction, however. This policy also dictated the relatively mild Soviet response almost a year later to the holding of the Palestine National Council (PNC) meeting in Aman. Arafat's decision to hold the PNC meeting meant that he had decided to go ahead with a majority rather than a consensus endorsement of his Jordanian–American plans. The significance of this was understood by Moscow, but the Soviets nonetheless urged Hawatmeh and Habash, in consultations in Moscow, not to formally split off and set up a rival organization, whatever the results of the PNC. This restraint on the part of Moscow, did not, however, continue much beyond the February 1985 Arafat–Hussein agreement, which outlined a joint plan for a Middle East peace settlement. Although this plan called for an international conference with the participation of the permanent members of the Security Council, it soon became clear that it was designed to pave the way for PLO cooperation with the United States.

There were some signs that Moscow actively sought Arafat's replacement at this time. There were, however, no serious candidates available. The Soviets did suspend their arms supplies to Arafat's forces, continuing training in Eastern Europe and the supply of arms to other components of the PLO. Moscow also refrained from inviting Arafat to Moscow so long as the Arafat–Hussein agreement was operative. With the breakdown of this accord in the spring of 1986, the Soviets began a gradual rapprochement, eventually mediating reconciliation meetings between Fatah and the PFLP and DFLP, with the participation of the Palestinian Communists, but without the Syrian-backed groups. Syria opposed Moscow's moves, but the Palestinian Communists, at least, benefited from the Soviet role. At the 1987 PNC which officially abrogated the Hussein–Arafat agreement and achieved the reunification of the major forces of the PLO, the Communists finally received a place on the PLO executive. This by no means gave them significant influence; nor did it ensure any Soviet control. Indeed, although the Soviets did resume aid to Fatah, and invited Arafat the following year to lead an official delegation to Moscow, a decided cautiousness, perhaps distrust, had entered Soviet treatment of the PLO leader. Inasmuch as the Soviet–PLO alliance had always been an uneasy one, it was not clear that Gorbachev's policies would bring about a significant change in either direction.

9   The Lebanon War, 1982

The Soviet Union had exhibited relatively little interest in Lebanon over the years. Its reporting of the civil war developing in that country, in the early 1970s, was scanty, although it did contain words of praise for what were called the patriotic-progressive forces. By this was meant the leftist Druze forces of Kamal Jumblatt and the pro-Soviet Communist Party of Lebanon (as distinct from other, non-Soviet Communists in the country). Moscow may even have provided this loose coalition with material aid, together with occasional propaganda support, but there appears to have been very little direct Soviet involvement. It is conceivable that the Soviets considered the domestic Lebanese scene to be too complex, contradictory and intractable to warrant Soviet involvement. In any case, there does not appear to have been any particular attempt to play a role in the Civil War even with the hope of promoting, perhaps, a left-wing government.

As already noted, the Soviets did not support the Syrian intervention in 1976, primarily for reasons connected with Soviet concern over Syrian aggrandizement, the possibility of Israeli retaliation, and even of a Syrian–American rapprochement. Thus even though a client state, such as Syria, was inherently more important to the pursuit of Soviet interests than a non-governmental movement or party, there were few reasons for the Soviets to support Syria's temporary but forceful alliance with the Christian forces in Lebanon against the Lebanese left and the PLO. To end the anomalous situation of two of its allies, the PLO and Syria, in open warfare with each other, as well as to defuse the situation and eliminate the temporary mutuality of Syrian–American interests, Moscow pressed for a cease-fire. Support, even encouragement, for a cease-fire was expressed despite the fact that it was the anti-Soviet, pro-American and pro-Egyptian Saudi Arabia that was most instrumental in the negotiating of a cease-fire, which also entailed some Egyptian–Syrian cooperation (at a time when the Soviet–Egyptian Treaty had just been abrogated by Sadat).

Once the Syrians abandoned their support for the Christian forces in Lebanon, Soviet policies regarding Lebanon were faced with somewhat fewer contradictions. At least Moscow assumed a more tolerant attitude to the Syrian presence in Lebanon, refraining from further public criticism. There was, however, little Soviet enthusiasm for the Syrian presence. This was especially the case when, in May 1981, Syria extended its SAM defence system to Lebanon itself, creating a new threat of Israeli–Syrian war. The provocative installation in Lebanon of the Soviet supplied anti-aircraft missiles was apparently undertaken without Soviet acquiescence or even foreknowledge. Israel responded with an ultimatum demanding the removal of the missiles or their destruction by Israel.

The threat of war was great, and the Soviet position was further complicated by Syrian references to the recently signed Soviet–Syrian Treaty of Friendship and Cooperation. Syria warned that an Israeli move against the SAMs would face not only Syrian retaliation and that of its Arab supporters, but 'the strategic world' of the Soviet–Syrian Treaty. Moscow, however, scrupuously refrained from any reference to the Treaty in its comments at the time, and Soviet Ambassador to Beirut, Aleksandr Soldatov, explicitly stated that the developments in Lebanon were 'unrelated' to the Soviet–Syrian Treaty. US mediation failed to resolve the crisis, but a flare-up in Israeli–PLO attacks and counterattacks to and from Lebanon (as well as the Israeli bombing of the Iraqi nuclear reactor in June) shifted attention elsewhere. The Soviets cannot have been pleased over the American mediation of a cease-fire between Israel and the PLO in July, but the danger of war over Lebanon appeared to have been defused.

If there was no real Soviet commitment to Syria in Lebanon, there was even less reason to expect a Soviet commitment to the PLO there. Soviet support for the PLO against Syrian attacks in 1976 had come, as we have seen, not out of enthusiasm for the PLO in Lebanon but rather out of opposition to the Syrian moves and, therefore, had not led to extensive assistance to the embattled PLO. This in fact had resulted in a strain in Soviet–PLO relations. Once the Syrian–PLO fighting had ended, Moscow favoured PLO observance of the cease-fire in the south, including abstention from operations into Israel, because of the risk of Israeli reprisal.

Whether a means of preparing the PLO for future attacks into Israel, or in an effort to restrain them from any immediate actions, or simply an example of the Soviets' preferred policy with regard to national liberation movements, Moscow began the conversion of the PLO forces into a conventional army at this time. As unlikely as it was that the PLO would ever be capable of facing the Israel Defence Forces in regular conventional warfare, the training, arming and planning accorded the PLO forces in Lebanon and in the Soviet bloc were clearly aimed in this direction. At the same time Moscow was selling the PLO arms, enabling the organization to stockpile enormous quantities of weapons in Lebanon, quantities well beyond PLO needs, stored in bunkers throughout Lebanon and under Beirut (and therefore clearly not intended for transfer to other movements – transfers which did occur in PLO training camps elsewhere). This stockpiling occurred at a time when the Soviets were advocating suspension of military action pending conversion of the PLO forces and, simultaneously, pressuring Arafat to moderate his attitude towards Israel so as to open the way to a political solution. Both of these were evident from documents found, and published by Israel, in Lebanon, including the protocol of a conversation between Gromyko and Arafat.

In this there was a similarity to past Soviet policies with Egypt (and other national liberation movements such as ZAPU in Zimbabwe). Moscow provided, possibly even at a profit, large supplies of arms, though not necessarily the types of arms requested. These provisions were meant to placate the client and, ostensibly, to strengthen it so that it might bargain from a position of strength and/or consolidate its internal power. At the same time, the Soviets nonetheless urged restraint. The problem with such a policy, apparent not only in the PLO case, was that such supplies also empowered the client to take action, whatever Soviet advice might be, while the supplies also created the impression on all concerned, that Moscow did approve of armed action. This did not in fact signify a Soviet commitment to the PLO in Lebanon or willingness to intervene on its behalf in the event of war.

The Israeli–PLO cease-fire broke down following a Palestinian assassination attempt in May 1982 against the Israeli Ambassador to London, which was answered by Israeli retaliatory strikes against PLO bases in southern Lebanon. This led to resumed PLO shelling of Israeli civilians in the northern Galilee and the reinforcement of Syria's SAM 6 network in Lebanon. Israel then invaded Lebanon on 6 June. With the outbreak of war, the Soviets' main concern was the danger of an all-out Israeli–Syrian conflict. Such a conflict might pose a serious threat to Damascus, leading possibly even to the downfall of the already weakened regime of Assad. The Israeli blow and these threats might be such as to prompt the Syrians to demand Soviet military intervention, resulting as in the cases of past wars with Israel, in the risk of super-power confrontation.

It was in the Soviet interest, therefore, that a cease-fire be obtained as quickly as possible, to stop the Israeli advance even before, but particularly after Syrian armour and aircraft had been engaged by the invading forces. There does not appear to have been any disagreement with the Syrians over these objectives; the Syrians themselves apparently were not interested in all-out war with Israel at this time. Thus it was not a case of Syria pressing to fight and Moscow holding it back but, perhaps, Syrian pressure on Moscow to press Washington to restrain Israel. Given the collapse of détente and the tension in Soviet–US relations after the Soviet invasion of Afghanistan, the election of Reagan, the US failure to ratify SALT II and the rocky arms talks underway between Washington and Moscow, the Soviets were not in an ideal position for pressing the Americans on anything. Nor was it certain just how much prior American collusion or agreement there had actually been between Jerusalem and Washington with regard to the Israeli invasion plans.

Disagreements did develop between Moscow and Damascus during the war. The Syrians became dissatisfied with the lack of direct Soviet involvement in the form of military moves – be it significant augmentation of the Soviet fleet in the Mediterranean or similar type of supportive action. Libyans and Palestinians, though not the Syrians themselves, openly expressed their disappointment that the Soviets did not send Syria a contingent of Soviet troops. Damascus apparently was not convinced that Moscow was bringing the full weight of its power to bear through Washington or directly on Israel in order to stop Israel and force its withdrawal.

Actual Soviet moves began only on 9 June, when Israeli and Syrian forces clashed in the Beka'a Valley of Lebanon, with the destruction of the Syrian SAM network there and what was subsequently called the largest single air battle since World War Two – in which Israel downed twenty-three Syrian MIGs (by the end of the war the Israelis had destroyed eighty-five Syrian planes without the loss of a single Israeli aircraft). It was this battle which presumably activated the Soviets into at least diplomatic moves. Brezhnev sent a message to Reagan on 9 June in which he called for a cease-fire and Israeli withdrawal. He underlined Moscow's concern by referring to the fact that this was a conflict located in close proximity to the Soviets' southern border.

Brezhnev did not, however, include anything which might be construed as an ultimatum or operative steps should the demand for a halt
to hostilities and Israeli withdrawal be ignored.

The Soviets sent a limited number of ships (reportedly five) to
reinforce their Mediterranean Squadron, but this second step was
probably designed to provide a certain amount of force to the diplomatic step and to signal Soviet support to its allies in the area. It was,
however, a basically symbolic act, limited in scope, so as not to alarm
the United States, and entirely in keeping with standard Soviet
procedures. It meant that the Soviet fleet was to an extent prepared
should the hostilities spread and require further symbolic gestures of a
military nature. In this sense it presumably was to be of deterrence
value, while more concretely it could monitor events. The move by no
means indicated any Soviet intention to intervene, and there was no
Soviet interference with the Israeli fleet, even when the latter imposed
a blockade of the Lebanese coast. There was a Soviet request to Turkey
for non-civilian overflights, and even a reported alert in two Soviet
airborne divisions – both steps presumably precautions taken in case
all-out war did break out between Israel and Syria.

The Soviets also undertook a limited resupply effort to Syria
following the Beka'a battle, but this was not carried out ostentatiously
or massively in the way the resupply effort had been implemented
during the Yom Kippur War. Nonetheless it could be said that
Moscow had fulfilled its commitment to Syria, albeit with little or no
risk to itself. The 13 June dispatch of a high-ranking Soviet military
official, deputy commander of the Soviet Air Defence Forces Colonel-
General Evgenii Yurasov was not part of these gestures – if Moscow
had wanted to signal its intention of guaranteeing Syria's air defences,
it would have done so more blatantly and officially. Rather this little
publicized visit, the first of four Soviet military delegations to Syria
over the following weeks, was most likely connected with Moscow's
concern over and interest in the Israeli destruction of the Soviet-
provided SAM system and the Syrian air-force losses in the Beka'a
battle.

The Soviets were presumably no less concerned than the Syrians
over the one-sided outcome of air battle, not only because of the
resulting Syrian vulnerability but also because of the blow to Soviet
prestige as well as the even more important consequences the failure
of the Soviet equipment – if indeed it had been a failure of the Soviet
equipment – might have for the Soviets' own military capabilities. A
reported trip to Syria by Soviet chief of staff Ogarkov in July may have

been related to this problem, although such a visit may also have been connected with later Soviet supplies. Actually, one of the signs of Soviet reticence with regard to its own involvement in the war was the conspicuous lack of any high-level exchange of visits in either direction.

Although the Soviet media reported Syrian references to the need for a 'strategic alliance', they did so without any comment or particular attention, giving no indication whatsoever of any Soviet intention of pursuing this idea. As might have been expected, they answered criticism of Soviet equipment with downright denials – claiming massive Syrian victories in the air and on the ground, and hinting that greater efficiency on the part of the users of this equipment might have produced better results. Inasmuch as the Soviets' greatest concern was the possibility of all-out Israeli–Syrian war and the attendant need for Soviet intervention, the Soviet media made little or no mention of Syrian involvement in the fighting in Lebanon until this danger had virtually passed (with Israel's declaration of a cease-fire on the Syrian front on 12 June). No mention was made until this time of the Soviet–Syrian Friendship and Cooperation Treaty, lest the connection be drawn and Soviet involvement demanded. Although it did not say so directly, the Soviet Union seemed to be limiting its commitment quite clearly to Syria proper; even its later efforts to defend the performance of Soviet weapons stated proudly that no Israeli planes had penetrated Syrian airspace.

In keeping with past policies, and despite the dire circumstances, the Soviets did even less for the PLO. Early in the war Moscow used two separate channels to make the limits of its support understood to the Palestinians. In response to what the PLO radio termed a call by Arafat to Moscow to 'help stop the Israeli aggression', the PLO representative in Moscow, Muhammed ash-Sha'ir, issued a statement on 8 June that the Soviet Union would continue to send military supplies to the Palestinians, but would send no troops, adding that no troops had been requested. None of the above appeared in the Soviet version of the Sha'ir statement, but this Soviet position was presumably also conveyed to PLO political department chief Faruk Kaddumi in his talk with Gromyko at the United Nations the next day. Exactly how arms were to reach the PLO in Lebanon given the Israeli blockade, control of the Damascus–Beirut road, and large parts if not all of southern Lebanon, is not clear. But the message was clear: do not expect anything more than supplies.

Palestinian dissatisfaction with the Soviet position became almost immediately apparent. Abu Iyyad, a critic of the Soviet Union in the past and one of the leading Fatah officials, on 11 June (according to Radio Monte Carlo) publicly expressed the PLO's disappointment with Moscow, saying that 'from the first hour, we wanted the Soviet position to be more radical, but our Soviet brothers have their own way of acting'. A few days later he was still more critical, expressing incomprehension over what he called the Soviets' silence and sluggishness, their purely symbolic encouragement and passiveness, concluding that although the Soviets could tell the United States 'to stop this massacre, it seems that we are not included within the framework of the red line' (referring perhaps to the Syrians' situation, which Abu Iyyad may have believed was within the Soviets' area of critical concern). Even the Soviets' closer ally in the PLO leadership, Nayif Hawatmeh, called on the Soviets to use 'all possible means including military power', and complained that the Soviets were contenting themselves with diplomatic and political pressures, the effect of which was 'limited if not zero'.

Soviet sensitivity to such criticism was one of the factors prompting the Soviet government statement issued on 14 June. Although its wording was to some degree the public expression of the note sent to Reagan a few days earlier (primarily out of concern over Israeli–Syrian fighting), the tone and timing were clearly designed to restore the shortlived cease-fire lest Israel take Beirut. Yet the statement's warning to Israel lacked the strong threat expressed at critical times in previous Arab–Israeli wars. Indeed, the PLO representative in the Persian Gulf was to make just this point, critical of Moscow, several days later. On the vital point of actual Soviet assistance to the Palestinians, the statement was vague, even defensive. It said only that 'The Soviet Union takes the side of the Arabs, not in words, but in deeds. It is working to bring about the withdrawal of the aggressor from Lebanon'. The 'deeds' referred to were limited to diplomatic action, although Soviet propaganda broadcasts implied, by reference to past cases, that this also meant Moscow's role in the creation of Arab military strength in general. Even this, however, said nothing of the present, prompting increasingly explicit Palestinian criticism over the following weeks.

The Soviet Union was apparently no more forthcoming in a letter Brezhnev sent to Arafat sometime in the last week of June, for Abu Iyyad said of the letter that it contained 'pretty words, but they have no basis on the ground'. Arafat reportedly halted all contact with the Soviet Ambassador in Beirut at one point, although he refrained from any public expression of his anger over Soviet inaction. Just prior to a trip to the Soviet Union in early July as part of an Arab League delegation designated to approach all permanent Security Council members regarding the Lebanon crisis, Kaddumi said that he planned to ask the Soviets for 'drastic action'. He added that condemnation of Israel was not sufficient. According to Arab sources quoted in the West, Gromyko told Kaddumi and the accompanying Moroccan and Kuwaiti Foreign Ministers in Moscow that Soviet military aid in the form of troops or combat ships was out of the question, refusing to change the Soviet position or increase its role in Lebanon in any way.

The Soviets offered little else in answer to Palestinian demands and criticism aside from protestations of how much the Soviet Union was doing, minimization of the Palestinians' losses, and the more frequent argument, employed implicitly and later explicitly, that the Arab states were supposed to be the Palestinians' great defenders. Thus citing help from its own allies, South Yemen and Syria, and its potential ally, Iran, the Soviet Union predictably tried to shift the criticism to the Arabs, bemoaning the lack of unity in the Arab world and its failure to act. It may have been true that if the Arab world had been united at the time, Israel may not have attacked; Soviet criticism of Egypt's defection from the anti-Israel camp may in this sense have been justifiable.

Yet inasmuch as Israel was now actually in Lebanon, it was by no means certain that the Soviets wanted other Arab states to become involved. The Soviets' main interest was, in fact, to limit the conflict, and therefore made no call to Syria to become fully involved – indeed the opposite was the case – nor to any other state. The appeal about the lack of Arab unity and therefore failure to act was to a large degree so much Soviet rhetoric, similar perhaps to Moscow's response to Boumedienne in the Yom Kippur War. The Soviets wanted the cease-fire to hold, but they themselves were unwilling to provide any more assistance to the PLO than they had in 1976, when they had idly watched the Palestinian camps be shelled and destroyed by Syrian-supported Christian forces, as indeed they had watched similar destruction by Jordanian forces during the Black September of 1970.

One type of aid that the Soviets did more genuinely encourage during the war was renewed use of the Arab oil weapon. While this promised to be less effective than in the 1973 war, when the western world was confronted with a serious energy crisis, the use of such a weapon now at least could serve Moscow's anti-western interests. Thus, on 8 June the Soviets appealed for Arab help to the beleaguered

Palestinians in the form not of military intervention but in the form of an oil boycott of the United States. There is little likelihood that Moscow believed that it could obtain such a boycott, but the idea presumably was deemed helpful to unite and concentrate the Arabs against the United States. And this was another major objective of Moscow during the war.

Once the initial crisis and risk of Israeli–Syrian war abated, the major Soviet concern revolved around American involvement. As in past wars, the Soviets most likely hoped to exploit the conflict, to use it against the United States to the degree that this was possible. At the same time they hoped to block or prevent any benefits the Americans might derive from the situation either with regard to US relations with the Arabs or as an opportunity to introduce an American presence.

Thus, encouragement of an Arab oil boycott was exploitation of the crisis, which probably carried with it Soviet hopes of engaging the conservative Arab states against the United States as well. Certainly the Soviets sought to exploit the conflict for this purpose by emphasizing the American influence over and collusion with Israel in the latter's aggressive action. Not only the fact of American arming of Israel over the years but also the US–Israeli alliance was emphasized, with the United States portrayed as the power, pulling the strings, behind Israel. Soviet commentators drew a straight line from Camp David through the US–Israeli strategic alliance to the Lebanon crisis thus holding the Americans indirectly as well as directly responsible for enabling Israel to take this action. These lines of argument were employed, however, also out of concern that the Americans might play a mediating role, thereby actually improving their position in what could be a zero-sum game with the Soviets. Criticism then of Washington, particularly emphasizing American support for and involvement with Israel, was designed to evoke Arab distrust and resistance to any American role.

Of greater and more immediate concern to the Soviets was the possibility of American intervention. Such a move was viewed by Moscow as constituting a serious change in the super-power status quo in the area, reminiscent perhaps of the days of powerful American intervention in the Middle East (for example, Lebanon in 1958) to prop up regimes of its choice against the threat of pro-Soviet developments in the region. This 'global' factor dictating Soviet behaviour was evidenced by the warning sent by Brezhnev to Reagan on 8 July. For weeks the PLO had been surrounded and bombarded in West Beirut, with the daily threat of Israeli occupation and destruction of the PLO strongholds in the city. Yet during all this time the Soviet Union did little or nothing, choosing to respond only when a new element appeared: the possibility of US forces being sent to Lebanon to assist in the evacuation of the PLO.

Brezhnev's 8 July warning was couched mainly in terms of preventing an Israeli move on West Beirut, and it was somewhat milder than the 14 June statement in that it omitted any reference to the proximity of the area to the Soviet Union. The warning was quite clear, however, in its objection to any importation of US forces into the area. Surprisingly this warning did not even mention Israeli withdrawal from Lebanon, an omission intended perhaps to lower the price necessary for American agreement to desist from sending troops. Obviously, such a move was more threatening to Soviet interests than the continued presence of the Israeli army in Lebanon.

The American troop threat was mitigated somewhat by their limitation in a temporary multinational supervisory force. The problem remained, however, of American domination and mediation of the negotiations to resolve the crisis. From the Soviet point of view, the problem was that the Americans might succeed in working out a solution to the PLO presence in Beirut, and even achieve a *modus operandi* with the Palestinian organization. Whereas Moscow, having no diplomatic relations with Israel and no patron-client relationship with Lebanon, would have no way of challenging the American-conducted talks. According to a Saudi source, the Soviet Union refused a Palestinian request to send a Soviet negotiator on the grounds that the absence of Soviet–Israeli relations would be an obstacle to the success of such an effort.

What the Soviets may have been doing was trying to discourage the Palestinians and the Syrians, as well as any state which was being approached as a potential host for the PLO forces, from accepting any kind of a settlement being proposed by the United States. Hoping thereby to prevent an American-mediated resolution of the conflict, Moscow could then claim that Washington in fact had nothing to offer the Arab world. At best then, the negotiations could be shifted to the UN or some other multinational forum which would include the Soviet Union. Indeed this was a suggestion raised by Brezhnev in an interview to *Pravda* late in July.

When, however, it became increasingly likely that Israel was going to move into West Beirut, and tensions rose again on the Syrian–Israeli front, Syria and others suddenly abandoned their recalcitrance regarding the evacuation of the Palestinians. The sudden change, which included a South Yemen offer to receive Palestinians, strongly suggested some type of Soviet intervention, presumably because Moscow became convinced that Israel had reached the limits of its patience and war was once again about to break out in full force.

In addition to the problem of American gains from the situation, far from resolved by the evacuation of the PLO, the Soviets also had to cope with some of the likely consequences of the war itself, at least for the PLO. There were signs that Israel's use of force had discredited Arafat's diplomatic–political tactic, strengthening the radical, rejectionist forces in the movement. Dispersion of the PLO after Beirut, with the radicals centered in Syria, would mean that Arafat would have less control over the more extremist elements. The likelihood of the radicalization of the PLO, or its split, and a probable return to terrorism as the only means of operating, was early perceived by the Soviets, but not necessarily as a positive development.

As we have seen, there was a wide gap between Moscow and the radicals on a whole spectrum of issues in the Arab–Israeli dispute, including the very idea of a negotiated settlement. Gromyko, in a press conference on 22 June, reiterated Moscow's positions, underlining the point of greatest conflict between the Soviets and the radical Palestinians: Moscow's recognition of Israel's right to exist. Presumably because of the danger of PLO radicalization and/or split, one of the themes of Soviet propaganda during the conflict, as well as of Brezhnev's *Pravda* interview, was that armed force could not solve the Middle East crisis; only a political settlement would do. While this line was employed primarily to criticize Israel's use of force, it could also have been directed against the radicals in the PLO. *Pravda*, for example, carefully omitted a remark by the PLO Moscow representative in a press conference to the effect that PLO forces would be kept in Beirut to defend against future Israeli and right-wing assaults. Moreover, there was much reporting in the Soviet media, and present also in Brezhnev's interview, of Israeli peace forces. Some of this reporting, and Brezhnev's comments, referred to this as a new and promising phenomenon for the possibility of a peaceful settlement.

Thus even as the Soviets were trying to discredit the United States as a legitimate mediator, they were encouraging the ideas of negotiations and compromise or the political over military solution policy. The two lines were not necessarily contradictory in that the Soviets hoped to head off a radicalization without having the PLO turn to the United States. Nonetheless there was the very real possibility – evidenced quite early by the Arafat–Hussein talks which began after the evacuation – that the moderate wing of the PLO, the Soviet-preferred Fatah, would find its way to the Americans. This would leave Moscow with the radical wing of a split PLO and thus few prospects for playing a significant role in peace negotiations.

During the war there were inconsistencies if not in actual Soviet policies, at least in the Soviet media, which suggested differences of opinion in Moscow. It is possible that the conflict in Lebanon strengthened those persons or forces which had all along opposed massive Soviet involvement with the Palestinians or in this region altogether. It has been argued over the years that elements of the Soviet military opposed such involvement on the grounds that it was too risky, that the Arab clients were too unstable and uncertain, and that war, including confrontation with the United States, or at the very least, loss of modern Soviet equipment, would be the result. Others were said to have opposed supporting non-Marxist groups, believing the investment to be worthless over the long run, while still others may in fact have pressed for greater support, as part of the Soviet–Chinese competition among the national liberation movements. Conversely there were those who preferred only state-to-state relations as the cornerstone of Soviet policy, no matter how progressive or Marxist the non-ruling client group.

There were signs of some of these differences, possibly of an ongoing debate, in the Soviet media in June and July. For example, in addition to the almost total absence of commentaries in *Pravda* in July, the formula for a Middle East settlement carried by the Soviet media in July omitted the customary call for a Palestinian state. Similarly, there seemed to be some confusion over the idea of an international conference: on 20 June, Central Committee expert Shishlin spoke positively on Moscow radio about such a conference but, in response, the more maverick journalist Bovin remarked that now was not the time for such a conference. The debate, if indeed there was one, was apparently closed by Brezhnev's *Pravda* interview, in which he spoke emphatically of the need for a Palestinian state and the desirability of a conference. Following this, the media fell obediently into line. Yet the whole period of the war was characterized by the phenomenon of moderate articles (regarding Israel, for example) almost side by side with virulently anti-Israel attacks; some commentaries suggested the possibility of peaceful settlement while others spoke only of Israel's aggressive intentions.

Discrepancies were also notable with regard to the United States. For many years there had been evidence of persons or groups favouring détente as distinct from those who had sought every opportunity to denigrate the possibility of détente with the United States. As during the Yom Kippur War, so too during this war, there were actually differences between the standard or official Soviet line and the comments of some individuals. This time, however, it was the dissenting individuals who expressed the pro-détente or more moderate view of the United States, as, for example, Bovin who several times tried to dissociate the United States from responsibility for the Israeli invasion. In an interview with senior Soviet Middle East expert Primakov, journalist Igor Beliaev also expressed the sentiment that the United States might not be entirely pleased with Israel's actions, although Primakov – in the past spokesperson for the moderate official position – now took the particularly anti-American official position of that period. Because Bovin's name had often been linked with Andropov as well as Brezhnev, it was possible that his remarks, and these discrepancies in general, reflected a power struggle connected with Andropov's ascendancy as a result of the death of Suslov some months earlier.

Be that as it may, Soviet behaviour during the Lebanon War did not reflect any significant changes in policy. The crisis may have triggered a debate and some rethinking, or contributed to a debate already in progress, but the Soviet–PLO relationship as well as the Soviet attitude toward Syria's presence in Lebanon were relatively consistent. In fact Soviet behaviour during the crisis was entirely consistent with and the logical outcome of the policies pursued by the Brezhnev regime in the area for some time. Put more bluntly, the failure of the Soviets to take a more active role to assist the PLO and even Syria may have appeared contradictory to their ostensible commitments and, therefore, contrary to expectations. It was in fact typical of the contradictions connected with Soviet–Arab relations altogether: Moscow's willingness to provide arms and political support for the Arabs, while being unwilling to approve of wars and to risk intervention which might endanger Moscow's primary interest of avoiding military confrontation with the United States.

The results of the war for Soviet policy were both negative and positive. On the negative side of the ledger, in the region, there was the Syrian dissatisfaction with the performance of Soviet equipment and Soviet concern as well over the ease with which the Israeli air force destroyed the advanced Soviet surface-to-air defence system. There were also the Syrian pressures for a more forthcoming alliance with Moscow, including a Soviet commitment to Syrian forces in Lebanon.

There was the PLO anger over the lack of Soviet assistance, and the negative phenomena of the ignoble retreat of the PLO from Beirut (through the mediation of the United States), the PLO's dispersion, and the likelihood of radicalization of the organization and possibly even a split. The Arab world in general was critical of Soviet inaction (the oil weapon was not activated), and the Soviets had clearly lost credibility and prestige. Moreover, the United States appeared to come out the winner, at least insofar as it was the mediating power throughout the crisis and had created a presence for itself not only politically but militarily as well.

The Soviets were able to reverse or minimize some of these negative phenomena relatively quickly, and there were indeed some positive results of the war for them. Compensation was quickly rendered the Syrians in the form of significantly new and better Soviet equipment. This included SAM-5s to improve Syria's air defences, SS-21s to provide greater surface-to-surface capability, and an additional 2000 Soviet advisers. The last were to have control of the new equipment, at least until Syrian personnel could be trained, but this also provided the Soviets with some control over the use of the equipment and possibly over Syrian actions. While these supplies represented an increased Soviet commitment to Syria, they also provided for greater Syrian dependence upon Moscow and, in this sense, an improvement of the Soviets' position.

In addition, the Americans quite rapidly became bogged down in Lebanon. Their troops were being hit, they were discredited as militarily impotent in the circumstances, and their mediation was failing as they found it virtually impossible to make their way between the warring Lebanese factions as well as between Israel and Lebanon. In time American efforts in Lebanon were to be seen, especially in the Arab world, as a total failure – a result which was to rebound to the Soviets' benefit, particularly among the conservative Persian Gulf states. Israel too had been badly discredited by the Lebanon venture and America's chief Middle East ally became a pariah among nations. From this came greater sympathy for the Arab and Palestinian causes and apparent justification of, as well as support for, the Soviets' anti-Israel and anti-Zionist positions. And Israel itself emerged badly divided internally, its government weakened, and those domestic forces interested in negotiations and territorial compromise with the Arabs greatly strengthened.

Nonetheless, even though the Soviets came out better regionally, the overall balance was somewhat mixed. If Moscow had in fact emerged as the winner of the conflict, one problem was how to maintain this advantage and at minimum costs. There were a number of serious concerns for the Soviets. The first was the American presence, however negative it was to prove for the Americans' good name. The United States, as a result of the war, had become more, not less, involved in the region. The Reagan administration, until then relatively inactive in the Arab–Israeli context, had now produced a peace plan, the 1 September Reagan Initiative, and it planned active mediation. It had placed military forces in the area, including a reinforced naval presence and the Marines. There had been a significant show of American strength, with the cooperation of the Americans' European allies.

These things meant not only important American gains but also serious risk of Soviet–American confrontation. There was the tense proximity of American forces near Syrian forces periodically accompanied by Soviet advisers. US–Syrian clashes, which did occur, carried with them the risk of a need for Soviet involvement, which could lead to Soviet–American clashes. There was also the risk that the United States would use Israeli forces to hit Syrian positions, leading once more to Israeli–Syrian confrontation and the dilemma of Soviet intervention, particularly with regard to the use of the missiles now under Soviet control. In this tense aftermath of the fighting, with American, Syrian and Israeli forces and Soviet advisers present, there were few assurances that the super-powers would be able to control their clients and prevent new, more dangerous confrontations.

Moreover, the regional picture was not entirely certain. As in the past, there was the danger, from Moscow's point of view, that Syria might respond positively to American offers and attempts to engage Damascus in a dialogue. The PLO was in fact moving in the direction of the United States, as Arafat began his dialogue with Hussein with the intention of at least partially accepting the Reagan Initiative. And, as we have seen, the fact that this might mean the splitting of the PLO did not promise much benefit to the Soviets.

The solutions sought by the Soviets to these problems were complex, often contradictory. The first objective was to eject the United States and the multinational force from Lebanon, without, however, so much tension or bloodshed as to cause confrontation. The latter condition led to Soviet warnings to the Syrians not to provoke the United States in December 1983–January 1984 when Syrian forces in Lebanon fired on US planes. The second objective was to generate multilateral negotiations, including of course the Soviet Union, as soon as possible. Once the US Marines were in fact withdrawn, and the immediate tensions relieved, Soviet policies and emphasis shifted to the competition with the United States in and over the Persian Gulf. With regard to Lebanon the Soviets emphasized the complexities of the domestic scene, calling occasionally for a united, neutral Lebanon. They demanded Israeli withdrawal and vigorously opposed the short-lived accord obtained by the Americans between Israel and the Lebanese government in May 1983.

In time the Soviets recognized and appeared to tolerate the Syrian presence in Lebanon without, however, showing much support or respect for the dominant position and power exercised by Damascus there. There was some increase in Soviet involvement in the domestic Lebanese conflict, but this was quite limited, particularly once Soviet personnel fell victim to the terrorist activity so characteristic of this conflict. By and large Lebanon was seen, or at least presented by the Soviets, as a distraction from the central problem in the area, that of the Arab–Israeli dispute, and it was to this issue, as well as to the conflict in the Persian Gulf that the Soviets turned their attention.

10   The Soviet Union and Syria

The Soviet relationship with Syria, like the one with Egypt, dated primarily back to the death of Stalin and the commencement of Soviet arms supplies to the Arabs in 1955. In fact the first arms deal with Syria was signed in 1954, preceding the Czechoslovak–Egyptian deal. The advent of a Ba'ath regime in Damascus had marked the opening of a positive Soviet–Syrian relationship. The Ba'ath ideology was one of Arab nationalism, Arab unity and strength. As such it was an anti-imperialist, anti-western ideology, with secular, socialist domestic aspirations. From the Soviet point of view, the Ba'athists represented the national bourgeoisie and petty bourgeoisie, fitting into the category of a bourgeois nationalist party, viewed favourably by the Soviets' post-Stalinist Third World policy. And, in keeping with this policy, the Syrian Communist Party was ordered to cooperate with the Ba'ath despite the fact that the two parties were in a competitive relationship. It is even possible that in this early period of Soviet–Arab cooperation Moscow viewed Syria rather than Egypt as the cornerstone of its Middle East policy. Ba'ath secularism and socialism may have appeared more promising than Nasserism, and Ba'ath willingness to cooperate with the legal and relatively strong Communist Party may have encouraged the Soviets. Egypt was more important strategically than Syria, but at this point political rather than primarily strategic interests were guiding Soviet policies in the area.

1957 was a peak year in this emerging relationship, when Moscow became involved in the Turkish–Syrian crisis. In this year the Soviets offered Syria the first credits accorded an Arab state by Moscow, in the range of $98 million. The Syrian Communist Party was brought into a coalition, with a person known for his connections with the Communists named to head the politically powerful army. An American–Syrian crisis developed as the United States viewed the deepening Soviet–Syrian relationship and the growing Communist–Ba'ath cooperation with some alarm, particularly in view of the Ba'ath's own socialist and anti-western orientation. There was concern that Syria was actually going Communist, and this concern in turn fuelled Syrian fears of American intervention, resulting in a heightened Syrian interest in or perhaps even dependence upon Soviet support.

In August 1957 the Syrians expelled three US diplomats on charges of organizing a coup attempt; the ensuing deterioration in Syrian–American relations led to Syrian fear that Washington would invoke the Eisenhower Doctrine in order to restore its interests. Presumably at the behest of Washington, but also out of its own concern over the possibility of a Communist regime on its southern border, Turkey began to mass troops on its border with Syria. In this tense atmosphere border incidents occurred between Turkish and Syrian forces, and Turkey threatened to invade should the Communists, or the Soviet Union, gain control over the Damascus government. The Soviet Union moved at this point to prevent what it claimed was to be an imminent American intervention. Moscow proposed negotiations with Washington, to include such issues as arms supplies to the Middle East. Dulles rejected this bid, and the Soviets warned both Turkey and the United States to expect a Soviet response if Syria were attacked. Giving this threat credibility the Soviets began troop movements on the Turkish–Soviet border and sent two warships into the Syrian port of Latakia. Yet the same day as the Soviet threat to Turkey, 10 September, Dulles announced that the Turkish–Syrian situation did not warrant US military action, and the Turkish government subsequently conveyed the message to Damascus that it too had no intention of invading Syria. The crisis gradually subsided by late October, and both Moscow and Damascus claimed credit for preventing American invasion.

It is doubtful that the Soviets would actually have intervened militarily had the Turkish–Syrian crisis erupted into war. Turkey was a member of NATO and was clearly backed if not actually inspired by Washington in this crisis. It is by no means certain that the Soviets actually believed that there was a serious threat of invasion, at least not by the time it sent its warning, which in any case was couched in vague, indirect terms. In this sense the threat was similar to the Soviet warning at the end of the Suez War, but the 1957 threat was somewhat more credible given Soviet troop movements on its common border with Turkey, and , therefore, the actual capability (provided America did not become involved). Moreover, this was a period in which Moscow was trying to improve its relations with Turkey, which point it emphasized in its threat to Ankara. On balance it would appear that

Khrushchev was perhaps engaging in sabre rattling, primarily trying to exploit the crisis in order to further Moscow's own positions and influence, to discredit the United States, and strengthen the anti-western regimes in Syria and Egypt. The Soviets subsequently supplemented this crisis support with additional military and economic contracts, demanding in return no more, apparently, than the anti-western position already adopted by Damascus.

The Soviet–Syrian honeymoon ended abruptly, however, with the union of Egypt and Syria, that is, the creation of the United Arab Republic (UAR) in 1958. It would appear that many in the Ba'ath leadership itself were disturbed by the growth of Communist influence in Syria, but the overriding motivation for the union with Egypt was pro-Nasserite pan-Arab nationalism. It is possible that if the Syrian proposal for a federated arrangement with Egypt had been accepted the Communists might have retained something of their position. With the complete union insisted upon by Nasser, however, Syria virtually ceased to exist as a political entity, and Nasser made sure that no competing, anti-union political groupings survived.

The very reasons presented for the rapidly and secretly planned union made it unacceptable to the Soviets. The step ostensibly came to forestall a Communist takeover attempt, and indeed Nasser was concerned over the increase in Communist influence particularly in the Syrian army. The outlawing of all political parties virtually eliminated the Soviets' political gains within the country and the domination by Egypt blocked Soviet access and influence. Thus the Soviet Union lost its ally, and it suffered still greater UAR hostility (and anti-Communist campaigns) after the Iraqi revolution. The latter heralded a period of cooperation between Moscow and the anti-Nasserite regime in Baghdad.

A military coup in Damascus took Syria out of the UAR in 1961, but relations with the Soviet Union did not return to the positive cooperation of the pre-UAR period. Moscow did support, and strive to improve relations with, a series of conservative governments, despite the anti-Communist policies of many of these regimes. In Syria, 1961–6 was a period of great instability (there were eight coups in this period), but the Soviets remained uninvolved in these domestic upheavals. They were apparently satisfied to maintain economic and cultural contacts, recognizing and renewing these contacts with each new government. Moreover, Egypt had begun gradually to take precedence over Syria by 1963 or 1964, both because of Cairo's greater stability and influence in the Arab world and the rise of Soviet strategic interests in the Mediterranean at this time.

Approximately a year after the return of the Ba'ath to power in 1963, the Soviets began to refer positively to the leftwing of the party. Though basically anti-Communist, the left-Ba'ath favoured an improvement of relations with the Soviet Union and was clearly anti-western. Under a left-Ba'ath Prime Minister in 1964, Syria nationalized western oil companies and then began normalization of relations with the Communists. Following a brief period of rightwing Ba'ath rule, the left returned to power under President Atassi, party chief Jedid, and Prime Minister Zu'ayyin in February 1966 heralding a new, this time lasting rapprochement with Moscow. Because of its pro-Soviet disposition, the new left-Ba'ath regime was hailed by the Soviets as progressive. It was generously provided with economic, military and, as we have seen in connection with the events leading up to the Six-Day War, significant political support.

It is not certain just how much basis there was for Soviet optimism regarding this regime. There were problems and differences between the two countries from the outset. In the realm of ideology, there was actually a certain indifference on the part of the Ba'ath with regard to Moscow, for Ba'ath socialism was a far cry from Soviet Marxism–Leninism. There was in fact little to bind the two sides ideologically except for the broadest interpretation of the Ba'ath's particular brand of Arab nationalist socialism. Further, although the Communists had one person in the cabinet, the party itself remained illegal and severely weakened. Indeed, Moscow's orders to the party to seek cooperation with the Ba'ath, even to the point of merger, if possible, was not well received by the party, on the grounds that the Ba'ath was not truly socialist and would in any case overpower the Communists.

There were also differences between Moscow and Damascus in the area of the Arab–Israeli conflict. The Soviet preference for a political solution was rejected by the Syrian regime, which believed in armed action, be it in the form of reprisals or all-out war. The Syrians actually boycotted the Khartoum Arab summit in the wake of the six-Day War because it feared the outcome would be too moderate on the issue of political versus military solutions. Similarly they opposed the 1970 cease-fire in the War of Attrition. The Syrians also rejected resolution 242 because of its recognition of Israel's right to exist (Syria even refused to use the name of Israel, as late as 1973, referring instead to occupied Palestine and, according to many observers, still harbouring dreams of United or Greater Syria which included Palestine). The

Syrians, including the Communists, were also more interested in the Palestinians, and armed actions by Fatah, in the 1960s than the Soviets, who condemned most of these actions and agreed to only limited if any support for the Palestinians at this time.

Despite the fact that Damascus was dependent upon Moscow for arms supplies and for virtually half of its foreign aid, the Soviets were apparently hesitant to press their own positions upon the Syrians. In view of the past fragility of their relations, the Soviets were mainly concerned with actually maintaining the relationship, that is concerned simultaneously with cementing relations and strengthening the regime itself. As with Egypt, there was the additional problem of gaining sufficient influence to prevent Syria from taking precipitous action in the Arab–Israeli context.

The situation was not helped, from the Soviet point of view, by the 1970 civil war in Jordan. On 18 September, during the Jordanian–PLO battles, Syrian forces invaded Jordan. The United States began to move its fleet eastward and Israel began to concentrate armour on its border with Jordan, accompanied by Israeli air surveillance. There were not only clear indications of US and Israeli military preparations for intervention on the side of Hussein but an American signal to Brezhnev that the United States would not tolerate a Soviet-backed Syrian battle against Jordan. Reportedly there was a joint US–Israeli plan to intervene if necessary although this proved unnecessary when, five days later, after encountering strong Jordanian defences, the Syrians withdrew.

Moscow would appear at the very least to have known of the Syrian invasion plans – through its own over 1000 advisers in the country and meetings held between the Soviet Ambassador and Atassi just hours before the invasion. It does not appear, however, that the Soviets supported the move, for they issued a statement less than twenty-four hours into the invasion expressing their opposition to any foreign military intervention. Moreover they informed the United States several times just prior to and during the invasion that they were trying to restrain the Syrians, publicly condemning the entire armed conflict in Jordan and any interference from outside. The Soviets did indeed press the Syrians to retreat, most likely because of the quite clearly threatened Israeli if not also American response.

While there were those in the Syrian leadership who shared Moscow's opposition to the Syrian move into Jordan, the crisis highlighted some of the basic differences between Moscow and Damascus – differences which were to continue to plague their relationship. Syrian action demonstrated the independence of Damascus *vis à vis* Moscow, and it also reflected the Syrians' greater, if self-serving interest in the Palestinians (one may assume that the Syrians moved into Jordan as much in pursuit of Greater Syrian goals as in support of the Palestinians against Hussein). Moscow shared neither of these objectives and even in the future was not to recognize Syrian claims to 'guardianship' of the Palestinians. More importantly, the crisis demonstrated the Syrians' willingness to use force as distinct from Moscow's preference for political methods or, more bluntly put, it demonstrated the Syrians' lack of caution, in a high-risk situation of war and even American involvement.

A political crisis was developing within the Ba'ath at this time with the potential for seriously affecting Soviet–Syrian relations. It was a complex situation which the Soviets apparently read incorrectly, and therefore intervened, albeit slightly, on behalf of the losing party. Atassi resigned the Presidency of the country in the middle of a power struggle between Jedid and Minister of Defence (former air force chief) Hafiz Assad. Jedid was seen as a strong supporter of the close Soviet–Syrian relationship which had developed since 1966, so much so that there were even accusations that he was a Soviet agent. Assad, however, was said to have been responsible for certain anti-Communist measures in 1969 and 1970; also he had sent his chief-of-staff Mustafa Tlas to China in 1969 in what was seen as an anti-Soviet move. It certainly appeared that Assad was less pro-Soviet than his rival Jedid, if for no other reason than that he was supremely determined to maintain Syrian independence.

Presumably for these reasons, Moscow, through the Syrian Communists, supported Jedid despite his differences with Moscow over the issues of the Arab–Israeli conflict. There was in fact little reason for the Soviets to think that Assad would take any more moderate positions than Jedid in this sphere, although Assad had at least shared Moscow's opposition to the Syrian move into Jordan. (He had actually withheld air support for the action.) As it turned out, there were no changes in Syria's policies in the Arab–Israeli context under Assad. What was more to the point for the Soviets, however, was the fact that although Assad did maintain the cooperation with Moscow initiated by Jedid, he was not willing to translate this into a formal alliance. For many years to come he jealously guarded Syrian independence by refusing to enter into a Friendship and Cooperation Treaty of the type negotiated by Moscow with Egypt in 1971 and Iraq in 1972 as well as a number of other Third World states.

With the rise of Sadat in Egypt, the deterioration in Soviet–Egyptian relations, particularly the expulsion of the Soviet advisers from Egypt, the Soviet–Syrian relationship assumed greater importance for Moscow. Syria began to act as something of a mediator for Moscow in cases of Soviet difficulties, such as the post-1971 deterioration with Numeri in the Sudan and with Egypt itself. Also some of the strategic losses in Egypt were to be compensated by facilities in Syria. The Soviets undertook the widening of Syrian ports, built air facilities, and increased the number of advisers in the country. Deliveries from a new, large arms deal, signed in July of 1972, began to arrive quite ostentatiously in the autumn of 1972 as Moscow strove, in propaganda as well, to prove that its relations with the Arab world were as close as ever, despite the falling out with Egypt.

Perhaps because of the augmented importance of Syria to the Soviet Union, and possibly also because of the setback in Egypt which triggered an overall reappraisal of Soviet policies towards Third World regimes, Moscow began to press for Communist participation in the Syrian regime. The objective was the creation of a National Front in which the Communists would participate together with the Ba'ath. This was not necessarily an anti-Ba'ath move; nor was it an attempt to stage or even prepare the ground for a Communist coup. It was intended by the Soviets as greater protection against abrupt ejection of the type experienced with Egypt, according, possibly, a channel for Soviet influence through at least Communist cooperation with the Ba'ath. In fact, however, the far superior position of the Ba'ath meant that the Communists could at best be only a junior partner. Carefully guarding its power base, the Ba'ath placed a ban on Communist activities, including recruitment, in the army and the government. In the eyes of many Syrian Communists, therefore, this cooperation with the Ba'ath was actually at the expense of the Communist Party. Such opposition to Moscow's orders led to a split in the party, with the dissenters breaking away. Nonetheless, when the Ba'ath did agree to Moscow's urgings for a National Front in 1972, Khalid Bakdesh led the Communist Party into the arrangement.

As the Yom Kippur War approached, Soviet–Syrian relations experienced similar if less severe strains as in the Egyptian case. There were Syrian complaints about the quantities and types of Soviet weapons provided prior to the war, although it is not certain that Assad was as demanding and disappointed as Sadat regarding newer surface-to-surface missiles, for example. During the war the Syrians successfully used the shorter-ranged FROG missiles, but they did not appear to have received any SCUDs, as the Egyptians had, prior to the war. Despite the steady stream of Soviet deliveries to Syria in the spring of 1973, which included MIG-21s and SAM-6 equipment, Assad hinted publicly that he was dissatisfied with the Soviets' arms policies. Shortly after this, Soviet air force chief Marshal Kutakhov led a delegation to Syria in May, presumably to assess Syrian capabilities and perhaps needs. Yet following the Syrian loss of thirteen aircraft in a scrap with the Israeli air force in September there were reportedly angry Syrian demands for MIG 23s.

In view of the arms deliveries in the spring, and the transport of Moroccan troops to Syria on Soviet vessels, in April and again in July, as well as Soviet media claims of hostile Israeli troop movements on the Syrian border, it appeared that there was greater Soviet–Syrian agreement over war plans than there was with Cairo. Yet, it appears that Assad made a secret trip to Moscow in May, at which time he was urged by the Soviets to postpone any war plans pending the upcoming summit in Washington. Somewhat stronger Soviet opposition to the war was reportedly expressed by Soviet Politburo member Kirilenko during his early July visit to Damascus for the opening of the Euphrates Dam. Assad was said to have been angry that the Soviets had not sent one of its three top leaders, as it had for the opening of the Aswan Dam, for example, but Syrian anger may have been more pointedly aroused by Kirilenko's message of continued Soviet opposition to the war. Some ten Soviet officials were actually declared *personnae non grata* and sent home from Damascus following the 13 September air battle with Israel, and a decided strain in relations was clearly developing, however much one might explain the publicity as simply disinformation to lull Israel into complacency.

There were, nonetheless, some signs of greater Soviet–Syrian than Soviet–Egyptian cooperation at this time, for example, the terrorist operation against Soviet Jewish *émigrés* in Austria, which was carried out by Palestinians belonging to the Syrian-sponsored Sai'qa group. The fact that the operation originated in Czechoslovakia, was Sai'qa's first overseas operation, and was meant to serve Soviet interests (reduction of Austrian cooperation with the emigration effort) all strongly suggested Soviet collusion. Moreover, according to the Soviets, though denied by Syrian sources, Moscow explicitly arranged with Damascus that the Soviet Union propose a cease-fire forty-eight hours after the outbreak of hostilities. This arrangement may have been worked out only on 4 October when the Syrians informed the Soviets of the exact time of the planned attack (the previous day Sadat had told them only that hostilities were imminent), but even so it would indicate a greater degree of coordination than was the case with the Egyptians.

During the war itself, there may have been less Soviet contact with Damascus than with Cairo, possibly because it was Sadat rather than Assad who, according to the Soviets, was refusing the Soviet bid for an early cease-fire. The Soviets did provide arms and equipment during the war, though somewhat less than that supplied to Egypt. Moscow also organized the supply of tanks from Iraq. Israeli hits on Soviet property and transport in Syria, including the sinking of a Soviet merchant ship in the port of Tartus, as well as the relatively rapid reversal of the Syrians' early victories prompted both the beginning of the airlift operation and Soviet political and diplomatic activity, until the Egyptians found themselves in even greater trouble (after the failure of the Sinai tank battle of 14 October).

For all that the Soviets were in close touch with and directly responded to the fortunes of the Syrian army, they were accused by Assad of neglecting to consult with him. He complained shortly after the war that the Soviet–American cease-fire proposal in the UN caught him by surprise, preventing the execution of what he claimed were plans with Iraq to launch a counter-offensive. Moreover, the Soviet–US sponsored resolution 338 called for the implementation of resolution 242 which had not yet been accepted by Damascus.

However genuine Syrian dissatisfaction with Moscow, it was nowhere near as great as that of Egypt. Nor did it occasion any deterioriation in Soviet–Syrian relations. On the contrary, Moscow compensated Damascus, partially also in response to the problems it continued to have with Sadat, by quickly and generously rearming the Syrians. These post-war deliveries included SCUDs and even the long-demanded MIG-23s, as well as the most advanced Soviet tanks and more SAM-6s. They were to a large degree financed by hard currency payments from Saudi Arabia, but when Damascus had difficulty meeting payment, the Soviets declared a moratorium on the debt. They refused to do the same for Sadat. In addition to the post-war arms, Moscow increased the number of its military advisers in Syria by approximately 3000.

Soviet–Syrian relations over the next years were characterized by conflicts or disagreements in a number of areas, including some quite basic to both Soviet and Syrian policies. In the area of the Arab–Israeli conflict, the more immediate issue was the Geneva Conference in December 1973, following the war. Syria simply refused to attend.

Inasmuch as the Soviet Union had been the initiator and co-sponsor of the Conference together with the United States, the Syrian refusal was a blow to Moscow's prestige as well as plans. Moreover it would appear that the Syrians' refusal came as a surprise to the Soviets, for Soviet media reported that the Syrians would attend, and the Syrian Communist Party publicly supported the convening of Geneva. A few years later, in 1975, the Soviets admitted that there were differences between the two countries on the issue of a conference, although there were also instances in the late 1970s and 1980s upon which Damascus expressed support for an international conference, presumably to please Moscow at least verbally.

The reason for the Syrian opposition to the Conference was the more fundamental disagreement with Moscow's positions on the existence of the State of Israel and, therefore, negotiations with this state. The first and third parts of Moscow's three-pronged position (Israeli withdrawal, Palestinian state, guarantees for all states) implied recognition of Israel, and challenged Syria's interests in United or Greater Syria or at the very least territorial claims beyond the 1967 lines. The differences on this matter were particularly clear when Syrian leaders visited Moscow, with the Soviets often emphasizing the specific borders referred to in the withdrawal clause and specifying Israel, by name, when speaking of guarantees for all states in the area. Similarly the Soviets made it quite clear that they preferred negotiations over military measures, opposing even the War of Attrition initiated by the Syrians on the Golan front in 1974 and later pointedly remarking in the presence of Syrian delegations that there was no military solution to the conflict in the Middle East.

Other areas of disagreement included the issue of détente and Syrian as well as Soviet relations with the West. Like Egypt, and other Third World states, Syria feared what it saw as a possible Soviet sellout of Syrian interests for the sake of Moscow's interest in cooperation with the United States. Repeated Soviet reassurances to Damascus on this point were, in fact, proof that there was Syrian concern. There was, however, also Soviet concern over just the opposite problem, that is, over the possibility of a Syrian–American rapprochement. Given Syria's more rejectionist position, the Soviets may have been less fearful that Damascus would emulate the Egyptian and even the less direct PLO moves towards Washington. Yet there were contacts between Washington and Damascus, such as the visit of President Nixon to the Middle East in 1974, and the opening of interest sections in the two countries, visits of the Syrian Foreign Minister Khaddem to

Washington in 1977. There were American–Syrian contacts over the possibility of a second Syrian-Israeli agreement similar to the Interim Agreement signed between Israel and Egypt in 1975, and Syria also began diversifying arms suppliers as well as trade, shopping in western Europe. These alarming signs prompted Moscow to warn the Syrians to distinguish between genuine friends and foes; it also urged Damacus once again to sign a Treaty of Friendship. Assad's continued independence on this point was further evidenced by his behaviour regarding Lebanon, as we shall see below, which included Syrian–American cooperation in defiance of Moscow.

Syria's relations with other Arab states, particularly Iraq, were often a source of difficulty for the Soviet Union as well. Syria and Iraq were at odds over a number of issues, such as the use of the Euphrates River, but the central cause of their mutual animosity was the fact that rival ideological factions of the Ba'ath movement ruled in each country. This was a source of concern to the Soviets when the competition threatened conflict, such as the time in 1975 when Syria moved to defend Kuwait in an Iraqi–Kuwaiti border crisis. Thus Moscow was often placed in the difficult position of facing two client states, both radical regimes formally or informally allied with the Soviet Union, at loggerheads, even open conflict with each other.

Beyond periodically complicating Soviet relations with each of the two, the Syrian–Iraqi hostility also impeded Soviet efforts to form a bloc of the radical states in the region. Even before Sadat's trip to Jerusalem, Moscow had sought the creation of an anti-Egyptian coalition, to include Syria, Iraq, the PLO and South Yemen. Syrian–Iraqi refusal to cooperate with each other interfered with this plan. In 1977 Syria accused Iraq of planning an assassination attempt against Foreign Minister Khaddem and, even as Sadat was visiting Jerusalem, Syria closed its border with Iraq, preventing any cooperation in the anti-Sadat campaign which followed.

There was a brief Syrian–Iraqi rapprochement after the Camp David accords were signed, but Moscow was skeptical and surprisingly unenthusiastic about it. One reason may have been that the Soviets were unable to gain Syrian agreement to what was apparently a Soviet attempt to exploit the rapprochement for greater control over the two countries' policies. Moscow reportedly proposed a tripartite committee, composed of Iraq, Syria and the Soviet Union to coordinate arms deliveries and, presumably, use. The plan, however, constituted a refusal of Syrian requests for more aircraft, in favour of Iraq, on the grounds that the two (with Moscow) would be working together. Thus

Moscow's view of Syrian–Iraqi cooperation was one which would accord the Soviets greater leverage, while Assad's was that the partnership might accord him greater strength and, therefore, independence from Moscow. The rapprochement did not last beyond the summer of 1979.

The most serious Soviet–Syrian differences occurred in connection with the Syrian invasion of Lebanon in 1976. As we have seen Moscow opposed this move for a number of reasons. The Soviets perceived it as an act of Syrian aggrandizement which would augment Assad's independence. Although it could be argued conversely that the invasion upset certain forces inside Syria, weakening Assad's own power base, while it overextended Syrian armed forces, and isolated Syria in the Arab world, at least among the more radical states. Whether it did or did not in fact weaken Assad, the Syrian move was viewed in Moscow as a sample of Assad's aspirations or perhaps pretensions for expansion of Syrian power. It was all the more unacceptable because it served certain American interests, providing a basis for Syrian cooperation with the United States. Indeed Saudi Arabia reportedly had cut off aid to Syria with the demand that it take steps in Lebanon to reach the Americans. And, in fact, Washington was to characterize the Syrian invasion as a 'constructive' act. In addition to the American side, there was also the danger of Syrian clashes with Israel, for Jerusalem could not be expected to view the expansion of Syrian forces into Lebanon with equanimity. At the same time the Soviets had to cope with the dilemma not only of fighting between two of its unofficial allies, Syria and the PLO, but of open military assistance provided by Syria to the Lebanese Christians in their battle against the Soviet-favoured Lebanese leftists and the PLO.

There were signs of Soviet annoyance with Syria's intermittent interventions in Lebanon between January and June 1976, but the real rift came over the massive intervention which began on 31 May–1 June, just as Soviet Premier Kosygin was en route from Iraq to Damascus as part of a Middle Eastern tour. Kosygin's comments before departing Iraq suggested Soviet opposition to any outside intervention; indeed there were some claims that Kosygin's trip was designed to stop a move by Assad. The Syrians may, therefore, have timed their move to prevent Soviet interference. In any case, Kosygin was reportedly angered by having been confronted with a *fait accompli* which left Moscow few alternatives for reacting.

There was speculation that the Soviets were not in fact opposed to what they thought was a limited, brief incursion, and they therefore refrained from condemning the move until it was clear that the Syrian forces were involved in a much more prolonged and broader action. There may even have been some differences of opinion within the Kremlin in response to the move, for *Izvestiia* refrained from criticism over the following weeks. Such hesitation would be easy enough to understand. Egypt had just abrogated its treaty with Moscow, and the Soviets cannot have been anxious to alienate another Arab state. Nor was there sufficient commitment to the struggling Lebanese left or even to the PLO to warrant jeopardizing relations with a radical Soviet client state such as Syria.

Yet the negative consequences of the invasion outweighed these reservations, leading to increasingly strong Soviet condemnation of the invasion and of continued Syrian action in Lebanon. *Pravda* even called it a stab in the back of the Palestinian movement, while the Soviet leadership dispatched a letter to Assad urging him to withdraw his forces. Beyond these admonitions the Soviets suspended arms deliveries to Syria for the remainder of the year, and no new arms agreement was negotiated between the two states until over a year later. In retaliation the Syrians expelled a large number of Soviet military advisers and, in January, ordered the Soviets to remove their naval vessels from the port of Tartus.

Moscow did not, however, become more directly involved in the Lebanon crisis. As we have seen, it did not provide the Palestinians with the aid they requested against the Syrians. Rather the Soviets advocated an immediate cease-fire, attempting to mediate and even supporting efforts by Saudi Arabia to bring the combatants to an agreement. The Soviets obviously had an interest in ending the polarization of its two clients and preventing the risks involved, particularly the risk of Syrian–American cooperation (as well as the Syrian–Egyptian rapprochement which was developing in the course of this crisis). Moscow also claimed that an end to the conflict was essential so as to bring attention back to the Arab-Israeli issue. While this was convenient propaganda it was also true inasmuch as there were renewed efforts at this time to reconvene the Geneva conference, and continued Syrian–PLO hostilities would hardly facilitate such a step.

The net result of the Syrian intervention in Lebanon for Soviet–Syrian relations was still greater Syrian independence *vis à vis* Moscow. Syrian relations with Washington gained momentum, with Assad making an official visit to the United States in 1977. Saudi Arabian–Egyptian–Syrian cooperation emerged in the Saudi-sponsored negotiations for a cease-fire; Syria also achieved a rapprochement with Jordan, which approved of any moves against the PLO. The Syrians extended their sphere of influence in Lebanon, at the expense of a weakened PLO. And Soviet pressures, through suspension of arms deliveries, were proven to be as ineffectual an instrument for influencing Assad as they had been with regard to Sadat some years earlier.

Once a cease-fire was achieved and, most importantly, Syria shifted to fighting the Lebanese Christians rather than the Left and the PLO, Soviet relations with Damascus were able gradually to return to normal. A contributing factor was undoubtedly the cooling of the nascent US–Syrian relationship in the summer and autumn of 1977, but the one event which triggered renewed cooperation was the American mediated Egyptian–Israeli peace talks following Sadat's visit to Jerusalem. Certain problems remained, however, in particular over Soviet arms deliveries. The Soviets were demanding payment, and Syria's hard currency sources such as Libya and Saudi Arabia were not always as forthcoming as necessary. The Soviets did, finally, write off 25 per cent of the estimated $2 billion debt in 1979. Beyond the financial side, the Soviets were resistant to Syrian demands for certain types of advanced weapons systems, including, according to some reports, demands for a nuclear capability.

While the arms issue was probably the major complaint the Syrians had, they reportedly sought, and publicly claimed to have already, greater Soviet commitment to their forces in Lebanon, particularly when Israel made a brief campaign into southern Lebanon in 1978. Irritants of lesser importance also appeared over issues such as Soviet suppression of the Eritrean rebellion supported by Syria, and other Arab parties, in Ethiopia. Yet Assad continued to resist Soviet pressures to enter into a treaty, specifically right after Camp David in October 1978 and again during his visit to Moscow in October 1979, despite or perhaps because of dissatisfaction over the Soviet response to Syrian grievances. These unsuccessful Soviet attempts to gain some control over Syrian policies may have been spurred by the Syrian repression of local Communists after the 1978 Marxist coups in South Yemen and Afghanistan (although there was no sign that Syrian Communists were planning similar measures).

Assad finally changed his mind and signed a Treaty of Friendship and Cooperation with the Soviet Union in October 1980. As far as can be determined it was not the result of any change in Soviet policies but rather a Syrian response to its own problems. Assad was faced with internal dissent including serious riots, particularly from anti-Ba'ath religious quarters such as the Muslim Brotherhood, but also simply in response to the abuses of the ruling minority, Alawis. Weakened at home, the Assad regime was becoming increasingly isolated once again in the Arab world, mainly because of its policies in Lebanon. It was at odds, occasionally even blows, with both Iraq and Jordan, and losing Saudi Arabia's support. Syria was now vulnerable as a result of the Egyptian–Israeli peace, which eliminated Israel's western front. Thus it was a weakened Assad who turned to Moscow in 1980.

From the Soviet point of view, the Friendship Treaty was at least some gain for Soviet policy as against the American successes of Camp David and the Egyptian–Israeli peace treaty. It also helped to counter Muslim criticism in the wake of the November 1979 Soviet invasion of Afghanistan. Indeed Syria was most cooperative in opposing condemnation and spearheading support for the Soviets with regard to Afghanistan. It abstained in the UN vote condemning the invasion, and it refused to attend the Islamic Conference devoted to the subject on the grounds that Syria's priorities lay with the struggle against Zionism.

Yet, even though Moscow had long sought and could derive benefits from the Treaty with Damascus, there were a number of reasons to give the matter some new consideration. The very reasons that prompted Assad to agree to the Treaty were those which may have given the Soviets second thoughts. Assad had been seriously weakened; the future of his regime was uncertain. The Soviet press even mentioned on one occasion that the era of stability in Damascus was over. Syria's isolation in the Arab world meant that the Soviets could expect to derive little benefit there from the alliance. The Soviet leadership had three options: to lower their profile with regard to Syria and await the new regime; to continue business as usual with Assad, despite the signs of the regime's decline; or to exploit the regime's weakened position to gain some leverage over the annoyingly independent Assad. Moscow chose the last option, probably on the basis of the evaluation that there were no readily available alternatives to Assad, domestically, nor to Syria, in the region, as allies for Moscow. Assad was anti-American, and in need of Soviet support. Both of these were factors which boded well for Moscow's policies.

There were signs, however, that the Soviets did not expect to gain much from the alliance, and did not give very much. There were no arms concessions of any significance. Syrian grumbling on these matters continued, as Libya assisted in the payments demanded by

Moscow (for example, $1,000 million, reportedly, in 1980). Syrian claims to the contrary, there were also no significant commitments made in the Treaty. It did not provide for Soviet intervention on behalf of Syria but rather said that in case of aggression, the two states would 'immediately enter into contact with each other with a view toward coordinating their positions and cooperating in order to remove the threat which has arisen and restore peace'.

As we have seen from the Lebanon crisis, beginning with the installation of Syrian missiles in Lebanon in the spring of 1981 and culminating in the Israeli invasion, the Soviet–Syrian Treaty provided neither the Soviets with control nor the Syrians with direct Soviet military assistance. The Syrian moves were apparently carried out without Soviet knowledge. Moreover, claims by the Syrians that Moscow would intervene on Syria's behalf were met with explicit denial by the Soviet Ambassador to Beirut that there was any connection between the Syrian presence in Lebanon and the Treaty. Following the Israeli war in Lebanon in 1982 Soviet advisers did spend time with Syrian forces in Lebanon, but all indications, including direct Soviet statements, were that Syria could not expect any direct Soviet assistance outside Syrian territory.

Following the war, and probably in compensation for the relative Soviet inactivity, Moscow did provide qualitatively new equipment, specifically SS-21s and SAM-5s, as well as replacements for the SAM-6s and other equipment lost. Initially Soviet personnel were sent to man these systems, which were also believed to be linked directly with the Soviet military command in southern Russia. Sometime later, however, when Syrian personnel were trained, this large contingent of advisers left. This would suggest that the Soviets did not significantly improve their direct control over Syrian military moves.

The post-Lebanon War arms deliveries and build-up of the Syrian army notwithstanding, Soviet–Syrian relations continued to be characterized by serious strains. Moscow apparently had some difficulties restraining the Syrians during the tension-filled months of the Israeli occupation of Lebanon, of particular concern while US forces were still in the area. Once these threats were relieved, the Soviets still had to contend with Syria's more bellicose policies *vis-à-vis* Israel, and particularly the Syrian demand for a new type of Soviet commitment. Assad apparently sought nuclear guarantees for Syria or some promise of Soviet intervention or enough supplies to create what the Syrians saw as strategic parity with Israel, or all of these things.

In addition, the Soviets did not fully accept Syria's influence in

Lebanon, preferring to deal directly with the government and the parties involved even to the point of insulting Syrian officials in Beirut. Indeed the Soviets were not always on the same side as the Syrians in the kaleidoscope of Lebanese factions, ethnic groups, and armed formations, especially when these included Islamic terrorist organizations. As we have seen, the Soviets also withheld support from the Syrian effort to take over the PLO, unseat Arafat and assist the rebels within the Palestinian camp. When Moscow finally succeeded in mediating a Palestinian reunification, it was not pleased with Assad's continued hostility. Somewhat different, but also a sign of diverging interests, was the Syrian opposition to Soviet efforts to improve relations with both Egypt and Jordan immediately after the war. At the same time, the Soviets were also shifting to Iraq in the Iran–Iraq conflict, resuming arms supplies to Baghdad and voicing criticism of Tehran. The latter continued to be supported by Damascus.

These differences, indeed tensions between Moscow and Damascus, were apparent during the various trips to Moscow by Syrian leaders, while Assad's failing health did little to strengthen the Soviets' confidence in the stability of their problematic relationship with Syria. Thus even as the Soviets found over the years that they had increasingly to rely on the Syrians as their only ally in the Arab–Israeli context, indeed their only state ally (aside from the virtually inconsequential South Yemenis) in the Middle East, they remained at loggerheads over a number of essential issues. Their mutual dependence had little to no effect on their conflicting objectives and interests; nor did it significantly restrict the actions or change the positions of either side. For this reason it remained uncertain, possibly to the Syrians themselves, just how far the Soviet commitment would go, in the case of armed conflict with Israel, for example, or in the conditions of negotiations with Jerusalem.

Similarly, Soviet leaders could be no more certain of their ability to prevent the Syrians from going to war or, conversely, to bring them to peace talks. Nor could they be certain of the future either of the regime or of its pro-Soviet orientation, particularly in view of Assad's personality and independence. For all of these reasons, perhaps, there were signs even in the months prior to Gorbachev's rise in the Kremlin, that Moscow hoped to broaden its options and friends in the area, even if this displeased Damascus. Under Gorbachev this was to transcend the realm of tactics, becoming theoretically rooted policy, the consequences of which, for Syria, were not entirely clear.

11 The Soviet Union and Iraq

Soviet interests in Iraq have been tied up with the fact that Iraq borders on a number of traditionally pro-western states: Jordan, Saudi Arabia, Kuwait, Turkey and Iran, the last two on the Soviets' own border. Its proximity not only to southern Russia but more directly to the Persian Gulf and the area of the Arab–Israeli conflict has heightened the country's strategic as well as political interests for Moscow. The pivotal role played by Iraq in' western alliance plans in the 1950s increased the importance of Baghdad. Its traditional rivalry with Egypt created certain possibilities for Soviet tactics in the region, be it the use of this rivalry to further Soviet–Egyptian relations in the period following Stalin's death, or the juggling of relations with Iraq as a lever on Egypt later in the 1950s or 1960s or even as a partial replacement for Egypt in the 1970s.

Since the 1960s, the anti-western ideology of Iraq's ruling Ba'ath Party has made the country a logical 'progressive' partner for Moscow. Its rejectionist position has given it something of a spoiler's power and leadership of the rejectionist camp, but with proper harnessing and exploitation this has also provided certain opportunities for the Soviets. Iraq's need for military assistance for its internal as well as external conflicts has made it a likely candidate for Soviet support, while its regional power, due to oil wealth and strong leadership, at various times has offered some advantages to the pursuit of Soviet policies in the area.

Soviet objectives with regard to Iraq have generally focused on keeping the country out of the western, mainly American, orbit, as well as seeking to gain a client-ally in competition with the West. In the military sphere the Soviets have sought to have Iraq look to the Soviet bloc rather than the West for arms, originally in order to create dependence but eventually also to gain hard currency profits. There has also been an interest in obtaining a naval base or at least facilities in the port of Umm Kasr. The Soviets did build a military infrastructure in Iraq, particularly Gulf bases and airfields which, theoretically, could be used for their own purposes. There have not been signs, however, that they were in fact ever permitted to do so in practice (with the exception of the Soviet airlift to Ethiopia in the late 1970s).

In the economic sphere, the Soviets eventually sought arms profits, and they had an interest of a kind in Iraqi oil. Moscow encouraged nationalization of the western oil companies in Iraq, and to promote this goal the Soviets provided an alternative market for Iraqi oil (in the early 1970s) as well as development aid and production assistance for Iraqi oil fields. The Soviets themselves were not in need of Iraqi oil and, by 1977, when Baghdad had succeeded in reviving its markets elsewhere, Soviet imports declined. This decline had been accelerated by Iraqi demands beginning in 1973 for hard currency payments from Moscow for these supplies.

In the political sphere, the Soviets sought an anti-western, anti-imperialist line from the Baghdad regime, as well as support for Soviet positions on such issues as Vietnam, Angola, Mozambique, disarmament, and other issues of East–West as well as regional interest. The Soviets saw a special role for Iraq in the Gulf, to help Moscow obtain a political foothold and bases. Iraq might also help the Soviets destabilize and/or thus promote a leftist or anti-western shift in the orientation of the Gulf states. This could be achieved by Soviet support for Iraqi encouragement of and aid to dissident groups such as the Arabs of Khuzistan in Iran or the Dhofar rebels in Oman (as well as the Eritreans in Ethiopia prior to the Ethiopian revolution of 1974). There was even a period of support for the Shi'a clergy and for Communists in Saudi Arabia. At the least Iraq could help Moscow sow opposition to the conservative regimes in the Gulf, such as that of Saudi Arabia, Kuwait, the United Arab Emirates and Bahrain.

While this may constitute a positive picture of what the Soviets hoped to achieve through Iraq over the years, many of the same interests and objectives have proven problematic, sometimes contradictory. There have also been a number of central issues which have been the source of serious dispute as well as interest to the Soviets in their relations with Baghdad. One of these was the Communist Party of Iraq, which the Soviet Union sought to protect if not actually promote. The Party was legalized and included in a National Front with the ruling Ba'ath in 1973, upon encouragement from the Soviet Union. This reflected the customary Soviet interest in preparing the ground for future Communist progress, pursued on a parallel basis with Soviet interests in state-to-state relations. Thus the party might even be brought into the government.

The question, however, was just how far would Moscow be willing to go in order to further the interests of the local party, particularly in the case of a clash with the government. In Iraq this problem was further complicated by the issue of the Kurdish minority, for many if not most of the members of the Iraqi Communist Party were themselves Kurds. They strongly supported the Kurdish rebellion even to the point of splitting off from the Party when Soviet policies dictated abandonment of the Kurdish cause. As we shall see, the Soviets tended to exploit Baghdad's Kurdish problem, possibly in order to create Iraqi dependence. Indeed it has been speculated that the Soviets aided in the suppression of the Kurds in the early 1970s in exchange for Iraqi agreement to create a National Front with the Communists. Yet the Communist Party also posed serious problems for Moscow in the latter's effort to maintain good relations with Baghdad, particularly in periods of Ba'ath oppression and periodic crack-downs, jealousy and rivalry with the Communists. On balance the Communists probably created more problems for the Soviets than influence or hope of influence for Moscow in Iraq.

The issue of the non-Arab Kurdish minority constituting 25 per cent of the population in Iraq has long been a source of serious internal conflict in the country. For a number of years the leadership and many of the members of the Kurdish national liberation movement found refuge, and training, in exile in the Soviet Union and Eastern Europe. Presumably equipped as well as trained, they returned to Iraq when the monarchy was overthrown in 1958. The Soviet Union advocated autonomy for the Kurds, rather than independence, for it rarely if ever supported fully secessionist demands. In fact Moscow usually portrayed what were in fact secessionist or separatist movements as national liberation movements seeking only autonomy.

Support for the Kurds suited Moscow's general policy of support for national liberation movements whereby the Soviets nurtured and assisted them, creating a stake in them as future allies. But such support was usually subject to tactical considerations, allocated when useful, denied when inconvenient. The tactical or instrumental approach was all the more applicable with regard to separatist movements, support for which was almost entirely a function of Moscow's interests and relations with the local central government. The ideological character of the movement was of only marginal importance for the Soviet Union. Although a large portion of the Communists were

Kurds, most Kurds were not Communists. In fact, the Communist Party was an alternative but not a substitute for the Kurdish national movement. And the national movement itself was not Marxist. Support for the Kurdish movement in Iraq was useful, nonetheless, not only for local purposes, for it occasionally served Moscow's interests in other areas of Kurdish minorities, for example in Iran and Turkey. To some degree, therefore, the Soviets sought to keep Kurdish nationalism alive, for use against the regimes in these countries, although it was often the case that Kurds from Iran or Turkey had greater influence on the Iraqi situation than the other way round.

It is probably true that the Soviets used the Kurdish issue as a lever on whatever government ruled in Baghdad. When the regime was unfavourable to the Soviets and state-to-state relations were poor, there was Soviet support for the Kurdish struggle and use of the issue against the regime. When relations were good, support was abandoned, while Moscow manipulated its aid to the regime against the Kurds so as to gain Iraqi dependence. It has been speculated that the Soviets wanted some degree of continued Kurdish unrest in the North of Iraq, possibly even seeking to prolong the war there in the 1970s, so as to create an Iraqi need for Soviet arms, political assistance and Communist support for the regime in order to stay in power. Such a policy created problems for the Iraqi Communists, in view of their Kurdish loyalties, although local Communists were usually but pawns in the service of Moscow's broader interests. It might also be argued that Soviet assistance to the government against the Kurds served to enhance the Party's position vis-à-vis the government. A somewhat Machiavellian view would have it that the Soviets not only welcomed ongoing unrest from the Kurds but actually encouraged it when Moscow–Baghdad relations declined, for example in the late 1970s.

The tactical nature of Soviet support did mean that the Soviet Union aided the government against the Kurds when asked, and they did sacrifice the Kurds for the sake of broader regional even global interests better served by the central government in Baghdad. Thus the Soviets never permitted the Kurdish issue to interfere with or harm Soviet–Iraqi relations; they supported the Kurds' demands only up to a point, never going beyond the idea of autonomy at most. They aided the government, militarily, in suppressing the Kurds in 1974, profiting from the Iraqi dependence upon this assistance. It has even been claimed that the Soviets manipulated this dependence to force an Iraq–Iran agreement in 1975, according to Iraqi leader Saddam

Hussein, withholding arms from Iraq which could not, alone, handle the Iranian-supported Kurds. By the same token, however, the Iraqi government was said to have become less friendly to Moscow in the late 1970s when it was no longer in need of Moscow's aid against the Kurds, and Iran.

The third major source of disagreement between the two countries was the Arab–Israeli conflict. As in the case of Soviet relations with Egypt and Syria, Moscow utilized this conflict as a means of opening and consolidating relations with Iraq. This was especially so when an anti-colonial appeal became less effective (following Iraqi independence and the revolution of 1958, as Iraqi Ba'ath emphasis on anti-colonialism became less pronounced). At the same time, and similarly to the other cases of Soviet–Arab cooperation, Moscow's use of the Arab–Israeli conflict could be risky, leading to encouragement of too bellicose a position. Although Iraq was not a direct combatant, it could influence as well as assist the parties involved, increasing the tension and volatility of an already volatile situation. Iraq was particularly dangerous because of its strong rejectionist position, contrary to Soviet positions. Thus it categorically opposed resolutions 242 and 338, including the cease-fire of the Yom Kippur War and the 1970 cease-fire in the War of Attrition; it opposed the Geneva Conference and any negotiations with Israel; it opposed the existence of the state of Israel altogether and was not interested in Israeli withdrawal only to the 4 June 1967 lines.

Baghdad was also more radical than Moscow on the Palestinian issue, supporting Palestinian terrorism and extremist factions, and it favoured the continued strife in Lebanon in the 1970s. These positions were not necessarily translated into deeds. For example, in the 1973 war the Soviets asked Iraq to send Syria 500 tanks but Iraq responded with less; in 1970 Iraqi forces in Jordan refrained from helping the Palestinians (this restraint was not a problem for the Soviets), and there was no Iraqi assistance during the trials and tribulations of Lebanon. Until the Camp David accords Iraqi rejectionism created obstacles for Soviet policies, such as efforts to reconvene the Geneva Conference or to moderate the Palestinians. After Camp David the Soviets were more tolerant of Iraqi intransigence, especially since Iraq played a major role in organizing Arab opposition to Egypt. Even then, however, Iraqi unwillingness to cooperate with various elements, even in the radical Arab camp, caused difficulties. And ultimate Soviet–Iraqi objectives in the Arab–Israeli context were not compatible. Iraq might cooperate with the Soviet Union in blocking

American mediation and successes, but Iraq's reasons were to prevent any settlement whatsoever with Israel, while Moscow's motives were to achieve participation in such settlement.

Still another source of conflict between the two countries was Iraqi Ba'athism. As in the case of the other issues (the Kurds, the Arab–Israeli conflict, even the Communist Party), there were both negative and positive aspects of Ba'athism in the eyes of the Soviet leadership. On the positive side, Ba'ath ideology was progressive, even socialist in orientation. It was not, however, 'scientific socialism' of the Soviet variety nor even Marxist. The Ba'ath rejected class struggle in favour of national unity of all classes and strata. Rather, the Ba'ath version of socialism, particularly the Iraqi wing of the Ba'ath as distinct from the more leftist Syrian wing, was perceived by the Soviets as some form of utopian state interventionism or welfarism, far removed from the Soviet model. Indeed from the Iraqi Ba'ath point of view, Communism was seen as a foreign, alien, sometimes even detrimental element to Arab history and culture. Friendship with the Soviet bloc was proclaimed in the 1968 Ba'ath programme, but this was to be posited on the basis of the mutual anti-imperialist struggle rather than any ideological affinity.

If Ba'ath socialism were not an entirely positive facet of Ba'ath ideology, two other components of that ideology were even less promising for the Soviets. The first was the idea of unity, specifically Arab unity, in the form of Pan-Arabism or Arab nationalism. These could be helpful forces when countering western imperialism, that is, the United States or Israel. However, it also implied an exclusivity which some Soviet theoreticians have even called racism. Thus Moscow sought to emphasize the anti-imperialist platform for unity rather than the purely Arab or nationalist interpretation. Similarly the Iraqi Ba'ath belief in freedom and independence could be problematic. Insofar as this was intended as independence from western imperialism, nationalization of foreign companies and the like, it was positive. But it also had a xenophobic streak, which could lead the Iraqis jealously to guard their freedom of action and independence from the Soviet Union as well.

It is unlikely that most of these issues or problems were entirely clear to the Soviet Union when it began its relationship with Iraq in 1958. Moscow could but welcome the revolution which brought the Ba'athists under Abd-al-Karim Kassem to power that year. Kassem took Iraq out of the Baghdad Pact in 1959, adhering to the Bandung non-aligned movement and adopting an anti-western position. The new regime also promised democratic reforms, which could mean freedom of action for the Communist Party. Indeed Kassem was in need of Communist support to consolidate the regime in the post-revolutionary domestic instability. The move away from the West also provided an opening for Moscow to become Iraq's new arms supplier, and the first Soviet–Iraqi arms deal was signed in November 1958. The timing of the revolution was also fortuitous, for it prevented Iraqi intervention in the Lebanon crisis in the summer of 1958, although there were fears in Moscow that the American intervention in Lebanon, and the British return to Jordan, might also lead to western intervention to protect their interests in Iraq against the new regime. The Soviets, therefore, accompanied their declarations of support for the new regime with mild warnings that 'the peace-loving peoples will come to the aid' of Iraq in case of attack.

An issue that drew the Soviet Union and the new regime together but also posed problems for Moscow, was the Egyptian–Iraqi rivalry in the Arab world. On the one hand, both Arab states could now be counted among Moscow's unofficial allies, and the Soviets did not want to be in the position of having to choose between them. Yet, on the other hand, Egyptian plans for a united Arab state, to include Iraq, were also alarming to the Soviets, for such a unit would in effect be an Egyptian empire under Nasser, closing off channels of Soviet influence in the new radical state, much as indeed occurred with regard to Syria. Kassem in fact opposed union with Egypt and, in accordance with Moscow's interests, the Iraqi Communists supported Kassem's anti-Nasserism. This did little to endear Communism to Nasser, who undertook bloody anti-Communist actions in Egypt and Syria. This in turn strengthened Soviet support for Iraq in its competition with Egypt. Whether the Soviets actually preferred Iraq over Egypt at this time is difficult to determine. At the very least, Iraq did provide an alternative when Soviet relations with Egypt sharply deteriorated at the end of the 1950s.

The positive relationship with Iraq did not last long, however, for Kassem turned on the Communists in 1960; in response to a local incident, he accused them of attempting a coup, and began a serious crack-down. There had been no coup attempt, and the Soviets had supported Kassem on the specific incident (a massacre which took place in the northern town of Kikuk, which in effect constituted a challenge to Kassem's ability to maintain order). Nonetheless the Soviets had to face what was to be a common dilemma: to support the local Communists under persecution, if not by terminating relations with the regime then by taking some drastic steps, such as suspension of arms supplies, or, rather, to opt for favourable relations with the regime and ignore the plight of the Communists. A middle road was chosen; some mild criticism of the regime was expressed but no drastic moves were undertaken.

While relations with Kassem became strained the Soviets continued to support Iraq regionally, in such things as the Iraqi dispute with Iran in 1960 and the dispute with Kuwait in 1961. A still more important sign of continued Soviet support despite the plight of the local Communists, was the lack of Soviet assistance to the Kurdish rebellion in 1961, which did receive support from the Iraqi Communists. Thus Moscow strove to maintain relations with Kassem, preferring his anti-western positions over the local Communists – whose chances for gaining power were in any case quite slim. It was Kassem, however, who moved away from the Soviet Union, becoming increasingly anti-Communist, anti-Soviet and far less radical in domestic policies, as well as weaker politically.

In February 1963 Kassem was overthrown, but a right-wing Ba'ath regime came to power, bringing relations with Moscow to a virtual halt. This was a regime of nine months of bloody suppression of the Communists; three thousand were said to have been killed. Soviet arms supplies ceased altogether, and Moscow offered assistance to the Kurds. This was clearly meant as a lever against the new regime, but the blossoming Sino-Soviet dispute was probably a contributing factor to the Soviets' inability to refrain from any response to the violence against the Communists. Another coup in November brought an end to the bloodshed and a slight improvement in relations. Moscow was cautious; some persecution of the Communists and the Kurds continued, although there was no open fighting. The new regime was independent of Egypt but favoured good relations – a policy now supported by Moscow in the aftermath of the failure of Nasser's united Arab idea. Moreover the new regime instituted some economic measures of a socialist nature, at least nationalizations. For these reasons, Moscow declared the regime a progressive one and resumed arms deliveries and economic aid in June 1964. These relations continued until the right-wing Ba'ath returned to power in 1968 under Ahmad Hassan Bakr. There was some evidence of Soviet support for the Kurds in this period, but it was certainly neither large nor open.

Following the 1967 Arab–Israeli War the Soviets increasingly emphasized the Arab–Israeli conflict as a lever or basis for Soviet–Iraqi cooperation, perhaps in part because Iraq's own anti-imperialist rhetoric was down, reducing the expediency or appeal of Moscow for Baghdad in that sphere. It has been claimed that another bond in this period was Iraqi need for arms, not only against the Kurds (whom the Soviets were still helping to some degree) but also to supply Iraqi forces spread out in Jordan and Syria. The return of the right-wing Ba'ath to power did not, this time, destroy the links with Moscow; the Soviets even committed themselves to development of much of the Iraqi oil potential, in order to encourage Baghdad to evict western oil firms.

Actually Moscow's investment in Iraq in the 1960s was quite extensive. There were some 1300 Soviet military advisers in the country and over half a billion dollars' worth of military aid was granted by the end of 1967 alone. Following a visit by Soviet Defence Minister Grechko in 1968, Soviet vessels were able to use Iraqi ports in the Gulf. Iraq reached eighth among Moscow's Third World trading partners, fifth among recipients of Soviet economic aid and fourth or fifth for military aid. Baghdad was one of the five recipients in the Third World of a nuclear reactor built by the Soviet Union. And Iraq sent more students to the Soviet Union than any other Arab state.

Thus the Soviet Union had extensive relations with and a large stake in a country which could not even be described as progressive, in Soviet terms. The Communist Party was illegal, and the Kurds, supported by the Soviets, were still oppressed. The only explanation to this paradox lay in Soviet interests both in the military and political spheres. With the expansion of the Soviet fleet in the 1960s and the blue waters or forward-deployment policy, Moscow was interested in the naval facilities which Iraq could offer in the Gulf. This became all the more important after Britain announced its East of Suez withdrawal plans at the end of the 1960s. The Soviets also hoped to prevent any Iraqi defection to the West, especially when Iraq became interested in purchasing French arms. There was also the Soviet hope that Iraq would nationalize the western oil companies, thus further limiting the western presence in the Gulf.

There were problems of course, as Soviet–Iraqi interests diverged on a number of issues. The 1969 Iraqi dispute with Iran was not entirely welcomed by the Soviets, for they were improving their relations with the Shah and preferred not to alienate him. Thus Moscow took a neutral position in the dispute hoping mainly to forestall the outbreak of war, which might have the added negative effect of alarming the British into postponing their withdrawal. The 1968–70 Kurdish War also posed problems. The Soviets championed the Kurds' demand for autonomy, but they were relieved by and welcomed the resolution of the conflict in 1970, despite the fact that the agreement reached was not particularly favourable to the Kurds. It is possible that at this time, the Soviets thought that resolution of the Kurdish issue would alleviate some of Baghdad's suspicions regarding the Communists and, therefore, lead to a less hostile, perhaps even more cooperative attitude towards the Party. Indeed at this time the Soviets began to press the regime to agree to a National Front including the Communists. In December 1969 the government did bring in one person who was a clandestine Communist, but arrests and persecutions nonetheless continued – and were generally ignored by Moscow.

The differences over the Arab–Israeli conflict occasionally became apparent. Iraq opposed the 1970 cease-fire in the War of Attrition between Egypt and Israel. *Pravda* described the Iraqi attitude as 'negative' and 'incomprehensible'. Iraq persisted in its opposition to resolution 242, and it even disrupted the creation of a unified Arab bloc because its positions were so extreme. At the same time, Iraqi foreign policy took turns which clearly distressed Moscow, such as the exchange of ambassadors with China in 1970 and the opening towards France. With diversification of Iraqi foreign trade, the Soviet Union's share of Iraqi trade declined, while the western countries, particularly France, accounted for an increasing percentage in the early 1970s. Iraq was in need of outside assistance, and apparently was not willing to seek this only from Moscow, presumably for reasons of national independence as well as underlying suspicions regarding Communist intentions.

Soviet interests in Iraq increased, however, in the 1970s. The death of Nasser and the advent of Sadat to power in Egypt was a blow to Moscow. The gradual deterioration of relations with Egypt culminating in the expulsion of the Soviet advisers led the Soviets to look elsewhere to fortify their positions in the region. Iraqi rivalry with Egypt had already resulted in a convergence of Iraqi–Soviet interests in the Sudan, when Iraq was the only Arab state to support the partially Communist coup attempt in the summer of 1971. Iraq's hostility to Egypt thus made it a willing alternative as Moscow sought compensation for its losses in Egypt. Morever, Soviet interests in the 1970s were shifting to the Persian Gulf–Indian Ocean region, for a number of reasons, including the withdrawal of the British, Soviet naval expansion, and the search for more profitable economic relationships in the Third World. Iraq therefore gained in importance with regard to shifting Soviet priorities in the region.

The most significant step towards the advancement of these interests was the Treaty of Friendship and Cooperation achieved with Iraq in 1972. It was as vague as the treaty with Egypt on the question of Soviet commitments, but it may have been seen by the Soviets as a framework for securing its military interest in the port of Umm Kasr, for example. From the Iraqi point of view, the Treaty may have been a precondition for the nationalization of western oil companies, for it provided some backing should Iraq come under pressure from the companies' countries. The Soviet Union had been urging nationalization as a major step against the West. Indeed in the early 1970s the Soviets advocated nationalization, not price rises or even boycotts, as the best application of the 'oil weapon'. Inasmuch as the Treaty came in April and the nationalization of the Iraq Petroleum Company in June, it did appear as if the first step had provided the protection for the second step.

The Soviets paid for the nationalization, quite literally, for they took on the commitment of replacing the lost western markets for Iraqi oil, at least until Iraq readjusted its relations with its previous clients. And until Iraq demanded hard currency payments, at the new higher prices, for its oil. Moscow also agreed to assist Iraq in drilling, refining and developing the Iraqi oil fields and oil industry, including the supply of equipment and tankers lost by the nationalization. Shortly after this, the two countries negotiated a large arms agreement and, in the period 1972–5, Iraq actually doubled the size of its armed forces through the doubling of Soviet arms supplies. It was at this time, however, that the Soviets began demanding hard currency payment for their arms, so these moves were not entirely a sacrifice on the part of Moscow.

The Soviet Union was further rewarded by Iraqi agreement in 1973 to the creation of a National Front, which included the Communists. A measure for which the Soviets had been pressing for some time, it was finally agreed to by Bakr, according to some interpretations, only after the regime experienced a near-successful coup attempt in 1973, necessitating a stronger political base. The Communist Party was thus finally legalized, but it was hardly accepted by the ruling Ba'ath as an equal partner. The Communists were not permitted to operate or recruit in the army or any other Ba'ath stronghold. Thus, despite the inclusion of two Communists in the government, the Party was still hamstrung by the ruling Ba'ath. Saddam Hussein, the leading power in the Ba'ath, was particularly wary of the Communists, and as his influence grew the fortunes of the Communists could be expected to decline.

The Soviets were to pay for their new alliance with Iraq, in more than oil- and arms-related concessions. While presumably not an explicit quid pro quo, Soviet support for the regime in Baghdad against both Iran and the Kurds appeared to be the price for the close relationship. Iraqi relations with Iran deteriorated seriously following the November 1971 Iranian takeover of three islands in the Straits of Hamouz. In time fighting actually broke out between the two countries on Iraq's southeastern border with the Arab-populated Khuzistan area of Iran. In the meantime Iran was also assisting the Kurdish rebellion which had resumed in Iraq. A further Iraqi problem with Iran was the Dhofar rebellion in Oman, where the two Persian Gulf rivals, Iraq and Iran, supported opposing sides (Iraq the rebels, Iran the ruling Sultan). While Iran sent troops to assist the Sultan, Iraq threatened Kuwait, also protected by Iran, over the islands in Shatt-al-Arab in a crisis that developed in the spring of 1973. In all of these Iran–Iraq problems the Soviets supported Iraq faithfully, even to the point of providing arms and material assistance such as Soviet fleet movements in the Kuwaiti crisis, and the training and arming of the Dhofar rebels in the Omani war. (The latter was also intended by Moscow to please the South Yemenis as we shall see below.)

It has even been argued that Moscow not only sided with Iraq against Iran but actually welcomed these conflicts as opportunities for creating Iraqi dependence upon Soviet aid. Yet, there were clear signs that Moscow sought to avoid the prospect of Iran–Iraq war. Aside from the dangers involved in open hostilities, the Soviets were still interested in the positive trade relationship they had developed with the Shah, and they were still pursuing the neutralization of Iran. They therefore moderated their positions somewhat and sought to placate Iran as well as Iraq. Saddam Hussein claimed, in a 1981 interview, that the Soviets went even further, actually cutting off arms supplies in 1975 to force Iraq to bring its conflict with Iran to a halt – and accept an accord which was less favourable to Iraq than to Iran. Opposite accounts, however, claim that Moscow in fact increased its support to Iraq, in an arms agreement announced in early 1975, as pressure upon Iran to agree to a settlement. It is possible that both versions are correct, if the Soviet Union in fact negotiated an arms deal but suspended deliveries pending Iraqi agreement to the settlement, which was signed in March 1975. Western figures are actually contradictory, some showing a minor rise and others a significant decline in arms transfers to Iraq in 1975, with a significant rise only the following year.

Moscow probably faced a similar dilemma or conflict of interests over the prolongation or cessation of the Kurdish rebellion, presumably an interest in Iraqi dependence operating against at least a past commitment to the Kurds. With the gradual breakdown of the 1970 agreement, full-scale hostilities broke out in 1973–4. The Iraqi army had, apparently, opposed the agreement to begin with, and the Kurds, for their part, were encouraged by Iran reportedly with the idea of keeping the Iraqi army occupied while Iran modernized its armed forces. Whatever the circumstances, the Baghdad regime launched an offensive in 1974 against the Kurds and received direct Soviet military assistance. Moscow provided not only aircraft but also according to some reports, pilots to fly sorties against the Kurds.

This reversal of previous support for the Kurds, even to the point of intervening directly against them, was a clear measure of the stake which Moscow now had in the regime in Baghdad. It was, however, typical of the tactical nature of Moscow's relationship with national liberation movements in general and even more so with secessionist movements in particular. The Kurds could expect Soviet help so long as this served Moscow's interests. When, however, a conflict arose between Moscow's interests in the central government and the movement, the movement could no longer expect support. The total pragmatism of the Soviet choice was all the more evident when the Soviets took an active military role against the same movement, led by the same people they had protected, armed and supported in the past. Such positions were somewhat more difficult for the local Communists to accept, not only because this represented a reversal but perhaps mainly because a very large portion of the Party was of Kurdish origin. There were those, therefore, who split off and continued to assist the Kurds.

The 1975 agreement between Iran and Iraq brought an end to the Kurdish rebellion as well as to the Iran–Iraq conflict, for without Iranian help the Kurds were without hope. Since both conflicts had put Moscow in a difficult position, one may assume that the Soviets welcomed the agreement. As we have seen Saddam Hussein even attributed the agreement to Soviet arms blackmail (although his statement was made in 1981, during a period of renewed Iran–Iraq war when Moscow suspended arms supplies to Iraq). Moscow did not, perhaps could not, anticipate that the agreement and end of hostilities was destined to impair rather than improve its position in Baghdad. For Iraq was no longer in need of Soviet military assistance, at least not to the degree or in the fashion that it was supplied during the conflicts.

If Saddam Hussein is to be believed, Iraq had bitterly resented its dependence upon Soviet arms, and strove to maintain some degree of independence. Thus it had resisted Soviet urgings to soften its positions on the Arab–Israeli dispute, and it had gradually broadened its relations with the West, particularly France but also the United States, even as it drew closer to Moscow. When the immediate need for Soviet military assistance passed, after the 1975 accord, Iraq was also less in need of Soviet assistance in the economic sphere. The energy crisis stimulated western willingness to provide the services offered by Moscow to Iraq's petroleum industry, and Iraq was able to profit from the new wealth of petro-dollars. It even demanded the new higher prices from the Soviets, although the Soviets certainly had no need to pay them, having purchased Iraqi oil mainly as an incentive to Iraq to nationalize. With this Soviet imports of Iraqi oil were substantially curtailed. Less to the Soviets' liking, however, Iraq drastically reduced the Soviets' share in Iraqi foreign trade to just 10 per cent, less than that of western Europe and even of France alone.

There was a temporary convergence of Soviet–Iraqi interests during the Syrian invasion of Lebanon in 1976. Iraq sent a symbolic force (around 100 troops) to assist the PLO and Lebanese Left against Syria, and it massed troops on the Syrian–Iraqi border reportedly in order to force Syria to draw troops out of Lebanon. This Iraqi support for Moscow's own opposition to the Syrian intervention may have contributed to the Soviets' willingness to sign a large arms deal with Baghdad. The previous year, according to some accounts, the Soviets had put off signing any arms agreement. The new arms deal was, by all accounts, significantly larger than any previous arms deal with Iraq. The agreement provided Baghdad with SCUDs, SAM-6s, advanced tanks and MIGs. Yet relations were strained, over old issues and new. In the Arab–Israeli context, Iraq opposed the Soviet–American effort to reconvene Geneva and the joint statement of 1977; it shared Moscow's objections to Sadat's visit to Jerusalem but it walked out of the founding meeting of the Steadfastness Front in December 1977, obstructing a unified effort against Egypt and engaging in factional activities within the PLO as well as the Arab world at large. Iraq also opposed Soviet policies in the Horn of Africa at this time, objecting to Moscow's assistance to Mengistu against the Eritreans and Somalis, whom Baghdad continued to support.

None of this was sufficient, however, to bring about a crisis in the relationship. That came only in 1978 when Saddam Hussein initiated a crackdown on the Communists, culminating in accusations against the Soviet Union, on the grounds that a coup against his regime had been planned. In May 1978 twenty-one Communists were executed and a purge of Communists was begun in the army. They were accused of setting up cells in the army with the intention of staging a coup. Drawing a direct link with the Soviet Union which signalled a serious rift in Soviet–Iraqi relations, Saddam Hussein said, 'The Soviet Union sees its security in spreading Communism . . . they won't be satisfied until the whole world becomes Communist.'

A number of hypotheses are possible regarding this crisis between the two countries:

(1) The Soviets may actually have been planning a Communist takeover. Following the expulsion of the advisers from Egypt there was a rethinking of Soviet Third World policy and a turn to a more ideological and activist approach. This led to such things as the reactivization of the Communist Party in Egypt, assistance to the Dergue in Ethiopia and encouragement of the creation of a Marxist-Leninist party there. According to some, the Marxist coups in South Yemen and Afghanistan in 1978 were also the result of this policy change. Thus there may have been orders from Moscow to take similar action in Iraq. Moreover the Iraqi Communist Party had become critical of the regime, particularly with regard to such issues as the lack of Iraqi cooperation with the Steadfastness Front, Iraqi trade with the West, and the Iraqi rapprochement with Iran and the Gulf states. It was rumoured that the Communists had resumed aid to the Kurds.

(2) The Communists may not have been planning a coup but may have been active within the army, setting up cells and expanding their support.

(3) The Communists may have been stirring up Shi'a opposition to the minority highly secular regime. This hypothesis would connect the Communists with the Shi'a protests of 1977 in Iraq.

(4) Saddam Hussein may have been fearful that the coups in South Yemen and Afghanistan were a sign of things to come in his own country.

(5) The moves against the Communists may have been intended merely as a signal to Moscow of Iraq's opposition to the Soviets' policies in the Horn of Africa.

(6) Or, finally, Saddam Hussein's acts may simply have been the result of his customary suspicions of the Communists aggravated perhaps by any of the above hypothetical reasons.

There are no certain answers to these theories. As to what actually motivated Hussein, it is difficult to know if he truly believed that there was a takeover plot. The twenty-one Communists executed were arrested some months earlier, prior to the upheavals in South Yemen and Afghanistan, so there was no question of an immediate threat or alarm specifically in response to the Aden and Kabul events. The purges, however, were a bit too long and extensive to have been merely a signal over Mengistu. There were no signs that the Soviets were actually encouraging Communist uprisings in the Third World. They may have urged greater Communist activity and recruitment – there were signs of this in Iraq – but the coups in South Yemen and Afghanistan were not the work of Moscow. While the Soviets supported these changes they may in fact have been surprised by them. Nor were there any signs that Moscow thought the situation ripe in Iraq for a Communist move. Indeed there has not been any evidence of plans, Soviet or Communist, for a coup. The hypothesis which would appear to be the strongest, therefore, is that of Hussein's chronic insecurity, augmented perhaps by the Shi'a riots of the previous year.

This rift led to a sharp deterioration in relations and open polemics. Oddly enough it did not lead to a break in relations or even to the suspension of arms supplies. Moscow still was unwilling to lose Iraq, even if relations remained strained. In the Arab–Israeli context the two countries actually came closer in the wake of the Camp David accords, for Iraq finally cooperated in efforts, supported by Moscow, for *unified* Arab steps against Egypt. At this point Moscow welcomed Baghdad's rejectionist position and the central role played by Iraq in the campaign against Camp David. Yet this convergence of interests was not only temporary but it also did little to alter the basic dispute between the two. Iraq was becoming a regional power or at least saw itself as such. It was mending fences with its neighbours in the Gulf and even with Syria, in response to fears over the rise of Khomeini and Shi'a strength. Saddam Hussein may even have had ambitions to fill the vacuum left by Iran as the dominant power in the Gulf. Little of this appeared to please the Soviets.

With regard to Syria, for example, Soviet reactions to the brief Iraqi–Syrian rapprochement at the end of the 1970s were surprisingly muted, as we have seen. While the reconciliation of two Soviet allies should have been a welcomed relief for Moscow, the Soviets in fact accorded it scant attention. Coming as it did at a period of strained Soviet–Iraqi relations, evidenced by the fact that Gromyko did not even include Iraq in his Middle Eastern trip in March 1979, the Soviets may have feared a turn in an anti-Soviet direction. Iraqi anti-Communism combined now with improved Iraqi relations with the conservative Gulf states may have led Moscow to view the new alliance with caution. A strong, united Ba'ath coalition of the two countries might well be a repeat of the anti-Communist rampage of the Egyptian–Syrian merger in 1958. Moscow may, however, simply have believed that the new alliance was highly fragile, most unlikely to last and, therefore, preferred simply to wait it out rather than support or oppose it. With the death of Bakr in the summer of 1979, and the rise of Saddam Hussein to full official power, the alliance with Syria did indeed come to a stormy end. Hussein accused the Syrians of planning a coup against him, and some even claimed the Soviets planned one. On this background, the signing of the Soviet–Syrian Treaty in 1980 did not help to allay Iraqi fears or improve Soviet–Iraqi relations.

With regard to Iraq's Gulf relations, there was Soviet concern over the rapprochement with Saudi Arabia. There is even reason to believe that the Soviets perceived the Iraqi anti-Communist and anti-Soviet moves as moves dictated by or undertaken to please the Saudis. Saddam Hussein did say that Iraq would 'protect' Saudi Arabia even from the Soviet Union, should such a threat arise, and Iraq mediated the North–South Yemen conflict in 1979 to a resolution favourable to North Yemen and Saudi Arabia (South Yemen forces had to withdraw having accomplished nothing by their invasion of the North). Iraq even got involved in a conflict with Moscow's ally, Aden, when Iraqi agents assassinated an Iraqi Communist lecturer in South Yemen, leading to a shoot-out with South Yemen troops which stormed the Iraqi Embassy.

Soviet–Iraqi tensions also rose over the issue of Iraq's deteriorating relationship with the new regime in Iran. There were differences of opinion between Baghdad and Moscow over the Khomeini revolution, for Moscow was still hopeful that the anti-imperialist, especially anti-American nature of the new regime held much potential for Soviet–Iranian relations. Iraq, however, was fearful of a spillover of Shi'a fundamentalism into Iraq with Khomeini's strong messianic streak and opposition to the secular Ba'ath. Baghdad was also worried that the Kurdish stirrings in Iran might spread to Iraq's Kurds, or lead to Kurdish aid to the Iraqi Kurds. In fact Iraq pursued its own Kurds into Iranian territory, even bombing Iranian Kurdish villages. At the same time Iraq apparently strove to incite the Arabs of Khuzistan against Khomeini.

Thus Baghdad's entire position regarding Khomeini ran counter to that of the Soviet Union at this time, and to Moscow's radical friends, Libya, Syria and the PLO. This became abundantly clear when Iraq invaded Iran in September 1980. It is not certain if the Soviets had prior knowledge of Iraqi plans or not (there were rumours that Moscow actually warned Iran of imminent Iraqi attack), but they clearly objected to the move against a country with which Moscow still hoped to develop positive relations. The Soviet response, as we shall see below, was the suspension of arms deliveries to Iraq and a further deterioration in bilateral relations.

The Soviet invasion of Afghanistan was a further source of strain in the already strained Soviet–Iraqi relationship. Iraq openly opposed the Soviet use of force, probably viewing it as an ominous example of what could happen to a Soviet ally which sought to exercise independence. The fact that the Soviets were fighting a Muslim uprising clearly did not help matters. Iraq voted for the UN condemnation of the invasion and engaged in open polemics with the Soviet media on the issue. There were also reports that Baghdad considered abrogation of its Treaty with Moscow, but no such break actually occurred.

As early as the end of 1979, as western analyst Robert Freedman has pointed out, it was clear that the Soviet–Iraqi relationship was no longer a normal patron-client one. Iraq issued no more pro-Soviet statements in any forum; it took its military aid mainly from the French; and its trade was primarily with the West. In the course of the war with Iran, it drew still closer to the West and, particularly, the conservative Gulf states. It also patched up its relations with Egypt, bowing out of the rejectionist anti-Camp David campaign. Only later, at a turning point both in Soviet–Iranian relations and in the Iran–Iraq War (which we shall examine below), did relations return to something of the former alliance. In late 1982-early 1983, discouraged over the anti-Communist, anti-Soviet policies of Khomeini, Moscow resumed arms deliveries and aid to what had become an Iraq defence against Iranian counter-invasion of Iraqi territory. Nonetheless, Baghdad maintained its independence, including its improved relations with both the West, typified by the renewal of diplomatic relations with the United States in 1984, and the conservative Gulf states.

On the whole the Soviets had not gained much from their investment in Iraq. Although the withholding of arms may have forced Iraq to end its conflict with Iran in 1975, generally it was the Iraqis who determined the nature of the alliance. When Baghdad found it expedient to have Soviet assistance, or actually needed it, relations with Moscow became positive. When Iraq no longer perceived such a need, it turned elsewhere. The attitude towards the Communists followed the same pattern. The Soviets did achieve some of their objectives in Iraq: there was nationalization of western oil interests; Iraq entered into a Treaty with Moscow; and it assisted in the anti-Camp David campaign. But the Soviets were never able to achieve Iraqi support for their overall position on the Arab–Israeli conflict, nor resolution of the Kurds' demands, nor lasting rights for the Communists – much less Communist influence.

The gains that the Soviets obtained through their arms deliveries and aid, that is, a National Front including the Communists plus Communist participation in the government, were shortlived. Nor did the Soviets ever obtain the military facilities that they apparently sought in Iraq, either in the form of a naval base at Umm Kasr or air bases. They reportedly used Iraqi air force bases for the dispatch of supplies to the Horn of Africa in 1977–8, to the consternation of Baghdad and possibly contributing to the 1978 rift. In time even Iraqi need for arms apparently was insufficient to warrant a positive Iraqi policy, perhaps because Iraq had both stockpiled and diversified its sources of arms over the years. Oil revenues aided this fortified independence. This is not to say that Iraq lost all interest in Soviet aid; its difficulties in the war with Iran presumably restored much of this interest. Yet even during that conflict, as we shall see, Iraq retained its independence and diversification. Interests tended to conflict on a number of issues, and the Soviet Union continued to have few means by which to dictate or ensure its own positions in Baghdad.

12   The Soviet Union and Iran

Much of the Soviet interest in Iran goes back to the days of the Russian Empire, predating the discovery of oil and, therefore, to some degree predating the vulnerability of the West, at least in this connection. Iran was and has remained primarily of geopolitical interest to Russia, because of its strategic location. Situated along a large part of the southern border, Iran (Persia) was contiguous to large areas of the Russian Empire, and these areas also included ethnic minorities to be found on both sides of the border and comprising much of the Islamic belt of Russia. This area on the southern border was also subject to Czarist expansion outward, as a land mass link to warm water ports and the open seas, the Indian Ocean. It was also a land mass leading to southwest Asia, but it may have held greater importance as an invasion route to Russia itself, leading more than one Russian leader to seek to convert this into a buffer zone, similar to Eastern Europe, for the security of Russia.

Persia was also a factor in the Russian competition with the British Empire, forming together with Turkey and Afghanistan a wedge between Russia and the British in India and the Middle East. It was the object of the competition between the two Empires, as the British themselves sought primacy in this area to the south of Russia. In 1907 the two powers reached agreement on a division of influence in Persia, which by World War One deteriorated to the point of Russian predominance with some British influence in the southern portion of Persia. After the Bolshevik Revolution the Soviets set up an independent Ghilan Soviet Republic on the Persian shore of the Caspian Sea adjacent to Azerbaijan, even as they declared all Czarist agreements null and void and promised to withdraw. Actually they did withdraw after the 1921 coup by the Reza Shah, at which time the Soviet–Iranian Treaty was signed.

The treaty, controversial to this day, was one of several treaties concluded by Moscow with its neighbours to the south (Afghanistan,

Turkey) designed to prevent any pretext for British intrusion. In this sense the Treaty with Persia could be perceived as defensive in nature, but the controversial articles five and six carried with them the potential for offensive action. They banned hostile activity on the soil of either state against the other, allowing that in the case of hostile action or the threat of a third state against Russia through Persia, Soviet troops could move in. Both this Treaty, and an agreement on neutrality added in 1927 calling for abstention from alliances hostile to either side, were subsequently invoked by the Soviet Union to justify measures against Iranian sovereignty, most notably the Soviet moves into Iran in 1941 and 1946, and to bring pressures in the 1950s. Iran unilaterally abrogated the Treaty in 1959 and again in 1979, but the Soviets refused recognition of these acts.

The aggressive Soviet moves in northern Iran after World War Two, thwarted by western, mainly American opposition, as we have seen in Chapter Two, led to an increasingly pro-American orientation in Tehran, only briefly checked by the Mossadeq period, 1951–3. During this period the Shah was eclipsed by his Prime Minister, Mossadeq, even fleeing the country for a few days in the summer of 1953. Mossadeq, a nationalist, leaned for his support upon both the clergy and the Tudeh (Communist) Party, adopting an anti-western, anti-imperialist posture.

Nonetheless there are different interpretations of the Soviet attitude towards the Mossadeq regime. Retrospective Soviet accounts are positive, but in fact at the time Moscow was relatively cautious, for although Mossadeq was anti-western, and permitted Tudeh activity, his was not actually a pro-Soviet policy. The Tudeh sought to stage a revolution when the Shah fled in the summer of 1953, but the Soviet Union was opposed. While this would suggest Soviet satisfaction with Mossadeq, the Soviets may in fact simply have been skeptical of the Tudeh's chances for success, or perhaps fearful of the American reaction. Moscow's hesitation may also have been one of the first signs of the less militant, post-Stalin policy. In any case, the Shah swiftly returned, Mossadeq fell from power, and the Tudeh was virtually destroyed in the aftermath. The subsequent Soviet–Iranian relationship was now determined by the post-Stalin changes in Third World policy.

It may be said that Soviet objectives did not change essentially, but rather the tactics. The traditional geopolitical and strategic interests remained, and the Soviets, even after Stalin, sought to block western, particularly American influence in the Gulf be it in the form of western alliances or friendship with Iran. The policy of peaceful coexistence dictated that these interests be pursued through political and economic competition rather than through military means. It also meant an ideological compromise in favour of relations with bourgeois nationalists, in this case, with the nearly feudal, anti-Communist monarchy. Therefore, negotiations for an improvement in Soviet–Iranian relations were initiated by Moscow as early as 1953, without, however, significant results.

A serious obstacle to progress was Tehran's decision to adhere to the Baghdad Pact in 1955. The Soviets responded to this with a note to the Iranian government invoking the 1927 accord against either country's joining hostile pacts. They did not accompany this with any serious threats, however, beyond economic sanctions. Moscow did campaign vigorously against the Baghdad Pact, claiming, justifiably, that it was anti-Soviet in nature. Indeed it was part of American Secretary of State Dulles' policy of surrounding the Soviet bloc with a network of alliances. Moreover, Iran presumably joined because of concern over its long border with the Soviet Union and fear of repetition of past Soviet actions, particularly with regard to the minorities in the border areas of Iran.

The issue of the Pact notwithstanding, post-Stalin Soviet policies did lead to a brief improvement of relations. In 1956 the Shah visited the Soviet Union, and a three-year commercial agreement was signed. The latter did not provide for any Soviet advisers, however, in view of the Shah's continued wariness. This wariness turned once again to more acute concern following the revolution in Iraq in 1958. Coming as it did on the heels of the significant inroads Moscow had made with Egypt and the crises developing in Lebanon and Jordan, the Shah apparently once again believed he was in need of fortification. He signed a mutual defence agreement with the United States in 1959 which allowed for the creation of American bases in Iran. This was, of course, just what the Soviets feared, and it came right after the Shah had refused a Soviet offer to sign a non-aggression pact. This time the Soviets invoked the 1921 treaty against Iran's move, but the Shah responded by unilaterally abrogating the relevant clauses of the treaty. Again there was no serious threat of Soviet action, although a deterioration in relations did occur. There was sharp Soviet criticism of the Iranian agreement with Washington, accompanied by the withdrawal of the Soviet Ambassador from Tehran for nine months.

The real turning point in relations between the two countries came only in 1962, when the Shah initiated a more neutral or balanced policy *vis à vis* the two super powers. The Shah had his own reasons for the change, connected apparently with disappointment over the American attitude and arms supplies, and reinforced, perhaps by a confidence that his 'White Revolution' domestically would reduce dangers from the left. Whatever his reasons, the Shah announced that he would no longer permit any American missile bases on Iranian soil. The Soviets knew and said that these bases were not particularly important now that the United States had ICBMs, and indeed the United States was pulling out many of its outdated missiles from the Middle East. Moreover, the United States would still be able to maintain its intelligence gathering facilities on the Iranian border with the Soviet Union.

Thus the importance of the Shah's decision was not so much substantive as symbolic, from the Soviet point of view. It could be seen as a signal and a gesture towards improving relations with Moscow, and the Soviets were more than willing to seize the opportunity. Since 1953 the Soviets had been seeking to weaken or block American influence and to eliminate Iranian dependence upon the United States. Now there was a clear opportunity, provided that Moscow did not push too hard by, for example, demanding total Iranian abandonment of ties with Washington, or by pursuing contacts which might arouse the Shah's latent anxieties about the minorities near the Soviet border or the Tudeh. Grasping this opportunity would also entail, at the ideological level, reversal of the critical attitude towards the White Revolution in favour of support for what could be called progressive elements of the Shah's programme, such as land reform.

A relatively positive relationship did develop after 1962, and it progressed – with ups and downs – until the fall of the Shah in 1978. The basis and dominant aspect of this relationship was in the economic sphere. In 1963 Khrushchev sent Brezhnev to Iran and the result was a number of agreements providing for trade and credits with the Soviet Union and Eastern Europe, as well as Soviet economic aid. The trade which had taken place in the 1953–8 period was increased seven-fold in the 1965–9 period. Indeed Iran became the Soviets' third largest trading partner in the Third World (after Egypt and India). While this trade was based primarily on Iranian exports with little importing of Soviet goods into Iran, Tehran did become the largest Third World purchaser of Soviet machinery and equipment. It also became the second largest Third World recipient of Soviet economic assistance. Moscow granted Tehran large credits, including a 1966 credit of $290 million (the second largest credit given a Third

World state by Moscow) and in 1968 a credit of $300 million. According to some calculations, the Soviets granted Iran $1 billion in credits by the end of the 1960s and reached a trade turnover of the same figure by 1978.

Most of the large 1966 and 1968 credits went for the building of Moscow's biggest showpiece in the Third World, the Isfahan Steel Works, which was a project the Americans had refused to finance. A second costly investment was the building of a 700-mile gas pipeline from the oil fields in southwest Iran to the northern border with the Soviet Union, intended for tripartite deals with the Soviet Union and western Europe. The laying of a second pipeline was contracted in 1977 for completion by 1980 but the ensuing revolution interfered in these plans. The Soviets also sold Iran arms, beginning with a $110 million arms deal in 1967. Iranian motivation for these purchases was apparently more political than economic, designed most likely not so much to diversify arms suppliers but rather to put pressure on the United States to be more forthcoming in its supplies.

The Soviets for their part did not supply anything in the way of particularly sophisticated weapons systems, limiting sales to APCs, trucks and some anti-aircraft weapons. It may be that the Soviets were hesitant to provide Iran with offensive or more sophisticated weapons because of the conflicts between Iran and some of the Soviets' Arab clients, notably Iraq. Nonetheless, economic relations thrived, and by the time of the 1978 revolution Moscow was supporting some 147 projects in Iran, which had become one of the Soviet Union's most important Third World partners.

There were many problems in the relationship, as well, even in the realm of economic relations. A minor crisis arose, for example, in 1974–5 when Iran tried to get the Soviet Union to pay a price closer to world energy prices for Iranian gas. After Tehran suspended shipments for a week in July 1974 the Soviets agreed to an 85 per cent price increase, somewhat short of Iranian demands but a Soviet compromise nonetheless. The issue basically demonstrated the importance with which Moscow regarded its relations with Iran, politically as well as economically; it was also an exercise in Iranian power inasmuch as Tehran was not in need of extra revenues but resented Soviet exploitation. While the Shah made his point, even the new price agreed to by Moscow was only, roughly, two-thirds the price the Soviets received for their gas in western Europe (57 cents instead of 75 cents per 1000 cubic feet).

More serious were the problems in the political and strategic spheres. Some of these problems resolved around the deepening Soviet relationship with Iraq, which was in a more or less constant state of conflict with Iran. In the 1969 crisis between the two states, the Soviets warned against the use of force but maintained a neutral position. Such neutrality was perceived by Iraq as less than the desired Soviet support, but Moscow's policy probably was not motivated by a desire to please Tehran. Although the Soviets had no wish to jeopardize the developing relationship with Iran and, therefore, were not anxious to take sides, the more important Soviet consideration was probably to avoid any action which might impede the announced British withdrawal from the Gulf.

Indeed Soviet preferences for Iraq over Iran were placed beyond question when Moscow and Baghdad signed their friendship treaty in 1972. Circumstances were different by this time; the Soviet–Egyptian rift had increased the importance of Iraq both strategically and politically for Moscow. Nevertheless, the negative implications of the pact for Soviet–Iranian relations were still of significance. The Soviets tried to mollify the Shah. Immediately after the signing of the pact with Iraq they invited him to the Soviet Union, and a fifteen-year economic agreement was reached. Less than half a year later, in March 1973, Iran negotiated a large arms deal with the United States, ostensibly – perhaps genuinely – to counter the Soviet–Iraqi alliance and military cooperation. Thus in the next Iraq–Iran crisis, in connection with an Iraq–Kuwait dispute in March 1973, the Soviets were somewhat less neutral. Although they reportedly sought to moderate Iraq, they sent their fleet to the area and naval chief Gorshkov to Baghdad in a gesture of support for Iraq. While this intervention occurred after the peak of the crisis, the gesture was not lost on the Shah. In response, he proposed the creation of a Gulf security pact which, under the circumstances, would have been of greater benefit to the West than to the Soviet Union.

Soviet–Iranian relations were further complicated by Iranian assistance to the Kurdish rebellion in Iraq, which was being put down by Iraqi forces with the direct assistance of the Soviet Union! Iranian aid was a key factor preventing an Iraqi successful suppression of the rebellion, Soviet help notwithstanding, and there was the continuous threat that Soviet-piloted missions would hit Iranian artillery supporting the Kurds from across the border. It would appear that Iranian aid to the Kurds was the main topic, and area of dispute, during the Shah's visit to Moscow in November 1974. According to some accounts, having failed to influence the Iranians to halt their aid to the

Kurds, Moscow signed a new arms agreement with Iraq just a few days later.

It has been argued that this arms assistance to Iraq did in fact constitute sufficient pressure to persuade Iran to reach its cease-fire agreement and a settlement with Baghdad in 1975. As we have already seen, however, Iraq has claimed just the opposite. According to Saddam Hussein, the 1975 settlement benefited Tehran more and was agreed to by Baghdad only because additional Soviet arms to Iraq, which would have permitted continuation of the conflict, had *not* been forthcoming. Most western analysts accept the Iraqi version and point to this as a sample of Soviet arms blackmail to bring about a desired policy change on the part of a client state, in this case Iraq. Just what role the Soviets played is, however, unclear. Nonetheless, Moscow did welcome the Iran–Iraq settlement, which promised to put an end to the dilemmas posed by a conflict between two Soviet client states, regardless of the differences in the relationship of each with Moscow.

The settlement relieved the Soviets of the burden of trying to maintain good relations with the Iranian government despite the fact that Tehran was directly assisting the rebellion the Soviets were helping to put down. It eliminated the risks of direct Soviet–Iranian confrontation in the Iraqi-Kurdish struggle, the danger of escalation of that struggle and the possibility of being drawn into a Gulf war. The settlement was also expected to bring an end to the long-term Iran–Iraq border problem. With regard to both Iran and Iraq, the Soviets hoped that the end of their conflict would pave the way for closer relations of each with Moscow. In fact, just the opposite occurred. Iraq no longer needed Soviet military aid in such an acute way, as we have seen, and Iran, frightened over the dimensions taken by the conflict, was spurred to strengthen its forces and, in particular, its power in the Gulf and with the Arab world.

It was Iran's aspirations as a Gulf power which provided the second source of problems between the Soviet Union and Iran. The Gulf arms race was of concern to Moscow, and the Soviets argued that Iran was purchasing more than necessary solely for defence. They also sought to reassure Tehran that it had nothing to fear from the Soviet Union and, therefore, did not need the arms build-up even for defensive purposes. Whether the Soviets genuinely opposed the build-up or objected merely because the source of the arms was the United States is difficult to determine. Inasmuch as the Soviets themselves made no counter offers of arms, it seems likely that Moscow's objections were directed to the raising of tensions in the area and a strengthening of

Iran that might not be in Soviet interests. One of the reasons was that Iran was beginning to act as an independent power in the Gulf. In 1971 it had simply taken the islands it claimed in the Straits of Hamouz, and it was patrolling the entrance to the Straits as a self-appointed watchdog. The Soviets viewed this as at worst surrogate action on behalf of the United States or, at best, an attempt by Iran to dictate to the rest of the world, including Soviet allies and the Soviet Union itself.

Iranian actions in the Gulf were directed against radical and national liberation groups, and this pertained to groups supported by the Soviet Union. Iran sent troops and air cover to the Sultan of Oman to assist him in putting down the Dhofar rebellion. The Soviets, however, were both arming and training the Dhofaris; in 1973 they transported South Yemeni troops to join the Dhofar rebels. Thus here too Soviet and Iranian interests were pitted against each other. The conservative (anti-leftist, pro-western) thrust of the Shah's moves in the Gulf went beyond this specific conflict, however. His efforts to establish a Gulf pact, of a military as well as economic and political nature, were of greater concern. Such a pact would presumably come instead of the Soviet-proposed Asian security system. More importantly, it might threaten Soviet interests in the Gulf. Moscow wanted an open Gulf, because of its proximity to the Indian Ocean and Soviet naval interests there. A Gulf pact would most likely favour, perhaps augment, a western presence and work against the Soviet Union inasmuch as the only Soviet friends in the Gulf were Iraq, Iran a great deal less, and Kuwait even less (an arms deal with Kuwait in 1975 only partially established a working relationship between the USSR and Kuwait). All the other Gulf states, Saudi Arabia, Bahrain, the United Arab Emirates, Qatar and Oman were pro-western; they were more likely to squeeze the Soviet Union out than accede to its interests in the Gulf. This was already apparent in the budding Iranian–Saudi relationship, part of the Shah's post-1975 moves in the Gulf. The pro-American Saudi influence had already worked against the Soviets in North Yemen and was at work even in South Yemen.

Concern over the possibility of Iranian-Saudi cooperation was part of another set of Soviet worries regarding Iran's role in the Arab world. The relationship between the Shah and Sadat, for example, was of concern. Iran had supported Sadat's American-mediated peace moves of 1971, his expulsion of the Soviet military advisers, and his exclusion of the Soviets from the Arab–Israeli peace process after 1973. The Shah contributed $1 billion to the reconstruction and reopening of the Suez

Canal so as to encourage Egypt to conclude the Kissinger-negotiated Interim Agreement with Israel in 1975, while as inducement to Israel he offered increased oil supplies to compensate for the loss of Sinai oil. Sadat's historical trip to Jerusalem in 1977, designed by the Egyptian President to avoid Soviet participation in the peace process, was reportedly facilitated by Iranian mediation; and the Shah fully supported the Camp David accords reached between Egypt and Israel. Not only were these positions all contrary to Soviet positions and interests; they also contributed to the Soviet concern over a conservative bloc, consisting of Iran, Egypt and Saudi Arabia, under the sponsorship of the United States.

Iran was also on the 'wrong' side and acting as a conservative, anti-Soviet force in a number of other disputes. For example, the Shah supported Numeri against the Communist-supported coup attempt in 1971 and subsequent anti-Soviet moves by the Sudan; he supported Somalia's moves away from Moscow and against Ethiopia. Iran also backed Pakistan in its struggle against Soviet-supported Baluchis as well as in its conflicts with Moscow's ally India. The Shah vigorously opposed the 1978 Marxist coup in Afghanistan and the Soviet-supported war against the Islamic rebels there. To top all this off, Iran opened relations with Peking in 1971 and sought to benefit from the Sino-Soviet competition. Iran thus opposed Moscow's proposal for an Asian security system, designed to isolate China, while China, for its part, terminated its support of the Dhofaris and South Yemen, calling for an end to outside (meaning Soviet) interference in the Gulf.

On all of these issues, the Soviets trod a very careful path, expressing only mild criticism, if any at all, of Iran's positions. With regard to domestic issues, Moscow was generally supportive. It sought positive points to note in the White Revolution, and it virtually ignored the Tudeh. In fact, the Soviets barely mentioned the Shah's repression of the Communists, sought no role for the Party in Iran, and did little to prevent its deterioration both inside Iran and in exile in East Germany. Soviet policy was clearly to support the Shah's regime, with no interest in promoting his overthrow. Yet as can be seen from the long list of policy differences Moscow had with Tehran, it is clear that the Soviets were not successful either in influencing the Shah or in severing Iran from the United States.

One can only speculate as to why Moscow persisted in what appeared to be a fruitless policy. Presumably the Soviets continued to believe that there was still a possibility of weakening the Iranian link with the United States. An independent Iran, even as leader of the

Gulf, was better than an Iran totally dependent upon Washington. Therefore there was reason to provide Tehran with the leverage necessary for it to stand up to the Americans, and to offer at least a potential alternative or option *vis à vis* the United States. At the same time, the Soviet–Iranian relationship was far from hostile. Their mutual border was quiet and stable, which was a priority consideration for Moscow. Moreover, their economic relationship was quite good, and that too was a priority consideration for the Soviet leadership for most of the 1970s.

There are different appraisals as to just how pleased or displeased the Soviets were to see the Shah toppled in late 1978. One thing that is certain is that the Soviets were not part of the revolution which removed him. Moreover, Moscow may have been no less surprised than many western governments. In the mid-1970s Soviet analysts were quite pessimistic as to the possibilities for a socialist revolution in Iran because of (a) the success of the Shah's reforms which appeared to quell class and other conflicts within the society; (b) the lack of mass interest in socialism; (c) the strength of the *ulama*, that is the religious leaders; and (d) the weakness of the Tudeh which was split between Maoists, Trotskyites, Guevera-ites, and Marxist-Leninists. Split-offs by such groups and others in the 1960s, and penetration by agents of the Shah, had seriously weakened the Party which itself had disagreed with Moscow over tactics and strategy. There were signs, however, that the Soviets did not expect any kind of revolution, including non-socialist. Their miscalculations were apparently based on the fact that all the opposition leaders were in exile abroad: the National Front (heirs to Mossadeq), the *ulama* (Khomeini, in Iraq), and the Tudeh (in East Germany). The Shah, with his strong intelligence and police forces appeared to have the remnants of or local supporters of these forces well under supervision if not actually in prison.

There were also reasons for the Soviets to be hesitant about the desirability as well as likelihood of a revolution. Moscow appeared to believe that the Shah's reforms had been successful and the Soviet–Iranian relationship satisfactory. The alternative, in their eyes, might be a feudal, clerical regime of reactionaries, with no guarantee whatsoever that the positive relationship with Moscow would be continued. Indeed the Soviets opposed democratic elections in Iran because they might bring in reactionary landlords and the *ulama*. The latter were termed by the Soviets fanatics and right-wing zealots; Khomeini was criticized directly for having claimed that the Shah's agrarian reforms ran counter to Islam. If the Soviets did not believe that the Tudeh were strong enough, and they opposed the *ulama*, they also had little hope with regard to the forces of the left. The Mojahdin were believers in modernization but they sought this through Islamic reforms, not Marxism. The Fedayin were Marxist and more secular than the Mojahdin, but they were generally anti-Tudeh and by no means pro-Soviet. On the whole, the Fedayin were too radical for Moscow.

The unrest, riots, demonstrations and killings which increased throughout 1978 were either ignored by the Soviet media or reported without comment. In April Moscow signed the agreement with the Shah for the construction of a second pipeline, and all signs indicated continued support for the Shah. The Soviet assessment changed, apparently, in August, when the riots began to be taken more seriously. In September the Soviet press carried at least indirect criticism of the Shah, and in November Moscow came out in favour of the revolution when Brezhnev issued a warning against outside interference in the situation in Iran. This warning, aimed at the United States and designed to protect the revolutionary forces, was accompanied by direct criticism of the Shah and a new, positive line regarding Khomeini. It came only once it was clear that the Shah would fall; it was very much a jumping on the bandwagon.

There were no signs that the Soviets intended in any way to implement Brezhnev's warning against outside interference. There were no unusual fleet or troop movements, for example. Rather, the November warning was an attempt, tried many times in the past and to be repeated even more intensely in the future, to play up the existence of an American threat. Thus Moscow not only prompted anti-Americanism but also could appear as the protector of the new regime. It cannot be ruled out, of course, that Brezhnev intended the warning as a genuine deterrent to any action the Americans might be contemplating on behalf of the Shah. There is no evidence, however, that this constituted direct Soviet involvement with the revolution.

The Soviets may also have misjudged the revolution once they accepted its inevitable success. They may have believed that Mossadeq's heirs, the National Front, would be the leading political force, with Khomeini playing the role only of spiritual leader. Soviet analysts and media spoke in terms of stages: this first stage would be the period of bourgeois nationalist rule, for which a united front of all revolutionary forces, including the Tudeh, would be formed. Later would come the ascendency of socialist forces to move the country onto the second stage, that of socialist orientation. Moscow appears to have believed that the Tudeh would participate in a broad coalition, and eventually dominate its policies. The Soviets appeared to ignore the many slights to the Tudeh on the part of the revolutionary forces, such as the refusal to permit the Tudeh to march in the January celebrations of the Shah's departure. They ignored the anti-Communist, even anti-Soviet comments of the new regime and down-played its Islamic character. Soviet media, for example, rarely employed the new official name of 'Islamic Republic' of Iran. Nonetheless, they did begin to discuss Islam more positively.

Soviet policy was based less on the actual situation than on hopes for the future, that is, the potential of the situation. Specifically it focused on the blow to US influence and the anti-American aspect of the new regime. Iran, the power of the Gulf, wealthy and influential, strategically located and militarily strong, was lost to the United States. And the zero-sum game assumption was that America's loss would be Moscow's gain. All other aspects of the new regime appeared to be secondary or perhaps were misunderstood as a result of overly optimistic expectations. Soviet objectives were, first of all, to prevent Iran from returning to the United States and, secondly, to seek influence for itself, that is, pro-Soviet policies and a strengthened Tudeh. Both presumably could be achieved through a broad left-wing coalition. The question posed by observers was whether the Soviets were banking on stability or instability within Iran.

If they were interested in instability, the Soviets could have used the Tudeh to obstruct the measures of the new regime, and they could have stirred up the minorities, possibly even moving in and taking territory in northern Iran. Yet actual Soviet behaviour did not seem to favour instability. Soviet broadcasts urged the minorities to remain loyal (although there were rumours of Soviet arms deliveries to the Kurds, which we shall discuss below), and the Tudeh was apparently also ordered to cooperate. Dismemberment of Iran, in the form of a Soviet move in the north, did not in fact promise much for the Soviets, for such a move might elicit an American response in the south. Moreover, there was no guarantee that an unstable government would remain suspicious of American assistance. The wiser option for the Soviets most likely was the one adopted by Moscow many times in the past: support for one, unified central government and an attempt to take it over from within rather than through dismemberment and short-term goals. In either case, instability promised little given the small size of the Tudeh.

There were a number of positive developments which suggested that the Soviets' acceptance of the new regime would lead to the desired results. In the realm of its anti-Americanism, Tehran pulled out of CENTO (the successor to the Baghdad Pact), it closed the US intelligence bases and abrogated the 1959 defence pact with Washington. Iran opposed the presence of American forces and facilities in the Gulf, and it joined the anti-American front in the Middle East. For example, it severed ties with Egypt, Israel and South Africa; transferred the Israeli Embassy in Tehran to the PLO; came out against the Camp David Accords, operated against US and Israeli moves in Lebanon, and generally vilified the United States. American credibility had also been badly hurt by Washington's failure to move on behalf of the Shah and its later impotence during the hostage crisis.

Domestically there were also a number of Iranian steps which were positively viewed by Moscow. Tehran closed the multi-nationals in Iran and nationalized the banks and heavy industry. It permitted the Communists abroad to return to the country and, for some time, the Tudeh was allowed to operate relatively freely. The new regime also, reportedly, permitted the Soviets to set up an intelligence-gathering station in the northeast, and the Soviets were also able to gain information about American equipment confiscated by Iran. A three-year military agreement was also rumoured to have been signed, providing for Soviet training and technical assistance to the Iranians and even some Soviet advisers in Iran. Reports of most of these direct benefits have never been confirmed. In the realm of indirect benefits one could claim that the Soviet invasion of Afghanistan in December 1979 was facilitated by the fact that Iranian and world attention were focused on the hostage crisis at the American Embassy. Yet this advantage was short-lived given Iran's opposition to the Soviet move. In the economic sphere, the new regime improved the Iranian–Soviet trade balance, raising imports from the Soviet Union from 4 per cent to 9 per cent of Iranian imports in 1980.

There were, however, many negative phenomena and developments in connection with the Khomeini regime. Anti-Americanism did not mean pro-Soviet policies. Khomeini pursued a policy of 'equidistance' from both super powers based on an ideological bias against both. For him, Islamic internationalism and identification with the Third World meant anti-Sovietism, Islamic messianism, and anti-Communism. The first had an ideological foundation which found expression in the clauses of the new Constitution and the Programme of the Islamic Republic Party critical of both super powers. Khomeini spoke of super-power domination and contended that the dangers emanating from the Communist powers were no less than those of the United States. He criticized the Soviet regime as atheistic, anti-Islamic, tyrannical, and exploitative. In a letter to Soviet Foreign Minister Gromyko from Iranian Foreign Minister Qutbzadah in August 1980, the Soviet Union was called imperialist. The Iranians said that the Soviet refusal to accept the 1979 abrogation of articles V and VI of the 1921 Treaty raised concern that the Soviet Union (and/or Afghanistan) had aggressive intentions with regard to Iran. The Soviets for their part had sought reaffirmation of the Treaty on the grounds that it was meant to protect Iran. The regime in Tehran was also critical of the fact that Moscow chose to ignore the Islamic nature of the Republic.

The Islamic nature of the regime was of concern to the Soviets, at least the element of messianism. Moscow was concerned over Khomeini's efforts to export his revolution, his stirring up of Shi'ites everywhere, and the threat Iran created to the secular, progressive Ba'ath regimes particularly in Iraq. Even if Khomeini's fanaticism was tactically useful in some cases, especially in its anti-American and anti-Israeli aspects, the Soviets appreciated its potential for creating chaos, stirring up forces which were not necessarily friendly to the Soviet Union, and disrupting stable relationships developed by Moscow over the years. Nor did the Soviets relish the idea of an Islamic bloc of states or alliance which might prove too strong and independent for Soviet influence, especially if such a bloc adopted Khomeini's idea of equidistance. The Soviets may also have been concerned that Islamic messianism would be targeted at the nearly fifty million Soviet Muslims; indeed Iran did publicly criticise Soviet treatment of its own Muslims.

Finally, Khomeini's anti-Communism was a serious problem. His opposition was based on ideology, but it also identified Communism with the Soviet Union, viewing local Communists as agents of Moscow. In this connection Tehran also accused Moscow of aggressive designs on Iran, accusing it of meddling in Iranian affairs through the Tudeh. Khomeini labelled the left 'the children of Satan', who did not support the revolution but only joined once it was successful. His anti-Communism was expressed in the exclusion of the Tudeh from the coalition government and a crackdown, at the time temporary, on the Party in the autumn of 1979. This included the closing of the Tudeh's main office and the banning of its paper. A second crackdown occurred in 1981, with arrests at the beginning of 1982. Communists were purged from government jobs, the media, and the university. At the beginning of 1983 Tudeh leaders were put on trial; over 1000 were arrested and forty-five executed for spying for the Soviet Union and plotting a takeover. On 4 May 1983 the Tudeh was dissolved by the regime.

The clamp-down and then virtual destruction of the Tudeh followed several anti-Soviet measures. In the summer of 1980 a Soviet diplomat was expelled and Moscow was ordered to reduce its Embassy staff in Tehran from forty to just fifteen people. There followed the Qutbzadah's letter to Gromyko complaining of hostile acts and 'unpardonable provocations'; then the closure of the Soviet consulate in Rasht. In 1982 Iran curtailed Soviet cultural activities and, more importantly, reduced trade with the Soviet Union while increasing the proportion of its trade with the Third World. In 1983 Tehran expelled eighteen Soviet diplomats and relations took a steep downhill dive.

The Soviets for their part were slow to respond to this anti-Communism and anti-Sovietism. From the outset, they were very supportive of the Khomeini regime; propaganda was favourable and progressive elements were found to exist even in Islam, in the area of social programmes and justice. The Soviets were careful not to get drawn into press polemics, responding only mildly when the Tudeh was restricted in 1979, refraining from criticizing Khomeini directly. Rather, Soviet media sought to blame American or generally western provocateurs. Yet, there were signs as early as 1981 of Soviet concern. In contrast to the effort to present positive sides of Islam, an important article appeared in the Soviet Union, written by CPSU International Department deputy chief and Third World specialist Ul'ianovskii, sharply critical of the reactionary elements of Islam. And Brezhnev, in his speech to the CPSU Congress in 1981 described the regime in Tehran as 'complex and contradictory' although essentially anti-imperialist. Open Soviet criticism, even of Khomeini, became frequent in 1982 and especially 1983, with the destruction of the Tudeh. Such criticism was still muted, however, and there were few concrete steps taken by the Soviets. Gromyko explained to the Supreme Soviet in June 1983 that Moscow wanted friendship with Iran and that the future would depend upon Iran's wishes.

In more concrete terms, the Soviets backed up the Tehran regime during the hostage crisis. Without actually condoning the taking of the American Embassy, Moscow exaggerated the American threat. To counter the American economic sanctions, the Soviets granted Iran transit rights, signing an agreement in September 1980. In addition to the already mentioned military agreement that was never denied, the Soviets reportedly offered Iran arms, and were refused; they reportedly did supply jet fuel. With the deterioration in relations, the Soviets sought to salvage whatever they could, and they strove primarily to direct Iranian approbation back in the direction of the United States. There were, however, several areas of dispute, beyond the ideological nature of the Khomeini regime.

In the economic sphere, Soviet exports to Iran did increase in 1980 as already noted, but in general the Iranians filled the gap left by the break with the United States by increasing trade with other Third World countries, notably pro-western countries such as Turkey and Pakistan, as well as Japan and China. Most of the old projects with the Soviet Union begun before the revolution were completed, but few new ones were agreed to. A serious problem arose over the gas pipelines. Pumping had been stopped during the revolution itself but resumed in April 1979 at somewhat lower than capacity. In July 1979 Iran asked for a price increase in the range of five times the former price (from $0.76 to the world price of $3.80 per 1000 cubic feet). In March 1980 the Soviets offered $2.66 as a final offer; the Iranians closed the pipeline. They also cancelled construction of the second pipeline. Soviet refusal to meet Iranian demands attests to the importance of economic considerations in Soviet policy at the time; but it may also be the case that Moscow believed Tehran would agree to a compromise. If so, this was but one of several misunderstandings which were to mark Soviet relations with the Khomeini regime. In June 1984, Iran sent an economic delegation for talks in Moscow, but nothing concrete apparently resulted; economic relations between the two did not improve prior to the Gorbachev period.

A source of dispute between the two countries was the Kurdish issue and perhaps that of other minorities in Iran which Tehran claimed were receiving Soviet support. In addition to the Kurds, the Baluchis, Turkomanis, Azerbaijanis, Arabs of Khuzistan and even others were all reported to have become active, with the advent of the revolution, demanding independence or some form of autonomy. And there were conflicting reports as to just what role, if any, the Soviet Union was playing in these demands. Once it became clear that the Khomeini regime had taken over, Moscow claimed that the Kurds and others were loyal to the new government; it may have been urging such loyalty. Soviet propaganda, at least, argued that Khomeini's plans for regional autonomy within Iran were satisfactory, and it advised the Kurds, Azerbaijanis and perhaps others to accept the plans. With this came denunciation of separatism as the counter-revolutionary work of Maoists, agents of the Shah's SAVAK, and so forth.

There were, nonetheless, reports that the Soviets actually strengthened their ties with the Kurds and some of the other minorities in the
immediate post-revolutionary period. The government in Tehran, for
one, claimed that Moscow was in fact arming the Kurds and Azerbaijanis, as well as the Arabs of Khuzistan, and it complained that Soviet
overflights in the border area were designed to assist the minorities
there. In 1979 there were, indeed, Soviet broadcasts favourable to the
idea of Kurdish independence, and the Iranian Communists did have
significant inroads into the Arab labourers in the oil fields of Khuzistan
(who were receiving support from Libya and possibly the PLO). There
were also some Soviet comments in 1982 favouring the idea of
Azerbaijani independence. According to some western sources,
Soviet arms accompanied some of the above propaganda support,
although these supplies may have been through third parties, such as
the Libyans or Palestinians, without, necessarily, Soviet knowledge or
at the Soviets' initiative.

It is possible to speculate that, as in the case of Soviet–Iraqi relations,
when Moscow's relations with Tehran were strained, the Soviets gave
support to the dissident minorities, and when relations were positive,
support was withheld. If this were, indeed, the case, the early period
of Khomeini's rule presumably would have been one of Soviet caution
regarding any encouragement of the minorities. One could argue that
the Soviets were optimistic, at this stage, with regard to the anti-
western, even pro-Soviet potential of the new regime – an optimism
which was evident in the revision of the Soviet depiction of Islam.
They therefore sought stability in Tehran and, presumably, refrained
from moves which might appear threatening so as to avoid any tilt
back towards the West in Iranian policies. The opposite was also
speculated by western analysts, that is that Moscow would try to take
advantage of the chaotic situation created by the revolution. It would,
according to this argument, encourage the minorities, creating a
pretext for a move into and the takeover of the northern areas of Iran
so long coveted by Moscow. Remaining in the realm of speculation,
however, it seems more likely that the Soviets would have preferred to
take advantage of the chaos to insert pro-Soviet elements into the
ruling bodies, seeking to gain influence with a stable new regime
rather than create a situation which might prompt counter American
moves or, at the least, alienate the new government in Tehran.

It is actually difficult to determine just what aid if any the Soviets did
render the minorities after Khomeini's rise to power. According to
Kurdish sources, the Soviets turned down the Kurds' request in 1980

for arms, particularly SA–7s although, following the deterioration in Soviet–Iranian relations in 1982–3, there was condemnation of Tehran's failure to meet what Soviet media termed the Kurd's 'just demands'. Denying that the Kurds pursued separatism, Moscow increasingly criticized Iran's treatment of the minority. Yet most western observers agreed that little if any material aid was in fact offered the Kurds by Moscow. The same would appear to have been the case with regard to the Azerbaijanis even in the pre-Gorbachev period. (Soviet motivation for encouragement of Azerbaijani or even Kurdish nationalism across its southern border would have dwindled with the outburst of Azerbaijani and other nationalist sentiment inside the Soviet Union itself during the Gorbachev era.)

There was also little motivation for the Soviets to support the Baluchis. Although the Iranians accused Moscow of arming the Baluchis in Iran, and there was at least one Soviet broadcast (in 1981) critical of the Khomeini regime's treatment of this group, public Soviet and Tudeh pronouncements were unsympathetic to the Baluchis. In fact, they condemned 'reactionary gangs' among the Baluchis and warned against outside plots to foment counter-revolution, in part traceable to the Baluchi refugees from Afghanistan. This was the main point for Moscow: the link between the Baluchis in Iran and their brethren in Afghanistan fighting the Soviet puppet regime and Soviet forces there. Whatever sympathies the Soviets may have had for this minority in the past and whatever manipulation of the minority problem in Iran that Moscow may – or may not – have pursued, the Afghan war precluded any Soviet support for this group in Iran. This was particularly the case after their ranks swelled by the addition of hundreds of thousands (reaching close to one million) of Baluchi refugees from Afghanistan over the years of the war.

The Soviet invasion of Afghanistan was another source of problems for Soviet–Iranian relations. The relative freedom with which Iran permitted Baluchis to transit the Iranian–Afghan border, as well as the reported direct assistance rendered the Afghan rebels by the government in Tehran were the concrete expressions of Iran's public criticism of the Soviet war in Afghanistan. Iran joined the United Nations and Islamic Conferences' condemnations of the invasion, boycotted the Moscow Olympics, and staged yearly demonstrations outside the Soviet Embassy in Tehran on the anniversary of the invasion. It also permitted the creation of refugee guerrilla camps on Iranian soil. Tehran even argued that the Soviet invasion of Afghanistan was a sign of Moscow's hostile designs on the whole region, directed against Iran and aimed at reaching the Indian Ocean. The invasion of one Muslim country was termed an attack on all Islam.

No amount of Soviet propaganda attempts to link the rebellion in Afghanistan with the United States could divert Tehran from this position. For its part, however, a cordial relationship with Iran was apparently more important than the concrete and verbal role played by Iran in connection with the war in Afghanistan. Thus, although Moscow's criticism of this role fluctuated in accord with the rise and fall of its relations with Tehran, it never became a central issue in Moscow's approach to Khomeini. As British expert Malcolm Yapp has pointed out, Soviet criticism of Iran's aid to Afghan rebels never came near the opposition expressed by Moscow to Pakistan's similar role, presumably because of the hopes that Moscow cherished for a relationship with the anti-American Iranian regime.

A similarly complex issue which disrupted Soviet–Iranian relations was the Iran–Iraq war, although Moscow's attitude and behaviour toward this conflict were greatly determined by the state of the Soviet–Iran relationship at any given time. When Iraq invaded Iranian territory in 1980, Soviet–Iraqi relations were already at an ebb. This was also a period when Moscow apparently still nurtured high hopes as to a possible relationship with Tehran. For these reasons, the Soviets declared themselves neutral in the conflict. In view of the fact that Moscow still had, at least formally, a Friendship and Cooperation Treaty with Baghdad, declaration of neutrality was virtually a declaration of support for Iran. Moreover, this neutrality was rendered militarily substantive by the suspension of Soviet arms deliveries to Iraq shortly after the outbreak of hostilities, although Soviet arms continued to reach Iraq from Eastern Europe. At the same time, Moscow reportedly offered direct arms supplies to Iran; indirect deliveries were undertaken from Eastern Europe, in addition to Syrian and Libyan deliveries. The Soviets also gave Tehran assurances regarding Soviet friendship, thereby enabling Iran to transfer forces from its common border with the Soviet Union for deployment against Iraq. And Moscow permitted expanded Iranian use of Soviet overland transit routes as an alternative to the disputed and dangerous Gulf waterways.

The outbreak of the Iran–Iraq War confronted Soviet decision-makers with a number of dilemmas. Aid and support for Iraq would endanger potential gains in Tehran; opposition to Iraq might push Soviet–Iraqi relations to the breaking point, with the negative implications such a rupture – and Soviet desertion – might have on other Third World states linked by treaty to Moscow. In either case, Soviet lack of help might result in pushing the neglected partner into the arms of the West, particularly the United States, as an alternative source of assistance. Neutrality meant, in effect, that Moscow opted for Iran as the most important prize, but the continuation of East European arms deliveries to Iraq presumably was designed to soften this blow and thus forestall a final break with Iraq. This dualistic policy, if indeed it was intended as such, met with little success. In fact it alienated both Iran and Iraq, for Iraq resented the suspension of direct arms supplies while Iran protested the continued deliveries to Iraq from Soviet bloc sources.

Moscow's problems with the war entailed not only which side to support or the danger that one or other might seek western assistance. Armed conflict and instability on its southern border was not a welcome phenomenon for the Soviet Union. Connected with this was also the concern that the United States might step in to protect the flow of oil through the Gulf, or that it would use such an objective as a pretext for a military build-up in the area. In addition, the war drew the Gulf states together, prompting the creation of the Gulf Cooperation Council. The Council itself was not a pro-Soviet body, and with the augmented importance of Saudi Arabia, also due to the war, the Council, at least initially, tended in a pro-American direction. While the war brought the basically conservative Gulf states together, it split the broader Arab world. This interfered with Soviet efforts to forge a united anti-American Arab bloc, and diverted attention, resources, and energies away from the Arab–Israeli front. Moreover the anti-Egyptian rejectionist bloc virtually disintegrated as Egypt and Jordan joined Saudi Arabia and the other Gulf states in support of Iraq against the Syrian, Libyan, PDRY-supported Iran.

Thus the Soviets' logical objective was to achieve a speedy end to the conflict. They tried to mediate a solution, arguing that the war only aided the imperialist world and, particularly, Israel. In time, Moscow openly called for negotiations and an immediate cease-fire. This, however, could be interpreted as a pro-Iraqi position for, with the turn of the battle against Iraq, it was Baghdad which sought negotiations while Iran insisted upon a fight to topple Saddam Hussein. By this time, summer 1982, the Soviets were beginning to change their position regarding the two protagonists. They resumed their direct arms supplies to Iraq and condemned the Iranian counter-offensive which crossed into Iraqi territory. While Soviet media remained relatively neutral in their coverage of the war, they did report that Iraq was the party seeking a negotiated settlement.

The Soviet switch has generally been attributed to the change in the course of the war, with Iran's move into Iraqi territory and the threat of an Iraqi defeat. Presumably this raised concern in Moscow regarding the possibility of an Iraqi call to Washington for assistance and increased American military involvement to protect United States allies and friends in the Gulf. Alternatively, the fall or overthrow of the Ba'ath regime in Baghdad would not have been a desirable development from the Soviet point of view. Nor would the strengthening and spread of Khomeini's fundamentalism which could be expected to accompany an Iranian victory. Yet it may be that the more important and operative reason for the Soviet shift back to Iraq was the deterioration which was taking place in Soviet–Iranian relations in 1982. The moves against the Tudeh, the sharp decline in economic relations, and the expulsion of Soviet officials, probably persuaded Moscow that it had little to hope for in pursuing its support of Tehran, particularly when the costs, in connection with Iraq, were so high.

There may have been a dispute or some indecision within the Soviet leadership over this decision. This was suggested by references in Soviet journals to the trials and tribulations faced by Communists in Iraq. Such criticism of Iraq may have been a sign of opposition to the change in the Soviet position. This opposition, if indeed that is what it was, could have been motivated by a belief that Iran was still the greater strategic and economic prize, worthy of continued pursuit. Another argument may have been that resumption of Soviet aid might enable and encourage Baghdad to escalate the war. The Soviets did take steps, not always successful, to restrain Iraq from escalating. And presumably in answer to the longer-range concerns over the future of Soviet–Iranian relations, Moscow was careful not to burn its bridges with Tehran. At least it did nothing to stop, and may actually have requested, the continuation of arms supplies to Iran from North Korea, Vietnam, Syria, Libya, Vietnam and, more directly linked with Moscow, Eastern Europe. Nevertheless, Soviet–Iranian relations remained strained until well into the Gorbachev period.

13   The Soviet attitude to Islam

The Soviet Union has a Muslim population of close to fifty million, most of whom reside in Soviet republics of the Caucasus, Azerbaidzhan, Central Asia and Kazkhstan, mainly in areas bordering on Iran, Afghanistan and China. The Soviet Union itself borders on the Muslim countries of Turkey, Iran and Afghanistan. Most Soviet Muslims belong to the Sunni branch of Islam; they fall into numerous ethnic groups (the most numerous of which are of Turkic origin), overlapping with ethnic groups just beyond the Soviet border. As followers of the religion of Islam, the Muslims have been treated and persecuted like most if not all other religionists in the Soviet Union; as peoples or Muslim 'nations', that is, ethnic groups which were traditionally Muslim, they have been accorded a degree of cultural expression, schools, use of their language, and so forth. Both as ethnic groups and religionists, Soviet Muslims have experienced significant vicissitudes throughout Soviet history.

Following the Bolshevik revolution, Islam as a religion was suppressed, Mosques were closed, and the clergy was severely persecuted. This, despite the fact that Lenin and the early Bolsheviks undertook an alliance with radical Muslim political groups, encouraging Muslims to rise up against their colonial oppressors, first in the Russian Empire and then, following the Bolshevik revolution, in countries of the Middle East and Asia. Lenin's policy, which in any case proved unsuccessful, was abandoned by the late 1920s. In the Stalin era, contact with co-religionists, usually of the same ethnic group just across the border, was forbidden, along with pilgrimages to Mecca and communication with Islamic centres abroad. The 1953 Soviet encyclopedia had the following to say about Islam:

Islam, like other religions, has always played a reactionary role, been an instrument in the hands of the exploiting classes for the spiritual oppression of the peoples of the East. [In the countries of the East] where Islam is the state religion, it continues to be a weapon in the hands of local reaction and foreign imperialism.

On the whole, in the Stalin era the attitude towards Islam – at home and abroad – was totally negative.

With the post-Stalin change in the Soviet attitude and policy towards the Third World, changes were gradually introduced in the attitude towards and relationship with Islam. The first such change was the use of Soviet Muslims for Moscow's foreign-policy purposes in the Third World. The Soviet Muslim republics were touted abroad as examples of the Soviet model of development. That is, the standard of living, social and economic conditions of Muslims living in the Soviet Union were presented to the underdeveloped Muslim world as selling points for the Soviet system. This was also, presumably, employed in defence of the Soviet treatment of its own Muslim population. Moscow could, and did, argue that Muslims in the Soviet Union had not suffered under atheistic Marxism-Leninism, and would not elsewhere. Thus the freedom and prosperity of the Soviet Muslim population was emphasized for foreign consumption. Such a tactic concentrated on material rather than spiritual issues, attempting at least to minimize the purely religious bonds or spiritual identity of Soviet Muslims with spiritual centres abroad. It, nonetheless, also included contacts of a purely religious nature to demonstrate Soviet tolerance and provide access to circles abroad which might otherwise be closed to Soviet emissaries.

Concretely, official Soviet Muslim bodies (four regional 'Spiritual Boards') were encouraged to send delegations to Muslim countries, including clergymen and pilgrims. Students were permitted to study in Islamic institutions abroad. The Soviet Muslim bodies were also encouraged to host visits from foreign Muslim organizations or countries, including the organization of Islamic conferences. Official visitors from Muslim countries were pointedly taken to the Muslim Soviet republics for visits which included not only historic Islamic sites but also participation in prayers at functioning Soviet Mosques. In addition, Soviet Muslims were employed for propaganda broadcasts to Muslim regions abroad.

Theoretically there was the risk of contamination of Soviet Muslims as a result of this contact, and there are in fact contradictory estimates in the West as to just how much Moscow did or did not limit the numbers of Soviet Muslims permitted to travel or study in Muslim countries abroad. The Soviets apparently calculated that the political benefits of such 'religious diplomacy', as British expert Fred Halliday has called it, outweighed the possibly nefarious effects on its own population. Not only could Islamic suspicions regarding Communism be, hopefully, allayed, but the contacts could be used constructively. The Soviet Union played on a cultural mutuality with visiting Muslim officials, to promote its relations with these countries. It also used these contacts, particularly the conferences, to promote the Soviet foreign-policy line, be it against the West or in support of Soviet actions. An example of the difficulties involved in this, but also its importance, was the effort to soften criticism by the Muslim countries of the Soviet invasion of Afghanistan at the Islamic conference held in Tashkent in August 1980.

Thus the Soviet attitude toward its own Muslims in relation to the world of Islam abroad was manipulative and instrumental. There is no evidence that Soviet Muslims themselves had any direct influence on Soviet policy making, no matter how much they were used as emissaries or even channels for Soviet policies abroad. Aside from the use of Muslims as ambassadors to some Muslim countries, those involved in foreign-policy decisions regarding these countries were not Muslims nor in any way linked culturally to the Muslim countries. As pointed out by Halliday, even the few Soviet Muslims who reached significant positions in Soviet foreign-policy matters, notably Geider Aliev who was named to the Politburo under Andropov and removed under Gorbachev, did not deal with this part of the world in particular. And even someone like Aliev, of former KGB as well as party importance in Azerbaijan, was hardly to be perceived as a representative of Islam. Those who were sent and employed as representatives of Soviet Islam were, like all other religious officials in the Soviet Union, state functionaries. They were clearly subordinate and limited by strict restrictions on their behaviour and pronouncements. While they may or may not have been respected in their own communities, it is most unlikely that they had any influence beyond these communities.

There was a gradual appearance of somewhat greater tolerance of Islam in the Soviet Union, possibly to facilitate this use of Islam for Soviet foreign-policy purposes. In 1971, for example, before and after the twenty-fourth CPSU Congress, a number of authoritative articles appeared which could be seen as somewhat positive in their discussion of Islam. It was explained that Islam had served and suited the Tzarist order of affairs in the Russian Empire, but this form of Islam had been virtually stamped out after the Revolution. At that time there had been two options for Islam: to disappear or to adapt to the new Communist order. The option chosen was to adapt, that is, to revise Islamic social principles to suit the new socialist society, to accept the idea of radical social–economic–political change and progress. With such an adjustment, it was claimed, Islam could go hand in hand with Communism

Even these relatively positive appraisals, however, ended with the proclamation that ultimately, as with every religion, Islam would gradually die out. Moreover, attacking the ideology rather than the religionists, Soviet sources continued to condemn formal Islam within the Soviet Union. Terming it a reactionary, anti-scientific belief system, like all religions, Soviet media dismissed the 'pretensions of the Muslim religious organizations to be a factor of social progress . . . Islam does not provide any positive program of social change, does not provide any ideal or organizing society.'

What emerged over time, and presumably in response to foreign-policy needs, was a dualistic attitude to the ideology: negative when dealing with domestic Islam, somewhat more positive when dealing with Islam abroad. To some degree this dualism was explained by a theory of stages of development. According to this, at the lower stage of social and political development existing abroad, Islam might serve a positive function for uniting and rallying the masses in their struggle for independence. Islam in this sense might play a similar role to that accorded by Lenin to nationalism. In certain circumstances, serving this positive function, it might be tolerated or even encouraged for this first stage, before going on to the second, socialist stage of universal proletarian goals. Soviet Muslims, according to this theory, were beyond the first stage; they were more advanced and no longer in need of religion as a rallying banner.

In any case, during the 1960s and 1970s, the Soviet Union was willing to acknowledge some positive aspects of Islam in the anti-colonialist, anti-imperialist struggle. Yet the picture presented of Islam abroad was far from uniform, inasmuch as Soviet foreign policy had to cope with Islam not only in countries still battling imperialism, but also in independent countries as diverse as, for example, Egypt, Syria, the PDRY, Afghanistan, Libya and Pakistan, whose approach to Islam, as well as to the Soviet Union, varied quite significantly. Therefore, particularly after the revolution in Iran but even as early as the 1960s, Soviet analyses distinguished between the progressive and the reactionary side of Islam, emphasizing one or the other in accord with the nature of Moscow's relations with the regime involved and the circumstances in each country.

The apparent contradiction was explained by what Lenin had pointed to as the varied pace of socio-economic development in the world, whereby remnants of different stages tended to mingle with each other. The Islamic world, as much of the Third World in general, contained societies wherein feudal and capitalist elements existed side by side with the remnants of earlier communal society, typical perhaps of patriarchal, nomadic tribes and earlier modes of production. These elements included such positive things as mutual assistance, common ownership of property, and collective decision-making. Thus, depending upon the circumstances, one aspect or another of Islamic society might be dominant, determining its constructive or destructive, progressive or reactionary characterization.

This flexible view of Islam, with particular attention to potentially progressive elements, was most notable after Khomeini's rise to power. Indeed this event occasioned quite a few analyses, often convoluted, to accommodate Moscow's early support of this fundamentalist regime. An early, albeit perhaps exceedingly liberal statement appeared in a Tashkent paper, claiming that 'Islam can now be regarded as a matter of individual conscience.' The official position was spelled out a bit more cautiously by Brezhnev at the 1981 CPSU Congress. He said:

Of late Islamic slogans are being actively put forward in some countries of the East. We Communists have every respect for the religious convictions of people professing Islam or any other religion . . . The main thing is what aims are pursued by the forces proclaiming various slogans. The banner of Islam may lead into the struggle for liberation; this is borne out by history. But it also shows that reaction, too, manipulates Islamic slogans and incite counter-revolutionary mutinies. Consequently, the whole thing depends on the real and actual content of this or that movement.

In this way, reminiscent of Lenin's words about nationalism Brezhnev sought to accommodate policies not only towards the new regime which it was wooing in Tehran, but also towards Islamic rebels fighting the pro-Soviet regime in Afghanistan, the pro-western Islamic state of Pakistan, and friendly states in the Arab world with their varying degrees of secularization and state religion. It also had to cope with anti-Soviet phenomena and certain dangers inherent in Khomeini's brand of Islam itself.

The authoritative theoretical approach was provided in 1980 by the then Oriental Institute head, Evgenii Primakov. He sought to explain Islam's persistent survival and power as well as the reasons for which it remained a factor with which one had to cope. Islam, he claimed, was not simply a religious system, but a way of life. The Koran and *Shari'a* provided not only religious rites but also a guide to moral ethical behaviour and norms relating to personal, economic and social life. Therefore, its influence went beyond the religious sphere. Moreover it encompassed hundreds of millions of people, with a long history as a guiding factor.

The influence of Islam, however, was due primarily to the historical, economic and political conditions of the Islamic countries. Inasmuch as imperialism was identified with the Western, non-Islamic world, Islam served as a rallying point in the struggle for independence, religious slogans becoming an integral part of this struggle. As with nationalism, the opposition to the outsider engendered anti-capitalist attitudes, for the foreigner was identified with exploitation and the poor conditions within the country. The colonizers had also brought with them their own religion; thus the issue of religion itself became intertwined with the struggle for liberation. In the case of Islam, however, this exploitation and religious oppression were compounded by what was seen as 'Westernization', which weakened the religious principles of Muslim society. Thus the traditional religious circles were prompted to take up the liberation banner.

On the negative side, this meant that it was the defenders of tradition, including the clergy, who led the anti-imperialist struggle, using religion as a means of reaching and rallying the masses. Thus more than anti-imperialism was involved. This was a struggle *for* Islam, cutting across class lines and, like nationalism, often contradicting a class approach. It juxtaposed the religious-exclusive principle over the universal class principle. Yet there was little alternative. Religious circles came to play this central role because of the absence of a large, indigenous proletariat able to provide either the leadership or content for such a struggle. Progressive organizations and parties were weak if at all existent. There had even been a tendency to erect a barrier against Communist ideology, preventing the penetration of Communist ideas. Rather, in order to involve the masses in the liberation struggle, it was necessary to speak to them in popular, religious terms.

All of the above came to explain the relative stability of Islam and why it could not be ignored as a factor in history. There were, however, positive elements inherent in Islam itself, at least as it had been affected by socio-economic changes over time. For example, the social elements of Islam had risen in importance as distinct from the purely religious elements. As a result, the 'Islamic state' and 'Islamic economy' were offered as an alternative, however utopian, to the western state and its exploitative economy.

'Islamic economy' was defined as the abolition of inequality based on the unity of production and consumption, that is, the principle of production according to one's ability, consumption according to one's piety. More specifically, it was said to mean that one's personal property consisted only of that which one produced by one's own labour; all other property belonged to God and was regulated by the State. This regulation, for the purpose of ensuring equilibrium and justice, was based on a taxation system determined by the Koran.

Primakov explained, however, the negative facets of this 'Islamic economy'. First of all, it could not be considered genuinely progressive, for it combined bourgeois requirements with support for the patriarchal peasantry as well as the petty bourgeoisie and urban proletariat. Secondly, the principle of 'consumption according to one's piety' left a good deal of room for inequality. Thirdly, there were those who opposed a progressive income tax, particularly as dictated by the rules of the Koran; and, fourthly, a form of state capitalism would emerge. In short, there were some positive elements to the 'Islamic economy' but there were definitely negative ones as well.

The same could be said of the idea of the 'Islamic state'. Primarily, it was criticized for allocating political power to the clergy in secular institutions. It was basically a combination of radical, progressive and conservative trends, which could be used by conservative elements of the bourgeoisie. These elements could accord these institutions a social content serving capitalists and landowners; they tended toward dictatorial forms of rule, as could be seen in Pakistan. This could be explained theoretically by the existence, historically, of diverse class and political interests in Islam. Islam was not, according to Primakov and other Soviet theoreticians, a single, whole entity; it contained two currents. One was a petty bourgeois current with a certain revolutionary democratic potential. The other was a capitalist, landowner current with reactionary, counter-revolutionary tendencies. Therefore, the same institutions and concepts, such as 'Islamic justice' and 'people's power', designed to implement the principle of the Koran, could be used by both currents, either against capitalism or against Communism. Everything depended upon the interpretation, which itself depended upon which of the class forces in the country achieved power.

By way of example, Primakov claimed that in Iran, some ideologists of the radical school emphasized those aspects which served the cause of anti-imperialism and anti-exploitation. In this sense, they were of the petty bourgeois current, with its revolutionary democratic potential. But this current itself had two aspects; petty-bourgeois movements themselves could go in two different directions. By definition the petty bourgeoisie had characteristics of the exploiter, that is, they were owners; they also had characteristics of the exploited, by the imperialist colonizers. Therefore, they might go in either a bourgeois, capitalist, reactionary direction or a revolutionary, progressive direction. The Iranian petty-bourgeois, Islamic movement had both possibilities. If the revolutionary current dominated, it could create the conditions for the emergence of a non-capitalist path of development. This might occur if there were unification of the forces on the left and mobilization of the workers, thereby introducing revolutionary substance to the movement. At the same time, there was also the potential in Iran for the convergence of the radical and reactionary currents. This could happen if the anti-Communists achieved dominance, joining with the other, reactionary current of Islam.

The conclusion was that Communists were to support the anti-imperialist current of Islam, assisting even religious believers in their struggle for independence. At the same time, they had to fight the use of religion for counter-revolutionary purposes and prevent the domination of the reactionary current. In this way, a distinction was made between support for anti-imperialism – what was called 'unity on anti-imperialism' – without support for religion, that is, 'unity of opinion on matters of heaven in the sky'. The idea was, as with bourgeois national movements, to strengthen the revolutionary democratic trend in the hope that this trend of even a religious movement, would progress from religion to socialism. While Soviet theoreticians hesitated to say at this point that socialism could not exist side by side with the religion of Islam, the implication was that it could not. Even the 'Islamic state', the 'Islamic economy', and 'Islamic justice' presumably would give way at some point to real socialism based on the proletariat.

The growing Soviet disappointment with the Khomeini regime, perhaps apparent as early as Brezhnev's 1981 warning of the dual nature of Islam, was reflected in subsequent discussion of Islam. The dualism argument remained the basis for analysis, but Party theoretician Rostislav Ul'ianovskii, for example, wrote about the 'highly contradictory ... politization of Islam' and the 'outdated moral and ethical standards of the Koran and *Shari'a*' in what he described as the increasing strength of the conservative wing in Iran as well as the totally counter-revolutionary character of Islam in a country like Afghanistan. Journalist Aleksandre Bovin, believed to be close to ruling circles in Moscow, said, on the august occasion of his receipt of the Order of Lenin, that the Islamic revival was 'an attempt to return to those times when Islamic dogmatists determined the character and system of political life'. He termed the Islamic revolution a 'theocratic renaissance', making no distinction between the conservative form of religious power pursued by the Muslim Brotherhood in Egypt or Syria, the Shi'ite clergy, or the Khomeini regime. Other analysts spoke of the 'considerable reserves of political extremism' being set in motion by Islamic 'traditionalist forces'.

It is far from clear as to whether the convolutions of Soviet analyses of the nature of Islam reflected concern over the potential influences of the Islamic revival on Soviet Muslims or the perception of fundamentalist Islam as comprising a threat to the Soviet Union. It is possible that Moscow was worried about the destabilizing effects of fundamentalist Islam on secular, progressive regimes in the Arab world. The Iraqi regime, of course, was directly threatened by the Holy War declared by Khomeini against Saddam Hussein after the Iraqi invasion of Iran. The stirring up of Shi'ites in Syria compounded the domestic difficulties faced by Moscow's ally Assad. And Moscow could not be entirely sanguine about the spread of Islamic terrorism, particularly in Lebanon where it hit Soviet as well as other targets. In addition, the Islamic revival provided impetus and sustenance to the rebellion against the pro-Soviet regime and Soviet troops in Afghanistan. The messianic designs of Islamic fundamentalism, that is, the quest for Islamization of the world and the building of an Islamic world order could not have been welcomed. Such designs clearly posed a threat to the secular, progressive regimes in Syria, Iraq and the PDRY, as well as to Soviet interests in the region. Any such expansion and consolidation of Islamic power threatened to create a strong, independent bloc with little promise of being pro-Soviet even if it were not pro-western in its orientation.

The more complicated question has been that concerning the effect of Islamic fundamentalism on the Soviet Muslim population, the Soviet fear of infection, and the possibility of Muslim unrest within the Soviet Union. There have been actually two conflicting views among outside analysts of Soviet affairs. A senior observer of Soviet Muslim society, Alexandre Bennigsen, has argued that Moscow did indeed become fearful after the Iranian revolution. Both the revolution and the war in Afghanistan rendered the borders between the Soviet Muslim republics and the Muslim world outside more penetrable. The fact that the Soviet Muslims have the same ethnic, cultural and religious characteristics as those on the other side of the border has made for particularly strong ties. Often the language is the same, and they belong to the same groupings, be they Shi'a or Sunni Muslims, Azerbaijanis, Turkmen or other. Thus these basically arbitrary state borders, now weakened, could not be expected to prevent contamination. Soviet Muslims have traditionally been aware of and interested in what occurs beyond the border, regarding the Muslim world beyond with a mixture of admiration and disdain. Moreover, Soviet Muslims were open to the influence of Islamic fundamentalism inasmuch as Soviet Islam had remained conservative and traditionalist. There was even an illegal group of highly traditionalist Muslim priests operating out of the Caucasus.

Bennigsen saw proof of Soviet concern in connection with Soviet Muslims serving in Afghanistan. After the 1978 coup in Afghanistan, Moscow sent Soviet Muslims to help with administration and various technical matters in Afghanistan, primarily because they were familiar with the language and customs. Some 30–40 per cent of the invading Soviet army in 1979 was Muslim, sent specially to fill out the Central Asian Republican Division which were *not* usually manned by Muslims. Other Soviet Muslims were sent to hold the border and, as occupying forces, to build airfields and so forth. In the winter of 1980 there were an estimated thirty to forty thousand Central Asians in Afghanistan, according to Bennigsen, but by February the Soviets began to pull them out. They were replaced by non-Muslim Soviet personnel.

Presumably the Muslims had fraternized too much, had identified with the Afghan rebels as fellow Muslims, and been upset by the tasks they had to carry out against them. According to this account, these tens of thousands of Soviet Muslims became infected with fundamentalism; some refused to fight, others deserted. Moreover, the flow of wounded and dead back to Central Asia had a similar affect of incitement; there were reports of riots in Khazakistan, for example. Thus Afghanistan may well have provoked concern in the Kremlin over the reliability of Soviet Muslims in Central Asia. The uncensored exchanges across the border raised the spectre of Islamic fundamentalism within the Soviet Union itself. There may even have been a fear that Soviet Muslims would try to emulate the Afghan rebels' Holy War to preserve Islam from Marxism.

The Islamic revival in Iran compounded the situation and, according to some interpretations, potentially posed an even greater threat. One reason for this was the immense prestige enjoyed by Iran among the Muslims particularly in the Caucasus, the only region where Shi'a out-

number Sunni Muslims. Many Soviet Muslims there, especially young
people, saw a resemblance between the fundamentalist movement in
Iran and the glorious radical religious movements of years past in the
Russian Empire. The anti-imperialism of the Iranian movement took
on the meaning of opposition to outside oppressors – for Soviet
Muslims the outside oppressors might well be the Russians. Indeed
the exaltation of Islamic values evoked and fortified Soviet Muslim
feelings of spiritual superiority to the Russians and other Europeans.
Moreover, the populist side of the Iranian movement was well suited
to the anti-bureaucratic, anti-urban attitudes of the Soviet Muslim. All
of this, according to Bennigsen, applied to the majority Sunni Muslims
as well as to the far less numerous Shi'ites, for the Shi'a–Sunni distinction was not of particular importance among Soviet Muslims.

There were certainly signs of Soviet concern. There was the withdrawal of Soviet Muslim personnel from Afghanistan. In the local
Central Asian press, there was an emphasis on the power of the KGB
and the security forces, suggesting that they were warning the local
population against any infringements of public order. There were
appeals for vigilance by border guards and the KGB with regard to
infiltrating agents. There were also many references to reactionary
Muslim clergy and to efforts from outside to spread revivalism within
the Soviet Union and thereby destabilize the country. In the early
1980s a central organ was created in Moscow to coordinate the international contacts of Soviet Muslims, although the contacts themselves
were not, apparently, reduced.

A 1978 Soviet study indicated that 10–15 per cent of secondary
school and university students in the Muslim areas were believers.
This was ten times the numbers claimed for other areas of the Soviet
Union. Presumably in response to this, an atheistic campaign was
undertaken, beginning in Central Asia in May 1979. A Centre for
Scientific Atheism was opened in the Turkman SSR in 1981 and one in
Tashkent in 1982. According to Ya'acov Ro'i, Israeli specialist on
Soviet Muslims, the campaign was begun with thousands of lectures
and meetings against religion, and articles appeared in this area
expressing concern over the growth of religious feelings. Accompanying the propaganda campaign was a clamp-down on illegal priests and
on the illegal opening of Mosques. Local Communist officials were
criticized for having closed their eyes to these activities or for having
actually joined in them.

Much of this criticism focused on the identification made by
Muslims between religion and nationality. The idea that religious rites

were taken as national customs, traditions and laws was condemned because it defined Muslims in national terms and thereby encouraged nationalism. It has been argued, however, that this very identification of the religion of Islam with Muslim nationhood is what distinguished the situation in the Soviet Union from the phenomenon of Islamic fundamentalism. According to a number of western experts such as Malcolm Yapp, Martha Olcott and James Chritchlow, the Soviet Muslim problem was an ethnic one, especially apparent among Muslims of Turkic origins (who constitute the largest group of Soviet Muslims). This was not a matter of religious revival or fundamentalism, in which Soviet Muslims showed little interest. It was, rather, a matter of national sentiments, of which Islam is an historically essential component.

Thus, it has been argued that decades of Soviet rule has weakened and changed Islam in the Soviet Union. The persistence of believers has been an indication of people who kept the customs as a matter of national culture, not as active believers. They were Muslim by practice; their faith was simplistic and focused on ritual. For the Soviet Muslim dogma has been unimportant. Indeed all these years of secularization has weakened the idea of Islamic law (*shari'a*) as the governing force of society. Yet *shari'a* is the cornerstone of Islamic fundamentalism. Therefore, there has been little impact of fundamentalism, as such, on Soviet Muslims. The religious arguments of the Wafd or Khomeini were little understood, and even the fanaticism of the illegal priests in Caucasus was more traditionalism than fundamentalism.

According to these observers, the Muslim masses and clergy had worked out a *modus vivendi* with the Communist authorities, who generally accepted Islam as a social phenomenon, so long as it remains unpolitical. For its part, the regime treated it as a national phenomenon rather than a religious one, channelling it into relatively acceptable ethnic lines of national customs. This too was dangerous for the Soviet regime, for there was the risk of Soviet Muslim sentiment erupting into national-political demands. There was evidence of concern over just this in the criticism noted above. Indeed the growth of national sentiments which has taken place, particularly among Soviet Muslims of Turkic origin, might ultimately be more serious a problem for Moscow than fundamentalism. The distinction between the two is an important one.

If the problem was a national rather than religious one, it was not entirely clear to what degree it had been affected by the rise of Islamic fundamentalism outside the Soviet Union or influenced Soviet policies towards the Islamic states. Aside from the general boost to national awareness, the religious fanaticism and violence of the fundamentalists may have little to offer Soviet Muslims. This need not mean that there has been no appeal or interest whatsoever. Moreover, any encouragement, even indirect, Islam outside might accord the problematic national issue inside the Soviet Union would be serious enough in the eyes of Kremlin leaders. Indeed the dangerous combination of nationalism and Islamic fundamentalism was to become evident in the Gorbachev period.

14 Arab Communism in the Middle East

The Soviet attitude towards Communism in the Middle East derived from Leninist concepts regarding Communism in the non-developed world. Marxism itself was a European-orientated theory. It foresaw a proletarian-socialist revolution as the inevitable outgrowth of advanced capitalist society. The under-developed world was seen as backward, feudal or semi-feudal, at a pre-capitalist stage and, as such, presumably unripe for socialist revolution. The existence of an advanced capitalist society was essential in Marxist theory, for the revolution was the direct result of a dialectic whereby conditions were created which could bring about revolution and socialism. In capitalist society, production technology would be sufficiently advanced to provide for all the needs of the people; monopolies would be sufficiently developed to facilitate planning and rational distribution. Thus the mechanism and material wherewithal for socialism would become present; only the profit-seeking of the ruling capitalists stood in the way of the creation of a socialist system which would provide rationally and justly for all.

Moreover, in advanced capitalist society, competition would virtually eliminate the small producer, devastating the middle class, as businessmen unable to compete fell into the proletariat. Thus the proletariat would grow, unemployment and poverty rise, while riches would be concentrated in the hands of the few. As the contrast and contradictions between the two classes grew, with the increased suffering of the majority proletariat, class consciousness would rise and revolution would erupt. In this way, capitalism created its own contradictions and a revolutionary situation, together with the mechanism and framework necessary for a socialist society.

Given this dialectic historical progression, one could posit the absolute necessity of capitalism as a prerequisite of socialism. There were some references in Marx's works to the possible telescoping of stages. Yet, basically, his theory was posited upon the unfolding of an

210

entire historical process, with capitalism emerging from feudal society, and socialism rising from the ashes of capitalism in an advanced industrial society such as the England of the nineteenth century in which he wrote.

Lenin sought to create a place in this theory for Russia, that is, for a country which was by no means at an advanced, industrialized stage of capitalism. Additionally, he sought to explain the failure as yet of Marx's predictions to materialize. In answer to the first problem, that of socialist revolution in Russia, Lenin produced the idea of the weak link. Only partially industrialized (and, later, weakened by World War One), Russia composed the weak link in world capitalism. Striking at the weakest link might break the whole chain, and figuratively provide the spark which would ignite world revolution.

The situation was a bit more complicated than that, however, and Lenin developed a theory of capitalist development to account for the failure of revolution to occur in an industrialized society as Marx had predicted. Instead of the virtual disappearance of the middle class, with a growing proletariat and increased class warfare, industrial societies were witness to a burgeoning middle class and a large degree of class cooperation in the form of trade union successes and labour cooperation with management in the interests of higher profits leading to greater advantages for the workers. The explanation, according to Lenin, lay in the phenomenon of imperialism, which he described as the highest stage of capitalism. As a result of imperialism, capitalists found cheap sources of labour, natural resources and new markets, rescuing capital from the inevitable problems of a diminishing market and rising costs at home. The capitalist metropole thrived as a result of colonial empires, leading to a rise in the standard of living in the metropole. Workers were thus lulled by improved conditions and willing to cooperate with management for continued improvements. The 'real' interests of the working class, the abolition of private property and capital, were forgotten as trade unionism met their more immediate interests in higher wages, shorter hours and better working conditions. Meanwhile the imperialists were dividing up the world and capitalist monopolies were becoming cartels.

According to Lenin, imperialism might temporarily save capitalism in the metropole, but the class struggle would be shifted to the colonies. In the colonies, the exploitation of the native people would provoke revolt. Costly colonial wars would endanger the standard of living in the metropole, 'awakening' the workers there and sparking the revolution. Weakened by the costs of empire and the putting down of overseas revolts, capitalists would find it even more difficult to withstand the inevitable revolution at home.

With this theory in mind, the question was not so much one of the relevance of the underdeveloped world – it was clear that something was to be found in the underdeveloped world. Rather, the questions became: how important was the struggle there in relation to the revolutionary effort in the developed world; how was one to work in the underdeveloped world (towards what objectives); and with whom was one to work there? These questions were the source of serious and devisive debate in the Comintern; indeed they remain so even in present-day Communist circles.

The first question was where to concentrate revolutionary efforts. Lenin argued that revolution in the underdeveloped world would facilitate and aid the revolution in the metropole. But the main effort would and should remain in the advanced European capitalist societies. Indian Communist Roy argued that revolution in the under-developed world was the only hope for revolution anywhere and, therefore, should be given exclusive priority. The debate, even as late as the early 1980s, in the Soviet Union revolved around the intrinsic value of the revolution in the colonies: could it substitute for or at least assume equal status with the proletarian struggle, or would it be merely an auxiliary to this struggle, not to be ignored but nonetheless secondary?

The second question was just how would the revolution in the colonies occur and what would be its nature. Would it be necessary to pass through stages of capitalism prior to socialist revolution? The answer was that the first revolution in the colonies would not, in fact, be socialist. It would be nationalist. In the colonies, the entire people, the nation as a whole, was exploited and oppressed by foreign domination. Class distinctions were blurred in the mutual suffering, shared even by the local bourgeoisie who were restrained by the imperialists. Nationalism, therefore, would spur the revolt. The reference was to 'positive' nationalism of the oppressed against the 'negative' nationalism of the oppressor, the imperialist power.

Basically Lenin's theory was tactically useful as a means of gaining the support of the oppressed nations within the Russian Empire. Their nationalism was to be encouraged and assisted for the purpose of weakening the Czarist regime and gaining allies for the socialist struggle. But within the theory of imperialism there was also the idea of national consciousness as the first stage of an anti-imperialist consciousness. Nationalism could be the banner rallying the people against imperialism and colonialism. Thus, nationalism, occasionally defined by Marx as a device created by the bourgeoisie to keep the workers loyal, contained also a progressive element. It was legitimate, perhaps even necessary, to satisfy national aspirations as a first stage, which would be the revolution for national liberation. Then one could go on to the satisfaction of universal aspirations, that is, stage two which would be the socialist, proletarian revolution.

This explanation of national revolution provides the answer to the third question: with whom to ally. Clearly revolutionaries should ally with the nationalists, particularly in the absence of a developed proletariat, even if these nationalists were bourgeois. Communists were to join with and assist the bourgeois nationalists in their revolution and then lead them, from within, on to the next stage which was the socialist revolution. While Lenin specified that the Communists were to maintain their independence in such an alliance, it was not entirely clear just what was meant by the word 'join'. In fact, the united front tactics of alliances and coalitions of the Communists with the bourgeois parties were occasionally supplemented by the idea of Communists actually joining the bourgeois parties. There was by no means full agreement on the idea of cooperation with the national bourgeoisie. Many Communists, in particular a Third World Communist such as Roy, were strongly opposed, arguing that the bourgeoisie, even if involved in the national liberation struggle, could not be trusted. The accuracy of this argument was more or less demonstrated when Stalin's albeit dogmatic application of the Leninist tactic led to the decimation of the Chinese Communist Party by its bourgeois nationalist ally, the Kuomintang, in the late 1920s.

With the post-Stalin return to Lenin's tactics, there was an attempt to come to grips theoretically with the phenomenon of the newly independent countries of the Third World, that is, the states born of the nationalist struggle. The new regimes were termed national democracies. They expressed the will of all strata and classes in society; they were neither capitalist nor socialist. Between the two systems, they were said to be on a non-capitalist path of development which was deemed pre-socialist. This meant that the content of the regime's policies was democratic but not socialist. Rather they were creating the necessary preconditions for the second stage, for social-ism, including the expansion of democracy (in which Communists could operate legally), socialist ownership of production, growth of the proletariat, and relations with the Soviet bloc. It was this last which would accord the necessary aid, and protection, to permit a peaceful progression to a socialist society without having to pass through a purely capitalist stage.

In time it became apparent that national democracy might develop in any direction; socialism was not the exclusive or inevitable end product. This was particularly true because of the dual nature of nationalism and of the bourgeoisie, both of which contained revolutionary elements at the stage of national revolution but were not inherently progressive. In view of this, there was no assurance as to the direction they would take in the future. Moscow began, therefore, to emphasize the requirement that national democracies be governed by revolutionary democrats. These were national democrats who believed in revolutionary change and socialism, though they were not necessarily Communists. Revolutionary democracy was thus that form of national democracy which had a socialist orientation, considered by some to be an additional stage or sub-stage on the path to socialism.

Even revolutionary democracy proved disappointing, however. Many of the so-called revolutionary democracies were intolerant of local Communists, not only unwilling to cooperate with them but actually outlawing and persecuting them. Revolutionary democrats might emit socialist slogans, even employ Marxist terminology, but the resemblance between their societies and real socialism was often remote. Moreover, it became increasingly clear that even a revolutionary democracy could abandon the path to socialism. The immediate source of this realization was the defection of Egypt, initiated with the expulsion of the Soviet military advisers in 1972. This move probably fortified those who had opposed the united front tactic all along, and it precipitated a rethinking among Soviet theoreticians over just who or what forces could be trusted to lead the way to socialism in the Third World.

The dominant conclusion was that it had been a mistake to rely on charismatic leaders and groups of a vague or dubious ideological nature, however revolutionary they may have been. What was required to ensure steady development in the right direction was a solid organization and a pure ideology, that is, a vanguard party based on Marxism-Leninism and orientated towards real socialism. This conclusion was not accepted by all those dealing with the subject in the Soviet Union; there were those who believed that Third World societies were not yet ready for such a leadership. They argued that the failure of the theory of revolutionary democracy was not that it expected too little but that it expected too much from the new societies. These were countries still tied to the western economic system, and often themselves only at a very early stage of development dominated by the bourgeoisie and lacking a mass proletarian base. These observers, therefore, argued for greater realism rather than more ideology. This view notwithstanding, the Soviet leadership in the Brezhnev era did opt for at least partial implementation of the more ideological approach. It is not entirely clear, however, just how much it was to be applied to the parties in the Middle East.

There existed a number of objective problems for Communists in the Middle East, aside from the vicissitudes of Soviet theoretical dictates. One of these was the fact that they were identified with the Soviet Union. Although the Soviet Union was not perceived as an imperialist power in the Middle East, as were the western states, it was nonetheless an 'outsider'. The 'foreign connection' of local Communists was a difficult image to combat, particularly in periods of strong nationalist sentiment. They were perceived as alien, rather than home-grown and, as such, possibly even a threat to the nation's sovereignty. In addition, the identification with Moscow included identification with Soviet policies, some of which were not the most popular or widely accepted in the Middle East, for example, Soviet positions regarding the existence of Israel or the Eritrean struggle or the Kurdish issue. For these reasons, many observers have concluded that the link with Moscow may actually have been a liability for local Communists.

Another problem was the atheistic nature of Communist ideology in this overwhelmingly Muslim world. The problems this created in the states ruled by Islam are obvious, but even in the less conservative, secular states ruled, for example, by the Ba'ath, or in its time, Nasserism, the heritage of Islam was not easily overcome. And the appeal of those aspects of Communism which called for change and reform tended to be usurped by these radical or 'leftist' regimes. Local Communists, therefore, had difficulty not only in getting their message across but in deciding which message to promulgate.

On the positive side of the ledger, it could be argued that a powerful ally like the Soviet Union could be an asset for a local Communist party. It could help the party achieve some of its demands and possibly concessions from the local government, if Moscow were willing to condition its aid to the government upon such things. The Soviet Union presumably had numerous means at its disposal for bringing pressures to bear in favour of the Communists. In this way, at a minimum it presumably could provide a degree of protection for the interests and well-being of the local Communists. In addition, the

Soviets could provide more direct assistance in the form of material and financial aid as well as political and other support.

From the Soviet point of view, the local Communist parties provided an additional vehicle for gaining support for Soviet positions, promulgating Soviet ideas, and augmenting Soviet influence. They could be used for dissemination of propaganda as well as for the testing of new ideas or policies that the Soviets themselves were as yet unwilling officially to espouse. They could also be used for political agitation, intelligence and covert action purposes. They could indeed serve as an arm as well as channel for Soviet policy in the country or region, providing contact with other groups or movements, often in cases where Soviet personnel or material might not be welcomed.

Yet the local Communist party was also capable of complicating Soviet relations with a local government. The very existence of a Communist party might render Soviet motives suspect in the eyes of a regime, fearful that Moscow had local ambitions. The Soviets might be blamed for activities undertaken by the local party. Because of this 'guilt by association', Soviet relations with the local government could suffer in the all too frequent periods of domestic anti-Communism. Failure of Moscow to take such a risk, and come to the aid of a local party, would be a blow to Soviet credibility, particularly in the Communist world. This in turn would fan the flames of the Sino-Soviet dispute, providing ammunition for the Chinese claims that Moscow cared little for the revolution and was willing to sacrifice local parties for the benefit of its own super-power interests. Conversely, Soviet intervention would disturb not only relations with the government concerned but raise the alarm in other countries of the region and, possibly, provoke western action.

To a large degree this was the basic dilemma: the potential conflict between Soviet interests and policies *vis-à-vis* the local government, often connected with broader regional and even global considerations, on the one hand and, on the other hand, the needs and interests of the local Communist party, with their implications for the Soviets' role as leader of the revolutionary world Communist movement. Since the Bolshevik revolution, Soviet policy has operated on two levels: the state-to-state level of a super-power and the party-to-party level of a revolutionary movement. And, since the signing of the Brest–Litovsk agreement taking Soviet Russia out of World War One, with only a few exceptions, priority has generally been accorded the first level in times of contradiction between the two. If, in the theoretical sphere, proletarian socialist revolution has had to take second place to bourgeois

national revolution, so too in the practical sphere local Communists
have had to subordinate their interests, sometimes their well-being
and very existence to Soviet interests and policies.

For most Middle Eastern parties, the Leninist united front tactic,
calling for the creation or joining of national fronts with local bourgeois nationalists, has meant serious limitations on their size, recruitment, propaganda and independence. This conflict of interests has led
upon occasion to dissent and division, even splits within the parties.
Similar problems have arisen over opposition to the content of Soviet
policies as well, be it on local domestic or foreign-policy issues. Few, if
any, are the cases, however, when the Soviets have adapted their own
policies to suit the needs or demands of a local party.

There is almost no country in the Middle East in which there have
not been periods of anti-Communism and persecution. Communist
parties have rarely been legal anywhere in the region and in the more
conservative Islamic states such as Saudi Arabia they have not existed
at all. Over time the Communists have probably fared the best in
Lebanon. There they have been a legal part of the parliamentary
system since 1970, although a very weak party. They probably
benefited from the fact that for many years Lebanon was relatively
uninvolved in the Arab–Israeli conflict or even inter-Arab affairs and,
as a result perhaps, their connection with Moscow was less salient.
They benefited from their alliance with the stronger, leftist Druse of
Kamal and then Walid Jumblatt. Nonetheless, there was some disagreement in the Party over the united front tactics of cooperating in
what the Soviets referred to as the 'progressive and national-patriotic'
forces. A number of more radical elements split off from the Party,
leading to the existence of more than one Communist group in
Lebanon, some of which were dominated by Palestinians. There was
also some reluctance to accept Moscow's positions on the Arab–Israeli
dispute, but on the whole the Lebanese Party remained a loyal ally of
the Soviet Union.

An example from the other end of the spectrum would be the Iraqi
Communist Party, which may have been the party to suffer the most
over the years. Although Kassem brought the Communists into the
government in 1958, he gradually turned against them. He viewed
them as a potential if not actual threat to his rule. Following the
massacre which occurred in the northern town of Kikuk in 1960,
Kassem accused the Communists of attempting a coup against him.
As we have seen, the Soviets now came face to face with the classical
dilemma of preferring the interests of a local party over the Soviet

effort to sustain a positive relationship with an increasingly anti-Communist government. The Soviet choice was to back the central government on the specific issue, eventually expressing only mild criticism of the growing animosity towards the Communists. Moscow even sided with the government when the local Communists supported the Kurdish revolt in 1961. Thus, it was more a result of Iraqi coolness than Soviet policy that a strain developed in Soviet–Iraqi relations. The reason may have been a low Soviet estimate regarding the Communists' chances to come to power or perhaps the risks of western involvement should the Communists make a bid for power. Whatever the underlying reasons, the Soviet leadership preferred to continue its support for the positions of the anti-western regime of Kassem, as we have seen.

The February 1963 coup, which brought the right-wing of the Ba'ath to power, led to bloody persecution of the Communists. As a result of the execution of a reported 3,000 Communists, Soviet–Iraqi relations came to a standstill. Soviet arms supplies were halted and aid to the Kurds resumed. At this point in time, the Sino-Soviet dispute had come out into the open, erupting into open competition and factionalism between the two Communist powers within the international Communist movement. This may account, in part, for the decisive action taken by the Soviets in response to the anti-Communist bloodbath, as the Soviets sought to prove that their policy of peaceful co-existence was not at the expense of local Communists. Yet the right-wing, anti-Soviet nature of the new regime in Baghdad may have had a good deal to do with the Soviets' response, for Moscow had little to hope for from this wing of the Ba'ath.

Soviet–Iraqi relations gradually improved with subsequent coups in Baghdad, including even the return of the right-wing Ba'ath to power in 1968. From June 1964 onwards Moscow became increasingly involved both militarily and politically with Iraq. Yet, locally, the Communists were actually calling for the overthrow of the government, as periodic persecution of the Party continued. Between 1968 and 1970 some thirty-five party activists were killed as part of a crackdown which culminated in 1970. These actions elicited a warning about the 'prejudices' of the Baghdad regime and some criticism from Moscow, but little else.

There does appear to have been at least one instance of Soviet pressures on behalf of the local Communists: in 1968 a number of Communists were released from prison, apparently in exchange for Soviet agreement to close down the Party's radio broadcasts from

Bulgaria. Moscow also began, around this time, to press for the creation of a National Front which would legalize and bring the Communists into some sort of government coalition. A clandestine Communist was brought into the government in December 1969, as we have seen. None of this, however, had any beneficial effect on the fate of the Iraqi Communists. Indeed, they reportedly were far from satisfied with Soviet positions. A group broke off from the Party in protest against Soviet policy regarding the Arab–Israeli conflict and to Moscow's opposition to revolutionary action. It has been claimed that the Soviets restrained the Iraqi Party from staging a takeover attempt both in 1959 and in 1967. It is difficult to know if that was in fact the case. The Party itself was probably too weak to have succeeded in taking power, but it is also true that Moscow's policy in those years did not encourage precipitous revolutionary action which might harm Soviet relations with the government.

The Soviets did achieve what they probably perceived as a major breakthrough for the Iraqi party when they finally obtained Baghdad's agreement to the creation of a National Front in 1973. The Party was thus legalized and two of its members were taken into the government. The problem was that the ruling Ba'ath, by now under the increasing influence of Saddam Hussein, did not view this as synonymous with granting the Communists either equality or even a free hand. The Party was barred from activities, including propaganda and recruitment, in the army or government, thus hampering its efforts in the major centres of power in the country. Moreover, the Communists were forced to subordinate their interest in the Kurds and accept the government's violent suppression, with Soviet help, of the Kurdish rebellion. This despite the fact that a large portion of the Iraqi Party was itself Kurdish, and renegade Communists were fighting with the previously Soviet-supported Kurds in the North.

The fate of the Iraqi Communists began to decline significantly in the period after the end of the Kurdish rebellion with the signing of the 1975 Iraq–Iran agreement. As already noted, Saddam Hussein may have assumed greater independence from Moscow in the wake of this agreement and his presumably reduced need for Soviet aid and arms. It is conceivable, therefore, that he also felt less restrained with regard to the local Communists, whom he had in any case always regarded with a large degree of suspicion. In 1978 he accused the Party of recruiting within the army, despite a ban on such activity, and preparing a coup against his regime. Arresting a number of Communists late in 1977, he had twenty-one Communists executed in

May 1978 and accused the Soviet Union of planning a Communist takeover.

Whether Saddam Hussein genuinely believed these accusations or not, is not clear. Many western observers did believe Hussein, in view of the general shift in Soviet Third World policy at the time to a greater emphasis on ideological purity through Communist dominance. Indeed there was increased activity on the part of the Iraqi Communists, particularly in the army, but it does not appear that they were actually planning a takeover attempt or any serious challenge to the regime. Moreover, the sharp deterioration in Soviet–Iraqi relations which ensued was initiated by Baghdad; Moscow did not seek a break nor limit its support to Iraq in any way, despite the persecution of the Iraqi Communists. This support was suspended, as we have already seen, only when Iraq invaded Iran in 1980. And once Moscow changed its attitude towards the Iraq–Iran conflict, it resumed its aid to Iraq without regard for the fate or wishes of the local Communists. In fact, in the course of the Iraq–Iran war – and Hussein's continued persecution of Iraqi Communists – the latter became increasingly involved in the Kurdish struggle against Baghdad, while Moscow ignored the conflict. There was some Soviet criticism of Iraqi treatment of the Communists and there were occasional efforts to restore the Communists' semi-accepted status in the Iraqi government, but Moscow apparently never permitted this to interfere with or overshadow its pursuit of improved relations with the Saddam Hussein regime.

As another example, there is the Syrian Communist Party which has enjoyed perhaps the greatest prestige among the Arab Communist parties, primarily because of its leader Khalid Bakdesh. Bakdesh, a Kurd trained in Moscow, is the longest serving, most respected leader of the Arab Communist parties. He is reported to have been an early supporter of the united front tactic and to have continued to advocate such a policy even in the post-World War Two period of Stalin's abandonment of the idea. Yet there have been contrary reports that in the early and mid-1960s, a very difficult period for Syrian Communists, he in fact opposed the concept of 'revolutionary democracy' and rejected the idea of cooperating with non-Communist parties. Certainly this was an issue which troubled and divided the Syrian Communist Party consistently over the years.

The Syrian Communists benefited from the opening of Soviet–Syrian ties in the post-Stalin era, and from 1954 to 1958 the Party grew in size and strength. This was due to Bakdesh's organizational abilities as well as to the positive relations between Damascus and Moscow at the time. With the Egyptian–Syrian union of 1958, pursued by Cairo and Damascus ostensibly and perhaps genuinely because of growing concern over the increasing strength of the Syrian Communists, the situation was to change drastically. There was a severe crackdown on the Communists, and Bakdesh was forced to flee the country along with many Communists taking refuge in the Soviet bloc. Although the union with Egypt did not last long, the situation did not change for the Communists until the leftwing of the Ba'ath party rose to power in 1966.

Bakdesh was permitted to return to Syria, at the same time that the Soviets granted a $132 million credit to Damascus; Soviet insistence upon a *quid pro quo* is strongly suggested. Similar concern for the fate of the Syrian Communists was also suggested by Soviet pressures upon Damascus to form a national front with the Communist Party. Yet the national front idea may well have been more to satisfy Moscow's search for accommodation with the new regime than to promote the interests of the Party, for the Syrian Communists, like those in Iraq, were not entirely in favour of the idea. It was the old conflict of Moscow perceiving the optimal path as alliance with nationalist forces while local Communists mistrusted these forces, preferring independence of action. The attitude of Bakdesh, himself, is not clear, but the Party was split over the issue.

In response to its own domestic weakness, if not to Soviet pressures, the Ba'ath regime under Atassi and Jedid did bring some Communists into the government. There were immediate tensions between the Ba'ath and the Communists, however, with public anti-Communist statements and frequent crises. These became more serious following the 1967 Six-Day War, presumably because of Ba'ath anger with Moscow over Syria's ignoble defeat and the Soviets' position on the Arab–Israeli conflict. There were demands in Syria, including pressures within the Ba'ath, to remove the 'atheistic Communists' from any positions of power and, in response, Moscow published criticism of the Ba'ath expressed by Bakdesh and the Syrian Communist Party. In late 1968 there were in fact some purges of Communists from leading positions.

It is generally believed that some of the Communists' developing problems with the Ba'ath at this time were connected with factional infighting within the Ba'ath. Assad, who was Defence Minister, was said to be the leader of a more military-nationalist anti-Communist faction opposed to Ba'ath party secretary-general Jedid who represented a civilian, more radical faction. The Communist Party supported Jedid in this internal competition, criticizing the more nationalist faction. This led to the obvious accusation by Assad that Jedid was receiving assistance from the Communists, to which accusation Jedid responded with some anti-Communist measures. Whatever the actual relations or sympathies, the Jedid regime was perceived by many as being too close to Moscow and the Communists. Both the Communist Party and the Soviet Ambassador (who became particularly active when Bakdesh suffered a heart attack at the end of 1968) were said to be actively helping Jedid against Assad in the power struggles of 1968–9.

At the end of 1969 there were rumours of coup plans by Assad, Communist plans to help Jedid should a battle ensue, and Soviet threats to suspend arms deliveries in such an event. In the midst of this crisis Bakdesh journeyed to Moscow, and upon his return the Communists adopted a more neutral position *vis à vis* the Ba'ath power struggle. Indeed, during the 1970 coup which brought Assad to power, the Communists played no role, merely calling for unity. Moscow may have urged the Party to refrain from contributing to the growing instability of the Damascus regime, but it is also likely that the Soviets did not want to jeopardize future relations with Syria by being associated with the losing faction, whichever that might turn out to be. The assumption presumably was that the Communists could not play a decisive role which would tip the scales in Jedid's favour. It is possible, however, that Moscow was not opposed to Assad's rise, diverging perhaps from the Syrian Communists' preferences for Jedid.

There were quite a few differences of opinion between Moscow and the Syrian Communists. Many of these came to a head in the early 1970s. In a meeting between Soviet officials and the leadership of the Syrian Party, the Soviets criticized the Party for (a) too activist a position on the Arab–Israeli conflict, arguing that the Arab states were not yet ready for another war and that such a war might lead to World War Three; (b) too extreme a position with regard to the existence of the State of Israel; (c) too great a concentration on the Palestinian issue and too much aid to extremist groups; and (d) too much emphasis on nationalist ideas of Arab unity, that is, support for the merger plans between Libya, Egypt, the Sudan, Syria and Iraq. The old differences – with at least many in the Party – remained regarding cooperation with the Ba'ath and the creation of a national front. The Syrian Party continued to fear that this would limit them to the role of junior partner and limit their freedom of action while binding them to an identification with the regime. From the Communists' point of view, there was little to be gained by this association, for the Ba'ath would maintain its majority in all the state institutions and a monopoly on recruitment, propaganda and political activity in the army and the universities.

The Syrian Party was split on many of these issues, Bakdesh apparently agreeing with Moscow on most of them. At least he used Moscow's criticism against at least one other faction in the Party, although the Soviets reportedly had to directly intervene and mediate in order to keep the Party together prior to the 1973 Arab–Israeli War. With the acceptance by the Syrian Communist Party of the post-war resolutions, that is, the principle of a negotiated settlement with Israel, the faction led by Riad Turk left the Party and set up a rival group. Following this split no more serious rifts with Moscow came to the surface. The Soviets continued to promote Communist cooperation with the Ba'ath, and Communists did serve in the government from 1972 onwards. Throughout Assad's rule, there have been periodic but relatively limited clamp-downs on Communist activities and even occasional arrests. Bakdesh has also expressed open criticism of the Ba'ath on a number of issues. Nonetheless the Soviets have not, apparently, intervened in any way and have generally ignored Communist complaints.

If the Iraqi Communist Party was virtually destroyed by the national front policy and the Syrian Party more or less neutralized by it, the Egyptian Communist Party provides a third example of the effects of Moscow's policies on Arab Communist parties in the Middle East. Although Egypt is the largest Arab country, the Communist Party there has been the smallest in the Arab world. The Party had to contend with the double obstacle of nationalism and Islam, in the form of Nasserite Arab nationalism which incorporated socio-economic reform, and the Wafd Islamic movement which incorporated a decree of liberal rather than conservative ideas regarding the organization of society. Never a large party, the Egyptian Communist Party suffered a serious blow in the 1958 crackdown which accompanied Nasser's unification with Syria. Inasmuch as Nasser pursued this unification in the name of stemming the alarming influence of Communism in Syria, as well as in the name of Arab nationalism, such events could but bode ill for the Egyptian party. When the Communists in Iraq supported Egypt's rival, the Kassem regime in Baghdad, against the unification of Egypt and Syria, Nasser began his arrests of Egyptian Communists.

There was a deterioration of Soviet–Egyptian relations at this time, but it is not certain that it was due to Soviet anger over Nasser's moves against Egyptian Communists, rather than his whole policy regarding Syria, as we have already seen. In any case, Soviet–Egyptian relations improved only after the union with Syria failed but before any change occurred in Cairo's behaviour towards local Communists. Nasser made it quite clear to Moscow that he would not tolerate Communist activity nor Soviet intervention on their behalf. And it was not until 1964, just prior to a visit to Egypt by Khrushchev and some years after the resumption of positive Soviet–Egyptian relations, that Egypt finally released most of the Communists held prisoner. At that time Moscow accorded Egypt a $277 million credit, possibly as a *quid pro quo*, but it must be remembered that this was a period when the Soviets were seeking other things from Egypt, specifically naval and air facilities, which may have been a greater incentive for granting the loan than the release of local Communists.

What followed was the most drastic action taken by any Communist party in implementing Moscow's orders to cooperate with ruling bourgeois-nationalists and revolutionary democrats. In 1965 the Egyptian Communist Party decided to disband, opting for individual membership in Nasser's Arab Socialist Union party. This appeared to be in keeping with the Soviets' policies at the time; the disappearance of the Party would certainly eliminate an irritant in Soviet–Egyptian relations. There were even rumours that Moscow had proposed the same idea to the Syrian and Sudanese Communists, both of which parties opposed it (the pro-Soviet head of the Sudanese Party was accused by a rival faction of supporting the idea). Yet, there is evidence that in fact the decision to disband was mainly an Egyptian Communist one. It is not even certain that Moscow fully approved, although the chronic weakness of the Party and the priority of Soviet interests with the Nasser regime presumably added some appeal to the move in the eyes of Moscow. The other Arab parties were, however, opposed, whatever the Soviet position.

The Communist Party of Egypt reemerged, underground, in the 1970s. It was associated with the National Progressive Unionist Party. Sadat was even less disposed to tolerate the Communists than was his predecessor Nasser. Accusing them of coup plans and subversion, Sadat subjected the Communists to persecution and periodic arrests. The decision to reconstitute the Party may have been a Soviet one, taken in the wake of Sadat's expulsion of the Soviet advisers and the later break in Soviet–Egyptian relations. Moscow certainly had less to lose, from the point of view of its strategic and political interests, by an active Communist party in the Sadat period. It might also be argued that the reformation of the Party was a result of the more ideologically motivated policy which emanated from Moscow (with regard to the Third World) after the expulsion. The theoretical explanation which had been given for the failure of the Soviet Union to maintain Egypt's loyalty was the absence of a Marxist-Leninist organizational structure underpinning the Cairo regime. It hardly seems likely, however, that the Soviets, even in a more ideological mood, believed that the Egyptian Communists could ever constitute a major power factor in the Egyptian political arena.

The examples of the Iraqi, Syrian and Egyptian Communist Parties may serve to demonstrate the subordinate role the Arab (or any other) Communist parties had to endure *vis à vis* Soviet state-to-state relations and interests. Thus even when these relations stood in contradiction to the fortunes of the local Communist party, Moscow maintained the priority of its own interests. It is not certain, however, that the Soviets totally ignored persecution of local Communists or refrained entirely from trying to help them. The sharp deteriorations in Soviet relations with the governments of Egypt and Iraq (and Iran) at various times were caused in part, though not wholly, by the crackdowns on local Communists. There were always other factors behind these deteriorations, including criticism of Moscow generally accompanying the anti-Communist actions, so that the Soviet response was not always traceable to anti-Communism alone.

On the whole, it would appear that Moscow chose to respond only when persecution became massive, perhaps because of concern for its reputation, particularly in the Sino-Soviet context. Even then, however, it sought to preserve something of the state-to-state relationship. Moreover, the Soviet Union never initiated a complete break in relations, however severe the anti-Communist repressions. The determining factor for the severity of the Soviet response may well have been the degree of accompanying anti-Sovietism on the part of the government involved. Arab accusations notwithstanding, a similar lack of active Soviet involvement with local Communists would appear to be the case with regard to revolutionary plans or preparations for coups and the like. There is no evidence that Moscow did in fact encourage such plans, be it because of the wish to preserve state-to-state relations and regional interests, fears of the western response, or simply a low estimate of Communist strength.

Indeed there were cases of Soviet restraining action and condemnation of too activist a policy on the part of local Communists.

Two possible exceptions to the above may be the cases of the Sudan and South Yemen. The 1971 coup attempt in the Sudan is often attributed to the Communists or at least to Communist support. In fact, because of factionalism in the Sudanese Communist Party and conflicting reports regarding who supported what and when, the perpetrators of the coup were associated with the Communist Party by reputation only; Party support for the coup came only after the fact and not necessarily with Moscow's approval. The Soviets did support the Party when Numeri conducted trials and persecution of the Communists following the failed coup, and Soviet–Sudanese (as well as Soviet–Egyptian) relations suffered from the attempt. Yet less public Soviet critiques of the event clearly stated that the time had not been ripe for revolution, that the united front tactic should have been maintained with regard to Numeri, and that the faction-ridden party had acted unwisely. It would appear, therefore, that whatever Communist involvement there was in the coup attempt was an unauthorized exception to the general Soviet restraint with regard to Communist action in the Arab world.

In the case of Marxist-Leninist South Yemen, the Soviets did not even support much less play a role in the advent to power of a Marxist leadership in Aden in the 1960s. The Communists (organized in the Popular Democratic Union), like the Marxists who took over in 1967, appeared to be of a pro-Chinese orientation. The ensuing close Soviet relationship and eventual alliance with the regime may have been a special case, and will be discussed in the following chapter. Even the 1978 coup by the more radical Marxist elements of the ruling party in Aden was not clearly the work of Moscow, although it has often been cited as a sign of a radicalization of Soviet policies, worrisome to leaders such as Saddam Hussein (who was already engaged in anti-Communist repressions when the coup occurred in Aden).

A final apparent exception to Moscow's overall deemphasis of Arab Communist parties may be the creation of the Palestinian Communist Party in the early 1980s. This was not an exception to the Soviets' restraint with regard to revolutionary or violent action. The policies of the new party kept entirely in line with the more moderate, political means-united front tactics dictated by Moscow. The very creation of a new Arab Communist Party could, however, be construed as part of the 1970s' bid for more ideologically motivated allies in the Third World. Particularly since the harbinger of this party, a Palestinian Communist Organization, was set up in the mid-1970s.

Yet, the creation of the Palestinian Communist Party may have had more of an administrative-political purpose than a tactical-ideological one. The Organization and then the Party had in fact been the West Bank wing of the Jordanian Communist Party. The gradual separation of the Palestinian Communists from the Jordanians to the point of setting up an independent party may, therefore, have been a function of the change in the Soviet position regarding the establishment of a Palestinian state on the West Bank and the separation of Palestinian affairs from those of Jordan. This included greater attention to the PLO as the future government of such a state and, therefore, promotion of the new Communist Party within the PLO. While the Soviets may have hoped, thereby, to influence the ideological colouring of the PLO, it continued to promote a united-front tactic even within the Palestinian national movement rather than encouraging precipitous action or parochial demands on the part of the Communists.

15 Marxist South Yemen and the Arabian Peninsula

Although the Soviets appear to have been wary, even critical of the apparently pro-Chinese Marxists who assumed power in 1969, Soviet relations with Aden began to develop towards increasing closeness, gradually overshadowing the Aden–Peking relationship. Competition with the Chinese, certainly an important factor at the time, was not the only reason for Soviet interest. This was a period of heightened Soviet interest in the Indian Ocean, in response to the imminent withdrawal of the British from the Gulf, the American plans for a base at Diego Garcia, and the placement of the American Polaris and then Poseidon nuclear missile submarines in the Indian Ocean. Moscow also pursued a close relationship with the new regime in Somalia which, together with Aden, offered significant possibilities for Soviet strategic, particularly naval interests in the Red Sea–Indian Ocean area.

Moreover South Yemen was rapidly moving in the direction of radical reform and socialism. This included nationalization and the beginning of collectivization of agriculture as well as the adoption in 1970 of a Soviet-type political system based on a new Constitution, with the declared goal of 'scientific socialism' and a new name: People's Democratic Republic of Yemen (PDRY). In 1970 Communists (from the Popular Democratic Union) and Ba'athists (from the Ba'ath People's Vanguard Party) were brought into the government in what was the first step towards the creation of a national front of the three parties. In foreign affairs the PDRY placed itself clearly in the socialist camp, proclaiming its affinity for the Soviet Union (while nonetheless maintaining some links with China). It had already broken diplomatic relations with the United States in 1969 and actively joined the ranks of the anti-imperialist struggle, including support for national liberation movements fighting western-backed regimes.

Actually, according to western expert Stephen Page, Moscow found the PDRY somewhat too radical in both its domestic and foreign policies. In the domestic area, Moscow's concerns were reminiscent of earlier warnings to Cuba, for example, about moving too fast and too drastically for the limited reserves and backward nature of the society and economy of the country. Aden held a more radical view than Moscow regarding the Arab–Israeli conflict and, like Iraq and other Soviet clients in the Arab world, it rejected the Soviet preference for a political solution. The PDRY was also less tolerant than the Soviet Union in its attitude towards the newly independent, conservative Gulf states of Bahrain and Qatar which were at least recognized by Moscow.

These differences or possibly concerns on the part of Moscow did not, however, prevent the Soviets from gradually taking the opportunity offered by the new regime in Aden, particularly after the expulsion of the Soviet military advisers from Egypt in 1972 which led to a general expansion of Soviet relations with radical states in the region, including the PDRY. Inasmuch as Sadat's act was claimed by Saudi Arabia to have been the result of the latter's efforts to reduce the Soviets' presence, to the benefit of the Americans, Moscow had all the more reason to link Egyptian events with Soviet interests in the Arabian peninsula. Conservative, Muslim Riyadh was the most powerful opponent to the Soviet Union in the Arab world, disdaining any revival of contacts since relations lapsed on the eve of World War Two. The emerging Egyptian–Saudi friendship of the post-Nasser period could not but be alarming to the Soviet leadership, fearing the spread of Riyadh's persuasive anti-Communism, anti-Sovietism and anti-radicalism.

Thus, Moscow began to expand its involvement and aid, particularly military aid, to Aden from 1972. In that year it delivered a $20 million arms deal, for which the South Yemenis apparently could not pay, doubling the sum the following year. Soviet, East European and Cuban military advisers began to arrive, though in numbers well below those dispatched to countries like Syria and Iraq. By the mid-1970s Soviet ships were plying the port of Aden on a regular basis. The interest in the strategic port was augmented by the reopening of the Suez Canal in 1974, and the increased strategic and economic interest of both super powers in the Red Sea–Arabian Peninsula waterways to the Horn of Africa, the Indian Ocean and the Persian Gulf.

Moscow also began to support the Dhofari rebellion in Oman, in conjunction with if not at the behest of South Yemen. Initially this was a secessionist rebellion begun in 1965 under the Dhofar Liberation Front (founded in 1962), and supported by the Chinese. In 1968 a more radical leadership took over the organization, expanding its goals to revolution in all of Oman and the Arab Gulf, in conjunction with the NLF of South Yemen, accordingly changing its name to the Popular Front for the Liberation of the Occupied Arab Gulf (PFLOAG). The Soviets did not demonstrate any interest in this movement, which continued to rely on the Chinese, until the 1969 change in regime in Aden and the beginning of Moscow's close relationship with the PDRY. Even then Soviet aid was relatively limited and indirect, channelled through supplies to the PDRY. Presumably the Soviets were not only suspicious of the overly radical pro-Chinese nature of the PFLOAG, but they were also wary of the Gulf-wide ambitions of the group which, among other things, threatened to complicate Soviet relations with Iran.

Nonetheless, contacts between the PFLOAG and the Soviets, including yearly visits by Dhofari leaders to the Soviet Union, began in 1969, eventually receiving Soviet publicity, that is, a publicly acknowledged link rarely accorded by Moscow to a secessionist movement. (The Soviets never advocated the secessionist objectives but, rather, called for a 'genuinely independent, democratic, and sovereign Oman', including the Dhofaris.) Just as the regime in Aden reduced its ties to China in favour of the Soviet Union, so too the Dhofaris shifted to Moscow. This process coincided with and was aided by a shift in Chinese policies in the Gulf which led to Chinese withdrawal of support for the Dhofaris. For its part, the Soviet Union also had an interest in weakening the pro-western British-backed regime in Oman. This may account for the fact that Moscow demonstrated increased interest in the organization when the PFLOAG changed its policies, and once again its name, in 1971, to concentrate more on revolution in Oman as distinct from its broader ambitions regarding the Gulf as a whole.

Aside from propaganda support, it is not clear just what material aid the Soviets actually gave the Dhofaris. Some accounts claim that the Soviets never accorded direct assistance, but rather aided South Yemen in its assistance to the movement. This indirect aid reportedly took the form of arms deliveries through the PDRY, training by Cubans in the PDRY and, in 1973, Soviet naval transport of PDRY troops and equipment to the Oman border. Libya and Iraq also provided aid, including, presumably, Soviet arms, but these were most likely independent acts. Dhofaris reportedly trained in the Soviet Union as well as in Cuba and Soviet bloc countries and, according to some accounts, there may have been direct arms shipments to the movement, although that appears to be doubtful.

In 1975 Soviet aid began to decline, simultaneously with reduction of PDRY support for the rebellion. There were reports that Aden was critical of the decreased Soviet aid to the Dhofaris and blamed Moscow for the virtual defeat of the movement by 1976. Yet there are other, probably more accurate accounts, which claim that Aden lost interest first, with Soviet support continuing, briefly, because of concern over the intensification of Omani ties with the United States in 1975. Soviet aid was not augmented, however, and there was no attempt by Moscow to replace the South Yemenis as primary supplier and supporter, suggesting that the main reason for Soviet involvement with the Dhofaris was the interest of the Aden regime – and with the disappearance of this interest, Moscow too virtually withdrew. One can only speculate as to whether the Soviet Union would have pursued an independent interest in the Dhofaris if they had possessed a genuine chance of overthrowing the Sultan of Oman.

The withdrawal of the PDRY from the Dhofari rebellion was the result of policy changes in Aden regarding its conservative neighbours on the Arabian peninsula; this in turn was the result of political and policy battles within the South Yemeni regime itself. The rivalry between the regime's two leading figures (from 1969 to 1978) Abd al-Fattah Ismail (head of the party) and Salim Rubay Ali (head of State) determined to a large degree relations with Moscow as well. A pro-Soviet Marxist, Ismail was a party man credited with the 1975 unification of the Communists and the Ba'ath with his own National Front in a new union called the United Political Organization-National Front (UPONF). He was a doctrinaire, ideologically orientated politician who sought to model the PDRY on the Soviet Union, the new party forming the basis for the creation of a workers' vanguard party which was to build 'scientific socialism'. Rubay Ali, a Marxist with somewhat closer affinity for the Chinese, was a pragmatist and, therefore, apparently more moderate. He was wary of too close an association with the Soviet Union; he was far more sanguine than Ismail about relations with the West and the conservative Arab states. As a corollary of the latter, he was decidedly less interested in supporting the Dhofaris and more interested in seeking economic assistance from the wealthy Gulf states, particularly Yemen's neighbour Saudi Arabia.

The Soviets were encouraged by the creation of the UPONF, which was a victory for Ismail and accorded with Soviet policy as well as personal preferences. They were presumably less encouraged, however, by the expansion of PDRY–Saudi relations the following

year, with the opening of diplomatic relations between the two
countries and promises of Saudi economic assistance which totalled
four times the amount offered by Moscow. At the time Saudi Arabia
was trying to persuade Somalia to follow Egypt's lead by expelling the
Soviets and shifting to the United States. Riyadh was also actively
involved with anti-Soviet regimes even beyond the Middle East,
supporting, for example, Zaire, as well as the anti-Communist UNITA
forces in Angola. Thus, although the PDRY continued to pursue a
close relationship with the Soviet Union, Moscow was most likely
concerned about Rubay Ali's emphasis upon relations with even the
conservative Arab world, and the foreign-policy course he was steer-
ing in that direction.

From the Soviet point of view, the old Sino-Soviet competition for
Aden was now transformed into something of a Soviet–Saudi competition. As Moscow sought to consolidate a bloc of radical states,
including in time an effort to create some form of cooperation between
Aden, Somalia, post-Haile Selassi Ethiopia, Djibouti (after its independence in 1976), and possibly even Eritrea, Saudi Arabia was trying to
turn the Red Sea into an 'Arab Lake' by the exclusion of outside
powers and the creation of a security pact linking Egypt, Sudan, both
Yemens, Somalia and Saudi Arabia. This conflict of interests became
more acute when the Soviets lost their naval facilities in Egypt,
including at least one facility on the Red Sea, in 1976, and shortly
thereafter their important military installations in Somalia. The
increased importance of sea and air facilities in South Yemen became
all the more evident when Moscow became involved in the fighting in
the Horn of Africa in 1977, using the PDRY as a launching point for its
aid to Ethiopia in the Ogadan War. Rubay Ali reportedly opposed this
assistance to Addis Ababa against Somalia, particularly as he was
pursuing a thaw in relations with both Saudi Arabia – which backed
Somalia – and with the West to the point of considering renewal of
diplomatic relations with the United States.

According to a number of accounts, however, it was clear by late
1977-early 1978 that Saudi Arabia had lost the competition with
Moscow. Although Aden had not agreed to join the Soviet–Ethiopian
suppression of the Eritreans (who had broad Arab support), it did
draw closer to Ethiopia not only by enabling the Soviets and Cubans to
use PDRY facilities for the war effort but also by dispatching their own
forces (reportedly 1000 troops) to Mengistu. There was little chance for
South Yemen participation in Saudi Red Sea plans under these
circumstances. Indeed PDRY cooperation with Ethiopia in direct

opposition to Arab interests led Saudi Arabia to cut off all its aid and contacts with Aden. Relations deteriorated to the point even of occasional armed clashes on their border. Moreover, domestically Ismail consolidated its strength in the party (and in the security forces), announcing in the autumn of 1977 that the long-awaited vanguard party would be formed (Rubay Ali's objections notwithstanding) within a year. This was but one of the signs that Ismail had strengthened his position at the expense of Rubay Ali and his policies.

While the rivalry between the two South Yemen leaders derived mainly from internal issues and personal as well as tribal disputes, each had come to represent a particular foreign-policy orientation. The victory of Ismail, with the execution of Rubay Ali on 26 June 1978 was, therefore, clearly a victory for Soviet interests and involvement in the PDRY. Beyond serving Soviet interests, the 1978 coup, according to some interpretations, was actually encouraged if not engineered by Moscow as part of a more activist, ideologically orientated policy in the Third World. The fact that it occurred just a few months after the Marxist coup in Afghanistan suggested that it was part of an overall Soviet plan. Yet the role actually played by the Soviet Union in the coup is not clear. The events were as follows. Rubay Ali was engaged in reconciliation talks with the leadership of the conservative North Yemeni regime; on 24 June 1978 a missive brought by a Rubay Ali emissary exploded, killing the YAR President. Ismail used this as a pretext for a move against Rubay Ali; the central committee of the party met and accused Rubay Ali of implication in the assassination. He defended himself against these charges and fighting broke out in Aden. The Presidential Palace was attacked by the air force and the militia, both loyal to Ismail. Rubay Ali was executed for allegedly planning an armed coup against his rivals, with the backing of the West and Saudi Arabia.

There were reports that Cuban pilots flew the planes which attacked the Presidential Palace; at the least, Cubans had played a large role in the development and leadership of both the militia and the air force. More directly, there were movements of the Soviet fleet off the coast of South Yemen, presumably to deter any outside interference in the events in the capital. And the Soviets reportedly flew in several hundred Cuban troops from Ethiopia as reinforcements for security forces protecting the victorious faction. At the same time, and in the weeks that followed, the Soviets provided strong, public political support, warning that the new regime in Aden would not stand alone should it find itself under threat.

Certainly Ismail was preferable to the Soviets over Rubay Ali. The latter was conducting a policy which could have, ultimately, moved Aden into the western camp. Indeed a United States envoy had been due to arrive in the capital just days after the coup for what Rubay Ali had designated as an examination of the possibility of renewed diplomatic relations between the two. He also opposed the Soviet–Ismail idea of a vanguard party. The timing also suggested more than a casual Soviet interest in the removal of Rubay Ali. At the height of its involvement in the Ogadan War, the Soviet Union needed a loyal South Yemen, at the very least as the transfer and launching point for the dispatch of Cuban and Soviet personnel, equipment and naval assistance to the Mengistu government. The visit to Aden by Soviet Navy Commander Gorshkov just one month before the coup was a reminder of the increased importance of Aden in the wake of the loss of Soviet naval rights in Somalia. And some months prior to this Castro had tried personally to persuade the PDRY leadership to accept the proposal for the union of the radical Red Sea states. Thus, it could be argued, given the increased importance of the PDRY to Moscow, the Kremlin could not afford to rely merely on the ever-changing balance between Rubay Ali and Ismail in hopes that the latter would somehow continue to prevail.

There were also reasons, however, for the Soviets not to play a role in the removal of Rubay Ali. There were elements in Ismail's radicalism which may not have been to Moscow's liking. Ismail's belligerent ambitions regarding North Yemen were not entirely acceptable to Moscow which, as we shall see below, pursued a less than hostile policy toward the YAR. In addition, the Soviets had to consider the effect the staging of a bloody coup in the PDRY would have on other Soviet clients in the Arab world. Especially as this was a period, following Sadat's visit to Jerusalem, in which Moscow had some hopes for a broad Arab coalition against the Washington–Cairo axis. There were even Soviet overtures at this time to Saudi Arabia in this connection, while, insofar as PDRY–Soviet relations were concerned, Saudi Arabia already posed less of a threat than previously.

It is entirely possible that the coup was wholly an internal affair, the natural result of the increasingly intense rivalry between the two South Yemen leaders. Inasmuch as the Soviets had clear preferences in this rivalry, there were certainly good reasons for them to assist, once events got underway. And such assistance did comply with the more general Soviet interest at the time in securing ideologically loyal regimes in the Third World. It must be noted, however, that this more ideologically orientated policy was not pursued uniformly throughout the Third World or the Arab world. While it may have rendered Moscow predisposed to support, and aid, the coup, it did not necessarily indicate a Soviet initiative or encouragement of the events in Aden.

Whether Soviet engineered or merely Soviet assisted, the coup produced a regime which was to draw still closer to Moscow than its predecessor. Although even the new regime refrained from according the Soviets more than use of South Yemeni ports, as distinct from actual Soviet bases, it was more generous with regard to air facilities. Moreover, it created the vanguard party long promised by Ismail and, in October 1979, the Ismail regime signed a Friendship and Cooperation Treaty with Moscow. It was also one of the very few Arab regimes to support the Soviet invasion of Afghanistan. For their part, the Soviets increased their military aid to the PDRY, virtually tripling the number of Soviet bloc and Cuban military advisers (according to conservative estimates bringing them up to 1100 and 1000 respectively). Increased economic aid was also promised, but Moscow did not agree to the PDRY request for membership in CMEA, granting it only observer status.

This last may have been an indication of certain reservations Moscow still had about Aden. The Soviets obviously did not want to take on the full burden of the primitive South Yemen economy, but there was an ideological issue as well. Despite the fact that a vanguard party based on 'scientific socialism' had been created, the Soviets continued to characterize the PDRY as a country with a 'socialist orientation', no more Marxist, therefore, than Syria, for example. The only recognition of Aden's ideological advantage was the placement of it in the category of states run by 'revolutionary democratic' regimes; this category included Angola, Mozambique and Ethiopia – all of which were similarly denied CMEA membership. Moscow apparently remained suspicious of the unstable, still faction-ridden regime in Aden. Moreover, although the PDRY could offer access to certain strategic facilities, it had little to no political significance in the broader context of the region, be it in the post-Camp David Soviet competition with the United States or the post-Iranian revolution developments in the Gulf. There may even have been occasions upon which Aden was a liability or at least troublesome rather than an asset to Soviet policies in the region.

An issue which loomed large in the Aden–Moscow relationship, with ramifications for Soviet relations with other countries in the region, was the PDRY–YAR conflict. The Soviet Union had actually been more directly involved in the internal struggle which established the Yemen Arab Republic than it had been with the creation of South Yemen. The reason was that the 1962 coup which created the YAR was conducted by pro-Nasserite (some say mainly pro-Soviet) officers, bringing the full support and direct military involvement of Moscow's ally Egypt in the ensuing civil war. The Soviet Union backed the Egyptian effort, signing a treaty of friendship and assistance with Sanaa in 1964 and providing military aid, channelled through the Egyptians, as well as direct economic aid. Although Egypt was clearly following its own interests and policy, it was also serving the interests of Moscow and, therefore, was viewed by as many as a proxy for Moscow in the Yemen Civil War. Moscow continued its aid even after Egypt's withdrawal in the wake of the latter's defeat in the Arab–Israeli war of 1967, and Soviet supplies played a major role in preserving the republican regime in power against its royalist, Saudi-supported opponents. The Soviets even went so far as to commit pilots to the intensive battles at the end of 1967 and the beginning of 1968, the first such direct involvement by Soviet military in a Third World conflict since the Korean War.

By the end of the 1960s the republican regime in Sanaa, which had undergone numerous personnel changes since its inception, was moving in a more conservative direction, seeking economic and other ties with the West in addition to a compromise with the Saudis and the Saudi-backed royalists. Moscow had already found greater potential for the pursuit of its own interests in the Marxist regime in the South. In any case there was little the Soviets could offer the North except continuation of the Civil War, which Sanaa no longer wanted, and economic aid which fell short of what could be found in the West and the conservative Arab states. Soviet–YAR relations, therefore, fell to a minimum, although Moscow avoided alienating Sanaa. Careful not to push North Yemen fully into western and Saudi hands, the Soviets may still have harboured hopes for a change in North Yemen policy. With the advent of Sadat to power in Egypt and the disruption of Soviet–Sudanese relations in the wake of the 1971 coup-attempt in Khartoum, the Soviets had good reason to strive for at least correct relations with this Red Sea state.

A number of factors militated against a smooth relationship with Sanaa. Aside from North Yemen's developing contacts with Saudi Arabia, the opening of diplomatic relations with Washington in July 1972, and growing dependence upon western aid, YAR–PDRY tension became an aggravating factor. The increasing radicalization of the regime in Aden and the deepening of Soviet–PDRY relations worried the regime in Sanaa. Tension between the two Yemens mounted, as *émigrés* fleeing the South ensconced themselves in North Yemen, organizing border incidents and terrorism back into the South, apparently with North Yemeni support. The PDRY also engaged in raids into the North and in 1972 these skirmishes erupted into a brief border war between the two countries. The three-week battle ended by means of Arab mediation and talks in Cairo. The South had had no serious problem militarily, eliminating the need for Moscow to take anything but a political stand on the events. Soviet loyalty to Aden was undisputed, but Moscow was careful to place the blame for the hostilities not on North Yemen but on outside interference, specifically that of Saudi Arabia and 'the imperialists'.

Despite the fact that animosity between the two Yemens put Moscow in an uncomfortable position, the Soviets showed little interest in Yemen unification plans which were discussed in the wake of the 1972 battle. Presumably the leadership in Moscow was uncertain about the ability of the regime in Aden to dominate such a new entity; it was, therefore, uninterested in a plan which might jeopardize the continued rule of a pro-Soviet, Marxist regime even if this regime had to be limited to the South. The Soviets do not appear, however, to have had any particular influence on the course of the unification talks. If the Soviets were worried about the effects of PDRY unity with the strongly Muslim North, Saudi Arabia was even more worried about the effects of YAR unity with the Marxist South. A Saudi-backed coup installed a more conservative leader in Sanaa, leading to the demise of the unity idea, at least temporarily. North Yemen drew still closer to Saudi Arabia as South Yemen drew still closer to the Soviet Union, and border incidents resumed in 1973.

Soviet competition with Saudi Arabia – and the United States – obviously had prompted Moscow to discourage efforts by Rubay Ali in Aden to improve relations with YAR. (There was, reportedly, a brief period in 1977 when both Rubay Ali and then YAR President al-Hamdi began rapprochement talks out of disappointment with Riyadh. The Soviets do not appear to have responded one way or another.) It was, in fact, this very competition which led the Soviets repeatedly to offer Sanaa arms sales, including the offer of supplies of at least MIG–21 air-craft. These offers were turned down in favour of arms deals with the United States, financed by and channelled through Saudi Arabia. Thus the Soviet response to Saudi, and western, inroads into the

North – which were strengthened once again in 1978 – was not hostility towards the regime in Sanaa but an effort to somehow win it over, or at least keep a foot in the door. For this reason, although it was wary of North–South unification, Moscow was not interested in North–South war.

There may have been still other factors dictating Soviet opposition to such a war in the late 1970s, when renewed border tensions led to the February 1979 PDRY invasion of the North. The Camp David accords of the previous autumn had precipitated an angry Arab stand, which was joined by Saudi Arabia, against the United States. Moscow sought to exploit this for a chance at improving Soviet–Saudi relations. At the very least, the Soviets did not want the eruption of a conflict which might disrupt this new-found but obviously delicate, united anti-American activity in the Arab world. There is, therefore, no reason to assume that the Soviet Union encouraged or even agreed to the PDRY action; there were even signs that Moscow was caught by surprise.

There had been Soviet ships in the area, sporadically, since the beginning of the government crisis in Aden in 1978, but there were no unusual movements by the Soviet fleet during the border war itself. Soviet and Cuban advisers in the South reportedly assisted in certain support roles, but Moscow assumed a very low profile in the crisis. As in 1972, it blamed the conflict on outside interference, proclaiming Aden's interest in peace and calling for a rapid cease-fire. An interest in a speedy end to the conflict not only accorded with Soviet opposition to the war, and PDRY war aims, but was also prompted by growing Soviet concern over the strong American reaction to the battle. Moscow was less than pleased over the US decision to send its fleet to the area and to dispatch arms and advisers to North Yemen on an emergency basis. The Soviets had benefited from America's loss of credibility as a result of Washington's inactivity during the Iranian revolution (and, perhaps, the Ogadan war). They, therefore, did not welcome any step which might help America recoup its losses, which is what this show of force in defence of Sanaa, and by implication Saudi Arabia, might do. Nor was Moscow interested in the existence of any pretext for an expanded US military presence in the region.

The results of the war were somewhat surprising, at least with regard to Soviet interests. Instead of gratitude for American aid and condemnation of Moscow as the principle backer of Aden, North Yemen and Saudi Arabia criticized the American action, and Riyadh even guardedly praised the Soviet Union. Both Arab states appeared to be genuinely intimidated by the PDRY's power. Perhaps uncertain of Washington's role in the region (after the failure of the United States to prevent the fall of the Shah and, before then, to stem the Soviet build-up in the Horn), also undoubtedly angry over American policies (Camp David), both states seemed hesitant to provoke or alienate the Soviet Union at this juncture. The surprising result of the war, therefore, was that six months later in September 1979 (after YAR–US arms talks broke down, in part because of a new cooling in YAR–Saudi relations), Sanaa agreed to a large arms deal with the Soviets, virtually inviting them back into the country. The YAR also abstained from the United Nations censure of the Soviet invasion of Afghanistan, assuming what was generally viewed as an ambiguous stand on the issue, as distinct from the vehement condemnation expressed by most of the Arab states.

Inasmuch as Moscow signed its Friendship Treaty with the PDRY the following month, it would appear that the Soviets' effort to deal with both Yemens, albeit more closely with the South, was beginning to succeed. The only Yemeni losers were the National Democratic Front (NDF) insurgents in the North. The NDF were generally left-leaning guerrillas opposed to the central government in Sanaa primarily on tribal rather than ideological grounds. They had been receiving aid from the South since their formation in 1976; they fought with the PDRY forces in the 1979 battles. Despite the PDRY support and the fact that the NDF often proclaimed loyalty to Marxism-Leninism, it does not appear that the Soviet Union rendered the organization any assistance. Moscow almost totally ignored the existence of the NDF in its public pronouncements, celebrations, conferences and front activities; NDF possession of Soviet weapons would appear to be the result purely of PDRY, and Libyan or Syrian, transfers. As in the case of Soviet reluctance to support active PDRY belligerency against the North, so too in the case of the NDF (indeed more so), the Soviets did not wish to jeopardize their relationship with Sanaa or push the latter irrevocably into the hands of the West or Saudi Arabia by supporting an effort to overthrow the government.

The YAR rapprochement with the Soviet Union in 1979 remained relatively secure; in 1984 Sanaa renewed its original, 1964, treaty of friendship with the Soviet Union. Moscow apparently was satisfied with the fact that theirs was a primarily military relationship (through virtual gifts of Soviet arms) while Sanaa continued to be dependent upon Saudi Arabia economically. This at least kept North Yemen out of the American orbit, particularly at a time of increased US military interests in the region. And this was Moscow's primary objective with regard to North Yemen. To a large degree it was North Yemen's desire to maintain some independence from Riyadh, and America's reluctance to deal directly with Sanaa against Saudi wishes, that led to this situation. Nonetheless, Moscow's restraint with regard to both the continued leftist-insurgency in North Yemen and the PDRY's aggressive ambitions against the North was an important contributing factor.

This clear priority of the Soviets' overall interests as distinct from those of their Marxist ally in the South may not have troubled the relationship so much as the continuing factionalism in the PDRY leadership. Within several months of the Soviet–PDRY Treaty, Moscow's primary ally, Ismail, was removed in a Palace coup. There were reports that the Soviets tried to intervene, and some attribute the fact that he was not executed to this intervention. Ismail was permitted to take refuge in the Soviet Union. The new leadership, under Ali Nasir Mohammed, was not necessarily any less pro-Soviet than Ismail, but he was considered more pragmatically than ideologically motivated. In this sense he was similar to Rubay Ali and, like the earlier opponent to Ismail, Ali Nasir Mohammed sought improved relations with Saudi Arabia and the conservative Gulf states, including Oman. He had to fight a rear-guard action against more radical colleagues who sought a revival of the Dhofar rebellion and hostilities with Oman, as well as active involvement with the NDF against the government in the North.

It is not entirely clear just how Moscow regarded Ali Nasir Mohammed's policies. The PDRY leader was a loyal Marxist who proclaimed his devotion to the Soviet Union and took steps to deepen the Soviet–Aden relationship. The Soviets presumably also favoured Ali Nasir Mohammed's more restrained position with regard to forays into the North and support for the NDF in view of Soviet–YAR relations. Indeed Karen Brutents, deputy head of the CPSU Central Committee International Department, reportedly threw his weight behind Ali Nasir Mohammed in his opposition to armed PDRY support for the NDF when Sanaa launched its successful suppression of the movement in the spring of 1982. It is possible that Moscow expressed the same caution regarding revival of the Dhofar rebellion in Oman. Aside from the fact that the PFLO (the former PFLOAG) had proven quite incapable of success, the Soviet leadership may have been hesitant at the time to provide further pretext for an American military presence in the Gulf (already provided by the Iran–Iraq war) or cause for alarm on the part of the newly formed Gulf Cooperation

Council (GCC). Thus when Aden encouraged the PFLO in 1981, the Soviets remained aloof. Even when fighting broke out in the PDRY–Omani border, there was no Soviet response. And by 1982 the government in Aden was pursuing a rapprochement with Oman.

The Soviet Union was not happy about the creation of the GCC and even less happy about the emerging US–Omani military cooperation. There were reports, however, that the Soviet leadership decided that the best way to handle these problems was by calming, rather than provoking, the fears of the states in the region. This was a particularly reasonable option given the unpopular Soviet involvement in Afghanistan. Moscow reportedly enlisted Kuwait in the pursuit of this moderate policy. Kuwait, unlike the other conservative states in the region, had maintained a correct, even positive relationship with the Soviet Union since independence in 1972. It has been claimed that Kuwait had special needs dictating such a connection. Its large non-Kuwaiti population (mainly Palestinian and Iranian) plus its location alongside two of the region's most powerful countries, one of which was a hostile Iraq, created a particular vulnerability for the small oil-rich country. Kuwait sought its security in genuine non-alignment, drawing on Soviet as well as American support. In border crises with Iraq in the 1960s and 1970s Kuwait had called upon Soviet mediation, and in 1975 it began to purchase arms from the Soviet Union. During a visit of the Kuwaiti Foreign Minister to the Soviet Union in April 1981, and alone of the states of the Arabian peninsula, Kuwait also supported Brezhnev's 1980 proposal for the non-interference of great powers in the Gulf. During this same visit, an agreement reportedly was reached according to which Kuwait promised to work against US–Omani cooperation and in favour of Gulf relations with Moscow provided the Soviet Union pressed the PDRY to abandon its pressures on Oman.

The entry of Aden into the short-lived Tripartite Alliance with Ethiopia and Libya in August 1981 – a pact which was in a way Moscow's answer to the creation of the GCC – did little to encourage rapprochement in the Gulf. However, as the GCC rejected American military cooperation and, in connection with the Lebanon War, American prestige declined significantly in the Gulf states, the Soviets may have perceived an opportunity for improving their position there. It was Kuwaiti–United Arab Emirate mediation which brought about the PDRY–Oman agreement of October 1982, and it is possible that the positive relationship the Soviets had developed with Kuwait encouraged Moscow as to the ultimate effects of the agreement. Especially since the United Arab Emirates, for the first time, had begun to consider Soviet offers for at least commercial relations. In addition, Soviet–Saudi relations were once again showing signs of thaw, as Moscow supported the Fahd peace plan for the Arab–Israeli conflict and moved to exploit the anti-American response of the Gulf states to the Lebanon War and America's failures in that arena. It was later revealed that talks for the opening of Soviet–Omani relations were begun in 1983 (under Brezhnev's successor, Andropov). Thus Ali Nasir Mohammed's Gulf policies may not have been objectionable in Soviet eyes.

Nonetheless, the Soviets were critical of the PDRY–Oman agreement, and there were rumours of a cooling of Soviet–PDRY (perhaps simply Soviet–Ali Nasir Mohammed) relations on this issue and, possibly, on the matter of the opening to Riyadh. According to a number of western observers, however, the problem between the two was not Ali Nasir Mohammed's foreign policies, or not these alone, but rather domestic policies which had foreign-policy implications as well. Neither the Soviets' economic model nor their relatively limited economic aid had been able to cope with Aden's acute economic problems and abject poverty. Nor was there any reason to expect Moscow to be more forthcoming in its assistance, particularly in view of the Soviets' own economic problems at the time, the need to assist its East European allies, especially crisis-ridden Poland, and the costly overseas burdens already assumed by Moscow from Ethiopia and Angola to Mozambique and, of course, Afghanistan. Therefore, Ali Nasir Mohammed undertook a domestic development programme based in no small part on outside aid and investments – from the wealthy Gulf states and the West. He also quietly permitted the growth of a private sector in the economy, in addition to introducing measures which weakened the state-sponsored social and labour mass organizations. According to his critics, he also demonstrated too great a tolerance of the role of Islam in the country.

In 1984 internal criticism of these socio-economic policies forced Ali Nasir to promote some of his more radical opponents in the government and party politburo. And in March 1985 Ismail himself was permitted to return to Aden. Soviet media joined in the criticism of at least the economic measures adopted by Ali Nasir Mohammed, warning against the growth of the private sector. There is reason to believe, therefore, that the Soviet leadership was sympathetic to efforts at restraining Ali Nasir, although it is not certain that it actually sought to overthrow him by returning Ismail to South Yemen. It is difficult to know if Moscow believed that the measures undertaken domestically actually constituted a threat to the continuation of Aden's 'socialist orientation'. Ali Nasir himself was sufficiently loyal to Moscow as to justify a Soviet preference for stability, both in the Gulf and in the PDRY itself, as the best means of safeguarding Soviet strategic interests in the region. Still another coup and the ascent, once again, of elements bent on the 'export of revolution' may not have been the preferred choice of Moscow's own changing leadership at the time.

It may be, therefore, that the Soviets were simply striving to follow rather than lead the ever-shifting factional-tribal politics of South Yemen when the bloody infighting broke out the following year. This conclusion is strongly suggested not only by the fact that Moscow was taken by surprise by events which later unfolded, but also by the fact that Soviet Third World policies in the mid-1980s were tending away from, not towards, radicalization. The late Brezhnev and early post-Brezhnev period was one in fact of slightly improved Soviet relations with virtually all of the states of the Arabian peninsula, in one form or another. These may well have been signs of what was to become a full-blown, and successful policy initiative under Gorbachev.

16   The Soviet Union and Turkey

The importance of Turkey for the Soviet Union has consisted of a number of factors. The first is the country's position on the Soviets' southern border, which entails a 'sharing' of the Black Sea and, together with the Soviet border with Iran and points east, is one of the longest land borders of any state in the world. As in the case of Iran, the vulnerability of the border places Turkey in a special category, from the Soviet point of view, but unlike the case of Iran, Moscow's agreements with Ankara never included the right of the Soviets to intervene in the event of the presence of hostile forces beyond the border. Moreover the 1925 Non-Aggression Pact with Turkey was not renewed by Stalin after World War Two. Thus, in theory at least, the Soviets had more to worry about on this border than on its continuation with Iran. The geographic position of Turkey, however, entailed a still greater sensitivity, for the Turkish Straits, the Bosphorus and the Dardanelles, controlled the entrance and the exit to Soviet waters. The Straits constituted the only sea passage between the Black Sea and the Mediterranean, a factor which became particularly important once the Soviet Navy opened its Mediterranean Squadron in the early 1960s. They also constituted a sea attack route from the Mediterranean, employed by enemy navies in the past and weakening Soviet defences in World War Two. Thus the Straits formed a part of Moscow's vital defence and commercial interests, with roughly half of Soviet sea-borne trade transiting the control points every year.

Aside from a brief period of mutual interests following World War One, the two countries were also traditional enemies. There was a history of competition, wars and threats between the Russian and Ottoman Empires. In more recent times, this was translated into membership in opposing world blocs and alliances, with Turkish membership in the Baghdad Pact, then CENTO, and in NATO. These brought with them American bases and missiles directly on the Soviet border. Thus Turkey held strategic interests for the Soviet Union as a NATO state on its border, also controlling the vitally strategic Straits.

Beyond these geostrategic interests, Turkey also fitted into Soviet policies as a part of the Third World more generally and of the Middle East more specifically. Within the latter, it belongs to what has been called the northern tier of the Middle East, together with Iran, or in Soviet terms the Near East, which related more clearly to the eastern Mediterranean. Bordering on the Soviet Union, the northern tier has often been viewed by outside observers as more important to Moscow than the southern tier, which includes Egypt, Syria and Iraq. Indeed in the early post-war period, as we have seen, this area certainly did take priority over the southern tier, as Stalin sought to expand Soviet influence on the periphery. Yet whatever the vicissitudes of Soviet relations with southern tier states, which appeared to claim greater importance under Stalin's successors, the northern tier was never neglected.

Given the above interests, the objectives of Soviet policies regarding Turkey have ranged from minimally defensive to maximally expansionist. At the maximum end of the spectrum, one might posit the idea of a Communist takeover in Turkey, which would create a Turkish member of the Warsaw Pact, dependent upon and loyal to the Soviet Union, according Moscow direct control of the Straits and insurance against the possibility of the presence of any hostile forces on this border. If not a full-fledged ally, then Moscow would presumably like to see an ideologically sympathetic regime in Ankara and, if not this, then at least a non-hostile, neutral regime. Minimally, if not neutral, then the regime might at least be one willing to maintain good relations with the Soviet Union. Indeed, in the post-Stalin period the Soviet objective appears to have been the securing of good relations and the good will of the government in Turkey while striving for the greater objective of Turkish neutrality, that is, an end to the American military presence in the country and to Turkish membership in NATO.

In the realm of tactics or more immediate Soviet objectives, there are a number of opinions amongst outside observers and the Turks, possibly even the Soviets themselves, as to Moscow's policies regarding Turkey. It has been argued that Moscow has sought a weak, unstable Turkey. Such a situation would not only render Turkey a poor NATO component but also prepare the ground for regime dissolution and Communist takeover. Accordingly, the Soviets are said to have encouraged and assisted dissident groups in Turkey, particularly national minorities such as the Kurds and the Armenians, as well as radical terrorist groups, all seeking to undermine the central regime primarily by violent means. Evidence substantiating this interpretation of Soviet policy may be found in the 'Bulgarian connection', that is, the smuggling of arms and the provision of other forms of aid by Bulgaria to dissidents in Turkey, as well as Soviet aid to the Kurds and Armenians operating in and out of Turkey. Indeed there have been claims, from Ankara itself, that the Soviets were behind the war of terrorism which took place inside Turkey in the 1970s.

A counter claim, however, has been that the Soviet Union has in fact preferred to have a degree of stability on its border with Turkey, as with Iran. Instability and anarchy on this border could lead to hard-line right-wing regimes in Ankara as well as to outside (western) intervention. Fortification or justification of the traditional suspicion and fear of the Russians would only bind Turkey more strongly to its NATO allies, impeding rather than enhancing Moscow's pursuit of its interests – indeed defeating its purpose altogether. Evidence for this interpretation of Soviet policy may be found in the advice given local Communists. Turkish Communists were encouraged to seek the formation of a national democratic front and to participate in legal activities in order to strengthen their position, rather than prepare for or pursue a revolutionary course. Communist aid to the Kurds, therefore, has been only small and sporadic, and Soviet aid to the Armenians limited and indirect. Even as the KGB and (or through) the Bulgarians have been connected in various, usually tenuous ways with some of the more radical or violent groups, the Soviet Union has condemned the use of violence in Turkey and sought a positive relationship with whatever government has been in power, including the military government which took over in 1980.

The latter was basically the policy introduced in the post-Stalin period, in keeping with Malenkov's new foreign policy regarding the Third World, including the Middle East. Stalin's more aggressive, expansionist and revolutionary policy had indeed failed, leading to the Truman Doctrine, the introduction of the US fleet on a permanent basis in the Mediterranean and, in 1952, Turkey's adherence to NATO. Malenkov reversed the policy, immediately withdrawing the 1945–6 Soviet demands for border changes and joint control of the Straits. Yet Turkey was suspicious and unreceptive to the new Soviet overtures. Strengthening its western orientation, Turkey joined the Baghdad Pact in 1955 and permitted the opening of US bases. Although Moscow sent an economic delegation to Ankara in July 1957 following Turkish problems with US aid, a serious crisis developed between the two countries just one month later. As we have already seen, during the Syrian–US crisis beginning in August 1957, the Turks massed troops along their border with Syria. Ankara presumably was acting out of its own concerns over the increasingly pro-Soviet regime in Damascus as well as at the behest of the Americans. Indeed the Turks had earlier threatened to invade Syria should the Communists or the Soviet Union gain control of the government in Damascus. The Soviets now accused Ankara of planning such an invasion and, on 10 September 1957, sent a note to the Turkish government with a not too veiled threat of Soviet invasion should Turkey move against Syria. Attributing the crisis and even Turkey's role to 'foreign circles', and thereby proclaiming Moscow's desire for 'friendly and good neighbourly relations' with Ankara, the Soviets promised 'great calamities' to be brought upon Turkey should it participate in a war against Syria. The note also referred to the Turks' geographic vulnerability, that is, their proximity to the Soviet Union, and the possibility of troop concentrations on their mutual border, as well as the impossibility of localizing a war only to Syria in the event of attack. This threat was indeed backed-up by Soviet troop movements on the Soviet-Turkish border. A few weeks later Khrushchev commented in an interview that the Turks had 'not been very sensible. They have concentrated so many Turkish forces against Syria that they have left their frontiers with us almost bare.' Yet the crisis petered out, without any precipitous action on any side. Khrushchev actually offered a gesture of rapprochement when he attended a reception at the Turkish Embassy in Moscow at the end of October.

It seems highly unlikely that the Soviets intended, in fact, to intervene militarily against a NATO state, just as it appears most unlikely that they genuinely believed the United States was planning a move against Syria. While there was the risk that the rhetoric and even border clashes between the Turks and the Syrians might erupt into something more serious, it is most likely that the Soviets merely sought to impress with bellicose statements and reinforce their credibility in the region as a counter to the recently introduced Eisenhower Doctrine and America's rejection of Soviet Middle East proposals. Turkey made it clear to Syria that it had no aggressive intentions against it, while the United States Secretary of State Dulles had said, the same day as the Soviet note to Turkey, that it was doubtful that the situation would demand US military intervention. The albeit unsuccessful Saudi attempt to mediate between Syria and Turkey, in addition to the failure of the United Nations to take any steps which might have promoted Moscow's anti-American interests, probably led the Soviets gradually to retreat from their own rhetoric. Moreover, the Soviets were not interested in alienating Ankara but rather in discrediting Washington, a factor which mitigated against continued accusations directed at Turkey.

Nonetheless, the crisis did impede Soviet–Turkish relations. The Turks, already suspicious of Moscow, responded to the Soviet statements and moves with accusations that the Soviet Union had recreated exactly the same atmosphere of insecurity for Turkey as in 1945. The Turks expelled some Soviet military personnel from the Embassy in Ankara, and continued to reject Soviet overtures be they in the economic or any other sphere. In fact the 1950s were a most unsuccessful period in Soviet–Turkish relations. The Turks drew still closer to NATO, permitting the Americans to place IRBMs with nuclear warheads in Turkey in 1959, and Ankara remained highly suspicious of Moscow. Unlike the Arabs, the Turks had experienced Russian and Soviet attempts at imperialism; like the Iranians they shared the fears of a border with the Soviet Union. Both conditions prompted extreme caution, even reticence on the part of Ankara. This has been suggested as at least a partial reason for a Soviet decision to leap-frog over the northern tier and concentrate, rather, on the Arab states of the southern tier. Yet the Soviets did not abandon their interest in the northern tier or in improving relations with Turkey; they sought an opportunity to promote their continued interest in this strategically important country.

This opportunity appears to have come with a change in Turkish policy in the mid-1960s. While the Soviets had been willing and actively seeking improved relations, their interest was presumably sharpened by the opening of their Mediterranean naval squadron in 1964 and the changes in Soviet military doctrine in the early 1960s which brought a heightened involvement in the Middle East altogether. The crucial change in the Turkish attitude may be attributable to three developments. The first two were the weakening of the CENTO alliance and the US withdrawal of its Jupiter missiles at the end of 1962 and the beginning of 1963. These may have been interpreted in Ankara as a downgrading of the American commitment to Turkey, signalling, perhaps, an unwillingness on the part of Washington to take too great a risk for Turkey. Thus, Ankara may well have felt less secure and, therefore, in need of placating the enemy on the border.

The third development was the Cyprus issue which erupted into a crisis in 1964 and proved to be the catalyst of shifts in Turkey's relations with both super powers. The Soviet Union was not directly involved in the 1964 Cyprus crisis, nor was its position consistent throughout. Rather, it was a case of exploiting a conflict in order to further Moscow's own interests, much the way the Arab–Israeli conflict was exploited to move into the southern tier. Although, unlike the case of the Arab–Israeli conflict, the Soviets were able to exploit the disaffection of an American ally rather than a straightforward East–West polarization.

Actually the Soviets opposed Turkey when the crisis broke out. In 1963 Cypriot President Makarios suspended the Constitution, which protected the legal rights of the Turkish community, in a period of civil strife on the island. A United Nations peace-keeping force was sent, but Turkey threatened to intervene on behalf of the Turkish Cypriots. Moscow supported Makarios's move, particularly because of the clauses in the Cypriot Constitution according the British bases on the island. The Soviets favoured full Cypriot independence and, in response to the mounting crisis, sent letters to this effect to the NATO countries, basing Soviet interest on proximity of the Mediterranean to the southern border of the Soviet Union. As in the 1957 crisis, Moscow at first placed all blame on 'outside', in this case NATO, machinations, but when the Turks began air forays against the island, the Soviets addressed them directly. In the summer of 1964 Khrushchev warned the Turks against any foreign intervention on the island, declaring that such intervention would be met with a Soviet response, in the interest of preserving stability on its southern border. Moscow reportedly even offered the Greek Cypriots arms, and a TASS statement of 8 August 1964 proclaimed Soviet willingness to defend the Makarios government if attacked from outside.

In the meantime, however, the United States had warned Turkey against intervention, suggesting that Ankara could not expect NATO assistance should Turkish moves on Cyprus provoke a Soviet response. Presumably this sign of a crack in the NATO alliance prompted the Soviets to alter their position. At the end of August Moscow reportedly assured Ankara orally of its neutrality in the crisis, hinting at a new position which was to emerge during the visit of the Turkish Foreign Minister Erkin to Moscow in November. This visit itself was a clear indication of the change taking place in Turkey's attitude, presumably in response to what Ankara perceived as American desertion over the Cyprus issue. Ankara was thus rewarded by a Soviet step closer to the Turkish position on Cyprus, in the form of the communique issued at the close of the Erkin visit containing a reference to 'the legal rights of the two national communities' on the island. This position was repeated by Soviet Politburo member and soon to be President Podgornyi during the visit of a Supreme Soviet delegation to Turkey in January 1965 and by Gromyko during his May 1965 visit to Turkey. Gromyko had also added a suggestion, in a January article in *Izvestiia*, that Moscow might support Ankara's idea of a federated Cyprus. At the United Nations the Soviets demonstrated their neutrality by abstaining in the General Assembly vote on Cyprus at the end of 1965.

It is possible to explain the change in the Soviet position as a result of the change of Soviet leadership, with the replacement of Khrushchev by Kosygin and Brezhnev in October 1964. There were already signs of a more neutral Soviet position as early as the end of August, although in September the Soviets declared their willingness to defend Makarios in the case of invasion. It is, therefore, possible that it took a new leadership to introduce a more decisive policy change, presumably based on the growing assessment, even in the last months of Khrushchev's rule, that Turkey's disillusionment with the nature of the NATO and especially American commitment to Ankara offered an opportunity to further Moscow's interests. The cost to Soviet–Cypriot, and Soviet–Greek, relations was deemed small compared to the possibilities of weaning Turkey away from NATO and the United States.

To a large degree the Soviet assessment was correct. Even as Podgornyi was visiting Turkey in January 1965 the Turks announced their decision to cancel their participation in the American plan for a NATO multi-lateral nuclear force. Progress then began, albeit slowly, in Soviet–Turkish relations. Turkish President Urguplu visited the Soviet Union in August, the first such visit since well before World War Two, and agreed to the opening of significant economic relations. After long negotiations and Turkish foot-dragging, these finally materialized in the form of a $200 million Soviet credit, with quite favourable conditions, for a number of mainly industrial projects to be undertaken with Soviet assistance in Turkey. Signed by President Demeril in March 1967, this was, according to western analyst Alvin Rubinstein, the most far-reaching accord for foreign industrial assistance ever undertaken by Turkey. It was virtually doubled in 1972 when the Soviets accorded an additional $280 million of aid for the Iskenderun iron and steel plant. As was the case with the Shah's Iran, economic assistance was to be the mainstay of improved Soviet relations with Turkey. By the end of the 1960s there were over 1000 Soviet economic advisers in Turkey, and Turkey was to become one of the largest Third World recipients of Soviet economic aid and trade.

Progress was also made in the political sphere, although of a more limited nature. Exchanges of high-level visits became relatively standard after Kosygin's 1966 visit, the first ever by a Soviet Premier, to Ankara. Numerous agreements were signed between the two countries in connection with minor border adjustments, and the tone of mutual propaganda criticism was decidedly muted. Turkey permitted the transfer of Soviet arms to both Syria and Iraq, via Turkey, in 1970, and Soviet overflights of equipment to the Arabs in the 1973 Yom Kippur War. There was a minor incident between the two governments in 1970, arising from the hi-jacking of a Soviet aircraft to Turkey by two Lithuanians. The Turks gave the hi-jackers sanctuary; the Soviets retaliated by shooting down an American military plane which overflew the border, with both American and Turkish officers aboard. Yet both sides avoided major crisis. The Soviets were unsuccessful, however, in their attempts in the 1960s and early 1970s to obtain a new non-aggression pact or friendship treaty with Ankara, obtaining in 1972 only a Declaration of Principles on Good Neighbourly Relations. Nor did they succeed in their encouragement of Turkey to eliminate the American military presence in the country.

It was once again a Cyprus crisis which gave new momentum to Soviet–Turkish relations, in the mid-1970s. The Soviet position on Cyprus was not totally consistent in the period between the two crises. Apparently to placate the Greeks or at least Makarios during the latter's official visit to the Soviet Union in 1971, Moscow back-tracked from its earlier tilt towards Turkey. Still ostensibly neutral, the Soviets joined Makarios in condemning all outside interference, calling for a solution to be reached by the people of Cyprus themselves and the removal of all foreign troops. The existence, and rights, of two distinct communities were ignored, while any role for Turkey was implicitly ruled out. The Soviets preferred to interpret the ban on outside interference as targeted only against the British, or NATO as such, but Ankara did not share this interpretation. The Soviets corrected matters when Podgornyi visited Turkey the following year. Claiming that there had been no change in the Soviet position, the Soviet President returned to the earlier formula regarding two communities, as preferred by Turkey, and refrained from any mention of foreign involvement. Moreover, the communique at the end of Podgornyi's visit explicitly ruled out the idea of Cypriot union with Greece and incorporated most of the Turkish demands.

In the summer of 1974 Cyprus erupted once again in crisis when Makarios was removed by a coup apparently engineered by the military rulers of Greece. Turkey responded by invading and occupying close to one-half of the island. Blaming NATO for the crisis, Moscow refrained from criticizing the Turks' move, thereby at least tacitly supporting it. It also sent an observer to the talks (in Geneva between Britain, Greece and Turkey) which ensued, seeking to play at least a small role – and thus have some say – in the determination of the future of the island *vis à vis* its two NATO rival-patrons. Presumably for the same reason, Moscow recommended internationalization of the issue, that is, an international conference within the framework of the United Nations, such as the one opened some months earlier on the Arab–Israeli conflict. The objective would be the return of Makarios and, as advocated by the Soviets in the past, an independent, non-aligned Cyprus devoid of foreign (British) bases.

Although the Soviet Union at least implicitly backed Turkey in the crisis, and was amply praised by Ankara for doing so, the situation was not entirely an easy one for Soviet policy-makers. Shortly after the outbreak of the crisis, the generals in Athens were replaced by a civilian government whose anti-American–anti-NATO tendencies were clearly of interest to Moscow. Thus the Soviets sought to focus the issue on NATO rather than Greece versus Turkey, hoping to exploit both the American opposition to the Turkish move and the new anti-Americanism in Athens. To this end and in justification of its own involvement, the Soviets spoke in terms of a NATO presence as a threat to the Soviet Union. Yet too strong a Soviet involvement carried with it the risk of pushing one or the other of the two protagonists back to the Americans for protection. Moreover, the Soviet demand for withdrawal of all foreign troops, although directed against the British, implicitly included the Turks, complicating matters somewhat for Moscow in Ankara. Nor were the Turks entirely happy with the idea of internationalizing the conflict by means of a UN-sponsored conference. And the Soviets were not too pleased with the *de facto* partition of the island, which seemed to be emerging, although they did have common ground with Ankara in their opposition to unification of any or all of Cyprus with Greece.

It is unlikely, however, that the Soviet leadership was particularly concerned about the resolution of the Cyprus problem. The island itself was not all that important, despite the growth of the Soviet naval presence in the eastern Mediterranean. The removal of NATO facilities on the island was desirable, but not a major matter. The continued conflict as a thorn in the side of NATO may have been more promising. At the same time, an acute conflict always ran the risk of precipitating direct American involvement, as well as creating a certain degree of instability and even insecurity regarding the vital Turkish Straits. Therefore, Moscow was probably interested in the conflict only to a limited degree, primarily to fan the flames of inner-NATO troubles, with little inherent interest beyond limiting the NATO presence and the effectiveness of the western alliance.

The greatest Soviet return on the Cyprus conflict was the sharp deterioration which occurred in US-Turkish relations. In response to the Turkish invasion of Cyprus, the American Congress cut off US military aid to Ankara at the beginning of 1975. The Turks responded by closing the American bases in Turkey. With little effort on the part of the Soviets, one of their major objectives – the removal of NATO facilities from this area to the south of their border – was achieved, at least temporarily. In addition, both the position of the Soviets in the Cyprus crisis and the Turkish rift with Washington led to a decided improvement in Soviet–Turkish relations. This was translated into another large economic agreement: a Soviet credit for $700 million for existing and new projects. In 1977 a ten-year economic agreement was negotiated for the sum of $1.3 billion and, two years later, a $3.8 billion agreement was signed for energy-related projects. By the beginning of the 1980s Turkey had received some $2 billion in Soviet economic assistance. There was renewed progress in the political sphere too, as Ankara declared its interest in a 'balanced' foreign policy. In 1976 a Turkish military delegation visited the Soviet Union, Turkish observers were invited to witness Warsaw Pact exercises in the Caucasus, and Soviet chief-of-staff Ogarkov was invited to Ankara in 1978. None of these things resulted in military relations, but they did indicate a more relaxed political relationship (and perhaps signalled Turkey's consideration, at least, of alternative sources for the suspended US aid). In this sense, the Soviet Union was beginning to appear as an alternative to the West.

The Soviet–Turkish border in the Black Sea was also amicably delineated in talks between the two countries in 1978, and Ankara appeared to take a more flexible attitude towards the movement of Soviet warships through the Straits. In 1976, for example, it allowed the passage of the aircraft carrier *Kiev*, accepting the Soviet classification of it as an anti-submarine vessel so as to circumvent the absence of clauses in the Montreux Treaty which would permit aircraft carriers to transit. Similar leniency had been shown during the 1973 war, when Turkey closed an eye to the time requirements for prior notification of the passage of Soviet warships.

The most significant political step forward, however, was the signing of a 'Political Document on the Principles of Good Neighbourly and Friendly Cooperation' in June 1978. Preceded by the 1972 Declaration and agreed upon in principle during a trip by Kosygin to Ankara in 1976, it took a good deal of negotiation and a few changes of the Turkish government finally to produce the political document. Although it was not the non-aggression pact sought by Moscow, nor a treaty of friendship of the type signed with Egypt and Iraq in the early 1970s and other Third World states, the Political Document was a break-through for Soviet relations with a NATO country. It even had a slight improvement over the 1925 Soviet–Turkish agreement; the latter had banned aggression or joining in third-party aggression against the signatories, while the 1978 Document banned the use of each country's territory for the perpetration of aggression or subversion against other countries. From the Soviet point of view, this was meant to prevent NATO activity or facilities in Turkey, although the Turks had a more limited interpretation. In any case, the Document was a political achievement from the Soviet point of view even if it proved to have little practical value.

Just two months after the signing of the Political Document, Turkey agreed to the reopening of American bases, inasmuch as Washington had lifted its embargo on arms sales to Ankara. This was a serious blow to what had appeared to be significant progress in the achievement of Soviet goals in Turkey. It also demonstrated the paucity of the actual achievements and the problematics of the relationship. Turkish President Ecevit had sent Brezhnev assurances that Turkey's membership in NATO would never be used in a way to create anxiety or insecurity for its neighbour, but the Soviets had sought much more. The return of the American bases threatened renewed American surveillance and monitoring of Soviet testing and troop movements; it also meant the rebuilding of American air and naval facilities. It clearly defeated Moscow's effort eventually to disengage Turkey from NATO altogether.

The Soviets invoked the new Good Neighbourly and Friendly Cooperation Political Document, but Ankara insisted that this did not apply. Moscow's gains regarding the Straits were similarly vulnerable; in the absence of any new treaty, Turkish flexibility was entirely dependent upon the goodwill of the government in Ankara at any given time. Thus, as in the past, these vital waterways were still greatly controlled by a NATO country acting according to its own interests. This became apparent in a less critical sphere when Turkey reversed its leniency of 1973 and, in 1978, refused the Soviets over-flight rights for the transfer of military aid to Ethiopia during the Ogadan War. Also on the negative side of the ledger, the Turks, reportedly, not only turned down Soviet offers of arms, but they also rejected Moscow's overtures for the use of Turkish facilities – and possibly facilities of their own – for the Soviet fleet. Nor did the Turkish Communist Party fare any better, or achieve legality, even in the period of improved Soviet–Turkish relations.

It would appear, therefore, that the ebb and flow of Soviet–Turkish relations were basically dependent upon and determined by the state of Turkish–American relations. Domestic Turkish factors do not appear to have played a significant role inasmuch as improvements and deteriorations in relations often occurred during the administration of one and the same government. While one Turkish party has been treated by Soviet media more favourably than another, the Turks for their part have shown only slightly varying degrees of suspicion regarding Moscow. Indeed their own negative attitude toward the local Communists, and even the vociferous objection to what many viewed as Soviet support for the flare-up of terrorism and civil disorder in the 1970s, did not prevent the kind of progress represented by the conclusion of the 1978 Political Document. Presumably it was this believed Soviet support for local dissidents that led to the clause in the Document calling for mutual respect for each other's 'public order', along with territorial integrity, security and so forth. It did not, however, prevent the signing of the Document. Rather, it was only after the United States resumed its interest in Turkey, particularly in the wake of events in the Persian Gulf and Afghanistan, that Ankara demonstrated decidedly less interest in Moscow.

With the United States once again willing to arm Turkey (the Cyprus issue was left at the 1974 stalemate, the island virtually divided but not formally partitioned), there were good reasons for Ankara to strengthen its ties to NATO once again. The military coup of September 1980 brought to power many of the very people who had been most critical of Soviet support for terrorism and the local Communists. Their suspicious attitude towards Moscow was presumably fortified by the Soviet invasion of Afghanistan at the end of 1979. Ankara strongly protested at the invasion and became the recipient of thousands of Afghan refugees. Past doubts about the American commitment may have been allayed by the US offer of a Defense Cooperation Agreement (signed in the spring of 1980) and, insofar as economic needs may have motivated the growth of ties with the Soviets, a new economic aid package negotiated with Washington apparently sealed Turkey's renewed unambiguous allegiance to the West.

This is not to say that Soviet–Turkish relations ceased or were even reversed in the 1980s. Moscow sought to maintain if not improve relations despite the Turkish–American rapprochement and the cold-war atmosphere which dominated the region in the early 1980s. Soviet propaganda vociferously castigated the military regime in Ankara for its domestic repressive measures but particularly for its cooperation with the United States, accusing it of expanding the US military presence beyond that demanded by its NATO commitments and converting Turkey into a base for the Americans' new Rapid Deployment Force. Presumably in deference to the leftist government in Athens at the time, Moscow also condemned what it called the 'illegal' creation of the Turkish Republic of Northern Cyprus in November 1983. Yet, at the same time, the Soviets proclaimed their interest in raising Soviet–Turkish relations to a 'new, higher level' than in the past, and Brezhnev told the 1981 CPSU Congress that the Soviet Union was (still) ready to develop good neighbourly relations with Turkey. This was evident in the increase which took place in Moscow's share of Turkey's foreign trade, which rose from 2 per cent in 1978 – the year of the signing of the Political Document – to 8 per cent (according to Soviet sources) in 1981 – the year after the military coup. A new three-year trade agreement was signed in 1983, and a scientific-cultural accord was also negotiated in 1982.

There was a brief hiatus in political contacts after the 1980 coup, but in late 1982 the Turkish Foreign Minister Ilter Turkmen visited Moscow, delcaring his interest in a stable relationship with Turkey's neighbour to the North. This resumption of normal relations was consummated after the return to restricted democracy in Turkey and the elections of November 1983. Following these elections, Soviet Premier Tikonov paid a visit to Ankara – the first visit by a Soviet Premier since Kosygin's 1976 trip. In 1984 the two countries signed their largest ever economic agreement, providing for Soviet crude oil and natural gas to Turkey in exchange for Turkish products. Implementation of this deal began only in 1987 with the export of 1.5 million tons of crude oil to Turkey and the signing of an agreement for

Turkey to build resort facilities in the Soviet Union. Turkish Premier Ozal visited the Soviet Union in 1986 and there was an exchange of military commanders in 1986 and 1987 as relations between the two countries steadily improved once again. The impact of Gorbachev's new policies was evident in this improvement when the Soviet Union agreed in 1988 to open a crossing point on its border with Turkey, which had been closed since 1937.

Soviet complaints about Turkey's military relations with Washington and its suppression of local Communists did continue. For its part, Ankara complained of Soviet support for the Turkish Kurds and Armenians. The former, including the sometimes Soviet–backed Workers Party of Kurdistan (PPK) had indeed become active once again when the Iran–Iraq war rekindled Kurdish insurgency in several countries. Both minorities apparently were receiving training and arms from the Soviets, with Bulgarian, Syrian and Palestinian help, although the last two may not have been at the behest of Moscow.

Despite these ties, it would appear that Moscow was still concentrating its primary efforts on improved relations, even during periods of tougher governments in Ankara, rather than on subversive activity. As in the past, the mainstay of Soviet policy was economic assistance, while striving to prove to Turkey that a stable relationship with Moscow would provide greater security for Turkey than the military aid or presence of the United States. In view of this argument, the Soviets chose a cautious even cooperative rather than confrontational approach to Ankara. The success of such an approach for the Soviet Union appeared to be dependent, however, more on the fluctuations in American–Turkish relations than decisions taken in Moscow at that time.

17 Gorbachev's Middle East policy

'New thinking' in Soviet foreign policy

Gorbachev and the foreign-policy people he brought to power after his own ascent in 1985 believed that Soviet foreign policy had been in a state of stagnation during the last years of the Brezhnev era. However Soviet ventures in Angola, Ethiopia, Mozambique, South Yemen, Afghanistan and elsewhere may have appeared in western eyes, as Soviet activism and perhaps success, to the Soviets they registered as failures or at the least as investments too great for the return received. There was an attempt by Gorbachev to revitalize Soviet foreign policy altogether, to invest it not only with a new, modern and internationally more acceptable image but also with originality and flexibility in order to break the many deadlocks binding the Kremlin, be they in arms control, the conflict with China, relations with Japan, the Third World or international trade. In addition to this overall revamping of policies, Gorbachev's massive reform programme of 'perestroika' dictated a concentration on domestic affairs and, consequently, an interest in international stability and quiet. Specifically these plans required a respite in relations with the West, in particular with the United States with whom improved relations were part of the economic as well as diplomatic cooperation deemed necessary for 'perestroika'.

Gorbachev also introduced a number of new concepts which went beyond the traditional peaceful coexistence ideas of earlier years. He spoke of the concept of 'interdependence' by which he meant the existence of bonds or at least interests of a universal nature, that superseded the particularistic interests and aspirations of individual states. Be it in connection with environment, natural resources, modern warfare or trade, the world could no longer be viewed in terms of blocs or even concepts of enemy or ally. Rather a 'mutual balance' was to be sought between the particular states, recognizing the interests of all, seeking to accommodate, through some sort of international balancing act, the various interests instead of the all-or-nothing, zero-sum game approach. Implicit in this view was the idea that socialism was no longer in a competitive position with capitalism; indeed it was recognition of the failure of socialism to supplant capitalism and an admission of capitalism's ability to overcome its contradictions, surviving, even thriving.

Within this new picture of interdependence and mutual balance, regional conflicts were viewed somewhat differently. Their interconnectedness with global conflict, primarily through the risk of escalation to global levels was of primary concern. Thus resolution of regional conflict was considered essential not only to gain stability and the respite necessary for internal Soviet development, but also in order to avoid global conflagration. Moreover, it was admitted that a competitive approach at the regional level, and the encouragement or involvement with such conflicts, interfered with and created obstacles to the pursuit of cooperation at the global level. These were theoretical supplements which went beyond the pragmatic considerations of 'perestroika', even if born of this consideration.

The new foreign policy or 'new thinking', as it was called, had a military side as well, for interdependence appeared to rule out the more aggressive and hostile theories of both deterrence and the so-called external function of the Soviet armed forces used to justify the power-projection practices of the 1970s. In place of deterrence came the concept of 'sufficient defence'. A vague term, open to varied interpretation, it nonetheless conveyed the idea that the primary if not sole function of the Soviet armed forces was to defend the Soviet state or, at most, the socialist bloc. Thus if deterrence were not to be sought in the sphere of the super-powers, power was not to be projected into the Third World. Here too a less competitive approach acknowledged the fact that socialism had not succeeded in supplanting capitalism as a model for development. Accommodation to this fact was to be sought, dictating a policy not of abandonment of interests in the Third World but of greater realism and pragmatism. As Soviet diplomats were instructed by the new Foreign Minister Shevardnadze, common sense, not ideology, was to dictate policy. The non-ideological approach, which eschewed the 1970s' effort to build Marxist-Leninist parties in the Third World and support only countries with a 'socialist orientation', was now embedded in the Party programme. The new programme, approved by the 1986 CPSU Congress, called for the development of favourable relations with capitalist countries in the Third World.

Most if not all of these ideas had been around before. Some were even adopted in the Khrushchev period, while others were increasingly discussed in the 1970s. In fact a pattern had begun to appear in the late 1970s when many of the above views concerning regional conflicts, power projection, Third World development and the non-ideological approach were argued, gradually finding their way from academic, military and Party discussions into leadership speeches by 1981. The last year of Brezhnev's life and the brief Andropov period saw references, possibly even the introduction of limited aspects of the new approach – what might be called a more realistic Soviet Union first policy, without, however, the conceptual innovations of the Gorbachev era.

Under Gorbachev many theorists of these ideas assumed central roles in the foreign-policy establishment: Karen Brutents, who became Central Committee International Department deputy chief, and later first deputy chief; Evgenii Primakov who was made candidate Central Committee member and then candidate Politburo member as well as head of the Institute for World Economy and International Relations (which he left in 1989 when elected chair of one of the chambers of the new Soviet parliament); his deputy V. V. Zhurkin was given a new Institute for European Affairs. These were people associated with ideas such as the linkage between regional and global conflicts, and the need, therefore, to eliminate regional strife. They had advocated the more realistic attitude towards the prospects for socialism in the Third World and the need for a less ideological, united front, pragmatic approach. Their superiors, Aleksandr Yakovlev in the Party and Foreign Minister Edward Shevardnadze clearly were receptive to their ideas, if not themselves the initiators.

There were undoubtedly opponents to the new ideas as well. Yegor Ligachev was the most senior and visible of these, attacking the 'non-class' approach of the new foreign policy. There were also numerous expressions of opposition among the military, who wrote of the continued legitimacy of certain types of military conflict as distinct from the blanket demand for purely political resolution of conflicts. They appeared to defend the 'external function' of the Soviet armed forces, implying if not stating that there should still be an active Soviet role in Third World conflicts. Most of this criticism, however, diminished if not totally disappeared after 1987, some critics even explicitly reversing their positions.

In late 1988 an authoritative article appeared in the Soviet journal *International Affairs* criticizing Soviet Third World policies under Brezhnev, admitting that Soviet activism had contributed to the continuation of regional conflicts as well as harmed détente. As this position was increasingly expressed, there were even those, from the Foreign Ministry as well as academia, who argued that Soviet arms supplies also played a contributory, detrimental role. Thus both the nature and the recipients of all types of Soviet support, it was urged, should be determined by a different set of non-ideological criteria in keeping with a new concept of the Soviets' role in the world.

Institutional changes were introduced as well, to accommodate the spirit of 'new thinking' and the application of 'perestroika' to the foreign-policy sphere. 'Perestroika' entailed a major change in the role of the Party altogether. Seeking to separate Party and government, to the advantage of the latter, Gorbachev sought to remove the Party from matters of day to day policy. He drastically reduced the size of the Central Committee departments, including the ID, augmenting both the independence and importance of the government ministries, including the Foreign Ministry. Within the Party, he further reduced the role of the ID by creating a Party commission for international affairs, under Politburo member Yakovlev, which was to serve as a foreign-policy consultative body for the Party First Secretary. At the same time, the Foreign Ministry itself was reorganized and genuinely upgraded, with Foreign Minister (and Politburo member) Shevardnadze playing an increasingly central role. A foreign affairs committee was created in the new Soviet parliament which, Gorbachev claimed, would have significant powers of review if not actual policy-making. It would have some control over the KGB and the military as well, in part of a broader effort to subordinate those two bureaucracies more strictly to the foreign-policy decisions of the government. Shevardnadze declared that foreign-policy decisions, such as the use of Soviet troops overseas, should also be subject to parliamentary approval. Within these institutional changes, the research institutes were also separated more clearly from the Party, their new independence meant to render them also more influential. Thus foreign-policy decisions were to be subject to the same democratization process as domestic decisions, including the liberalized dissemination of information necessary for greater public discussion.

The new leadership began to innovate concrete new policies, in accord with the new concepts and ideas. The results could be seen, directly or indirectly, in such things as the INF agreement of December 1987 with Washington, the withdrawal from Afghanistan, the resolution of the Angola conflict, the beginning of Vietnamese withdrawal from Kampuchea, and even the beginning of talks to end the Western Sahara conflict and a number of other such conflicts, as well as the improvement of relations with China, talks with Japan, and the opening or improvement of relations with many capitalist and/or conservative states, from Mexico and Brazil to Qatar and South Korea. According to Gorbachev, the Middle East was on the same agenda, to be directly linked with the improved super-power relationship and the need to resolve regional conflicts. Moscow's claim was that a new Soviet policy was now operative in the Middle East.

The Arab–Israeli conflict

These claims notwithstanding, it was not entirely clear just how new – or totally new– Soviet Middle East policies were under Gorbachev. As we have seen with regard to the Arab–Israeli conflict, the Soviet attitude toward a settlement had gradually shifted over the years, and in the 1970s Moscow, on balance, preferred to see a settlement. The reasons could be traced to a number of factors: the growing independence of the Arab states, due in part to the benefits of petro-dollars; the diminishing Soviet control and heightened dangers of war, with its risks of super-power confrontation; declining Soviet positions in the Arab world, countered by an increase in American gains in the area; shifting Soviet interests in the direction of the Indian Ocean–Persian Gulf area; and possibly concern over the nuclearization of the conflict.

By achieving resolution of the conflict with Soviet participation, Moscow may have hoped to be able to stem its own retreat, shore up what assets it had and ensure its continued presence by being part of an internationally recognized agreement. Soviet naval and air facilities presumably could be maintained, even as these assets became somewhat less vital, with increasing Soviet logistics capabilities, and their purpose somewhat reduced – from comprising part of overall Soviet power projection, to the more limited traditional protection of the Soviet southern perimeter facing NATO's southern flank. The Soviet Union might continue to sell arms, preserving whatever profits were derived in this way, while perhaps limiting American sales to the area and relieving the pressures placed upon Moscow by the growing arms race pursued by its own clients. A settlement may not have been viewed as an ideal objective for the Soviet Union, but it was probably seen as preferable to the more likely alternative: a *Pax Americana*.

Thus the Soviets' main objective prior to Gorbachev had been to prevent an American-mediated settlement, and the vehicle by which to achieve this was the convening of an international conference. Soviet interest in such a conference was in direct proportion to American successes in the region, waning when such progress appeared impeded. The tactic employed to bloc American progress in the absence of a conference or Soviet participation was the attempted creation of a radical bloc. Such a bloc could be used to pressure the United States to agree to a conference, if the Soviets could appear to hold the war option, control the threat of war or the key to moderation of the Arabs. At the same time détente was invoked as the basis for the demand for super-power cooperation, that is, inclusion of Moscow.

Yet the Soviets demonstrated surprisingly little imagination or originality in this period. The only concession they offered as an inducement to Israel to agree to Soviet participation was Soviet recognition of the country's 1949–67 borders. Even as Moscow did this, however, it sought favour with the Arabs by supporting the demand for a Palestinian state. Its substantive positions basically were altered only in response to the United States' positions. This was particularly the case with regard to the Palestinian issue, which was the Achilles' heel of Washington's Middle East policy. A glaring example of this was Moscow's official recognition of the PLO as the sole legitimate representative of the Palestinian people, only in 1978 – just within weeks of the Camp David accords.

Under Gorbachev, Soviet policy with regard to the Arab–Israeli conflict appeared to be guided by the same overall objectives: to prevent a *Pax Americana* and to prevent instability in an area close to the Soviet border, in which both super-powers were involved. Additional motivation and new tactics were to appear, however. 'Perestroika' at home, that is the need for a stable international environment so as to concentrate on domestic reform, improved relations with the United States, the idea of interdependence and the need to resolve regional conflict all constituted new elements motivating Soviet policy in the Middle East. Tactics too were to be determined by the new theories of balance, adjustment if not abandonment of the zero-sum game adversary approach, and flexibility characterized by a pragmatic willingness to make concessions in order to achieve Soviet objectives.

Policy towards Israel

The new tactics, consistent with overall Soviet foreign policy and policy towards the Third World, were readily apparent in Soviet relations with Israel. Diplomatic relations had been broken with Jerusalem at the close of the Six Day War, as a symbolic step which hardly compensated the Arabs for the lack of Soviet assistance in that war. Nonetheless, having severed relations, it would take a political act of some significance to renew them without alienating the Arabs and further damaging what had become over the years relatively strained relations between Moscow and many states in the Arab world. It is difficult to know if Moscow viewed the absence of relations as a particular hardship. Indirect contacts with Israel had been maintained; in some years the foreign ministers had met within the framework of the opening of the General Assembly of the United Nations, and the Soviets had been able even to co-chair the Geneva Conference of 1973 despite the absence of relations with Israel.

Yet Moscow had indicated to the Arabs, at least during the Lebanon War if not earlier, that it could not actively intercede because of the absence of relations with Israel. Whereas this was probably merely an excuse for inaction, as well, perhaps, as pressure on the Arabs to accept more moderate positions (similar to Moscow's consistent rejection of Arab urging to withdraw recognition of Israel altogether), it did suggest Soviet discomfort with the situation. This presumably derived from the disadvantage Moscow may have felt it suffered from the fact that Washington could deal with all parties to the conflict, with the exception of the PLO. It may also have derived from other side effects of the absence of relations, such as the lack of direct control of intelligence and clandestine activities inside Israel and, more importantly, the transfer of the Soviet Jewish emigration issue to the realm of Soviet–American relations in part because of the absence of Soviet–Israeli relations. Yet whatever discomfort did exist had clearly been insufficient to offset the losses Moscow might incur by resuming relations.

While the absence of relations with Israel was by no means a priority issue, even if something of an anomaly in Soviet foreign policy, the Soviets set certain conditions for the renewal of relations. In conversation with Israeli Foreign Minister Abba Eban at the Geneva Conference, Soviet Foreign Minister Gromyko said that progress in the peace process would bring about formal renewal of ties; later Israel's return to the 4 June 1967 lines was made a condition and, later still, during the Lebanon crisis in the early 1980s, abandonment of Israel's close relationship with the United States.

The Gorbachev period saw a gradual reduction of the conditions set by Moscow. First Soviet officials dropped the US-connected demand, then they spoke of renewed relations when the state of aggression, initiated they claimed by Israel, came to an end – specifically the withdrawal to the 1967 lines. Increasingly, however, the only condition referred to was progress in the peace process such as the opening of an international conference or even simply Israeli agreement to such a forum. In April 1987 Gorbachev stated, in the presence of Syrian President Assad, that the absence of Soviet relations with Israel was 'abnormal', and this became the common phrase in subsequent Soviet references.

Beyond the realm of words, small but increasingly significant steps were undertaken, in effect opening direct and even official relations with Israel, beginning in mid-1985. Surprisingly positive references to Israel in the Soviet press were accompanied by meetings between Soviet and Israeli diplomats, beyond the usual UN venue, leading to an official meeting in Helsinki in 1986 to discuss the possibility of a Soviet consular delegation to Tel Aviv, upon Soviet request. These meetings assumed more significant proportions when in April 1987 Foreign Minister Shimon Peres met with Karen Brutents in Rome, opening what were to become relatively regular consultations between Israeli and Soviet officials. Going beyond the customary meetings at the United Nations, Shevardnadze met with Israeli Foreign Minister Moshe Arens in France in January 1989 and then just a month later in Cairo during the Soviet Foreign Minister's Middle East tour. Indeed this last meeting appeared to place Israel, along with Jordan, Egypt, Syria and Iraq, among those nations with which Moscow sought to pursue its peace initiatives. While far short of a trip to Israel itself, the meeting did appear to elevate the place Israel held in Moscow's thinking. The converse was also true, for by agreeing to meet Shevardnadze during what was publicized as his Middle East peace-seeking tour, Israel appeared to be according Moscow a new status, close to that of mediator, previously accorded Washington exclusively. The symbolic nature of the Shevardnadze–Arens meeting in Cairo was not lost on Moscow's allies, however, and the temporary addition of a new precondition for the resumption of Soviet–Israeli relations (Shevardnadze demanded Israel speak with the PLO) was apparently the concession made to Arab, particularly PLO sensitivities.

At the formal diplomatic level a Soviet consular delegation arrived in Israel in July 1987, ostensibly to remain only temporarily in order to deal with Soviet properties and citizens in Israel. In fact the delegation repeatedly renewed its visas, adding at least one delegate from the

Foreign Ministry's political rather than consular section. After repeatedly refusing reciprocity, Moscow finally agreed in 1988 to an Israeli consular delegation, which was granted its visas to the Soviet Union exactly one year after the Soviet delegation began its stay in Israel. Israeli cooperation with Soviet authorities in the incident of the hijacking of a Soviet aircraft to Tel Aviv late in 1988, as well as Israeli aid to Armenian earthquake victims, led the Soviets to remove most of the technical obstacles faced by Israeli diplomats in Moscow. This included the permission for the Israeli delegation to use the premises of the former Israeli chancellory, openly acknowledged as part of an overall improvement in relations and indicative of a willingness eventually to resume full diplomatic relations. Cultural ties were resumed after the break of some twenty years, as Soviet performing groups, delegations and some academics were permitted to visit Israel, with reciprocity for groups and visitors from Israel. Moscow expressed an interest in purchasing Israeli agricultural products and know-how.

Similar contacts resumed between Israel and Eastern Europe, with Hungary and Poland permitting the opening of interest sections with Israel. These eventually became embassies as full diplomatic relations were restored between Israel and these two countries in 1989. Even before its revolution in November 1989, Czechoslovakia expressed an interest in joining the new contacts with Israel. It too resumed full diplomatic relations by 1990. Bulgaria and East Germany joined these moves and altogether Israeli–East European commercial as well as academic, cultural and tourist exchanges underwent significant progress, even prior to the free election held in 1990 in these countries.

At the same time the press of the Soviet bloc assumed a new tone towards Israel, and the central press in the Soviet Union abandoned its formerly virulent anti-Zionist diatribes. While the Committee for Anti-Zionism was not disbanded (although the contrary was reported by the Soviet press on a number of occasions), a new approach even to the ideology of Zionism seemed to be emerging. An article appearing in 1988 spoke of the need to acknowledge the complexities of this ideology and the different streams which had developed in Zionist thinking. A few months later this argument was taken further, condemning the pre-Gorbachev anti-Zionist campaign as anti-Semitic and, thus, similar to Nazism. While this second article was aimed at domestic anti-Semites, it carried extraordinary ramifications regarding Israel given the fact that Leninists since pre-revolutionary days had completely rejected the ideology of Zionism, upon which the state of

Israel was eventually founded. The Soviet media also began to carry decidedly more objective, varied, even occasionally positive accounts of Israeli society.

Much of the improvement in Soviet–Israeli relations was an effort to meet, at least partially, Israeli demands for the resumption of diplomatic ties as a condition for Soviet participation in the Middle East peace process, specifically an international conference. Israel set a second condition, however, and here too Gorbachev appeared to be willing to meet the Israelis at least part way. This second condition was the emigration of those Soviet Jews wishing to leave the USSR. This was an issue which, in the absence of Soviet–Israeli relations, had become a matter for US–Soviet relations and could, therefore, now be seen as part of the East–West relationship. Soviet moves on Jewish emigration were directed not only at pleasing Washington but also at attracting western Jewish businessmen into industrial and technological ventures with the Soviet Union. In time these moves also became part of Gorbachev's effort to demonstrate Moscow's new, sensible and liberal emigration policy regarding not only Jews. Nonetheless, Soviet moves in this sphere, too, became part of the new effort to improve relations with Israel.

It was not initially clear that Gorbachev had any plans to compromise on the Jewish emigration issue; he appeared to share Andropov's view that the détente-related emigration of over 250,000 Jews in the 1970s had been a mistake. It had created domestic problems, and had not even been rewarded with what the Soviets had seen as American promises of *quid pro quo* trade and credit benefits. The only change Gorbachev appeared willing to make at first was the improvement of the life of the Jews inside the Soviet Union, to some degree as part of 'perestroika' and *glasnost*, ending the official anti-Semitism of the Andropov period. By permitting greater religious and cultural freedom, largely in response to western Jewish demands, the new Soviet leader seemed to be offering integration and relative well-being for those who chose to remain.

Gradually, however, this policy was changed, and Gorbachev began the resumption of some emigration (as he did with regard to Germans and Armenians). At first this was sporadic and individual emigration only, limited to some of the more famous persons long refused emigration or even imprisoned, such as Anatolii Sharansky. In time, however, this increased to a steady stream, with the Soviets promising to allow all of the 'refusniks' (estimated at between 12,000 to 20,000), to be followed by new, greatly liberalized regulations. In

1987 8,011 Jews were permitted to emigrate on exit visas to Israel; this
number was almost doubled in 1988. The sharp and alarming rise in
popular anti-Semitism in the Soviet Union led to massive demand for
emigration, resulting in the immigration of almost 10,000 Jews per
month into Israel.

Israel sought direct transportation to accommodate the large
numbers, particularly in view of the fears spreading through the
Soviet Jewish population in the face of growing anti-Semitism. Agreement was reached between Aeroflot and El Al for direct flights, but the
Soviet leadership withheld approval because of vociferous Arab opposition to the influx of Jews to Israel. Unwilling to impede its developing relationship with Israel or its improved image on freedom of
movement, Moscow did not comply with Arab demands to halt the
emigration. Refusal to permit direct flights was the limit to Gorbachev's concession to the Arabs (and domestic opponents to the
rapprochement with Israel). He did, however, join the Arab effort to
obtain international guarantees that emigrating Soviet Jews would not
be settled in the occupied territories, that is, the West Bank and Gaza.

Both the improvement in relations with Israel and the stand on
emigration represented a clear change in policy, meeting at least
partially Israeli demands with the open promise of renewal of full
diplomatic relations. In part what was new was the willingness to
make concessions in the pursuit of many of the old objectives. This
itself was characteristic of changes in Soviet policies towards a number
of states, in every part of the world. It also reflected a new approach to
Israel's position. Moscow no longer viewed Israel as an object, to be
dealt with indirectly, through the Americans. Rather, the Soviets now
opted to deal directly with Israel, suggesting that it intended to pursue
a resolution of the conflict with greater seriousness.

Change regarding Egypt

The same, new, flexibility became apparent in Soviet relations with
Egypt. While Moscow had long sought to repair and restore its
relations with Cairo, particularly after Sadat's death, it had not been
willing to reduce its own demands in any significant way. In 1987,
however, the Soviets agreed to the Egyptian request, of many years
standing, to reschedule the Egyptian debt (believed to total approximately $3 billion) and to permit repayment over a twenty-five-year
period after a six-year grace period. Soviet consulates were reopened
in Alexandria and Port Said, economic relations were reopened with
Soviet contracts to expand factories in Egypt and, according to

rumours, resume supplies of military spare parts and even some military equipment. In the political sphere, Brutents met with Egyptian President Mubarak in Cairo during his January 1988 trip to the Middle East; Egyptian Foreign Minister Esmat Abdel Meguid made an official visit to Moscow in May. The latter signed a number of accords with the Soviets, in the economic, cultural and scientific fields. In February 1989 Shevardnadze returned the visit, the first of a Soviet Foreign Minister to Egypt since 1974 and the rift with Sadat.

Shevardnadze's visit in a sense sealed the normalization process that had taken place, as the Soviet Foreign Minister officially declared the former rift totally mended. Evidence of this was an invitation from Gorbachev to President Mubarak to visit the Soviet Union. Indirectly critical of over-ambitious efforts to woo Egypt in the past, however, Shevardnadze explicitly rejected a description of the two countries' new relationship as 'special'. Whether meant to allay fears in Washington, or in Damascus, or simply to create a modest level of expectations, Shevardnadze's comments concentrated rather on the positive role Egypt might play in furthering the peace process.

These and other moves towards Egypt were themselves part of a broader change in Soviet tactics in the region. The attempt to create a bloc of radical states, which in any case had failed, was now replaced by a move to reach the conservative and pro-western states in the region. This effort to broaden Soviet options had its ideological and practical basis in the new Third World policies of Gorbachev, and it entailed improvement of relations with a number of Middle Eastern states including the conservative Gulf states (as we shall see below) as well as Israel.

Settlement of the Arab–Israeli conflict

As a result of these changes, the Soviet approach to the resolution of the Arab–Israeli conflict was also altered somewhat. On the whole there was no new sense of urgency under Gorbachev; the Middle East was by no means first on the Soviets' list of priorities, and there were no American breakthroughs which might arouse Soviet alarm. Yet there were a number of factors which did elicit a steady, possibly more intense ongoing Soviet effort to move the peace process forward. Events in the area, particularly the Palestinian uprising in the territories occupied by Israel, with the signs of radicalization in some Arab circles, and the growth of Islamic fundamentalism, augured against delaying an effort towards solution too long.

In addition, Gorbachev appeared to link progress at the super-power level with resolution of regional conflict: following the INF agreement he spoke of the need to resolve regional conflicts. Shevardnadze, in his speech in Cairo as well as in his March 1989 Vienna talks with US Secretary of State James Baker, made a similar linkage, speaking of impediments to super-power disarmament caused by the presence of certain missiles in the Middle East. The dual argument was that progress at the super-power level facilitated resolution of regional conflict, providing an example as well as a vehicle for cooperative rather than competitive behaviour; at the same time regional instability threatened to impede current and future progress at the super-power level. Brezhnev, too, had occasionally invoked super-power détente as a basis for co-participation in the Middle East, but under Gorbachev this was part not only of an overall theory of super-power resolution of regional conflicts but also of what may have been a genuine concern over the types of weapons – and their use – appearing in the Middle East. This included not only Soviet concern over the Israeli Jericho missiles but also dissatisfaction with the Iraqi alterations of Soviet surface-to-surface missiles for use against Iranian cities as well as the use of chemical warfare.

Priority specifically of the Arab–Israeli conflict was linked to Soviet withdrawal from Afghanistan. Following the announcement of the Soviet decision to withdraw, it became increasingly clear that this Middle East conflict would be next on the agenda. More than once Shevardnadze made such a connection, invoking the Afghan accord as a model for resolving regional difficulties such as the Arab–Israeli conflict. After Afghanistan, the Middle East dispute was perceived as one of the remaining few (if not the only) conflicts which threatened to obstruct super-power relations. Moreover, the withdrawal from Afghanistan provided a boost in Soviet credibility, particularly in the eyes of influential Arab states such as Saudi Arabia. It was, thus, no coincidence that just two days after the Soviet withdrawal from Afghanistan the Soviet Foreign Minister made his tour of the Middle East.

Yet the 'new thinking' produced no new idea for a framework suitable for talks on the Arab–Israeli conflict. There were numerous meetings between Soviet and Israeli officials under Gorbachev which could be perceived as Soviet efforts to mediate by speaking with all the sides involved in an effort to find compromise formula for convening talks. And there were numerous meetings with the Americans, be it talks at the Foreign Ministry level between Richard Murphy and Vladimir Poliakov or even at the summit level between Reagan and

Gorbachev and later between Baker and Shevardnadze. All of these were designed, however, to bring about the convening of an international conference, and the Soviets undertook an extensive campaign to generate support for the idea from states throughout the Middle East and Europe. Indeed the only 'innovation' the Soviets offered was the proposal brought by Shevardnadze to the Middle East in February 1989 for preparatory talks in the Security Council (as well as bilateral and other talks), with a six- to nine-month timetable for convening the Conference.

Moscow's preference for an international forum derived, of course, from its desire to be a party to any settlement, as distinct from the American-mediated Camp David Israeli–Egyptian peace agreement. The addition of the demand for participation of all the permanent members of the Security Council may not have been a Soviet demand, although Brezhnev had occasionally, in 1976 and later, suggested British and French participation, presumably to bring additional pressure on the Americans to agree. Rather, the expanded version of the conference was probably an Arab idea, of particular importance to Jordan, which feared a super-power deal, possibly at the expense of Jordan, and therefore sought the active participation of its strong advocate, Great Britain.

Basically, however, it was the Americans, not the Soviets, who demanded detailed clarifications regarding rules of procedure, issues, participants and the like, for the proposed conference. This may simply have been an American ploy to prevent the convening of such a conference and thus maintain Washington's exclusive role in the peace process; the American claim was that careful and detailed planning would prevent the conference from failing. Whatever the reason, the Americans only very gradually came around to agreeing to a conference, as evidenced by the Shultz initiative of 1988, but they continued to insist upon detailed advanced planning.

Washington was supported to some degree in this demand by Israel, whose government was split for and against the conference idea – mainly because it was split for and against any kind of Israeli territorial concessions in exchange for peace. Acting Prime Minister-Foreign Minister Shimon Peres, even as Prime Minister from 1984 to 1986, had become an advocate of an international conference not out of any great conviction that this would be the ideal forum or that international participation would be more effective than bilateral or purely American-mediated talks. Rather his support was the result of demands made by King Hussein for such a forum, and Peres, and his

Labour Party, were traditionally committed to what Labour called the 'Jordanian option', that is a peace agreement with Jordan. If Jordan were willing only in the framework of an international conference, for inter-Arab as well as international reasons, then Peres was willing to press for such a forum.

Thus, procedural issues became of the essence as Peres sought to convince both the Israeli public and government that there was nothing to fear from the conference, describing it merely as an opening umbrella for what would in fact become bilateral talks much the way the 1973 Geneva Conference had eventually become. King Hussein, anxious for international pressure as well as backing for resolution of the conflict even initialled an agreement with Peres in April 1987 for the convening of a largely ceremonial conference. The Americans, however, gave this only moderate support, and Peres was uanble to persuade the divided Israeli government to adopt the accord.

The Soviets, for their part, most likely did not want a repeat of the 1973–4 proceedings in which the Geneva Conference had deteriorated to US-mediated bilateral talks in the region, excluding Moscow until the final ceremonial signing of agreements, back in Geneva. For this reason they spoke of a conference which would have plenipotentiary powers, that is, the plenum of the conference would have such powers over whatever accords were worked out in bilateral sessions. As the most interested party with regard to the international framework, however, the Soviets were not anxious to become bogged down in detailed formulations and preparatory issues which continuously delayed if not actually prevented the convening of a conference. They therefore sought general, relatively minimal guidelines; and they gradually conceded on a number of points raised by Washington.

By 1987 Soviet officials were speaking not of a plenipotential plenum but of an 'authoritative' one; by the May 1988 summit, this became an 'effective' plenum. (Some of the Soviet press continued to write of a 'fully authoritative' plenum, suggesting that either indecision or differences of opinion still remained on this issue.) Bi-lateral meetings within the overall framework of the conference, a concession already made in the Soviets' 1984 proposals, now became increasingly dominant as the forum for negotiations acceptable to Moscow. Shevardnadze explained that the plenary would not exercise veto power over – or interfere in – agreements worked out in bilateral sessions. Interim accords, as proposed by US Secretary of State George Shultz, were agreed to if not championed, and even the Shultz initiative itself was not thoroughly condemned by Moscow, so long as it envisaged the convening of an international conference.

In the summer of 1989, however, the Soviets appeared to be willing to retreat somewhat from the international conference idea and even from the Shevardnadze proposal for preliminary talks in the Security Council. Referring only vaguely to an eventual conference, Moscow encouraged discussions even outside the UN framework. The change in the Soviet position presumably was the result of Baker's expressed agreement to the Soviets playing a role in the peace process, and the progress actually made in American talks with both Israel and the PLO. The Soviets also were more forthcoming on the idea of an interim agreement which was basically what was proposed by the Israeli government in the form of the Shamir Plan in May 1989. The Soviet Union gradually supported (with some conditions) the Plan's proposal for elections in the occupied territories. Thus the Soviets appeared willing to seek what would in effect be a step by step solution.

With regard to the substantive issues of the Arab–Israeli conflict, it is not certain that the Gorbachev era produced many changes. On the whole, the substantive issues were not of primary importance to Moscow. As we have already seen, the Soviets developed positions over the years regarding Israel's borders and the possibility of a Palestinian state beyond these borders, the resolution of the refugee problem in the context of a Palestinian state, the inclusion of East Jerusalem in such a state, the possibility of demilitarization, and so forth. Yet they had no vital or intrinsic interest in any of these issues. Rather, their positions appear to have been dictated by the interests of their clients, the competition with the United States and, perhaps primarily, by the limits of what Moscow deemed achievable, realistic and viable. Exactly where the Israeli border would run, even, possibly, whether there were a Palestinian state under any circumstances, might be of little genuine concern to them. If there were anything new under Gorbachev, it may have been that this position, or lack of position, was made clearer. The Soviets, for the first time, conveyed to Israel as well as stated publicly that whatever arrangements were worked out by the parties concerned would be acceptable to Moscow. Even the official formula for a resolution of the conflict referred only generally to self-determination for the Palestinians, resolutions 242 and 338, and the need for Israeli withdrawal, without specific mention of the form of Palestinian self-determination or any of the formerly mentioned issues such as Jerusalem or the refugee problem. Purposely vague and general, the Soviets claimed to have no iron-clad positions or conditions of their own, or as Shevardnadze put it in Cairo, 'no magic formula'.

To back up this claim and prove that there was a 'new thinking' on the Arab–Israeli conflict, a second tack was taken. Usually beginning with Gorbachev, followed by lower officials, journalists and academics, new formulations, expressions and phrases were introduced into the discussion of a settlement. A striking example of this occurred during Arafat's visit to Moscow in April 1988, upon which occasion Gorbachev explicitly juxtaposed Israel's right to recognition and security with the Palestinians' right to self-determination. In the communique on the talks, Gorbachev was said to have spoken of the need to satisfy the interests of both sides, that is, those of Israel as well as the Palestinians, and the need to achieve a 'balance of interests' of the parties to the conflict.

This position was repeated by Shevardnadze in the Middle East, where the only details he offered to his vision of a settlement were such new ideas as a 'regional military risk-reduction center', on-site monitoring and mutual inspections, and other suggestions all connected with allaying Israel's concerns over security. No mention was made of borders, Jerusalem, refugees or even a Palestinian state (beyond noting the PLO declaration of a state). These were clearly new formulations, presumably designed to impress Israel and the United States and thus inject new life into the idea of an international conference. Such equanimity cannot, however, have pleased the Soviets' Arab clients.

The Palestinians

As in the past, Soviet relations with the Palestinians were of a complex nature. Gorbachev's attitude to the Palestinian issue was no more – and possibly less – tolerant than that of his predecessors with regard to the lack of PLO unity and therefore immobilism. Gorbachev may also have been wary of Arafat's loyalty to Moscow, in view of the PLO leader's flirtation with the Reagan Initiative after the Lebanon War. In fact, until the collapse of the Hussein–Arafat agreement in the spring of 1986, Gorbachev had little to do with the PLO leader. He refused to have Arafat lead a delegation to the Soviet Union, and he suspended aid and training to Fatah. At the same time, Moscow drew closer to Hawatmeh and Habash, and brought the relatively new Palestinian Communist Party into deliberations.

Gorbachev did not reverse his predecessors' opposition to a formal split in the PLO, but he was even more adamant about internal PLO reunification and reconciliation with the Syrians. Once the Arafat–Hussein accord collapsed, the Soviets assumed an active role in bringing about reunification of the PLO. Gorbachev's predecessors may well have done the same, for Moscow certainly had an interest in a united Palestinian and Arab camp. What apparently had not been done before was intensive and persistent Soviet mediation, bringing together the different factions of the PLO, at least those willing to enter such talks, in Prague and in Moscow.

The major Soviet demand was official abrogation by the PLO of the Arafat–Hussein agreement. This was achieved, along with reunification of the major PLO factions, at the PNC meeting in Algiers in April 1987. The Soviets also received, finally, inclusion of one Communist and one fellow traveller in the PLO executive. For their part the Soviets resumed their aid to Fatah and, within a year, Arafat was finally once again invited to lead an official delegation to Moscow to meet with Gorbachev, the already mentioned April 1988 visit. A new PLO chargé d'affaires, Nabil Amar, was also allowed to present his credentials to the Kremlin (officially becoming an Ambassador in 1990).

The active role played by the Soviets in the reunification of the PLO was but the first step in a new activism regarding the organization, suggesting that under Gorbachev the Palestinians were to be viewed more than instrumentally. This was not because the Soviets had higher regard for the PLO or greater sympathy for its cause. Indeed Gorbachev exhibited much less interest than his predecessors in national liberation movements in general, and took a much firmer, less tolerant position with the PLO in particular. Soviet activism actually took the form of persistent and even public pressure upon the PLO to moderate its positions, beginning with the Arafat visit to Moscow in April 1988 and culminating in talks with the DFLP and PFLP prior to the November 1988 meeting of the PNC.

The new activism and the pressures for moderation appeared to be based on two ideas in Soviet thinking. The first, presumably conveyed to the PLO, was that a new wave of conciliation and compromise was afoot in the world, demanding a change in the PLO commensurate with worldwide movement towards resolution of conflicts. The second may have been the conviction that the Palestinian issue was the central problem in the Arab–Israeli conflict, demanding resolution if the conflict itself were to be seriously addressed. Therefore, PLO immobility, created, previously, by its disunity, and by its continued official intransigence, would have to give way to the steps necessary for a breakthrough in the peace process. These were, specifically, acceptance of resolution 242 and recognition of Israel's right to exist.

Therefore, Soviet pressures upon the PLO were to a large degree dictated less by the long-standing dissatisfaction with the movement (frequently apparent under Brezhnev) than by a desire effectively to deal with the issue now believed to be essential to a settlement of the conflict: the Palestinian issue. The Palestinian uprising ('intifada') in the occupied territories only strengthened such a belief. Moscow did not, however, posit its positions upon this uprising. While it gave due press coverage and praise to the acts of the indigenous population in the territories, frequently reporting severe Israeli responses, it was surprisingly restrained in doing so. This may have been because the uprising *initially* was not under PLO control or that of the local Communists but was, rather, a spontaneous outburst led at times and in some places by quite radical elements and Muslim fundamentalists. A more likely reason may have been that Gorbachev's policies were focused on achieving negotiations, urging movements in many areas of the world to emphasize talks rather than armed struggle or even action in the field. This in itself was not an entirely new position for Moscow, but Gorbachev was engaged in a diplomatic offensive on a number of fronts, with little interest in pressures in the nature of civil disorder or paramilitary action. Indeed he was unwilling to let the uprising interfere with his rapprochement with Israel, for example, announcing agreement to the Israel consular delegation in February 1988, at the height of the 'intifada' and the peak of international condemnation of Israeli actions against the uprising.

Gorbachev probably shared his predecessors' conviction that the PLO, united even under Arafat, was the only address for the Palestinians. But also like his predecessors, Gorbachev did not appear to be willing to have the issue of PLO participation block the path to an international conference. Thus, on this issue too, an effort to find new formulations was apparent. The Soviets agreed to the formula used at the 1973 Geneva Conference, to the effect that additional invitees would be decided at the conference itself; they also spoke of the possibility of a joint Arab delegation, or a delegation acceptable to the PLO even if not an official PLO delegation. They were willing to add Palestinian self-determination to resolution 242 as the basis for participation, but they were adamant, even according to TASS, about the need for the PLO to accept 242 and recognition of Israel.

The 'self-determination–resolution 242' formula was also connected with the 'new thinking' regarding this conflict. It did not rule out but it did not explicitly demand the creation of an independent Palestinian state. A call for such a state was missing from the communique on Gorbachev's talks with Arafat and from subsequent official pronouncements such as Shevardnadze's major Middle East policy address in Cairo, as we have seen above. In keeping with this, Moscow tried to dissuade the PLO leadership from formally declaring such a state, responding only reservedly when the PLO nonetheless went ahead with the proclamation at the November 1988 PNC meeting in Algiers. The new, perhaps surprising Soviet reticence on this issue did not signify abandonment of Soviet support for the creation of an independent Palestinian state. What it did signify was a preference for more open formulations which might be easier for Israel to consider and, therefore, facilitate the opening of negotiations.

Both the 'loosening' of the Soviet position on a state and the effort to moderate the PLO (as well as the new approach to Israel) were signs of a search for an effective means of resolving the conflict. In the past Moscow had accorded increasing support to PLO demands in an attempt to block American progress. The Palestinian issue had been viewed as the weak point in United States policy and therefore was exploited in Moscow's competition with Washington. Under Gorbachev it was no longer clear that the PLO was viewed in this tactical way, as a means of crippling the Americans. In part, this may have been due to a genuine Soviet interest in resolution of regional conflicts and, therefore, the belief that the Palestinian issue must be addressed. In part, it may have been due to the proclaimed abandonment of the 'zero-sum-game' approach, that is, a shift from a competitive mode *vis à vis* Washington to a cooperative one.

Such conclusions were strongly suggested by the fact that the Soviet Union did not oppose or even criticize the opening of the US–PLO dialogue following the PLO's dramatic policy changes at the end of 1988. It did not appear to be fearful of losing the PLO, as it had been in the earlier PLO consideration of the Reagan plan. Having played a role in the PLO's 1988 recognition of Israel's right to exist and renunciation of the use of terror, Moscow officially welcomed the American response. It supported the Palestinian demand that substantive issues be addressed, seeking to engage the Americans in what was developing as unusual combinations of four-way talks between the United States, the PLO, the Soviet Union and Israel. Still a further sign that the Soviets were less interested in competing with the Americans over the Palestinians and more interested in reaching a solution was

Moscow's encouragement of the PLO to accept (with realistic conditions) the elections proposal contained in the Shamir Plan. The Soviet position came despite the fact that the Plan had been produced at the Americans' behest, had full support of Washington, and ignored the idea of an international conference.

Soviet–Syrian relations

The other essential party to the conflict, Syria, took a less sanguine attitude toward these developments and Gorbachev's 'new thinking' in the Middle East. Syria was opposed to the PLO declaring an independent state; it had in fact withstood intensive Soviet efforts to strike a reconciliation with Arafat. This caused some strain in Soviet–Syrian relations, for it not only meant that the Syrian–sponsored PLO factions remained outside the reunification accords of Algiers, but it also was perceived in Moscow as a rejection of Soviet policies and an affront to Soviet efforts. This was but one source of tension between Damascus and Moscow, not necessarily the result of Gorbachev's new policies, but in no way improved by these policies.

In the first year of Gorbachev's rule there had actually been some signs of warmer relations with Syria, based on what was seen as the emergence of a good personal relationship between the two leaders. The communique following the trip to Moscow by Syrian Vice President Khaddem in May 1986 spoke of the 'trust between the leadership of the two countries'. Nevertheless, the by now standard differences between the two countries were quick to reappear: over Assad's ambitions in Lebanon, the demands of Damascus for 'strategic parity' with Israel, and Syria's fundamental hostility to Israel as well as to many of the countries, from Egypt to the Gulf, with which Moscow was now pursuing improved relations.

Under Gorbachev as well as under his predecessors, Moscow refrained from acknowledging Syrian domination of Lebanon. The Soviets sought, instead, to maintain their own independent channels to the Lebanese government and various factions in the country, occasionally even snubbing the senior Syrian representatives in Beirut. They were also critical of Syrian policy there, urging Damascus to adopt greater openness towards the various factions vying for political power. Both in the media and political discussions, Moscow made it clear that Syria was acting on its own in Lebanon, the implication being that Moscow considered the situation in that country too complex and hopeless to warrant any association with

Syria's moves. In July 1989 the Soviet Union sent first deputy Foreign Minister Aleksandr Bessmertnykh to discuss the Lebanon situation in Damascus, having told Arab League leaders that it would press Syria to end the violence in Lebanon.

The Soviets rejected Assad's repeated demands for 'strategic parity' with Israel. At first Gorbachev appeared to be continuing the arms build-up of Syria begun in the wake of the Lebanon war. Gradually, however, actual arms deliveries fell from the previous average of $2.3 billion per year to no more than $1 billion per year in the period 1985–9. Further, Moscow apparently delayed deliveries of Syrian-requested MIG-29 aircraft, providing them first to India and Iraq. Some of the planes reportedly were delivered finally in August 1987, but reports of an unsuccessful trip by Syrian Defence Minister Tlas to Moscow late in 1988 claimed that Damascus was still dissatisfied with Soviet supplies of missiles, aircraft, bombers, tanks and advanced air defence systems. The MIG-29 and other aircraft were reportedly still the source of disagreement during Soviet Defence Minister Yazov's trip to Damascus in March, although Yazov finally did promise at least some SU-24 bombers. Moscow also balked at supplying Syria with SS-23 intermediate-range ballistic missiles, which would contradict the INF accord with Washington. Syria appears to have found a substitute from China.

In Israel there were claims that Moscow had agreed to supply Damascus with the means for chemical warfare, evidenced by two visits to Syria by the chief of chemical warfare in the Soviet army. The trips may have been a sign of Soviet concern over the proliferation of chemical warfare (after its use by Iraq) rather than an indication of Soviet supplies to Syria. At least that is what Soviet military sources claimed publicly, in accord with positions enunciated by the Soviets in 1988 and 1989. Indeed, the Syrians exhibited some dismay over Soviet reticence to meet all their demands, slow arms deliveries, and, particularly, Soviet demands for prompt hard currency payments. Repayment of Syria's roughly $15 billion debt to the Soviet Union, or at least the interest due, was destined to be the source of some problems.

The US State Department revealed in August 1988 that the Soviets had greatly expanded the Syrian port of Tartus. This, however, was for the purpose of servicing the Soviet fleet in the Mediterranean, similar to the improvements made in the Syrian port of Latakia following the Soviets' loss of naval facilities in Egypt in the 1970s. In itself, this appeared to be a deviation from the general pull back from power projection characteristic of Soviet military policy since the early

1980s, and part of Gorbachev's policy as well. Yet the Soviet military presence in the eastern Mediterranean had not been connected exclusively with Soviet power projection, given the importance of the area for Soviet defence *vis à vis* the US Sixth fleet and strategic positions *vis à vis* NATO in what comprised the south-western theatre of warfare in Soviet military planning. Moreover, US officials themselves later minimized the importance of the Tartus facilities for the Soviets, supporting Soviet denials that these constituted a Soviet base.

Continued Soviet refusal to meet all of Syria's military demands was connected, under Gorbachev as well as under Brezhnev, with Moscow's opposition to another Arab–Israeli war. Whatever intentions Assad may have had, Gorbachev made it clear that he would not support a new military action against Israel. This was conveyed most directly and publicly to Assad during the Syrian President's April 1987 visit to Moscow, at which time Gorbachev said: 'the reliance on military force has completely lost its credibility as a way of solving the Middle East conflict'. It was in the same speech that Gorbachev said that the absence of Soviet relations with Israel was abnormal. Neither remark could have been welcomed by Assad, and the talks between the two leaders were said to have been difficult.

This was apparently the case also when Tlas was reportedly told in Moscow that the supply of the armaments requested by Damascus would be perceived as a provocation by Israel and lead to an Israeli preemptive attack. Shevardnadze apparently presented a similar argument when he visited Damascus in February 1989, remarking, a few days later, that 'more arms' clearly did not mean 'greater security'. Just prior to the subsequent visit by Yazov, the Soviet Defence Minister repeated Shevardnadze's Cairo comments regarding the dangers and futility of the Middle East arms build-up. Thus the Soviets remained consistent in their refusal to respond to Assad's long-standing demand for 'strategic parity' with Israel.

Gorbachev could not be totally indifferent to Syria's wishes; Damascus was not only Moscow's sole state ally in the area but also an important party to whatever international forum the Soviets might succeed in convening. Yet what was striking under Gorbachev was that the new Soviet leader was even less willing then his predecessors to forego Soviet interests, be they with regard to the Arab–Israeli conflict or efforts to improve relations with states opposed by Damascus, or even renewed relations with Arafat, whatever the Syrian position. One might argue that this demonstrated confidence on Moscow's part that Syria did not have an American option of the type taken by Sadat when strains had developed in that relationship. It may indeed be true that Soviet analysts estimated little likelihood of Syria shifting towards Washington. Yet it may also be the case that the Kremlin merely sought to place all of its foreign relations on a more business-like basis, preferring a broad spectrum of clients with a lower level of Soviet commitment than exclusive or near exclusive dependence upon an ally such as Assad – whose own health, political stability, economic well-being and international standing were not above concern.

This did not mean that the Soviets were no longer responsive to Syrian military and political needs. Albeit reduced, supplies to the Syrian armed forces, in the area of at least $1 billion a year, continued, and efforts to resolve some of the problems between the two countries, regarding for example, the PLO issue, were apparent. Moreover meetings and consultations between the two continued on a regular basis, with Syria even declaratively supporting most of Moscow's positions, such as the need for an international conference, although there was no indication that Damascus actually accepted these positions.

Another problem, though perhaps not always a central one, in Soviet–Syrian relations which remained unresolved was that of Iraq: Syria's continued hostility to its rival faction of the Ba'ath in Baghdad despite Moscow's rapprochement with Saddam Hussein after 1982. This hostility had dictated a pro-Iranian Syrian position in the Iran–Iraq war, bringing Syria into conflict with virtually all of the Gulf states, as well as Jordan and Egypt. All of these were states with which Gorbachev sought improved or even the initiation of relations. Syrian support of Iran complicated Soviet relations with the Arab world and isolated Syria, reducing whatever effectiveness the latter might have in aiding the Soviets in the Arab arena. Moreover, it also ran counter to Moscow's support for, at times even attempts to mediate, a resolution of the Iran–Iraq war. This issue was still more complex, however, for Moscow's own positions on the Iran–Iraq war, and particularly Iran, underwent so many shifts that there were in fact times when the Soviets were able clandestinely to exploit Syrian assistance to Iran, primarily, perhaps, in the realm of arms transfers.

Iran–Iraq war

When Gorbachev assumed power in 1985, the Soviets were already well into their pro-Iraqi phase of the war. They were openly and generously supplying arms to Iraq and supporting Iraq's call for a cease-fire (generated by the fact that Iraq was now on the defensive). Moscow's relations with Iran had seriously deteriorated, the Tudeh virtually destroyed, trade virtually halted, and the Soviet press stridently critical of the Khomeini regime. Nonetheless, the Soviets had not burned their bridges entirely with Tehran. Moscow had received an Iranian economic delegation in June 1984, though little was to come of it at the time. More importantly, arms supplies to Iran from Syria, Libya and North Korea may have had some Soviet approval, constituting, according to some interpretations, indirect Soviet arms supplies. It was most likely that Syria, Libya and North Korea, all singularly independent of Moscow, were acting in their own interests and at their own initiative. In any case, these were channels by which Iran received Soviet-made arms, and there was no known attempt by Moscow to prevent such deliveries.

Actually it would appear that the Soviets were engaged in a dualistic policy of arms supplies, that is providing the wherewithal to continue, possibly escalate the war, even as they urged a cease-fire and solution to the conflict. This was not the first time Moscow had adopted such a dualistic policy, as we have seen in the Arab–Israeli conflict; nor was it the first time it had tried to maintain relations with both sides to a conflict in the Middle East, for example Iraqi conflicts with Kuwait or even past Iraqi conflicts with Iran.

Nevertheless, there were signs that the Soviet Union, after as well as before Gorbachev took power, tried to prevent escalation of the war. Moscow supplied Iraq with surface-to-surface missiles, but it reportedly pressured the Iraqis to suspend their use of them against Iran in the spring of 1985. Indeed it has also been said that Moscow expressed anger over the Iraqis' modification of the range of the SCUDs, that is, the doubling of their range to 650 kilometres (by reducing the strength of the warheads) so as to reach Iranian cities. (Although one source did claim that East German forces had made the necessary adjustments for the Iraqis.)

Gorbachev had basically the same interest as his predecessors to see an end to the war. Even a dualistic Soviet policy pleased neither party to the conflict, each of which objected to arms deliveries of any type reaching the other side. It was almost a no win situation from the Soviet point of view, presenting Moscow with the continuous dilemma of choosing between an ally, Iraq, and the potentially bigger prize, Iran. The war also complicated Gorbachev's effort to improve relations with the Gulf states, interfering also in plans for Arab unity.

An additional though, under the circumstances, less serious problem was the fact that the Chinese had also entered the picture, providing arms to both belligerents but most notably Iran.

The major problems created by the continuation of the war, however, were those connected directly or indirectly with the ramifications of the war for the super-power competition. Aside from generally adding insecurity to a region on the Soviets' border, the war precipitated the increasing presence of a hostile power in the Gulf: the US military build-up in the Gulf. Moreover, although the war drew the Gulf states together, this was basically a pro-western alliance. Indeed the need for support against Iran led to greater American military access to Saudi Arabia as well as a softening of Saudi and Iraqi attitudes towards Egypt. This in turn assisted American political interests in the region. Iraq renewed diplomatic relations with Washington and increased its diversification composed of economic and military purchases from the West, particularly the NATO state, Turkey.

An Iranian victory at any point threatened to push the states of the region towards the United States, for protection. In addition, the fall of the Ba'ath regime in Iraq, however uncertain an ally to Moscow, would amount to a net loss for Soviet interests. Nor would such a victory for Khomeini's messianic Islamic state have been particularly welcomed by Moscow. As claimed by some, the Soviets' problems with their large Muslim minority derive less from the appeal of the Shi'a Islamic fundamentalism promulgated by Tehran than from the growth of nationalism among the close to 50 million Soviet Muslims, primarily of Turkic origin. Nonetheless, the fortification and aggrandizement of Islam threatened to fan the flames of this nationalism, particularly of those Muslim peoples whose populations resided partially in the Middle East as well as in the Soviet Union. Indeed such a development became more than a theoretical concern when in June 1989 Uzbeks conducted a bloody pogrom against the small Meskhetian minority (a Turkic people transferred from Georgia by Stalin after World War Two). Economic problems as well as Uzbek Communist officials' opposition to the anti-corruption campaign of Gorbachev in Uzbekistan apparently contributed to what Moscow condemned as a well-planned and organized 'political action' that took the lives of over one hundred Meskhetians. Soviet officials also claimed, however, that Islamic fundamentalism was a factor, and it was reported that some of the Uzbek attackers carried portraits of Khomeini into the fray. Some months later, in January 1990, the attacks of Azeris on Armenians in the Armenian enclave inside Soviet Azerbaijan, and the near rebellion of the Azeris bordering on Iran, clearly had fundamentalist overtones. Destroying the border fences, large numbers of Azeris poured into Iran carrying portraits of Khomeini. Gorbachev employed the army to restore order to Azerbaijan, but the explosive combination of Islamic fundamentalism and nationalism remained a serious problem.

While the list of reasons for Soviet opposition to the prolongation of the Iran–Iraq war was long, there were nonetheless some advantages to be gained. The Kuwaiti request in 1987 for Soviet protection for its tankers offered an opportunity for Moscow, particularly when it appeared that Washington had refused such a request. The Soviets complied by chartering three Kuwaiti tankers, although the advantage gained proved to be shortlived once the United States reacted and agreed to reflag Kuwaiti vessels. More important was the improvement Moscow was finally able to achieve in relations with Iran as a result of Tehran's growing need for assistance and the developing confrontation between Iran and the United States in the wake of the revelations of the Iran–Contra deal.

Policy towards the Gulf States

The renewed Soviet drive, begun in 1986, to ameliorate relations with Tehran was part of Gorbachev's new policy of broadening Soviet options and extending them to a variety of states regardless of ideological considerations. This policy had led to the opening of Soviet diplomatic relations with Oman and the United Arab Emirates in late 1985, and in 1988 with Qatar, as well as significant improvement of relations with Kuwait and North Yemen, together with contacts with Bahrain and even Saudi Arabia. The Soviets reached an agreement with OPEC for which the Saudi Petroleum Minister had travelled to Moscow in January 1987. At the same time Soviet diplomats in the Gulf publicly stated that Moscow sought the resumption of diplomatic relations with Saudi Arabia, claiming that such relations had never been formally broken. Riyadh appeared to be responding favourably when, the following January, the Saudi Foreign Minister Prince Saud al-Feisal visited the Soviet Union, carrying a message from King Fahd, albeit in his capacity as chairman of the Gulf Cooperation Council. More direct contacts were made when Soviet deputy Foreign Minister and Ambassador to Afghanistan Yuli Vorontsov travelled to Saudi Arabia in 1988, engaging Riyadh in the negotiations surrounding the Soviet withdrawal from Afghanistan.

These limited but growing successes for the Soviets in the Gulf were due in no small degree to a new receptiveness on the part of these conservative, traditionally pro-western states. Their receptiveness may in turn have been the result of a certain disappointment with American performance in the Middle East, particularly in connection with Lebanon, or perhaps a response to vulnerabilities generated by the Iran–Iraq war. Most of these states, however, continued to be critical of the Soviet invasion of Afghanistan, and there was no slackening of their bonds with the United States or their basically pro-western orientation. This was evidenced by Kuwait's preference for US reflagging when faced with a choice between the two super-powers.

Moscow's limited but indisputable progress among the conservative Gulf states was also apparently due to a gradually changing per-ception of the Soviet Union by these countries. At least under Gorbachev, the Soviet Union was perceived as less menacing than in the past. The bloody 1986 coup in the PDRY did not appear to alter this new view of Moscow, despite the fact that the conservative Gulf states had reason to be concerned over the return to power of more radical forces in Aden. Within the long-standing policy as well as tribal and personal disputes in South Yemen, the overthrown PDRY leader, Ali Nasir Mohammed, had favoured improved relations with these Gulf states. Moscow, for its part, had no reason to oppose such an approach at the time, inasmuch as it suited Soviet policies themselves, under Gorbachev. Indeed, as we have already seen, it was not certain that the Soviets in fact supported Ali Nasir Mohammed's replacement by more radical elements; and there were a number of indications that the coup caught Moscow by surprise. It was only after an initial few days of neutrality – in which there were some signs that Moscow might actually try to preserve Ali Nasir's rule in one form or another – that the Soviets finally threw their weight behind the victorious coup forces (whom they had called 'putchists' only days before). Still they did not formally condemn Ali Nasir for many months after the coup and, although they aided the new regime, it was some time before a new working relationship was secured between Moscow and Aden. Moreover, they encouraged even the new regime to continue the policy of improving relations with such states as Oman, Kuwait, Saudi Arabia and North Yemen. This presumably allayed any fears the Gulf states may have had that the radical (though mainly tribal as distinct from ideological) coup in Aden might have been a sign of potentially nefarious Soviet plans in the Gulf. In fact, the steady opening and improving of Soviet relations with the Gulf states continued and even accelerated.

With regard to the Soviets' renewed drive for rapprochement with Iran, the relative success, perhaps even the initiative, originated with Tehran, as Iran began to feel the economic as well as military burden of the long war. Both states were to benefit from the economic agreement signed in December 1986 which allowed for the reopening of the gas pipeline from Iran to the Soviet Union. Indeed the February 1987 trip to Moscow by Iranian Foreign Minister Ali Akbar Velayati led to reports that Soviet technicians were returning to the sites of steelworks under construction at Isfahan and elsewhere, and that the Soviet–Iranian Chamber of Commerce had reopened in Moscow.

In the summer of 1987 deputy Foreign Ministers of the two countries exchanged visits and, in August, the Soviets announced that a second visit to Tehran in two months by deputy Foreign Minister Yuli Vorontsov had resulted in agreements for 'large-scale projects of mutually beneficial economic cooperation', including apparently a new rail line and an oil pipeline from Iran to the Soviet Union. Indirect arms shipments, from Libya, Syria and North Korea, were increased and, more directly connected with Moscow, some East European countries reportedly joined the supply effort. The Soviets denied any connection with these supplies, including and particularly the Syrian transfer of surface-to-surface missiles to Tehran.

The Soviet press also continued, somewhat reduced, its critical appraisal of the regime in Tehran, and the Tudeh programme issued in 1986 maintained its call for the overthrow of the Khomeini regime. This suggested that the rapprochement had not extended to the political sphere, and that Moscow was still quite wary as to just what might be achieved politically from the improvement in economic, even diplomatic relations. Indeed anti-Soviet riots in Tehran in May 1988 in response to renewed Iraqi attacks on Iranian cities, with Soviet-made surface-to-surface missiles, demonstrated the validity of such wariness.

Nonetheless, Moscow's policy in 1986–8 had clearly tilted, once again, towards Iran in the context of the war. In June 1987 the Soviets called for an end to the tanker war – a move which would favour Iran over Iraq, and they refrained from any significant reaction when a Soviet freighter in the Gulf was attacked by Iran or Soviet ships ran into trouble over Iranian mines. In December the Soviets proposed a UN flotilla to replace the American – and by now west European – naval forces in the Gulf, an idea which would relieve American pressure on Iran even as it served Moscow's interest in removing the western military presence. At the same time, the Soviet Union dragged its feet on the idea of a UN resolution to impose sanctions – an arms embargo – on Iran, which would have led to the implementation of resolution 598 calling for an end to the war.

All of this led to what Iraqi Foreign Minister Tariq Aziz described in a New York news conference in October 1987 as a 'mini-crisis' in Iraqi relations with Moscow. The crisis did not last long, and Moscow demonstrated its continued interest in Iraq, despite the aid to Iran, by totally ignoring Baghdad's later inhuman suppression of the Kurds and, with them, much of the Iraqi Communist Party. The 1987 crisis may, however, have accounted, at least in part, for Baghdad's resumption of the Soviet-opposed use of SSMs against Iranian cities in March and April 1988. Certainly – and ironically – the Iranians blamed the Soviets for failing to prevent the renewed Iraqi use of these Soviet weapons. The Soviet response to this was criticism once again of the Khomeini regime, in *Pravda* 3 June 1988, blaming Tehran for refusing to end the war. This may have been a signal that the Soviets were finally ready to help impose a cease-fire. By the summer of 1988 the Soviets' indirect arms deliveries to Iran had been gradually reduced, leaving only China and North Korea as Iran's suppliers; Soviet criticism of the US military presence was muted after the May summit in Moscow, and the Soviets may have believed that Iran was now in fact ready to give in. In July Tehran did indeed agree to resolution 598, paving the way for peace talks with Iraq under UN auspices.

Having calculated correctly, Moscow did not endanger its developing rapprochement with Iran. The overall improvement in their relations was symbolized by Khomeini's agreement to meet with Shevardnadze during his 1989 Middle East tour. The picture of the Soviet Foreign Minister locked in conversation with the fanatic leader of Islamic fundamentalism clearly demonstrated both the benefits Moscow had managed to derive from the Iran–Iraq war and just how far 'new thinking' might carry the Soviets in expanding their options abroad. In the wake of the withdrawal from Afghanistan, however, the Soviet Union was presumably particularly interested in as good a relationship with Iran as possible – in order to forestall an anti-Soviet fundamentalist Iranian–Afghani bloc on its border. Hopes that the improving relationship with Iran would continue, and perhaps deepen, after Khomeini's death were clear from the Soviet visit of the new leader Ali Akbar Rafsanjani in June 1989. During this visit, which was highly publicized by the Soviets, a number of accords were signed including a defence and cooperation agreement. The details of the agreement were not revealed, but it reportedly included Soviet supplies of anti-tank and surface-to-air missiles and other arms described by the Soviets as purely defensive. After two days of talks with Gorbachev, the two countries also agreed to refrain from interference in the domestic affairs of the other. Although this could be meant to restrain encouragement of Islamic fundamentalism in the Soviet Union, the agreement also called for exchanges of religious figures between the two, and Rafsanjani was taken to visit the predominantly Shi'ite region of Azerbaijan neighbouring on Iran. Iran's objections to Soviet activation of the Tudeh were clearly an important reason for the agreement against domestic interference.

On balance Soviet policy towards the Iran–Iraq war under Gorbachev did not undergo essential changes. Rather the tilt towards Iran, part of the more general attempt to improve relations, probably did not signify abandonment of the more basic interest in seeing an end to the war and, in particular, the end of the American military build-up in the Gulf. More likely it was the temporary exploitation of the perhaps irresistible opportunity presented by Iran's escalating conflict with the United States after the Irangate affair. The Soviets did not attempt to compete with the United States militarily in the Gulf. In fact they were relatively unconfrontational and cooperative in their behaviour towards the American fleet, warning them of mines and avoiding clashes. One western analyst called this 'complementary intervention' rather than 'competitive intervention'. Instead they chose the less dangerous or costly path of political-competition, cooperating to produce a UN resolution to end the war but refusing to jeopardize the opportunity to curry favour with Iran by agreeing to such drastic action as sanctions.

The Soviets might have preferred to bring about an end to the war in their own way, through their offer of a Tashkent-type meeting or Soviet mediation. In any case they had no interest in a decisive victory by either side. In time, and it would appear to be when Iran was finally ready, Gorbachev's general interest in the resolution of regional conflicts, accelerated after the withdrawal from Afghanistan, became the dominant Soviet position.

Implications and conclusions

It has been argued that Soviet behaviour in the Iran–Iraq war, particularly the virulent propaganda campaign against the US presence in the Gulf, as well as the dualistic, opportunistic manipulation of arms supplies, the refusal to apply sanctions against Iran, and the general effort to turn the Americans' situation to Moscow's advantage were proof of continued Soviet aggressiveness, the 'new thinking' notwithstanding. As least they represented the same zero-sum-game propensities on the part of Gorbachev as in the era of power projection under Brezhnev, suggesting that no change had taken place in Soviet policies in the Third World in general or the Middle East in particular.

Such a conclusion may have erred in the same direction as the many misinterpretations of détente in the early 1970s. A retreat from an activist Third World policy and power projection did not mean an abandonment of all interests abroad, particularly in areas adjacent to the Soviet border. Nor did greater flexibility and pragmatism mean the absence of any concern over western military moves. Indeed a policy could be competitive and cooperative at the same time, as Soviet policy had been at various times in connection with the Arab-Israeli conflict. Soviet or, for that matter, American competition need not entail expansionism or aggressiveness; indeed it often accorded priority to low-risk, non-confrontational postures.

In viewing Gorbachev's policies toward the Iran–Iraq and Arab–Israeli conflicts, it might be best to bear in mind that a Soviet interest in the end of these conflicts, like other regional conflicts, need not mean Soviet abandonment of competition with the United States, in the Gulf or the Middle East as a whole. The interest in ending regional conflicts did, however, reflect efforts to cultivate favourable relations with a maximum number of states, regardless of the nature of their regimes, to eliminate pretexts for American military interventions or presence, and to seek measures, including those of a cooperative nature, for the reduction of international and regional tensions in favour of a 'Soviet Union-first' preoccupation with 'perestroika'.

The Soviet withdrawal from Afghanistan, while prompted by a number of domestic factors, including the unpopularity of the war among the Soviet leadership as well as the public, was an impressive sign that Gorbachev's 'new thinking' constituted more than mere public relations or propaganda. It provided much substance to the conclusion that Gorbachev's policies in the Middle East, an area close to Soviet borders and of strategic as well as economic and political value, would be more open to cooperation and accommodation. It was this openness, combined with a willingness to make compromises or bring pressures avoided in the past, which constituted the change in policy under Gorbachev. It was designed to render the Soviet role in the region effective rather than merely symbolic. And, if Gorbachev was to be believed, the goal of such effectiveness was the resolution of conflict and the end of super-power confrontation and even 'zero-sum' competition in the area.

Guide to further reading

1 Soviet policy-making in the Middle East: from Stalin to Brezhnev

M. Confino and S. Shamir (eds.), *The USSR and the Middle East*, Israel Universities Press, Jerusalem, 1973.

Robert Harkavy, *Great Power Competition for Overseas Bases*, Pergamon Press, New York, 1983.

J. C. Hurewitz (ed.), *Soviet–American Rivalry in the Middle East*, Praeger Publishers, New York, 1969.

Walter Laqueur, *Struggle for the Middle East: The Soviet Union in the Mediterranean*, Macmillan, London, 1969.

Neil Malcolm, 'Soviet Decision-making and the Middle East', in P. Shearman and P. Williams (eds.), *The Superpowers, Central America and the Middle East*, Brassey's Defence Publishers, London, 1988, pp. 90–104.

Yaacov Ro'i (ed.), *The Limits to Power*, Croom-Helm, London, 1979.

2 The immediate post-war period: Iran–Turkey–Palestine

J. C. Hurewitz, 'Russia and the Turkish Straits: A Reevaluation of the Origins of the Problem', *World Politics*, 14, 4, July 1962, pp. 605–32.

Arthur Klinghoffer, *Israel and the Soviet Union: Alienation or Reconciliation?*, Westview Press, Boulder, 1985.

George Lenczowski, *The Middle East in World Affairs*, Cornell University Press, Ithaca, 1962.

Yaacov Ro'i, *Soviet Decision Making in Practice: The USSR and Israel*, Transaction Books, New Brunswick, N.J., 1980.

Alvin Rubinstein, *Soviet Policy Toward Turkey, Iran and Afghanistan: The Dynamics of Influence*, Praeger, New York, 1982.

Soviet documents in Yaacov Ro'i, *From Encroachment to Involvement: A Documentary Study of Soviet Policy in the Middle East, 1945–1973*, John Wiley and Sons, London, 1974, pp. 3–9, 11–27, 31–40, 48–65.

3 The Soviet–Egyptian relationship

Mohamed Heikal, *Sphinx and Commissar: The Rise and Fall of Soviet Influence*, Collins, London, 1978.

Charles McLane, *Soviet–Middle East Relations*, Central Asian Research Centre, London, 1973.

Oles Smolansky, *The Soviet Union and the Arab East Under Khrushchev*, Bucknell University Press, Lewisburg, 1974.
Ilan Troen and Moshe Shemesh, *The Suez–Sinai Crisis: A Retrospective*, Frank Cass, London, 1990.
Soviet documents in Yaacov Ro'i, *From Encroachment to Involvement: A Documentary Study of Soviet Policy in the Middle East, 1945–1973*, John Wiley and Sons, London, 1974, pp. 174–97.

4 The Six-Day War, 1967

Arnold Horelick, 'Soviet Policy in the Middle East', in Paul Hammond and Sidney Alexander (eds.), *Political Dynamics in the Middle East*, American Elsevier, New York, 1972, pp. 581–91.
P. Jabber and R. Kolkowicz, 'The Arab–Israeli Wars of 1967 and 1973', in S. Kaplan (ed.), *Diplomacy of Power*, Brookings Institution, Washington, D.C., 1980, pp. 419–37.
Arthur Klinghoffer, *Israel and the Soviet Union: Alienation or Reconciliation?*, Westview Press, Boulder, 1985.
Soviet documents in Yaacov Ro'i, *From Encroachment to Involvement: A Documentary Study of Soviet Policy in the Middle East, 1945–1973*, John Wiley and Sons, London, 1974, pp. 436–46 and in *The Policy of the Soviet Union in the Arab World: A Short Collection of Foreign Policy Documents*, Progress Publishers, Moscow, 1975, pp. 129–43.

5 The inter-war period, 1967–1973

George Breslauer, 'Soviet Policy in the Middle East, 1967–1972: Unalterable Antagonism or Collaborative Competition?', in A. George (ed.), *Managing US–Soviet Rivalry*, Westview Press, Boulder, 1983, pp. 65–102.
Galia Golan, *Yom Kippur and After: The Soviet Union and the Middle East Crisis*, Cambridge University Press, Cambridge, 1977.
Mohamed Heikal, *Road to Ramadan*, Ballantine Books, New York, 1975.
Anwar Sadat, *In Search of Identity: An Autobiography*, Harper and Row, New York, 1977.
Lawrence Whetten, *The Canal War: Four Power Conflict in the Middle East*, MIT University Press, Boston, 1974.
Soviet documents in John Norton Moore, *The Arab–Israeli Conflict: Readings and Documents*, Princeton University Press, Princeton, 1977, pp. 786–93 and Igor Beliaev, 'Middle East Crisis and Washington's Manoeuvres', *International Affairs*, March 1970, pp. 30–9.

6 The Yom Kippur War, 1973

Galia Golan, *Yom Kippur and After: The Soviet Union and the Middle East Crisis*, Cambridge University Press, Cambridge, 1977.
Galia Golan, 'Soviet Decision-making in the Yom Kippur War', in Jiri Valenta and William Potter (eds.), *Soviet Decision-making for National Security*, George Allen and Unwin, London, 1985, pp. 185–217.

Mohamed Heikal, *The Road to Ramadan*, Quadrangle Books, New York, 1975.
Anwar Sadat, *In Search of Identity: An Autobiography*, Harper and Row, New York, 1977.
Dina Spechler, *Domestic Influences on Soviet Foreign Policy*, University Press of America, New York, 1978.
Soviet documents in Yaacov Ro'i, *From Encroachment to Involvement: A Documentary Study of Soviet Policy in the Middle East, 1945–1973*, John Wiley and Sons, London, 1974, pp. 578–88.

7 Settlement of the Arab–Israeli conflict

George Breslauer, 'Soviet Policy in the Middle East, 1967–1972: Unalterable Antagonism or Collaborative Competition?', in A. George, *Managing US—Soviet Rivalry*, Westview Press, Boulder, 1983, pp. 65–102.
Robert Freedman, 'The Soviet Conception of a Middle East Settlement', in Roi'i (ed.), *The Limits to Power*, Croom-Helm, London, 1979, pp. 282–330.
Galia, Golan, 'Soviet Power and Policies in the Third World: The Middle East', *Adelphi Papers*, No. 152 (1979), pp. 47–54.
Peter Mangold, 'The Soviet Record in the Middle East', *Survival*, 10, 3 (1978), pp. 98–104.
Lawrence Whetten, *The Canal War: Four Power Conflict in the Middle East*, MIT University Press, Boston, 1974.
Soviet documents in *New Times*, 13 (1977), pp. 4–7; O. Fomin, 'Stop The Aggressor, Ensure the Peace', *New Times*, 39 (1982), pp. 7–8; *New Times*, 32 (1984), pp. 4–5.

8 The Palestinians and the PLO

Helena Cobban, *The Palestine Liberation Organization*, Cambridge University Press, Cambridge, 1984.
Robert Freedman, 'Soviet Policy Toward International Terrorism', in Y. Alexander (ed.), *International Terrorism*, Praeger, New York, 1976, pp. 115–50.
Galia Golan, *The Soviet Union and the Palestine Liberation Organization*, Praeger, New York, 1980.
Soviet documents in 'Special Document: The Soviet Attitude Towards the Palestine Problem', *Journal of Palestine Studies*, 6, 1 (1972), pp. 187–212 and Raphael Israeli, *PLO in Lebanon: Selected Documents*, Weidenfeld and Nicolson, London, 1983, pp. 34–55.

9 The Lebanon War, 1982

Karen Dawisha, 'The USSR in the Middle East: Superpower in Eclipse?', *Foreign Affairs*, 61, 2 (1982), pp. 438–52.
Galia Golan, 'The Soviet Union and the Israeli Action in Lebanon', *International Affairs*, 59 (Winter 1982), pp. 11–16.

Ilana Kass, 'Moscow and the Lebanese Triangle', *Middle East Journal*, 33, 2 (1979), pp. 164–88.

Dina Spechler, 'The Politics of Intervention: The Soviet Union and the Crisis in Lebanon', *Studies in Comparative Communism*, 20, 22 (Summer 1987), pp. 115–43.

Soviet sources: Victor Bukharov, 'The Palestine Movement Shapes its Course', *New Times*, 52 (1976), pp. 26–7; V. Volgin, 'Conspiracy of Zionism, Imperialism and Reaction', *International Affairs*, 10 (1982), pp. 83–7; Alexander Soldatov, 'In the Fighting City', *International Affairs*, 8 (1988), pp. 128–34.

10 The Soviet Union and Syria

Robert Freedman, *Soviet Policy Toward the Middle East Since 1970*, Praeger, New York, 1978.

G. Golan and I. Rabinovich, 'The Soviet Union and Syria: The Limits of Cooperation', in Ro'i (ed.), *The Limits to Power*, Croom-Helm, London, 1979, pp. 213–31.

Pedro Ramet, 'The Soviet Syrian Relationship', *Problems of Communism*, Vol. 35, 5 (September–October 1986), pp. 35–46.

Oles Smolansky, *The Soviet Union and the Arab East Under Khrushchev*, Bucknell University Press, Lewisburg, 1974.

Soviet documents in Yaacov Ro'i, *From Encroachment to Involvement: A Documentary Study of Soviet Policy in the Middle East, 1945–1973*, John Wiley and Sons, London, 1974, pp. 361–6, 400–2, 419–24, 505–9, 536–9 and in *Current Digest of the Soviet Press*, 32, 41 (1980), pp. 6–7.

11 The Soviet Union and Iraq

Robert Freedman, 'Soviet Policy Toward Ba'athist Iraq', in R. Donaldson (ed.), *The Soviet Union in the Third World*, Westview Press, Boulder, 1981, p. 161–91.

Francis Fukuyama, *The Soviet Union and Iraq Since 1968*, Rand Corporation, Santa Monica, 1980.

Oles Smolansky, *The Soviet Union and the Arab East Under Khrushchev*, Bucknell University Press, Lewisburg, 1974.

Soviet documents in *The Policy of the Soviet Union in the Arab World: A Short Collection of Foreign Policy Documents*, Progress Publishers, Moscow, 178–83; Yaacov Ro'i, *From Encroachment to Involvement: A Documentary Study of Soviet Policy in the Middle East, 1945–1973*, John Wiley and Sons, London, 1974, pp. 258–64, 355–8, 361–6.

12 The Soviet Union and Iran

Karen Dawisha, 'Moscow and the Gulf War', *World Today*, January 1981, pp. 8–14.

Zalmay Khalilizad, 'Islamic Iran: Soviet Dilemma', *Problems of Communism*, 33, 1 (January–February 1984), pp. 1–20.

Dennis Ross, 'Soviet Views Toward the Gulf War', *Orbis*, 28, 3 (Autumn 1984), pp. 437–47.

Alvin Rubinstein, *Soviet Policy Toward Turkey, Iran and Afghanistan: The Dynamics of Influence*, Praeger, New York, 1982.

Malcolm Yapp, 'The Soviet Union and Iran Since 1978', in M. Kauppi and R. Nation (eds.), *The Soviet Union and the Middle East in the 1980s*, Lexington Books, Lexington, Mass., 1983, pp. 222–45.

Soviet documents in Yaacov Ro'i, *From Encroachment to Involvement: A Documentary Study of Soviet Policy in the Middle East, 1945–1973*, John Wiley and Sons, London, 1974, pp. 288–95, 405–9, 435–6; P. Demchenko, 'Iran Takes a New Road', *International Affairs*, 10 (1979), pp. 80–6, and V. Gurev, 'In Defiance of National Interests', *International Affairs*, 4 (1984), pp. 116–24.

13 The Soviet attitude to Islam

A. Bennigsen and M. Broxup, *The Islamic Threat to the Soviet State*, St Martin's Press, New York, 1983.

Fred Halliday, 'Islam and Soviet Foreign Policy', *Asian Studies Quarterly*, 19, 3 (1986), pp. 217–33.

Martha Brill Olcott, 'Soviet Islam and World Revolution', *World Politics*, 34, 4 (July 1982), pp. 487–504.

Yaacov Ro'i (ed.), *The USSR and the Muslim World: Issues in Domestic and Foreign Policy*, George Allen and Unwin, London, 1984.

Soviet sources: E. M. Primakov, 'Islam i protsessy obshchestvennogo razvitiia stran zarubezhnogo Vostoka', ('Islam and Processes of Social Development of Foreign Countries in the East'), *Voprosy filosofii*, 8 (1980), pp. 60–71 translated in *Soviet Law and Government*, 1981; G. Kim, 'Social Development and Ideological Struggle in the Developing Countries', *International Affairs*, 4 (1980), pp. 65–75; Alla Ionova, 'Islam and the Contemporary World', *International Affairs*, 11 (1986), pp. 145–6, 83.

14 Arab Communism in the Middle East

M. S. Agwani, *Communism in the Arab East*, Asia Publishing House, London, 1969.

John Cooley, 'The Shifting Sands of Arab Communism', *Problems of Communism*, 24, 2 (March–April 1975), pp. 22–42.

Robert Freedman, 'The Soviet Union and the Communist Parties of the Arab World', in R. Kanet and D. Bahry (eds.), *Soviet Economic and Political Relations with the Developing Countries*, Praeger, New York, 1974, pp. 100–34.

Arnold Hottinger, 'Arab Communism at Low Ebb', *Problems of Communism*, 30, 4 (July–August 1981), pp. 17–32.

Jaan Pennar, *The USSR and the Arabs: The Ideological Dimension*, Crane Russet New York, 1973.

Soviet sources: Georgii Kim, *The Socialist World and the National Liberation Movement*, Progress Publishers, Moscow, 1978; Rostislav Ulyanovsky,

National Liberation: Essays on Theory and Practice, Progress Publishers, Moscow, 1978.

15 Marxist South Yemen and the Arabian Peninsula

Norman Cigar, 'South Yemen and the USSR: Prospects for the Relationship', *The Middle East Journal*, 39, 4 (Autumn 1985), pp. 775–95.

Mark Kartz, *Russia and Arabia: Soviet Foreign Policy Toward the Arabian Peninsula*, Johns Hopkins University Press, Baltimore, 1986.

Stephen Page, *The Soviet Union and the Yemens: Influence in Asymmetrical Relationships*, Praeger, New York, 1985.

William Quandt, 'Riyadh Between the Superpowers', *Foreign Policy*, Autumn 1981, pp. 37–56.

Dennis Ross, 'The Soviet Union and the Persian Gulf', *Political Science Quarterly*, 99, 4 (Winter, 1984–5), pp. 615–36.

Paul Viotti, 'Politics in the Yemens and the Horn of Africa', in M. Kauppi and R. Nation (eds.), *The Soviet Union and the Middle East in the 1980s*, Lexington Books, Lexington, Mass., 1983, pp. 211–26.

Soviet documents in Yaacov Ro'i, *From Encroachment to Involvement: A Documentary Study of Soviet Policy in the Middle East, 1945–1973*, John Wiley and Sons, London, 1974, pp. 410–12, 496–98; *Current Digest of the Soviet Press*, 31, 43 (1979), pp. 13–14; V. Naumkin, 'Southern Yemen: The Road to Progress', *International Affairs*, 1 (1978), p. 64–9; 'North Yemen', *New Times*, 2 (January 1979), p. 7.

16 The Soviet Union and Turkey

George Harns, 'The Soviet Union and Turkey', in I. Lederer and W. Vucinich (eds.), *The Soviet Union and the Middle East*, Hoover Institution, Stanford, 1974, pp. 25–54.

Alvin Rubinstein, *Soviet Policy Toward Turkey, Iran and Afghanistan: The Dynamics of Influence*, Praeger, New York, 1982.

Duygu Sezer, 'Peaceful Coexistence: Turkey and the Near East in Soviet Foreign Policy', *Annals of the American Academy of Political and Social Sciences*, 481 (September 1985), pp. 117–26.

Malcolm Yapp, 'Soviet Relations with the Northern Tier', in A. Dawisha and K. Dawisha (eds.), *The Soviet Union in the Middle East*, Heinemann, London, 1982, pp. 24–44.

Soviet documents in Yaacov Ro'i, *From Encroachment to Involvement: A Documentary Study of Soviet Policy in the Middle East, 1945–1973*, John Wiley and Sons, London, 1974, pp. 310–14, 330–3, 405–9; *Current Digest of the Soviet Press*, 30, 26 (1978), pp. 8–9; Y. Gavrilov, 'The Republic of Cyprus', *International Affairs*, 12 (1974), pp. 137–8; and Vitali Alexandrov, 'Soviet–Turkish Cooperation', *International Affairs*, 12 (1986), p. 35–8.

17 Gorbachev's Middle East policy

Graham Fuller, 'The Case for Optimism', *National Interest*, 12 (Summer 1988), pp. 73–82.

Galia Golan, 'Gorbachev's Middle East Strategy', *Foreign Affairs*, 66, 1 (Autumn 1987), pp. 41–57.

Fred Halliday, 'Gorbachev and the "Arab Syndrome": Soviet Policy in the Middle East', *World Policy Journal*, Summer 1987, pp. 416–42.

Soviet sources: *Current Digest of the Soviet Press*, 41, 9 (29 March 1989); Dmitry Zgersky, 'Peace at the Height of War', *New Times*, 32 (August 1988), pp. 5–6; Igor Belyayev, 'Mid-East Versions', *International Affairs*, 6 (1988), pp. 55–63, 79; Alexander Zotov and Vladimir Nosenko, 'Israel Forty Years Later', *New Times*, 20 (May 1988), pp. 13–15; Grigori Alyoshin, 'A Mission to Israel', *International Affairs*, 5 (1988), pp. 103–7, 144; Alexei Vasilyev, 'A Chance Not To Be Missed', *New Times*, 10 (March 1989), p. 8.

Bibliography
(Western sources in English)

Books

Alexander, Yonah (ed.), *International Terrorism: National, Regional and Global Perspectives*, Praeger Publishers, New York, 1976.

Bar-Siman-Tov, Yaacov, *Israel, the Superpowers and the Middle East*, Praeger Publishers, New York, 1987.

Becker, Abraham S., *Oil and the Persian Gulf in Soviet Policy in the 1970s*, Rand Corporation, Santa Monica, 1972.

Becker, Abraham and Arnold Horelick, *Soviet Policy in the Middle East*, Rand Corporation, Santa Monica, 1970.

Ben-Dor, Gabriel (ed.), *The Palestinians and the Middle East Conflict*, Turtledove Press, Ramat Gan, 1978.

Bennigsen, Alexander and Marie Broxup, *The Islamic Threat to the Soviet State*, St Martin's Press, New York, 1983.

Bidwell, Robin, *The Two Yemens*, Westview Press, Boulder, 1983.

Braun, Aurel (ed.), *The Middle East in Global Strategy*, Westview Press, Boulder, 1987.

Brown, Carl L., *International Politics and the Middle East: Old Rules, Dangerous Game*, I. B. Tamris Publishers, London, 1984.

Calvocoressi, Peter, *Suez Ten Years After: Broadcasts From the BBC Third Programme*, British Broadcasting Corporation, London, 1967.

Chubin, Shahram, *Soviet Policy Towards Iran and the Gulf*, Adelphi Paper 157, International Institute for Strategic Studies, London, 1980.

Cline, Ray and Yonah Alexander, *Terrorism: The Soviet Connection*, Crane Russak, New York, 1984.

Cobban, Helena, *The Palestinian Liberation Organization*, Cambridge University Press, Cambridge, 1984.

Confino, Michel and Shimon Shamir (eds.), *The USSR and the Middle East*, Israel Universities Press, Jerusalem, 1973.

Cooley, John, *Green March, Black September*, Frank Cass, London, 1973.

Dagan, Avigdor, *Moscow and Jerusalem*, Abelard-Schuman, New York, 1970.

Dawisha, Adeed (ed.), *Islam in Foreign Policy*, Cambridge University Press, Cambridge, 1983.

Dawisha, Adeed and Karen Dawisha (eds.). *The Soviet Union in the Arab World*, Holmes and Meier, New York, 1982.

Dawisha, Karen, *Soviet Foreign Policy Towards Egypt*, Macmillan Press, London 1979.

Dismukes, Bradford and James McConnell, *Soviet Naval Diplomacy*, Pergamon Press, New York, 1979.

Duncan, Raymond (ed.), *Soviet Policy in Developing Countries*, Ginn-Blaisdell, Waltham, 1970.

Eagleton, William, *The Kurdish Republic of 1946*, Oxford University Press, New York, 1963.

Eden, Sir Anthony, *Full Circle: The Memoirs of the Rt Hon. Sir Anthony Eden*, Houghton Mifflin, Boston, 1960.

Elad, Shlomo and Ariel Merari, *The Soviet Bloc and World Terrorism*, Jaffee Center for Strategic Studies, Tel Aviv, 1984.

Fatemi, Faramarz, *The USSR in Iran*, A. S. Barnes, Cranbury, N.J., 1980.

Freedman, Robert O. (ed), *The Middle East After the Israeli Invasion of Lebanon*, Syracuse University Press, New York, 1986.

Freedman, Robert, *Soviet Policy Towards the Middle East*, Praeger Publishers, New York, 1975.

Fukuyama, Francis, *Gorbachev and the New Soviet Agenda in the Third World*, Rand Corporation, Santa Monica, 1988.

The Soviet Union and Iraq since 1968, Rand Corporation, Santa Monica, 1980.

Garthoff, Raymond, *Détente and Confrontation*, Brookings Institution, Washington, D.C., 1985.

Soviet Military Policy, Faber and Faber, London, 1966.

George, Alexander, *Managing Soviet–US Rivalry*, Westview Press, Boulder, 1983.

Gibert , Stephen and Wynfred Joshua, *Arms for the Third World: Soviet Military Aid Diplomacy*, Johns Hopkins University Press, Baltimore, 1969.

Golan, Galia, *The Soviet Union and National Liberation Movements in the Third World*, Unwin and Hyman, London, 1988.

Gorbachev's New Thinking on Terrorism, Praeger Publishers, New York, 1990.

The Soviet Union and the Palestine Liberation Organization: An Uneasy Alliance, Praeger Publishers, New York, 1980.

Yom Kippur and After: The Soviet Union and the Middle East Crisis, Cambridge University Press, Cambridge, 1977.

Goren, Roberta, *The Soviet Union and Terrorism*, George Allen and Unwin, London, 1984.

Hammond, Paul and Sidney Alexander (eds.), *Political Dynamics in the Middle East*, American Elsevier, New York, 1972.

Harkavy, Robert, *Great Power Competition for Overseas Bases*, Pergamon Press, New York, 1983.

Harris, George, *The Origins of Communism in Turkey*, Hoover Institution, Stanford, 1967.

Heikal, Hassan, *The Road to Ramadan*, Collins, London, 1975.

Sphinx and Commissar: The Rise and Fall of Soviet Influence in the Middle East, Collins, London, 1978.

Hirst, David, *The Gun and the Olive Branch: The Roots of Violence in the Middle East*, Faber and Faber, New York, 1977.

Hosmer, Stephen and Thomas Wolfe, *Soviet Policy and Practice Toward Third World Countries*, Lexington Books, Lexington, 1982.

Hunter, Robert E., *The Soviet Dilemma in the Middle East*, Part 1: *Problems of Commitment*, Part 2: *Oil and the Persian Gulf*, Adelphi Paper, nos. 59, 60, Institute for Strategic Studies, London, 1969.

Hurewitz, Jacob C., *Diplomacy in the Near and Middle East: A Documentary Record*, Octagon, New York, 1972.

Soviet–American Rivalry in the Middle East, Praeger Publishers, 1969.

Israeli, Raphael, *The PLO in Lebanon, Selected Documents*, Weidenfeld and Nicolson, London, 1983.

Kanet, Roger and Donna Bahry (eds.), *Soviet Economic and Political Relations with the Developing World*, Praeger Publishers, New York, 1974.

Kanet, Roger, *The Soviet Union and Developing Nations*, Johns Hopkins University Press, Baltimore, 1974.

Kaplan, Stephen S., *Diplomacy of Power*, Brookings Institution, Washington, D.C., 1981.

Karsh, Efraim, *The Cautious Bear: Soviet Military Engagement in the Middle East*, Jaffe Center for Strategic Studies, Tel Aviv, 1985.

Kass, Ilana, *Soviet Involvement in the Middle East: Policy Formulation*, Westview Press, Boulder, 1978.

Katz, Mark, *Russia and Arabia: Soviet Policy Toward the Arabian Penninsula*, Johns Hopkins University Press, Baltimore, 1986.

The Third World in Soviet Military Thinking, Johns Hopkins, Baltimore, 1982.

Kauppi M. and R. Nation, *The Soviet Union and the Middle East in the 1980s*, Lexington Books, Lexington, 1983.

Kazziha, Walid, *Revolutionary Transformation in the Arab World: Habash and His Comrades from Nationalism to Marxism*, Charles Knight, London, 1975.

Klieman, Aaron S., *Soviet Russia and the Middle East*, Johns Hopkins University Press, Baltimore, 1970.

Klinghoffer, Arthur J., *Israel and the Soviet Union*, Westview Press, Boulder, 1985.

Krammer, Arnold, *The Forgotten Friendship: Israel and the Soviet Bloc 1947–1953*, University of Illinois Press, Urbana, 1974.

Kuniholm, Bruce, *The Origins of the Cold War in the Near East: Great Power Conflict and Diplomacy in Iran, Turkey, and Greece*, Princeton University Press, Princeton, 1980.

Landis, Lincoln, *Politics and Oil: Moscow in the Middle East*, Dunellen, New York, 1973.

Laqueur, Walter, *Confrontation: The Middle East and World Politics*, Bubler and Tanner, London, 1974.

Guerrilla, Little Brown, Boston, 1976

Terrorism, Weidenfeld and Nicolson, London, 1978.

The Road to War: The Origins and Aftermath of the Arab–Israeli Conflict, 1967–68, Penguin, Harmondsworth, 1969.

The Soviet Union and the Middle East, Praeger Publishers, New York, 1959.

The Struggle for the Middle East: The Soviet Union and the Middle East, 1958–1968, Routledge & K. Paul, London, 1969.

Lenczowski, George, *Russia and the West in Iran, 1918–1948: A Study in Big-power Rivalry*, Greenwood Press, New York, 1968.

The Middle East in World Affairs, Cornell University Press, Ithaca, 1985.

Love, Kennett, *Suez: The Twice-fought War*, McGraw-Hill, New York, 1969.

McClane, Charles B., *Soviet–Third World Relations, Vol. 1: Soviet–Middle East Relations*, Columbia University Press, New York, 1973.

McClellan, Grant, S. (ed.), *The Middle East in the Cold War*, H. W. Wilson Co., New York, 1956.

MccGwire, Michael, Ken Booth and John McDonnell (eds.), *Soviet Naval Policy: Objectives and Constraints*, Praeger Publishers, New York, 1975.

McLaurin, R., *The Middle East in Soviet Policy*, D.C. Heath, Lexington, Mass., 1975.

Malik, Hafees (ed.), *Soviet–American Relations with Pakistan, Iran and Afghanistan*, St Martin's Press, New York, 1987.

Maoz, Moshe, *Palestinian Arab Politics*, Jerusalem Academic Press, Jerusalem, 1975.

Marantz, Paul and Blema S. Steinberg (eds.), *Superpower Involvement in the Middle East*, Westview Press, Boulder, 1985.

Menon, Rajan, *Soviet Power and the Third World: Aspects of Theory and Practice*, Yale University Press, New Haven, 1986.

Moore, John Norton (ed.), *The Arab–Israeli Conflict*, 1–3, Princeton University Press, Princeton, 1972.

Nollau, Gunther, *Russia's South Flank: Soviet Operations in Iran, Turkey and Afghanistan*, Praeger Publishers, New York, 1963.

Odell, Peter R., *Oil and World Power: A Geographical Interpretation*, Penguin, Baltimore, 1970.

Page, Stephen, *The Soviet Union and the Yemens: Influence on Asymmetrical Relationships*, Praeger Publishers, New York, 1985.

The USSR in Arabia: The Development of Soviet Policies and Attitudes Towards the Countries of the Arabian Peninsula, Central Asian Research Center, London, 1972.

Pennar, Jaan, *The USSR and the Arabs: The Ideological Dimension*, Crane Russak and Co., New York, 1973.

Quandt, William B. (ed.), *The Middle East: Ten Years After Camp David*, The Brookings Institution, Washington D.C., 1988.

Quandt, William, Faud Jabber and Ann Morley Lesch, *The Politics of Palestinian Nationalism*, University of California Press, Berkeley, 1973.

Ra'anan, Uri, *The USSR Arms the Third World: Case Studies in Soviet Foreign Policy*, MIT University Press, Cambridge, Mass., 1969.

Rabinovich, Itamar, *The War in Lebanon: 1970–1983*, Cornell University Press, Ithaca, 1988.

Ramazani, Rouhollah, *Iran's Foreign Policy 1941–1973*, University Press of Virginia, Charlottesville, 1975.

Ro'i, Yaacov, *Soviet Decision-Making in Practice*, Transaction Books, New Brunswick, 1980.

From Encroachment to Involvement: A Documentary Study of Soviet Policy in the Middle East, 1945–1973, John Wiley, New York, 1974.

(ed.), *The Limits to Power*, Croom-Helm, London, 1979.

(ed.), *The USSR and the Muslim World*, Allen & Unwin, London, 1984.

Rubinstein, Alvin (ed.), *Soviet and Chinese Influence in the Third World*, Praeger Publishers, New York, 1975.

Red Star On the Nile, Princeton University Press, Princeton, 1977.

Soviet Policy Toward Turkey, Iran and Afghanistan: The Dynamics of Influence, Praeger Publishers, New York, 1982.

Sadat, Anwar, *In Search of Identity*, Harper and Row, New York, 1977.

Sezer, Duygu Bazoghu, *Turkey's Security Policies*, International Institute for Strategic Studies, London, 1981.

Shearman, Peter and Phil Williams (eds.), *The Superpowers, Central America and the Middle East*, Brassey's Defence Publishers, London, 1988.

Smolansky, Oles, *The Soviet Union and the Arab East Under Khrushchev*, Bucknell University Press, Lewisburg, Pa., 1974.

Spechler, Dina Rome, *Domestic Influences on Soviet Foreign Policy*, University Press of America, Washington, DC, 1978.

Spector, Ivar, *The Soviet Union and the Muslim World, 1917–1958*, University of Washington Press, Seattle, 1959.

Stein, Janice Gross and David B. Dewitt (eds.), *The Middle East at the Crossroads – Regional Forces and External Powers*, Mosaic Press, Oakville, Ontario, 1983.

Stookey, Robert, *South Yemen: A Marxist Republic in Arabia*, Westview Press, Boulder, 1982.

Troen, Ilan and Moshe Shemesh, *The Suez–Sinai Crisis: A Retrospective*, Frank Cass, London, 1990.

Vali, Ferenc A., *The Turkish Straits and NATO*, Hoover Institution Press, Stanford, Calif., 1972.

Van Wagenen, Richard W., *The Iranian Case, 1946*, Carnegie Endowment for International Peace, New York, 1952.

Wells, Samuel F. Jun., and Mark Bruzonsky (eds.), *Security in the Middle East: Regional Change and Great Power Strategies*, Westview Press, Boulder, 1987.

Whetten, Lawrence, *The Canal War: Four Power Conflict in the Middle East*, MIT University Press, Cambridge, Mass., 1974.

Wolfe, Thomas W., *Soviet Goals and Politics in the Middle East*, Rand Corporation, Santa Monica, 1970.

Yodfat, Aryeh, *Arab Politics in the Soviet Mirror*, Israel Universities Press, Jerusalem, 1973.

Articles

Abu 'Amr, Ziad, 'Notes on Palestinian Political Leadership', *Middle East Report*, 154 (September–October 1988), pp. 23–5.

Abu-Jaber, Faiz S., 'Soviet Attitude Toward Arab Revolutions: Yemen, Egypt, Algeria, Iraq and Palestine', *Middle East Forum*, 46, 4 (1970), pp. 41–65.

'The Soviets and the Arabs, 1917–1955', *Middle East Forum*, 45, 1 (1969), pp. 13–44.

Allen, Robin, 'Gulf States Warm to the Soviet Union', *Middle East Economic Digest*, 31, 4 (24 January 1987), pp. 2–4.

Apremont, B., 'La Penetration des pays du bloc Sovietique au Moyen-Orient et dans le Sud-Est Asiatique', *Politique etrangere*, 21, 2 (avril 1956), pp. 201–14.

Atherton, Alfred L., 'The Soviet Role in the Middle East: An American Perspective', *Middle East Journal*, 39, 4 (1985), pp. 688–714.

Azar, Edward, 'Soviet and Chinese Roles in the Middle East', *Problems of Communism*, 28, 3 (May–June 1979), pp. 18–30.

Barkey, Henri J., 'The Silent Victor: Turkey's Role in the Gulf War', unpublished paper, Jaffee Center for Strategic Studies, Tel Aviv, September 1988.

Bennett, Alexander J., 'Arms Transfer As An Instrument of Soviet Policy in the Middle East', *Middle East Journal*, 39, 4 (1985), pp. 745–74.

Berry, John A., 'The Growing Importance of Oil', *Military Review*, 52 (Oct. 1972), pp. 2–16.

Bilsel, Cemil, 'The Turkish Straits in the Light of Recent Turkish–Soviet Russian Correspondence', *American Journal of International Law*, 41, 4 (Oct. 1947), pp. 727–47.

Breslauer, George, 'The Dynamics of Soviet Policy Towards the Arab–Israeli Conflict: Lessons of the Brezhnev Era', in D. Coldwell (ed.), *Soviet International Behavior and US Policy Options*, Lexington Books, Lexington, 1985.

Bruzonsky, Mark and Stephen Green, 'Why the USSR Eyes the Gulf', *Middle East International*, 313 (21 November 1987), pp. 15–17.

Brynen, Rex, 'PLO Policies in Lebanon: Legacies and Lessons', *Journal of Palestine Studies*, 70 (Winter 1989), pp. 48–70.

Campbell, John C., 'The Communist Powers and the Middle East: Moscow's Purposes', *Problems of Communism*, 21, 5 (September–October 1972), pp. 40–54.

'Soviet Strategy in the Middle East', *American–Arab Affairs*, 8 (1984), pp. 74–82.

'The Soviet Union and the Middle East: In the General Direction of the Persian Gulf.' *Russian Review*, part 1, 29, 2 (April 1970), pp. 143–54; part 2, 29, 3 (July 1970), pp. 247–61.

'The Soviet Union and the United States in the Middle East', *The Annals of the American Academy of Political and Social Sciences*, 401 (May 1972), pp. 126–35.

Carrere D'encausse, H., 'L'URSS et le Moyen-Orient', *l'Orient*, 37 (1966), pp. 7–25.

Chritchlow, James, 'Minarets and Marx', *Washington Quarterly*, 3, 2 (Spring 1980), pp. 47–57.

Chubin, Shahram, 'The Soviet Union and Iran', *Foreign Affairs*, 61, 4 (Spring 1983), pp. 921–49.

Cigar, Norman, 'South Yemen and the USSR: Prospects for the Relationship', *Middle East Journal*, 39, 4 (1985), pp. 775–95.

Cooley, John, 'The Shifting Sands of Arab Communism', *Problems of Communism*, 24, 2 (March–April 1975), pp. 22–42.

Cottrell, Alvin, J., 'Soviet–Egyptian Relations', *Military Review*, 49, 12 (1969), pp. 69–76.

'The Soviet Union in the Middle East.' *Orbis*. 14 (Autumn 1970), pp. 588–98.

'Conflict in the Persian Gulf', *Military Review*, 51, 2 (1971), pp. 33–41.

Daneshku, Scheherazade, 'Gorbachev's Iran Dilemma', *Middle East International*, 320 (1988), pp. 16–17.

Dawisha, Karen, 'Moscow Moves in the Direction of the Gulf', *Journal of International Affairs*, 34, 2 (Autumn–Winter 1980), pp. 219–33.

'The USSR in the Middle East: Superpower in Eclipse', *Foreign Affairs*, 61, 2 (1982), pp. 438–52.

Dunn, Michael Collins, 'Soviet Interests in the Arabian Peninsula: The Aden Pact and Other Paper Tigers', *American–Arab Affairs*, 8 (1984), pp. 92–8.

Eran, Oded, and Jerome Singer, 'Soviet Policy Towards the Arab World 1955–71', *Survey*, 17 (Aug. 1971), pp. 10–29.

Farouq, M., 'Palestine and the Soviet Union', *Palestine*, 3 (January 1977), pp. 34–41.

Forsythe, David P., 'The Soviets and the Arab–Israeli conflict,' *Middle East Forum*, 46, 4 (1970), pp. 29–39.

Freedman, Robert O., 'Is Gorbachev Changing Soviet–Israeli Relations?' *Middle East International*, 305 (1987), pp. 14–15.

'Moscow and a Middle East Peace Settlement', *Washington Quarterly*, 8, 3 (1985), pp. 143–61.

'Moscow, Damascus and the Lebanese Crisis 1982–1984', *Middle East Review*, 17, (1984), pp. 22–39.

'Patterns of Soviet Policy Toward the Middle East', *The Annals of the American Academy of Political and Social Sciences*, 482, (1985), pp. 40–64.

'Soviet Policy Toward Syria Since Camp David', *Middle East Review*, 14, 1 (1981–2), pp. 31–42.

'The Soviet Union and the Civil War in Lebanon', *Jerusalem Journal of International Relations*, 3 (Summer 1976), pp. 60–93.

Fukuyama, Francis, 'Nuclear Shadowboxing: Soviet Intervention Threats in the Middle East', *Orbis*, 25, 3 (Autumn 1981), pp. 579–605.

Fuller, Graham, 'The United States and the Soviet Union in the Middle East: Prospects for Cooperation', *Middle East Insight*, 6, 4 (Winter 1989), pp. 3–8.

Gasteyger, Curt, 'Moscow and the Mediterranean', *Foreign Affairs*, 46, 4 (July 68), pp. 676–87.

Gawad, Atef, 'Moscow's Arms-for-oil Diplomacy', *Foreign Policy*, 63 (Summer 1986), pp. 147–68.

Glassman, Jon, *Arms for the Arabs*, Johns Hopkins University Press, Baltimore, 1975.

Golan, Galia, 'Soviet Policy in the Middle East: Growing Difficulties and Changing Interests', *The World Today*, 33 (September 1977), pp. 335–42.

'Syria and the Soviet Union since the Yom Kippur War', *Orbis*, 21 (Winter 1978), pp. 777–801.

'The Soviet Union and the Israeli Action in Lebanon', *International Affairs*, 59, 1, (1982/3), pp. 7–16.

'The Soviet Union and the Palestine Question', in George Breslauer (ed.),
The Soviet Strategy in the Middle East, Cornell University Press, Ithaca, 1990.

'The Soviet Union and the PLO since Lebanon', *Middle East Journal*, 40, 2
(1986), pp. 285–305.

'The Soviet Union in the Middle East After Thirty Years', in A. Korbonski
and F. Fukuyama (eds.), *The Soviet Union and the Third World After Thirty
Years*, Cornell University Press, Ithaca, 1987.

'The Soviet Union, Israel and Gorbachev's Middle East Policy', *Foreign
Affairs*, 66, 1 (Autumn 1987), pp. 41–57.

'Soviet Decision-making in the Yom Kippur War', in William Potter and Jiri
Valenta, *Soviet Decision-making for National Security*, George Allen and
Unwin, London, 1983.

Goodman, Melvin A., 'Gorbachev's "New Directions" in the Middle East',
Middle East Journal, 42, 4 (1988), pp. 571–86.

Graz, Liesl, 'South Yemen's New Leaders Seeking Legitimacy', *Middle East
International*, 24 October 1987, p. 13–15.

'The Soviets and the Middle East', *Swiss Review of World Affairs*, 34, 5
(August 1989), pp. 7–10.

Green, Stephen, 'Strategic Asset, Soviet Opportunity', *American–Arab Affairs*,
9 (1984), pp. 46–54.

Gresh, Alain, 'Palestinian Communists and the Intifada', *Middle East Report*,
157 (March–April 1989), pp. 34–6.

Halliday, Fred, 'Gorbachev and the "Arab Syndrome": Soviet Policy in the
Middle East', *World Policy Journal*, Summer 1987, pp. 415–42.

'"Islam" and Soviet Foreign Policy', *Asian Studies Quarterly*, 3 (1986),
pp. 217–33.

'Moscow's Crisis Management: The Case of South Yemen', *Middle East
Report*, 151 (1988), pp. 18–22.

'The Great Powers and the Middle East', *Middle East Report*, 151 (1988),
pp. 3–6.

'The USSR and the Gulf War: Moscow's Growing Concern', *Merip Report*,
148 (1987), pp. 10–11.

Hannah, John, 'Soviet–Syrian Relations Under Gorbachev', Washington Institute for Near East Policy, Washington, 1989.

Harris, George, 'The Left in Turkey', *Problems of Communism*, 29, 4 (July–
August 1980), pp. 26–32.

Hirshfeld, Yair, 'Soviet–Iranian Relations in Historical Perspective', *Orbis*, 24,
2 (Summer 1980), pp. 219–40.

Hoffman, Stefani, 'Shades of Gray: The Current Soviet Press on Israel and
Zionism', Marjorie Mayrock Center for Soviet and East European
Research, Jerusalem, 1989.

Horelick, Arnold, 'Moscow's New Time of Troubles in the Middle East',
Middle East Review, 8 (Spring–Summer 1976), pp. 42–51.

Hoskins, Halford L., 'Soviet Economic Penetration in the Middle East', *Orbis*,
3, 4 (Winter 1960), pp. 458–68.

Hottinger, Arnold, 'Arab Communism at Low Ebb', *Problems of Communism*,
30, 4 (July–August 1981), pp. 17–32.

'Moscow's New Effort in the Middle East', *Swiss Review*, 37, 5 (1987), pp. 8–9.

Hudson, Michael, 'The Palestinian Factor in the Lebanese Civil War', *Middle East Journal*, 32 (Summer 1978), pp. 261–78.

Hurewitz, Jacob C., 'Russia and the Turkish Straits: A Revaluation of the Origins of the Problem', *World Politics*, 14, 4 (July 1962), pp. 605–32.

Hutton, C. Powell, 'Changing Soviet Oil Interests: Implications for the Middle East', *Naval War College Review*, 24 (Oct. 1971), pp. 76–93.

Ibrahim, Saad E. M., 'Arab Images of the United States and the Soviet Union Before and After the June War of 1967', *Journal of Conflict Resolution*, 16, 2 (June 1972), pp. 227–40.

Indyk, Martin, 'Glasnost and the Middle East; How Should the US Respond?' *Middle East Insight*, 5, 4 (1987), pp. 14–21.

Irwin, Zachary, 'The USSR and Israel', *Problems of Communism*, 36, 1 (January–February 1987), pp. 36–45.

Jabber, F., 'The Soviet Attitude toward Arab Revolution: Yemen, Egypt, Algeria, Iraq and Palestine', *Middle East Forum*, 46, 4 (1971), pp. 41–67.

Jansen, Godfrey, 'Moving Towards an Inevitable Clash?', *Middle East International*, 11 July 1987, pp. 3–5.

'The Gulf: Superpower Involvement', *Middle East International*, 3 April 1987, pp. 5–7.

Kanet, Rogert E., 'The Soviet Union and the Developing Countries: Policy or Policies', *The World Today*, 31, (August 1975), pp. 338–46.

Kass, Ilana, 'Moscow and the Lebanese Triangle', *Middle East Journal*, 33, 2 (Spring 1979), pp. 164–88.

'The Lebanon Civil War 1975–76', *Jerusalem Papers on Peace*, Leonard Davis Institute for International Relations, (1979), pp. 26–7.

Katz, Mark K., 'The Soviet Challenge in the Gulf', *Middle East Insight*, 5, 4 (1987), pp. 24–7.

'Civil Conflict in South Yemen', *Middle East Review*, 14, 1 (Autumn 1986), pp. 7–14.

'The USSR and the Iran–Iraq War: Short-term Benefits', *Middle East Insight*, 5, 1 (1987), pp. 8–13.

Keep, John, 'The Soviet Union and the Third World', *Survey*, 72 (1969), pp. 19–38.

Kerim, Mohammed, 'Soviets and South Yemen', *Jane's Defense Weekly*, 15 February 1986, pp. 263–67.

Khalidi, Walid, 'Thinking The Unthinkable: A Sovereign Palestinian State', *Foreign Affairs*, 56 (July 1978), pp. 695–713.

Khalilzad, Zalmay, 'Islamic Iran: Soviet Dilemma', *Problems of Communism*, 33, 1 (January-February 1984), pp. 1–20.

Kielmas, Maria, 'The Soviet–Iranian Deal', *Middle East International*, 355 (1989), pp. 16–17.

Klinghoffer, Arthur J., 'Soviet–Israeli Relations and a Middle East Peace Settlement', *Crossroads*, 23 (1987), pp. 1–14.

'The Dynamics of Quiet Diplomacy: The Soviet Union and Israel', *Middle East Review*, 18, 4 (1986), pp. 34–42.

Krammer, Arnold, 'Soviet Motives in the Partition of Palestine 1947–8', *Journal of Palestine Studies*, 2, 2 (1973), pp. 102–19.

Lawson, Fred, 'South Yemen's Troubles', *Orient*, 27, 3 (September 1986), pp. 441–49.

MccGwire, Michael, 'The Middle East and Soviet Military Strategy', *Middle East Report*, 151 (1988), pp. 11–17.

McDermott, Anthony, 'Sadat and the Soviet Union', *The World Today*, 28, 9 (Sept. 1972), pp. 404–10.

Millar, T. B., 'Soviet Policies South and East of Suez', *Foreign Affairs*, 49, 1 (Oct. 1970), pp. 70–80.

Murarka, Dev, 'Soviet Perceptions of the Gulf', *Middle East International*, 187 (12 November 1982), pp. 12–13.

Napper, Larry C., 'The Arab Autumn of 1984: A Case Study of Soviet Middle East Policy', *Middle East Journal*, 39, 4 (1985), pp. 733–44.

Nasrallah, Fida, 'The USSR and Lebanon', *Middle East International*, 356 (4 August 1989), pp. 17–18.

Neff, Donald, 'The Soviet Bear Burrows Ever Deeper', *Middle East International* (27 June 1987), pp. 15–17.

Olcott, Martha Brill, 'Soviet Islam and World Revolution', *World Politics*, 34, 4 (July 1982), pp. 487–504.

Padelford, Norman J., 'Solutions to the Problems of the Turkish Straits: A Brief Appraisal', *Middle East Journal*, 2, 2 (April 1948), pp. 175–90.

Page, Stephen, 'Moscow and the Arabian Peninsula', *American–Arab Affairs*, 8 (Spring 1984), pp. 83–91.

'The Soviet Union and the GCC States: A Search for Openings', *American–Arab Affairs*, 20 (Spring 1987), pp. 38–56.

Pennar, Jaan, 'Moscow and Socialism in Egypt', *Problems of Communism*, 15, 5 (September-October 1966), pp. 41–7.

Pipes, Daniel, 'Syria – The Cuba of the Middle East?' *Commentary*, 82, 1 (1986), pp. 15–22.

Pitty, Roderic, 'Soviet Perspectives of Iraq', *Middle East Report*, 151 (1988), pp. 23–8.

Pollock, David, 'Moscow and Aden: Coping with a Coup', *Problems of Communism*, 35, 3 (May-June 1986), pp. 50–70.

Quandt, William, 'Riyadh Between the Superpowers', *Foreign Policy*, 59 (Autumn 1981), pp. 37–56.

Rafael, Gideon, 'Divergence and Convergence of American–Soviet Interests in the Middle East', *Political Science Quarterly*, 100, 4 (Winter 1985–6), pp. 561–74.

Ramet, Pedro, 'The Soviet–Syrian Relationship', *Problems of Communism*, 35, 5 (September-October 1986), pp. 35–46.

Ro'i, Yaacov, 'The Role of Islam and the Soviet Muslims in Soviet Arab Policy', Parts 1 and 2, *Asian and African Studies*, 10, 2, 3 (1974–5), pp. 157–89, 259–80.

Ross, Dennis, 'Soviet Views Toward the Gulf War', *Orbis*, 28, 3 (Autumn 1984), pp. 437–47.

'Soviet Union and the Persian Gulf', *Political Science Quarterly*, 99, 4 (1984–5), pp. 615–36.

Rossow, Robert, Jun., 'The Battle of Azerbaijan, 1946', *Middle East Journal*, 10, 1 (1956), pp. 17–32.

Rothenberg, Morris, 'Recent Soviet Relations with Syria', *Middle East Review*, 10 (Summer 1978), pp. 5–9.

Rouleau, Eric, 'The Palestinian Quest', *Foreign Affairs*, 53 (January 1975), pp. 254–83.

Rubinstein, Alvin, 'Soviet Policy in the Third World in the 1970s', *Orbis*, 15, 1 (1971), pp. 104–17.

Safran, Nadav, 'The Soviet–Egyptian Treaty – as seen from Washington', *The New Middle East*, 34 (July 1971), pp. 10–13.

Saivetz, Carol R., 'Islam and Gorbachev's Policy in the Middle East', *Journal of International Affairs*, 42, 2 (1987), pp. 435–44.

Schapiro, Leonard, 'The Soviet Union and the PLO', *Survey*, 23 (Summer 1977–8), pp. 193–207.

Schopflin, George, 'Russia's Expendable Arab Communists', *The New Middle East*, 35 (June 1972), pp. 20–1.

Sezer, Duygu, 'Peaceful Coexistence: Turkey and the Near East in Soviet Foreign Policy', *The Annals of the American Academy of Political and Social Science*, 481 (September 1985), pp. 117–26.

Shoumikhin, Andrey V., 'Soviet Perceptions of US Middle East Policy', *Middle East Journal*, 43, 1 (1989), pp. 16–19.

Smolansky, Oles M., 'Moscow and the Persian Gulf: An Analysis of Soviet Ambitions and Potential', *Orbis*, 14, 1 (Spring 1970), pp. 92–108.

'Moscow and the Suez Crisis 1956: A Reappraisal', *Political Science Quarterly*, 80, 4 (Dec. 1965), pp. 581–605.

'The Kremlin and Iraqi Ba'ath 1968–1982: An Influence Relationship., *Middle East Review*, 15 (Spring/Summer 1983), pp. 622–8.

Spechler, Dina Rome, 'The Politics of Intervention', *Studies in Comparative Communism*, 20, 2 (Summer 1987), pp. 115–43.

Stein, Georg, 'The Spectrum of Palestinian Opinion', *The Middle East*, (March 1989), pp. 15–17.

Sukru, Esmer Ahmet, 'The Straits: Crux of World Politics', *Foreign Affairs*, 25, 2 (January 1947), pp. 290–303.

Tekiner, Suleiman, 'Soviet–Iranian Relations Over the Last Half Century', *Studies on the Soviet Union*, 8, 4 (1969), pp. 36–45.

'Soviet–Turkish Relations and Kosygin's Trip to Turkey', *Bulletin. Institute for the Study of the USSR*, 14, 3 (March 1967), pp. 3–13.

Valkenier, Elizabeth, 'New Trends in Soviet Economic Relations with the Third World', *World Politics*, 22, 3 (1970), pp. 415–32.

van Bruinessen, Martin, 'The Kurds in Turkey', *Merip Reports*, (February 1984), p. 8.

'The Kurds', *Merip Reports*, (February 1984), pp. 6–12.

Walker, Martin, 'Mikhail's Middle East', *The Middle East*, 145 (1986), pp. 39–43.

Whetten, Lawrence, 'Changing Soviet Attitudes Towards Radical Arab Movements', *The New Middle East*, 18 (March 1970), pp. 29–8.

Wittman, George, 'The Emerging Superpower Concensus', *The Middle East* (March 1989), pp. 11–12.

Wright, Marcus, 'Moscow Loan Splits the Gulf', *Meed*, 28, 23 (1984), pp. 8–10.

Xydis, Stephen G., 'New Light on the Big Three Crisis Over Turkey in 1945', *Middle East Journal*, 14, 4 (1960), pp. 416–32.

Yodfat, Aryeh, 'The USSR and Arab Communist Parties', *The New Middle East*, 32 (May 1971), pp. 29–33.

'The USSR and the Palestinians', *New Outlook*, 19 (June 1976), pp. 30–3.

'The Soviet Presence in Syria', *East Europe*, 20, 7 (July 1971), pp. 9–12.

Yorke, Valerie, 'The Sultan Keeps His Eye on Dhofar', *Middle East International* (March 1982), p. 12.

Zoppo, Ciro, 'Soviet Ships in the Mediterranean and the US–Soviet Confrontation in the Middle East', *Orbis*, 14, 1 (Spring 1970), pp. 109–28.

Index

CPSIA information can be obtained at www.ICGtesting.com
Printed in the USA
LVOW080935100712

289452LV00001BA/8/P